# Policing Developing Democracies

There is now a very considerable and varied body of literature exploring the nature, style, tactics, make-up and impact of policing. Indeed, arguably, this is the largest sub-area of criminological scholarship. However, as is true of the subject more generally, policing literature has been dominated by research and writing from the United States and the Anglophone world and has tended to focus on the police forces in those parts of the world: primarily the USA, Canada, the UK and Australia. Although there has been a long-standing interest in comparative policing questions, this literature remains relatively sparse.

The end of the Cold War led some commentators – with more than a degree of hyperbole – to argue that we were witnessing 'the end of history'. In particular, such events were taken as evidence of the triumph of the liberal democratic political model over its main alternative: communism. While such claims were exaggerated, it is nevertheless the case that throughout the developing world, countries are struggling to craft new democracies and social orders. In established liberal democracies 'the police' have long been seen as a staple element in the maintenance of order and in the preservation of the rights and freedoms upon which a democratic system depends.

Yet, there are enormous challenges in establishing policing systems in young democracies. In such polities there are typically a host of unresolved pressing social, economic and political questions that impinge on policing and the prospects for reform. Such societies are often characterized by weak rule of law, precarious citizenship rights, significant levels of poverty and inequality, rampant corruption, contentious police legitimacy and continuing military involvement in policing. In addition to the challenges inherent to this context are the hugely important questions arising from the emergence of the new security agenda, the problems of transnational crime and international terrorism.

There is an emergent literature in this field, but until now no single volume encompassing the central developments. *Policing Developing Democracies* brings together scholars from political science, international relations and criminology to focus on the issues raised by policing within developing democracies.

**Mercedes S. Hinton** is Nuffield Research Fellow in the Department of Law at the London School of Economics. Her previous book is the prize-winning *The State on the Streets: Police and Politics in Argentina and Brazil* (Lynne Rienner Publishers: 2006).

**Tim Newburn** is Professor of Criminology and Social Policy and Director of the Mannheim Centre for Criminology at the London School of Economics.

D1022633

# Policing Developing Democracies

Edited by Mercedes S. Hinton and
Tim Newburn

Routledge
Taylor & Francis Group

LONDON AND NEW YORK

First published 2009 by Routledge
2 Park Square, Milton Park, Abingdon, Oxon OX14 4RN

Simultaneously published in the USA and Canada
by Routledge
270 Madison Ave, New York, NY 10016

*Routledge is an imprint of the Taylor & Francis Group, an informa business*

© 2009 Mercedes S. Hinton and Tim Newburn

Typeset in Garamond by
RefineCatch Limited, Bungay, Suffolk
Printed and bound in Great Britain by
CPI Antony Rowe, Chippenham, Wiltshire

All rights reserved. No part of this book may be reprinted or
reproduced or utilized in any form or by any electronic,
mechanical, or other means, now known or hereafter
invented, including photocopying and recording, or in any
information storage or retrieval system, without permission in
writing from the publishers.

*British Library Cataloguing in Publication Data*
A catalogue record for this book is available from the British Library

*Library of Congress Cataloging in Publication Data*
Hinton, Mercedes S., 1977–
Policing developing democracies / Mercedes S. Hinton, Tim
Newburn.
     p. cm.
   1. Police—Developing countries. 2. New democracies. I.
Newburn, Tim. II. Title.
   HV7921.H57 2008
   363.2'3091724—dc22
   2008008940

ISBN10: 0–415–42848–3 (hbk)
ISBN10: 0–415–42849–1 (pbk)
ISBN10: 0–203–92693–5 (ebk)

ISBN13: 978–0–415–42848–4 (hbk)
ISBN13: 978–0–415–42849–1 (pbk)
ISBN13: 978–0–203–92693–2 (ebk)

# Contents

# Figures

# Tables

# Contributors

**Mercedes S. Hinton** is Nuffield Research Fellow at the Department of Law of the London School of Economics and Political Science (LSE). Her first book, *The State on the Streets: Police and Politics in Argentina and Brazil* (Lynne Rienner Publishers, 2006) was awarded the British Society of Criminology's prize for best book of 2006.

**Tim Newburn** is Professor of Criminology and Social Policy and Director of the Mannheim Centre for Criminology at the London School of Economics. He is the author of over 30 books on topics including policing and security, youth crime and justice and comparative criminal justice policy.

**Antony Altbeker** is the author of *The Dirty Work of Democracy: A Year on the Streets with the SAPS* (Jonathan Ball Publishers, 2005). After the transition to democracy in South Africa in 1994, he worked as an advisor to the Minister for Safety and Security until 1998. Since then he has worked at the National Treasury, as a researcher first at the Centre for the Study of Violence and Reconciliation and then at the Institute for Security Studies.

**Kemi Asiwaju** is Senior Programme Manager/Altus Regional Representative at the CLEEN Foundation. She trained as a lawyer and graduated from the Faculty of Law, University of Lagos. She has a Bachelor of Law Degree from the Nigeria Law School, Abuja and a Masters degree in Humanitarian and Refugee Studies from the Univeristy of Lagos.

**Adrian Beck** is Reader in Criminology at the Department of Criminology at the University of Leicester. His research interests are focused on crime against the retail sector and policing transitional societies. He has received a number of research grants to look at issues of crime and policing in Eastern Europe.

**Christopher Birkbeck** is Reader in Criminology at the University of Salford, UK. He is also Emeritus Professor of Criminology at the Universidad de Los Andes, in Venezuela, where he was based between 1980 and 2005. His current research interests include: use of force by the police;

Latin American criminology; and the discursive structure of the crime problem.

**Diane E. Davis** is Professor of Political Sociology and Head of the International Development Group in the Department of Urban Studies at MIT. Her many publications include *Urban Leviathan: Mexico City in the Twentieth Century* (Temple University Press, 1994; Spanish translation 1999) and *Discipline and Development: Middle Classes and Prosperity in East Asia and Latin America* (Cambridge University Press, 2004).

**Mark Downes** currently works for the OECD Development Cooperation Directorate on conflict, peace and security issues. He was one of the architects of the *OECD DAC Handbook on Security System Reform: Supporting Security and Justice* (www.oecd.org/dac/conflict/if-ssr), a multi-donor initiative to develop practical tools to make support to security (police, military, parliamentary oversight) and justice (rule of law, prisons) reform more effective, coordinated and coherent.

**Andrew Goldsmith** is Professor of Law and Criminal Justice at Flinders University, Adelaide, Australia. He has been interested in police governance issues in developing and transitional countries for more than a decade. He has previously conducted research or consultancies in Colombia and Turkey and is currently conducting research on Australian police assistance missions in Timor-Leste, Papua New Guinea and the Solomon Islands.

**Luis Gerardo Gabaldón** is Professor of Criminal Law and Criminology in the University of Los Andes, Mérida, and University Andrés Bello, Caracas, Venezuela. He has been Visiting Professor and Research Associate in the University of New Mexico, in 1991–92 and 1997. He is a consultant on police issues and public safety for the Andean Community, Nueva Sociedad and the Police Reform Commission in Venezuela.

**Alice Hills** is Professor of Conflict and Security at the University of Leeds. Her publications include monographs on public policing in Africa and on urban operations. She is currently a member of the UN Department of Peacekeeping Operations' International Policing Advisory Council.

**Otwin Marenin** is Professor of Political Science and Criminal Justice at Washington State University. He has taught at Ahmadu Bello University and the University of Benin in Nigeria, as well as the Universities of Baltimore, California, Colorado and Alaska-Fairbanks. His recent research and publications have focused on developments in international policing, transnational police assistance programmes and efforts to reform the policing systems in failed, transitional and developing states.

**Byongook Moon** is an Assistant Professor at the Department of Criminal Justice at the University of Texas at San Antonio. He has been involved in research on community policing, efficacy of mini-police stations, stress in policing and the process of recruiting police in South Korea.

**Merry Morash** is Professor at the School of Criminal Justice at Michigan State University. She is Director of the Michigan Regional Community Policing Institute and the Michigan Victim Assistance Academy, which provides education and training for professionals who work with crime victims.

**Gordon Peake** is a Senior Associate at Libra Advisory Group, a justice and security consulting company based in London. He is a fellow at the Bobst Center for Peace and Justice, Woodrow Wilson School, Princeton University, USA. He received his doctorate from Oxford University, writing on international assistance to the establishment of police services in Kosovo and the Palestinian territories.

**Annette Robertson** is Senior Lecturer in Criminology in the Division of Law, School of Law and Social Sciences, Glasgow Caledonian University. Her main research interests are: crime and policing in Russia and the former Soviet states, victimization and crime prevention in transitional societies, and comparative criminology. She is currently writing a book, co-authored by Adrian Beck, on police reform in Russia and the FSU.

**Sonja Stojanovic** is currently the Director of the Centre for Civil-Military Relations (CCMR) (www.ccmr-bg.org), a leading Serbian think-tank specializing in security studies. She also works as a Deputy Dean of Belgrade School of Security Studies, the first civilian research centre on security matters in the Western Balkan region, and as a part-time teaching assistant at the Faculty of Political Science, University of Belgrade.

**Arvind Verma** is Associate Professor of Criminal Justice and Director of the India Studies Academic Program at Indiana University, Bloomington. He served in the Indian Police Service for several years and was Superintendent of Police in a number of districts in the state of Bihar, India. He is the author of three books.

# 1 Introduction

## Policing developing democracies

*Mercedes S. Hinton and Tim Newburn*

## Introduction

In 2007, the chief U.S. training officer for the Iraqi National Police characterized his experiences of police capacity building as similar to "trying to build
an airplane while you're flying it" (Col. Chip Lewis quoted in Frayer 2007).
After the overthrow of Saddam Hussein's military dictatorship, the coalition
had envisioned the rapid development of an impartial and professional local
police force that would be capable of providing security, committed to
the rule of law, and supportive of the goal of building a democratic Iraq
(U.S. House of Representatives 2007: 71). The U.S. government spent
$19 billion to develop the capacity of the Iraqi armed forces and police
between 2003 and 2007 (ibid., 41).

However, because of massive planning failures based partly on an unrealistic
assessment of Iraq's political and sectarian landscape, followed by poor coalition oversight of the subcontracted security and reconstruction agencies,
devastation of the economy, and a growing insurgency, the coalition's
goals proved extremely elusive. An independent audit by the Independent
Commission on the Security Forces of Iraq mandated by the U.S. Congress
found that the Iraqi Police Service is "incapable today of providing security at
a level sufficient to protect Iraqi neighborhoods from insurgents and sectarian
violence" (Independent Commission 2007: 10). The commission found it
to be compromised by criminal elements, militia, and insurgent infiltration,
to be underequipped and undertrained, and that the police were counter-
productively transferred from U.S. coalition oversight to premature control
by a "dysfunctional," "sectarian," and "corrupt" Iraqi Ministry of the Interior.

While the situation in Iraq is certainly extreme, what it reveals is the
impossibility of institutional transplant and rapid-fire reform in a setting ill-
prepared to absorb such changes. Yet unrealistic police reform proposals are
devised on a routine basis throughout the developing world. Some are drafted
to score political points at home while others are propelled by international
institutions, bilateral agreements with foreign governments, and international security consultants. Indeed, inflated expectations for police reform
are frequently trumpeted by domestic politicians and international policy

elites, regardless of how staggering the rates of crime, how politicized and heavy-handed the police force, and how corrupt and lawless the government that is meant to enact and monitor the promised reforms.

Money and expertise from donor nations are parachuted in with the aim of aiding transformation. David Bayley (2006) estimates that in 2002–3 the United Nations spent over two billion dollars on civilian police operations. He estimates that in 2004 the U.S. government spent upward of $635 million on development and support of police agencies abroad. However, the nature of such activity is highly variable and, as Bayley notes, quoting Carothers (1999), it appears to have "an uncertain and sometimes contradictory relation to democracy goals." Taking the specific example of international efforts to promulgate community policing models, Brogden points out the very real dangers of such aid becoming another form of colonialism:

> New missionaries have spread a particular policing creed. A uni-linear perception of police development has been assumed, a process occurring largely independently of local police mandates, cultures and patterns of organization. What appeared to offer promise in small-town America, and in the prosperous white suburbs, is being exported by a new brand of academic and police salespeople to all and sundry.
>
> (1999: 179)

The limits and frequent absurdities of reform transplantation are clearly reflected in Gordon Peake's East Timor chapter. Peake describes the reform process that followed the United Nations 1999 intervention to create a provisional police force. This force was to be responsible for all local policing, but it was staffed by officers from fifty different countries, most of whom lacked local knowledge and language. These international officers arrived with wildly diverse skills, ages, ranges of experience, standards, policing styles, and educational backgrounds, in a "merry-go-round" of different arrival and departure dates and lengths of mission; there was little agreement in theory or practice about even basic issues such as how to perform a traffic stop (Peake, Chapter 7).

As if the bureaucratic challenges were not Herculean enough, the UN was also mandated with the parallel task of building from the ground up a professional, accountable, politically neutral, rights-respecting domestic police force that would be capable of taking over local policing responsibilities in a multiethnic, multilingual society—this in a postconflict newly independent country with fragile state institutions, few resources, scant rural penetration, and deep economic, social, and governance problems. Six-and-a-half years and four separate UN missions later, the newly created national police force still lacked basic infrastructure, communications systems, "legal frameworks, mechanisms for control, and well-functioning managerial systems." After the country suffered a wholesale breakdown of law and order in 2006, the UN returned for a fifth mission to try again. Peake's assessment of preliminary results leads him to conclude that "the do-over may not work" and that "the current model of police rebuilding needs rethinking in terms of its contextual appropriateness and actual feasibility."

While a cynic, with the benefit of hindsight, may ask if some of these reforms are set up to fail, these efforts also reflect a lack of scholarly knowledge about policing systems in the developing world or their interaction with the local political environment, particularly within young democracies. Policing literature has been dominated by research and writing from the United States and the Anglophone world and has tended to focus on the police forces in those parts of the world: primarily the United States, Canada, the United Kingdom, and Australia. Although there has been a long-standing interest in comparative policing questions, this literature remains relatively sparse (though see Bayley 1985; Mawby 1990; Baker 2002; Caparini and Marenin 2004; Sheptycki and Wardak 2005; Bayley 2006; Hinton 2006). This gap represents a sophisticated level of knowledge that has not been transmitted to policymakers, journalists, teachers, and students, and it contributes to the perpetuation of the transplantation practices discussed above.

This volume takes up this story.

In the twelve chapters that form the body of this book, a variety of experts examine policing in young democracies across four continents: Latin America, Africa, Europe, and Asia. Each of these substantive chapters focuses on one particular jurisdiction and seeks to examine a number of questions:

- What is the historical and politico-economic context of the country in question?
- What is the predominant model of policing?
- What is the relationship of the police with the military?
- What are the major domestic challenges to achieving democratic forms of accountability over the police?
- To what extent are national policing practices affected by regional and international issues and actors?
- What has given the main impetus for police reform, and what processes of reform are under way?
- Finally, what are the prospects for police reform?

An overview of the role and nature of the police in the advanced industrialized democratic context will help us understand the key differences within the developing democracy context.

## Police and democracy

It is hard to imagine the modern state without some form of established policing service. But "how and for what this is used speaks to the very heart of a condition of a political order" (Reiner 1993: 1). The police are the state's primary legal enforcers and embodiment of the law, providing in principal protection, access to justice, and redress. Police actions to detect crime and bring perpetrators to the attention of the courts for punishment are critical to the effective functioning of any criminal justice system.

In addition to upholding due process, freedom of speech and assembly and managing public gatherings and demonstrations, a well-functioning police force that enjoys civic trust affords society the degree of order, predictability, and accountability needed for the functioning of a market economy in a democratic system. The treatment people receive from the police and other agents of the criminal justice system has an important effect on their perception of the government's fairness and effectiveness and, correspondingly, on whether they accept the right of the state and its enforcers to govern behavior (Bayley 1995; Marenin 1996; Tyler 1990). If people can have trust and confidence in rules, institutions, and authorities, they are likely to believe that their long-term personal interests will be well served by voluntary compliance with the laws of the state.

The rule of law is especially important to the democratic process if one accepts that the main feature of a democracy is a government's continuing responsiveness to the preferences of its citizens—who are considered to be political equals. This is the starting point of Dahl's (1971) conception of political democracy. He defines it as a system of government where there are free and fair elections for most positions of governmental power, and he specifies that elections must occur on a regular basis under conditions allowing candidates and organized groups to compete meaningfully and freely in a polity where no major adult group is excluded from the right to vote. Underpinning political competition and participation is a guarantee of the civil and political liberties necessary for political debate and competition, such as freedom of speech, freedom of the press, and freedom of association and assembly (Dahl 1971: 3).

These characteristics of the democratic process hold several implications for police functioning. Jones *et al.* (1994: 185–86) identify seven criteria for democratic police service provision:

- *equity*—the fair allocation of services in relation to needs and enforcement that is proportionate to the frequency and severity of offenses;
- *delivery of service*—efficient and effective delivery of police services, given that a "well policed society is more just than a badly policed one";
- *responsiveness*—based on the democratic principle that government should reflect the wishes of the citizenry;
- *distribution of power*—preventing the police from buttressing a repressive complex;
- *information* about the police and their activities—enabling the achievement of many key democratic criteria;
- *redress*—public complaints about police wrongdoing are addressed, unfair

and malevolent policies are reversed, and some form of compensation is provided where appropriate;

- *participation*—some mechanism for public input into policing policies.

Examining the extent to which these values are visible within policing policies and practices is one potentially important approach to assessing the democratic nature of policing. Arguably, it is precisely the absence of some or all of these values in many of the policing systems described in this volume that underpins calls for reform.

## The controversies of policing

While this volume explores the situation of developing democracies, it is important to note from the outset that even in the advanced industrialized democratic context the role of the police is riddled with controversy and contradiction. The coercive capabilities of the police highlight the tension present within all democracies between the state's power to compel through force and its representative, consensual, and liberal character. In the words of Goldstein,

> The police, by the very nature of their function, are an anomaly in a free society. . . . The specific form of their authority—to arrest, to search, to detain, and to use force—is awesome in the degree to which it can be disruptive of freedom, invasive of privacy, and sudden and direct in its impact upon the individual. And this awesome authority, of necessity, is delegated to individuals at the lowest level of the bureaucracy, to be exercised, in most instances, without prior review and control.
>
> (1977: 1)

The powers given to the police for protecting freedom contain very real potential for the abuse of such power. This paradox is evident in the field of civil liberties more generally: the expression of such liberties contains within itself the potential seeds of its own destruction (Gearty 2007).

In their adversarial role, the police direct much of their surveillance and actions toward the underclass, minorities, young people, and other groups that are perceived to contribute most to criminality. In so doing, they constitute a socially divisive force and add to structural tensions latent in society (Bittner 1975: 10).

There are a number of other aspects of the police organization that complicate any discussion of the proper police role in a democracy. Even in most developed countries, the police are on the whole hierarchically organized, secretive in their esprit de corps, jealous of external interference, and on many occasions contemptuous of legal and procedural constraints on the gathering of criminal evidence and treatment of suspects and criminals (Skolnick and Bayley 1988: 49–51).

The police are also subject to intense pressures: the public and politicians demand results, while they are required to comply with procedural laws concerning arrests, the treatment of suspects, and other human rights standards, even during fast-paced operations dealing with individuals who confront them with verbal or physical aggression. Accountability may be undermined if the police circumvent these laws in the course of their work, as is possible simply through the exploitation of the wide discretion police officers typically have in their day-to-day activities (Goldstein 1977; Skolnick 1966).

Thus the police role in any democracy is bound to be contentious and imperfectly aligned with the broader procedures, objectives, and practices of a democratic polity. In the developed economies scandals concerning overpolicing, underprotection, racial and ethnic profiling, lack of respect for legal procedures, capitulation to political pressure, and arbitrary and abusive practices are far from uncommon. But if these issues are a challenge in the First World, where the factors that work to restrict the coercive potential of the police are well-established, they are all the more complicated in developing countries whose democratic institutions are still young.

## Characteristics of developing democracies

Developing democracies typically suffer from a range of intractable political and socioeconomic problems. Certainly these societies are not a monolithic block; they vary from region to region, by the strength of their institutions, their political culture, ethnic homogeneity, their level of industrialization and wealth, and by how this wealth is distributed among the population. But generally speaking, developing democracies tend to exhibit the following characteristics to a greater or lesser extent:

1   weak democratic institutions
2   corruption and weak rule of law
3   significant levels of poverty and inequality
4   high crime and societal instability
5   poorly institutionalized channels of police accountability and responsiveness.

We discuss each of these below.

### Weak democratic institutions

In the late 1970s and 1980s, much of the developing world began to leave behind an era of military rule, ushering in the "third wave" of democratization (Huntington 1991). Elections were held, constitutions redrawn, political parties reinstated, and civic groups allowed greater voice.

Despite popular hopes and expectations, however, today few of the third wave democracies meet the criteria of competition, participation, and respect for liberties considered to underpin robust political democracies (Carothers 2007; Schedler 2002; Zakaria 1997). Even as the threat of military rule has diminished in many countries due to more robust forms of civil–military control, the insidious effects of authoritarian historical legacies remain.

A number of young democracies found their transitions constrained by authoritarian provisions written into their constitution and institutional architecture to guarantee a certain measure of continuing power for the military or ruling elites. In Kenya, for example, the first multiparty elections in thirty-one years were allowed in 1992, but structural power was so heavily tilted in favor of the incumbent President Daniel Arap Moi—who had been in office since 1978—that he won in 1992 and again in 1997 (Hills, Chapter 11).

Elections in many young democracies remain flawed by political intimidation, manipulation of media and harassment of the press, fraud, and vote buying. The instilling of democratic values and experience in monitoring government are not accomplished overnight. It can take decades for civil society to become effectively organized and adept at mobilizing the population or at holding government accountable, particularly in nations with lower GDP where economic resources are scarce.

In the aftermath of dictatorship, parliamentarians are typically unaccustomed to functioning independently of the executive and to forming the coalitions needed in a consensus-based regime. Young democracies' public accounting systems and judiciaries may well be weak from decades of political interference and a lack of independence and resources. Further, legal codes that were designed to maintain political order and control need substantial post-transition updating so as to provide effective, political and civil freedoms and human rights, a process that can take years. In Russia, the government and public "inherited more than four thousand pieces of Soviet legislation, most of which had never been made available to the public and many of which directly breached civil rights" (Beck and Robertson, Chapter 3).

Clearly the political circumstances in which policing has developed are crucial. In many cases, the colonial legacy continues to play an important role in contemporary policing. Colonial policing models were typically centered on power maintenance, protection of the colonizer's holdings, suppression of disorder, and control and regulation of the population.

In reference to South Korea, Moon and Morash observe that "the thirty years of brutality and suppression that Koreans experienced from the Japanese-led police [1910 to 1945] created a deep hostility of Koreans toward the police, and this hostility was passed from generation to generation" (Chapter 5). During the years following independence and the subsequent Korean War, the military staged several successful coups, and active and retired military personnel filled the police hierarchy such that the "police were mobilized to collect information about political dissent, labor movements, and antigovernment student movements." While South Korea has more successfully democratized post transition than have the majority of developing countries, the legacy of authoritarianism on policing has not entirely been eclipsed. In the far more extreme African context, Kemi Asiwaju and Otwin Marenin write that even forty-seven years after Nigeria's independence in 1960, "the Nigerian Police Force still struggles with an image derived from its colonial origins as a repressive, brutal, semimilitary, politically controlled force which served the interests of the colonial British administration and, after independence, the new political elites" (Chapter 13).

Stojanovic and Downes find an apt description of the police role during dictatorship in Serbia in the deputy chief of the Belgrade police's observation that "Milošević's police was a repression machine, a civil war army, an immense riot squad. No wonder the citizenry was alienated: the cops were either beating them up—or sneering behind the administration counters" (Chapter 4). Altbeker, in his chapter on South Africa, identifies the police role in enforcing the hated policies of apartheid and repression of popular resistance during the 1970s and 1980s as a critical factor underpinning policing's lack of social and political legitimacy in the country (Chapter 12).

In all the countries examined in this book, whether postcolonial or not, police involvement in repression associated with authoritarian regimes has cast a long shadow over police–community relations, generating enduring patterns of mutual suspicion, fear, and mistrust. In the majority of cases, the histories of policing described here begin with militarized origins in nondemocratic political circumstances.

### Corruption and weak rule of law

In a context of newly democratic societies, the rule of law is typically weaker than in the advanced industrialized context. As O'Donnell has highlighted, such "horizontal" mechanisms of accountability not only promote responsiveness to public agendas but enable the government to police itself effectively to prevent, detect, and punish malfeasance. Because state agencies have greater access to public information (such as financial receipts and contractual documentation) than does the general electorate, an effective system of checks and balances affords the government an important means of promoting transparency, responsibility, and self-control (1998: 119).

While abuse of public power for private gain can certainly be found in the countries of the First World, it is even more widespread in the developing democracy context, where the rule of law is weaker and checks and balances are less established. Table 1.1 shows Transparency International's corruption rankings for the countries examined in our volume in relation to selected other countries.

As the table reveals, in the majority of countries described in the chapters of this book corruption is a deeply embedded problem. This tends to be seen in the wider political system as well as within criminal justice. In the chapter

*Table 1.1* Corruption perceptions index, 2007

|  | Country Rank | Country | CPI 2003 Score |
|---|---|---|---|
| *Least Corrupt* | 1 | Denmark | 9.4 |
|  | 1 | Finland | 9.4 |
|  | 1 | New Zealand | 9.4 |
|  | [. . .] | [. . .] | [. . .] |
|  | 9 | Canada | 8.7 |
|  | [. . .] | [. . .] | [. . .] |
|  | 12 | United Kingdom | 8.4 |
|  | [. . .] | [. . .] | [. . .] |
|  | 19 | France | 7.3 |
|  | 20 | United States | 7.2 |
|  | [. . .] | [. . .] | [. . .] |
|  | 43 | South Africa | 5.1 |
|  | 43 | South Korea | 5.1 |
|  | [. . .] | [. . .] | [. . .] |
|  | 64 | Turkey | 4.1 |
|  | [. . .] | [. . .] | [. . .] |
|  | 72 | Brazil | 3.5 |
|  | 72 | India | 3.5 |
|  | 72 | Mexico | 3.5 |
|  | [. . .] | [. . .] | [. . .] |
|  | 79 | Serbia | 3.4 |
|  | [. . .] | [. . .] | [. . .] |
|  | 123 | East Timor | 2.6 |
|  | [. . .] | [. . .] | [. . .] |
|  | 143 | Russia | 2.3 |
|  | [. . .] | [. . .] | [. . .] |
|  | 147 | Nigeria | 2.2 |
|  | [. . .] | [. . .] | [. . .] |
|  | 150 | Kenya | 2.1 |
|  | [. . .] | [. . .] | [. . .] |
|  | 162 | Venezuela | 2.0 |
|  | [. . .] | [. . .] | [. . .] |
|  | 178 | Iraq | 1.5 |
|  | 179 | Myanmar | 1.4 |
| *Most Corrupt* | 179 | Somalia | 1.4 |

*Source:* Transparency International 2007.

on Brazil, Hinton notes widespread "particularistic, venal, or elite-interest capture of public policy" and comment that "all levels of the Brazilian state, not just the police, operate in a climate of deficient checks and balances and pervasive corruption" (Chapter 10). With respect to India, Verma writes of a dangerous "criminalization of politics," a nexus between crime syndicates and elected members of Parliament (Chapter 6).

Corruption can also arise out of the disorder inherent to regime transition itself. Beck and Robertson note the case of the widening sphere of organized crime in Russia since the collapse of the Soviet Union and the extreme corruption of administrative, government, and law-enforcement bodies that took root in the wake of transition to a market economy (Chapter 3).

## Significant levels of poverty and inequality

The problems of weak democratic institutions, tenuous rule of law, and corruption—and the resulting implications for policing—are exacerbated in contexts of significant poverty and inequality. Generally speaking, where the per capita income is very low, a government will lack the necessary funds to provide for basic needs, educate its population, and maintain infrastructure and functioning public services in the health, public transportation, housing, and criminal justice sectors.

Societies with low per capita GDP tend to have less robust democracies, if they have any democracy at all (Dahl 1971; Huntington 1991; Lipset 1981). If democracy depends on the link between the citizenry and those who govern, this connection is more effectively maintained where citizens enjoy educational opportunities and time to participate and make informed voting decisions, to evaluate publicly available information, and monitor the government. When a significant percentage of the population is preoccupied with subsistence and survival, such things as reading about politics, participating in public life, and joining trades unions, political associations, and NGOs slide down the priority scale. In such contexts, citizens are also more vulnerable to personalistic and populist appeals from politicians who make inflated promises challenging the existing order. Similarly, they are vulnerable to clientelistic forms of power relations, with politicians essentially trading public services, jobs, cash, and other state largesse for political support.

It is not surprising that the wealthiest and most equitable country considered in this volume, South Korea, is also considered to possess the strongest democratic freedoms of the countries surveyed here (Freedom House 2007). South Korea's per capita gross national product, which rose from $79 in 1960 to $10,000 in 1995, led to critical societal and political changes that smoothed the country's process of democratic transition in 1992, when the first civilian head of state in thirty-two years was elected by democratic vote (Moon and Morash, Chapter 5). Reflecting macro-political and economic realities, the Korean police force today, while not without its problems, is the least wracked by controversy of those examined here.

In countries at the opposite end of the spectrum, such as Kenya, Nigeria, and East Timor, we find immense economic and governance problems in addressing the basic needs of large segments of the population. In East Timor, half of the population lacks access to safe drinking water, per capita GDP is only $350 a year, and unemployment is running at about 40 percent (Peake, Chapter 7). Further hampering political participation is the fact that 90 percent of the population lacks fluency in Portuguese, the official language of the courts and police. To put some of these issues in perspective, Table 1.2 compares poverty levels in the countries examined this volume.

*Table 1.2* Percentage of population living below the international poverty line ($2 a day)

|  | Country | Year | Less than $2 per day (Purchasing Power Parity Adjusted) % of population |
|---|---|---|---|
| Least Poor | South Korea | 1998 | 2.0 |
|  | Mexico | 2004 | 11.7 |
|  | Russia | 2002 | 12.1 |
|  | Turkey | 2003 | 18.7 |
|  | Brazil | 2004 | 21.2 |
|  | South Africa | 2000 | 34.1 |
|  | Venezuela | 2003 | 40.1 |
|  | Kenya | 1997 | 58.3 |
|  | India | 2004 | 80.4 |
| Most Poor | Nigeria | 2003 | 92.4 |

*Note:* Data refer to most recent year available; data for Serbia and East Timor not available.

*Source:* World Bank 2007.

*Table 1.3* Inequality of Income

|  | Country | Survey Year | Poorest 20% | Richest 20% | Ratio of Richest 20% to poorest 20% |
|---|---|---|---|---|---|
| Least Unequal | South Korea | 1998 | 7.9 | 37.5 | 4.7 |
|  | Canada | 2000 | 7.2 | 39.9 | 5.5 |
|  | France | 1995 | 7.2 | 40.2 | 5.6 |
|  | India | 2004 | 8.1 | 45.3 | 5.6 |
|  | United Kingdom | 1999 | 6.1 | 44.0 | 7.2 |
|  | Russia | 2002 | 6.1 | 46.6 | 7.6 |
|  | Kenya | 1997 | 6.0 | 49.1 | 8.2 |
|  | United States | 2000 | 5.4 | 45.8 | 8.4 |
|  | Turkey | 2003 | 5.3 | 49.7 | 9.3 |
|  | Nigeria | 2003 | 5.0 | 49.2 | 9.7 |
|  | Mexico | 2004 | 4.3 | 55.1 | 12.8 |
|  | Venezuela | 2003 | 3.3 | 52.1 | 16.0 |
|  | South Africa | 2000 | 3.5 | 62.2 | 17.9 |
| Most Unequal | Brazil | 2004 | 2.8 | 61.1 | 21.8 |

*Note:* Data refer to most recent year available; data for Serbia and East Timor not available.

*Source:* World Bank 2007.

For a number of countries discussed in this book, poverty is itself exacerbated by extreme levels of inequality. Brazil, South Africa, Venezuela, and Mexico particularly are characterized by pockets of First World consumption and living standards coexisting side by side with Third World conditions. Table 1.3 indicates the levels of inequality levels for countries considered here as compared to selected First World countries.

High levels of inequality skew a country's power relations, with knock-on effects for the rule of law and democracy. Where inequities are very pronounced, economic and political elites have a more marked tendency to bend laws, enfeeble courts, violate rights and constitutions, and corrupt politicians (Karl 2000: 155). "Where income inequality is greatest, people are more willing to accept authoritarian rule, less likely to be satisfied with the way democracy works, less trusting of their political institutions, and more willing to violate human rights" (ibid., 156).

### High crime and societal disorder

Economic inequality and the multiple political and societal problems discussed above can generate a number of crime-accelerating pressures. Table 1.4 is suggestive of the higher crime levels found in the countries examined here and in the developing-democracy context more generally, although the available data underrepresent the magnitude of the problem because of poor statistical recording practices and political tampering.

High rates of violent crime tend to generate enormous pressure on the police to achieve "results" (Skolnick 1966: 42). High levels of crime and public fear have a tendency to generate moral panics among the affluent (Cohen 1972) but can also have a conservatizing tendency among the poorest members of society, who are most vulnerable to violent crime. While such a

*Table 1.4* International homicide rates

| Country | Year | Rate per 100,000 inhabitants |
| --- | --- | --- |
| Australia | 2006 | 1.4 |
| England and Wales | 2006 | 1.4 |
| Serbia | 2004 | 1.8 |
| Canada | 2006 | 1.9 |
| South Korea | 2004 | 2.2 |
| India | 2006 | 2.9 |
| Spain | 2003 | 3.2 |
| Germany | 2003 | 3.4 |
| Turkey | 2004 | 3.9 |
| France | 2003 | 3.9 |
| United States | 2006 | 6.1 |
| Mexico | 2002 | 13.0 |
| Russia | 2003 | 21.9 |
| Brazil | 2004 | 27.0 |
| Venezuela | 2005 | 37.0 |
| South Africa | 2006 | 40.0 |

*Source:* Germany, France, Spain, and Russia: *European Sourcebook of Crime* 2006; South Korea, Turkey: UNODC 2007b; Mexico: UNODC 2005; Venezuela, South Africa, India, Serbia: chapters in this volume; Canada: Statistics Canada 2007; Australia: Australian Bureau of Statistics 2006; England and Wales: United Kingdom Home Office 2007; United States: FBI 2006.

context can produce an impetus for police reforms leading to greater efficiency, it more often leads to the generation of inflated public discourses about crime and control that create false expectations regarding police capabilities which, in turn, may stimulate actions which prove costly for accountability and human rights.

In the case of South Africa, Altbeker observes that public confidence in the police has been undermined by high levels of crime. This is particularly worrying in view of the fact that "for many in the middle classes, crime and, by extension, law enforcement have become litmus tests of the capacity and legitimacy of democracy itself" (Chapter 12). High crime levels also tend to politicize the police and lead to crackdowns on classes, racial and ethnic groups, or regional groups whom the more vocal and powerful members of society associate with crime and disorder, as seen particularly in the chapters on Brazil, India, Kenya, and Nigeria. High crime may also elicit calls for increased military involvement in policing, which weakens democratic institutions as it widens the sphere of military influence and often leads to heavy-handed and 'zero tolerance' approaches to crime control.

In developing democracies, high crime rates in urban centers are often accompanied by societal instability and political unrest. This can be a function of structural inequalities, as mentioned earlier, which tend to give rise to class-based politics and populist appeals. It can also be a legacy of dictatorship. Central American countries such as Guatemala, El Salvador, and Nicaragua experienced their democratic transitions as they struggled to rebuild from ruinous and protracted civil wars amid all the postconflict issues of disarmament and demobilization.

Instability may also be generated by a nation's ethnic or racial balance of power. While South Korea and other countries in South East Asia have benefited from relative racial and ethnic homogeneity, societies in Africa, South Asia, and Latin America are very much segmented along ethnic lines. In many countries, colonial powers drew boundaries with little regard for the ethnic or tribal makeup of a given area. In others, one ethnic or racial group was deliberately privileged over another by colonial and post-independence powers. In a contemporary context of weak democratic institutions and economic inequality, these historical conditions can give rise to abuse of power by those who govern in favor of one racial or ethnic group to the detriment of others and to the drafting of particularistic legal rules. Such dynamics are most clearly reflected in the African country case studies of this volume, alongside the Serbian, Indian, and East Timor cases. Internecine tension serves as another source of political instability, disorder, democratic weakening, and crime-accelerating pressure, particularly when fused with situations of high poverty and unemployment, large informal economies, low investment in the educational sector, and poor funding for the criminal justice system.

A related issue is the fact that many developing countries, whether because of their artificially drawn colonial boundaries, the legacies of expansionist military dictatorships, or geographical and cultural factors, tend to suffer from a variety of border-related or spillover conflicts. In a context of scarce resources, these situations become all the more difficult to deal with and can generate an important measure of political instability and temptation to militarize public security or, conversely, draft in police forces to deal with issues that are military in nature.

In Serbia, for example, the Milošević regime mobilized the police in combat operations on the side of ethnic Serbs to fight in Croatia, Bosnia, and Kosovo. "The common experience of participation in the Yugoslav conflicts and the obligation to serve in Kosovo during the ten-year-long state of emergency led to the socialization of literally the whole police force into the military style of command and control" (Chapter 4). In the case of Turkey, borders shared with parts of the former Soviet Union and with Syria, Iran, and Iraq are a source of instability. This and the home-grown terrorist threat emanating from the activities of the Kurdish separatist movement has tended to justify military involvement in matters of day-to-day policing (Chapter 2). In the case of Mexico, Diane Davis explains that pressure to contain human smuggling and drug trafficking between the United States and the impoverished countries of Central and South America has contributed to a militarization of public security (Chapter 9). India, for its part, has undergone a militarization of public security owing to conflict with Pakistan over the disputed territory of Kashmir, concerns over pan-Islamic terrorism, and civil strife spilling over from Nepal, Sri Lanka, and Bangladesh. Verma explains how skewed economic development has further exacerbated this situation: the feelings of "neglect, exclusion, and injustice" it generates contribute to a high volume of street protests, rallies, and intercaste, intragroup, and communal riots, often involving violent confrontation with the police. In the year 2005 alone the police recorded 56,235 riots in the country (Chapter 6).

Governing in such a context presents acute challenges. In situations of economic and political turmoil, scarce resources, divided societies, tenuous governmental legitimacy, and historical traumas, it is more difficult for the state to craft effective public policy and pattern social relations through law.

## Accountability and responsiveness

The kinds of democratic deficits and macro-political and economic problems outlined above hold numerous implications for police accountability and responsiveness to the needs of the population. In particular, control over police forces in developing democracies is all too often exercised in a personalistic fashion. Statistics are generally not well developed, resources are insufficient and inappropriately assigned, and police forces are corrupt, partisan, and heavy-handed. Each of these issues will be discussed below.

*Personalistic control*

As suggested earlier, in a democracy one expects police forces that are accountable to a body of democratic law, reliable, and universalistic in orientation. Yet as chapter after chapter in this volume indicates, these criteria are very much wanting in developing democracies. Certainly the systemic factors discussed in the preceding sections have a bearing on this, but politicized management of the police also plays an important role. That is, in many developing democracies the police are typically subject to the control or patronage of individual politicians rather than to institutionalized forms of accountability.

In Korea, as Moon and Morash note, prior to a 2003 reform the average period of tenure of Korean police commissioner generals was less than a year. "Promotions and assignments to important positions have been based on officers' relationships with ruling parties and their loyalty to regimes in power," thus compromising the political neutrality of the police (Chapter 5).

In India, Verma explains, police officers cannot be posted in their "home district" and must be transferred every three years to another post. This policy, a vestige of colonial efforts to keep tight controls over the loyalties of native personnel, "prevents police officers from developing local links and effectively creates a situation where an officer has no stake in the local community" (Chapter 6). It has also provided politicians with opportunities to interfere in police operations through threats of transfer to undesirable locations or promises of attractive postings. Such centralized forms of control are more common to police forces in developing democracies because of fears that police power will be usurped by local political bosses or will weaken the integrity of the national territory, especially where there are the types of major societal cleavages discussed earlier. Very direct political control has also enabled politicians in India to use the police for political intelligence gathering and to harass political opponents through arrests, threats and intimidation. Indeed, of the twelve cases analyzed in this volume, police forces are organized primarily at the national level through central control in all but the three South American countries—and in the Brazilian context, the geographic territories involved are so large that provincial control can hardly be considered a decentralized system.

Centralized and distant directives hamper the ability of the police to address local needs and priorities. In the case of Turkey, Goldsmith analyzes a strong police and justice system orientation toward punishing political offenses and preventing public denigration of Turkishness or Turkey's state institutions (Chapter 2). In Nigeria, as Asiwaju and Marenin explain, "control of the police helps ensure that [politicians] end up on the winning side, and that the police will not be used against you once, as they always arise, accusations of abuse and corruption are leveled against those in power" (Chapter 13).

Similarly, Beck and Robertson note a lack of political neutrality on the part of the Russian militia (police). "Political affiliation appears as strong as it was during Soviet times," they say, citing militia campaigning during elections. Power remains heavily concentrated in the hands of the Russian president, and legislative control over policing is very weak; informal oversight by the media and NGOs is also hampered by increasing restrictions on government critics (Chapter 3).

Concentration of power in the executive is an issue raised in several of the country case studies, because of the challenges this poses for police oversight. Bayley has suggested that a democratic police force is characterized by accountability to "multiple audiences through multiple mechanisms" (1996: 5). Greater control over the police would be reflected, inter alia, by mechanisms to hold the police accountable to the budget committees of the legislature, to courts and prosecutors, to ombudsmen and oversight commissions. Nongovernmental or social control of the police is also fundamental and can include such actors as the press, human and civil rights organizations, and external auditors. Achieving such accountability has proved problematic in numerous of the countries examined here.

While civil society organizations have mushroomed in many post transition countries, they face an uphill struggle against state deficiencies and gaping social needs and many remain under-resourced and subject to state co-optation. Vis-à-vis the judiciary, particular difficulties arise where prosecutors, courts, and public defenders (where they exist) are overwhelmed, backlogged, and besieged by political interference, poor internal administration, and complex legal procedures, as so often the case in developing democracies.

Verma reports an extremely high volume of judicial backlog in India, massive delays, and periods of pretrial detention that can last ten to fifteen years. Poverty and illiteracy in that country have created enormous systemic barriers to judicial relief for injustice. Highlighting the fragility of state institutions in East Timor, Peake notes that there are just three working courts and one ramshackle prison in the whole country. "Six years after independence, the majority of everyday disputes in the country are still dealt with largely by informal means rather than through an underresourced formal justice system" (Chapter 7). Where the broader judicial system is experiencing dysfunction, whether because of politicization, corruption, heavy caseloads, poor management practices and training, or inadequate/inequitable distribution of resources, the citizenry will have difficulty in securing access to justice for wrongs they suffer.

Frustration with the courts can also strain police performance and distort police attitudes. Police officers may feel compelled to take the law into their own hands and beat out confessions from suspects, frame them, or otherwise make use of excessive or lethal force (Hinton 2006: 112). Moreover, as illustrated in the majority of cases in this volume, judicial weakness may encourage the police to feel they can behave in such ways with relative impunity.

*Statistical deficiencies*

The absence of reliable statistics about levels of crime and police performance is both a part and a reflection of inadequate systems of governance. Accountability implies effective analysis of key indicators so that resources can be appropriately allocated, rewards can be given or sanctions issued to personnel and leaders, and suitable strategies of reform can be devised and monitored. Virtually all the authors in this book note major deficiencies in this area.

Basic deployment data, performance indicators, and figures to indicate gun use and lethal force are often not publicly available; where found, they are patchy and marred by manipulation and poor recording practices. National victimization surveys, which in the First World are regarded as an important tool to gauge the reliability of police statistics, either do not exist or are very limited in their frequency or geographical coverage. Despite international treaty obligations to do so, of the countries studied in our volume, only Mexico, South Africa, Korea, and Turkey provided homicide rates as part of the 2001–2 eighth United Nations Crime Trends Survey; only Turkey and South Korea did so in response to the ninth survey the following year (see UNODC 2005 and 2007b).

The situation in Africa vis-à-vis crime and justice statistics is the most extreme. Although a quarter of the world's countries are in Africa and the region contains one-fifth of the world's population, the continent is, "by far, the least documented region in terms of data and information on crime and drugs" (UNODC 2007a). Many governments are unwilling or unable to supply this information; even when available, the limited resources and data-collection systems of many African governments lead to statistics that do not reflect the true scale of the problem.

In 2005 the Nigerian Police Force, for example, recorded only 2,074 murders (see Chapter 13). In a country of some 140 million, this suggests a homicide rate of 1.6 per 100,000 inhabitants—lower than Canada's. Considering the cycles of political violence, coups and countercoups, ethnic conflict, riots, land conflict, corruption, and vigilantism that characterize Nigeria, the homicide data illustrate the general unreliability of crime-related information.

Though criminal justice data collection is more developed in Brazil than in African countries, Hinton notes a number of statistical irregularities there as well. In 2004 the Brazilian police recorded some twenty thousand fewer homicides than were registered by national health agencies. Even more troubling is the federal government's report that "the police in Rio killed no civilians in 2004 or 2005, when separate statistics published at the state level indicate that 983 and 1,098 civilians were killed by Rio police in these years respectively" (Chapter 10).

## *Poor resources and allocation*

Given the expenses involved in developing, monitoring, and training authorities in data collection systems, in part poor statistics can be seen as a
symptom of under-resourcing. It is also a sign, however, of the politically
motivated resource allocation and diversion of funds that characterize many
developing democracies. Beck and Robertson note that shortages of basic
equipment are readily apparent in any Russian police station and show that
this may be as much a function of financial misappropriation and mismanagement as of a general lack of funding.

Underfunding or misfunding naturally affects policing in ways beyond
data collection; it affects the choice, stock, and use of equipment and the
quality of training. Where training and resources for forensics and investigations are inadequate, police are more prone to reliance on forced confessions.
Inadequate funding also keeps police pay (and the caliber of recruits) low and
hampers police responsiveness to the needs and emergencies of the population. All these problems are more acute in rural areas, where roads, bridges,
and general infrastructure are more precarious. Under such conditions, it is
unlikely that the police will arrive with any speed in times of trouble. During
the January 2008 violence that shook Kenya following hotly contested
presidential elections marred by ballot rigging, some fifty people from the
incumbent's tribe were burned alive as an angry mob barricaded and set fire
to a church in a rural area. It was several hours before the police arrived
(Gettleman 2008).

Prisons are another area typically plagued by poor resourcing. Relatedly,
Hinton notes that Brazilian prisons are notoriously overcrowded, under-
staffed, violent, and corrupt places ridden by disease and lack of investment, where prisoners must often buy their own food or rely on their
relatives to bring it. A recent case in Brazil brought attention to these
issues and to the failure of provincial governments to find the funding to
build separate prison and jail facilities for women, even though federal law
requires it. In the northeastern Amazon state of Pará, federal investigators
discovered that a fifteen-year-old girl had been illegally placed in a police
jail among thirty-four male inmates in October 2007. For twenty-six days
she was raped and tortured repeatedly by the male prisoners, who would
deny her food unless she consented to sex. Equally disturbing was the
role that authorities played; it had been the judge who heard the charges
of petty theft against her who placed her in the all-male setting, a situation
also known to the police and a public defender who visited the jail. The
police even shaved her head to make her look more like a boy and
blamed her for lying about her age when federal authorities became involved
(Barrionuevo 2007).

Prisons in the developing world are typically not given priority in investment and reform, given other pressing social problems. Under such conditions the rehabilitative capacity of incarceration, which is disputed even in

the First World, is nonexistent. "Instead, individuals behind bars are further brutalized in prisons and presented with new opportunities for criminal networking" (Chapter 10).

## *Corruption, partisanship, and violence*

In a context of poor police oversight, weak checks and balances across government, halting performance of courts, and insufficient resources, the police are more prone to corruption and violence—particularly in societies where there is substantial inequality. Corruption is of course a means of income supplementation, and it thrives in environments of low pay, few controls, and numerous opportunities.

According to Goldsmith, Turkish police officers are widely known to supplement income "through selective enforcement (or nonenforcement) of the law" (Chapter 2), and notes that such bribery is common in interactions between public servants and the citizenry.

Certain police powers can facilitate bribery. In the case of Russia, the former Soviet system of "totalitarian control and supervision over the population" continues to cast a shadow on contemporary policing (Chapter 3). The militia (police) in Russia continue to be responsible for issuing visas, internal passports, residence permits, licenses for printing presses, and vehicle registration. The system of internal residence permits, in particular, provides ample opportunity for abuse, as bribery of a militia officer may be the only way of remaining in certain cities. As Beck and Robertson point out, however, the huge scale of police deviancy and corruption in Russia must be seen in the wider context of a "culture of corruption" and lack of respect for the law throughout society and the government.

Indeed, in all of the societies where political and societal corruption was a problem, it was also endemic within the police. While some might see bribery as a relatively benign phenomenon that can keep business and government running and help to unblock bureaucratic transactions, it contains enormous inherent dangers.

In a climate of weak controls and relative impunity, bribery can easily lead to direct police involvement in criminal activities. The chapters in this volume note police involvement to various degrees in criminal activities such as contract killings, drug trafficking, arms dealing, smuggling, kidnapping rings, and protection rackets. Widespread corruption also erodes the public service and universalistic protection of all neighborhoods that one would expect a democratic police force to embody.

Where police presence and intervention in commercial and interpersonal disputes and investigations can be bought by private citizens or politicians, the rule of law is eroded, power relations become more skewed still, and poorer members of society suffer further. These forms of "privatization" of public security are common to many of the countries considered in this book, particularly given environments of weak state checks and balances. In developing democracies it is not uncommon to find retired or active-duty police personnel moonlighting as private security guards.

The Serbia chapter in particular notes that following that country's democratic transition in 2000, International Monetary Fund pressure on the state to reduce public spending contributed to a reduction in police salaries and to income supplementation in the private security sector by police personnel. Stojanovic and Downes find this development especially worrisome because "many of these companies served as conduits for money laundering and extortion by the nexus of organized crime and extreme nationalistic forces" (Chapter 4).

An unregulated private security sector and inappropriately channeled public security resources are also very disruptive of efforts to increase equity in law enforcement. The South Africa chapter notes that while the wealthy are relying increasingly on private security guards, the poor are forced to turn to vigilante groups.

Unfortunately, in some developing democracies, unequal power relations are so much a part of the political fabric that the very idea of policing as a public service lacks foundation. Birkbeck and Gabaldón observe that in Venezuela there is little cultural support for a universalistic form of policing and highlight the problematical nature of the very concept of "community." They claim that among the citizenry there appears to be a widespread desire "to treat the police as social capital for policing others" (Chapter 8). Venezuela's high levels of social inequality "provides the structural foundation for many current arrangements (and problems) in policing." Similarly in Nigeria, "the diversion of police resources to serve the powerful and well-off is massive. . . . Most patrol officers are deployed to protect the persons and property of the well-off (who also use their own resources to buy private protection or fortify their homes), while the poor are left to fend for themselves by creating and supporting their own informal control mechanisms" (Chapter 13).

Not surprisingly, police violence is associated with corruption and nonuniversalistic policing. To varying degrees, all the countries we study cite this as a problem. Indeed, in all societies "the potential for police violence and the rhetoric that would justify it are endemic" (Chevigny 1995: 26), and particularly in settings where violent crime, social instability, inequality, and impunity are problems of a large magnitude (Hinton 2006: 33).

Verma emphasizes that the growing threat of terrorism in India has contributed to a reluctance on the part of successive governments, whether from the right or left, to limit police use of force. Police violence can manifest itself in protest and riot control, heavy-handed arrests, illegal searches, and torture during interrogations and detention (Chapter 6). In Venezuela, "the rules for the use of force are usually so vague or incomplete that it is difficult to specify a clear situational standard for police behavior against which to hold officers accountable" (Chapter 8). In a climate in which judges are generally unwilling to prosecute defendants and there is public support for "cleansing" of "antisocial elements" and criminals in poor neighborhoods, this contributes to high rates of police use of lethal force and impunity for extrajudicial executions. Birkbeck and Gabaldón find that in 2005, the rate of civilian deaths at the hands of the police for "resisting authority" was 5 per 100,000 inhabitants in Venezuela—higher than the national murder rate in countries such as France and England.

Extrajudicial killings by police, whether through death squads, contract killings, or social cleansing, are also serious problems in Brazil, India, Kenya, and Nigeria, and to a lesser extent in Russia, Serbia, and Turkey. In the Hobbesian view (1991 [1651]), it is people's need for protection from the predatory activities of others that leads them to consent to the state. Where citizens believe that their physical security is threatened by the very state agencies meant to safeguard them, the legitimacy of government and laws is at risk, as is the democratic system itself. Moreover, a predominantly unlawful, corrupt, and brutal police force decreases the public's respect for legality and increases reliance on private vengeance and vigilante groups, as do police forces that are unavailable or unwilling to enter dangerous or remote areas (Hinton 2006: 6).

Inadequate police presence, lack of confidence in the police, and weak state penetration in rural areas, slums, and shantytowns has led to an explosion of vigilante groups in many developing democracies, as seen most particularly in the Africa and South America chapters. While certain groups may provide needed dispute settlement and security in areas where there is little alternative, vigilante groups ultimately represent a challenge to the authority and laws of the state and to human rights.

They can also quickly become as much of a security threat as that which they emerged to disrupt. Vigilante groups easily degenerate into lynch mobs or criminal gangs that extort local residents, exact beatings, unlawfully detain and kill suspected criminals and rivals, or morph into private militias that support the local power elite, reinforcing unequal power relations, patterns of patriarchy and ethnic hatred, and unlawful social practices.

## Conclusion and prospects for reform

In a study of democratic police building, Bayley (2006) identifies four major sets of reforms that he considers to be the minimum requirement for the establishment of such institutions and processes. Reforms must ensure that police

- are accountable to law rather than to government
- protect human rights, especially those rights that are required for the sort of political activity that is the hallmark of democracy
- be accountable to people outside their organization who are specifically designated and empowered to regulate police activity
- give top operational priority to servicing the needs of individual citizens and private groups (2006: 19–20).

It would be difficult to disagree with any of these reform objectives, and indeed the countries we examine here abound with measures espousing these principles to address the multiple problems discussed in the preceding sections.

Several countries have adopted reforms to create ties between the police and the communities they serve through participative forums and recruitment changes. South Africa, for example, launched an aggressive program of affirmative action to increase demographic, racial, and linguistic representation on the South African police force and thus enhance legitimacy and effectiveness. During apartheid it had been official "police policy that white police officers could never be under the command of black officers," so the majority of the force's training and managerial experience was held by whites. Affirmative action to address this inequality was accompanied by initiatives to bring in elements of community policing models, such as increased foot and vehicle patrol, partnerships with civil society, and community police forums to be held at every station (Chapter 12).

Others countries brought in new police complaint commissions, monitoring bodies, and human rights agencies. Venezuela, for example, created the National Commission for Police Reform to produce a comprehensive strategy for reform based on extensive data canvassing and consultation. Most countries considered here have also endeavored to enact reforms to professionalize police forces and provide improved training. Legal codes have been reformed, in some countries to restrict police powers and in others to ensure that police are mindful of human rights.

But the effects of these efforts in most of the countries here have not been as promising or sustainable as hoped. Asiwaju and Marenin find that Nigerian political and police management discourse is "replete with the correct aspirational rhetoric, critiques of the current goals, practices, and cultures of the force, and exhortations to do better" but that successful pilot projects are not always reproduced or routinized once media attention and political priorities shift or foreign funding fades (Chapter 13). In some cases the local context transformed internationally-espoused reforms into local authoritarian variants; in others the reforms succeeded on some level but were undercut by parallel measures that perpetuated old patterns of policing and control. While organizational and legislative change is relatively easy and rapid, generating substantive changes in the culture and mindset of the police and the ways they do their job and relate to the public is far more arduous, and even when achieved difficult to sustain, particularly where political authorities send conflicting signals and maintain practices that perpetuate political and particularistic use of policing.

Beck and Robertson find that even after fifteen years of criminal justice sector reform in Russia, "much of the police reform has in fact been superficial or involved the continuation—and even the reinforcement—of Soviet trends and traditions" (Chapter 3). Most particularly, as this introduction and chapter after chapter in this volume show, the police reflect many aspects of the political and socioeconomic climate in which they operate. Governments struggling with massive social blight, political unrest, and scarce resources typically have more pressing priorities than democratic police reform, particularly where the status quo enables political elites to retain their existing power. As Hinton observes in reference to Brazil, "in the context of few systematic attempts to deal with inequality, social exclusion, or massive political corruption at all levels of the state, it is unrealistic to expect that the police could become a vanguard of democratic values and probity" (Chapter 10).

The bottom line of reform is that the emergence of something that looks akin to what we might describe as "democratic policing" will be unlikely without fairly systemic political and cultural change, ensuring that political and civil institutions are themselves democratic in their operation. Asiwaju and Marenin's account of the April 2007 general elections in Nigeria—beset by extensive violence, corruption, intimidation of voters, ballot stuffing, and fraud, and resulting in overwhelming victory for the ruling party—reflects the scale of the problem in some regimes (Chapter 13). That same year in Kenya, incumbent President Mwai Kibaki was perceived to have stolen the presidential elections, a conviction that unleashed tribal conflict that resulted in the killing of hundreds and the displacement of several hundred thousand people from their homes.

While an unreformed political system can stymie democratization of policing, it is also true that a violent and corrupt police force can also be a major blockage to political change, as it relegates segments of the population to chronic insecurity, violence, and victimization by extortionary practices and hampers effective political voice. While this indeed suggests a "chicken and egg problem" (see Stenning 2006) regarding which should come first, the reality is that democratic political and police reform are intertwined. One cannot endure without the other. Reform is thus a process of shifting sands, as old habits and cultural patterns die hard and traditional practices often re-emerge under a different guise. Reflecting this is the fact that the majority of contributors to this volume offer pessimistic conclusions regarding the short- to medium-term prospects for democratic police reform in the countries they study.

One of the few optimistic pictures is that of South Korea, owing to the country's success with structural and functional changes to encourage greater police neutrality, improve handling of public demonstrations, prevent police corruption and brutality, and separate military operations from policing. South Korea, however, has benefited from a historically high degree of societal homogeneity and equitable land distribution; as Table 1.3 shows, it possesses the lowest levels of income inequality of the countries we consider here. As noted by Moon and Morash, in its post-independence period a strong developmental state successfully stewarded tremendous economic growth (Chapter 5). Economic prosperity and more equitable distribution of such has made for more stable democratic political reforms than seen in many other developing countries and more successful democratic consolidation. Most developing countries lack these conditions, and their police forces and political masters have struggled a great deal more to cast off large authoritarian shadows.

The intrinsic difficulties of police reform in the developing democracy context can certainly be mitigated by international influences. In the case of Turkey, the European Union has lent substantial impetus and momentum to efforts to strengthen civilian democratic control over the country's security forces. But still, Goldsmith observes, unresolved tensions concerning the Kurdish question and others arising out of the Middle East "continue to legitimate taking hard, militarized stances against perceived threats to state security" (Chapter 2). In the case of Serbia, prospects of EU accession have also played an important role in encouraging police reform. But as illustrated in East Timor, international police reform efforts cannot create the requisite domestic political and cultural conditions for reform. They often focus efforts too narrowly on the police, without taking appropriate stock of the context. Stojanovic and Downes' assessment of international efforts in Serbia suggest that a series of barriers—including lack of coordination among donors, the international community's failure to conceive of police reform as a political process rather than only a technical one, community policing models that revived memories of systematic neighbor-on-neighbor spying during the communist period, and donor fears of investment in equipment that could be used for repressive purposes—all contributed to the failure of transfer projects (Chapter 4).

In addition to such barriers, the international climate is no longer as conducive to democratization as it was in the years immediately following the end of the Cold War. Fear of terrorism is creating new incentives for establishing hard-line security policies, centralizing policing, and supporting hard and soft dictatorships throughout the world. Arguably, it is also the case that the 'war on terror' and developments such as Abu Ghraib, Guantánamo Bay, international rendition of terrorism suspects to authoritarian countries for torture, and First World moves to increase periods of police detention without charge are undermining First World claims in connection with human rights and the rule of law and potentially eroding their credibility in relation to democratization movements in the Third World. For example, the United States recently barred UN inspectors from visiting some of its own immigration detention facilities—a move that undercuts developing-country incentives to allow UN inspections of their agencies and practices.

These challenges, however, make the study of policing and politics in the developing world all the more urgent. The majority of the world's population is concentrated in these areas, and deeper knowledge of conditions there is thus crucial to human welfare. Study of these regions will also shed light on some of today's most pressing global political problems, in addition to offering the potential to awaken First World citizens to the dangers of democratic erosion and rising inequality in their own societies. Without realistic assessments of the conditions that prevail outside the small islands of prosperity of the First World, moreover, global issues such as transnational migration, organized crime, terrorism, the spread of disease, and environmental degradation stand to worsen. In this climate, further study of international and comparative criminal-justice issues become all the more important.

# References

Australian Bureau of Statistics (ABS). 2006. *Recorded Crime, Victims, Australia.* Various issues, ABS 4510.0. Canberra: ABS.

Baker, Bruce. 2002. *Taking the Law into Their Own Hands: Lawless Law Enforcement in Africa.* London: Ashgate.

Barrionuevo, Alexei. 2007. "Rape of Girl, 15, Exposes Abuses in Brazil Prison System." *New York Times*, December 12.

Bayley, David H. 1985. *Patterns of Policing: A Comparative International Analysis.* New Brunswick, NJ: Rutgers University Press.

——. 1995. "A Foreign Policy for Democratic Policing." *Policing and Society* 5: 7–93.

——. 1996. "The Contemporary Practices of Policing: A Comparative View." In *Civilian Police and Multinational Peacekeeping: A Role for Democratic Policing.* Washington, DC: National Institute of Justice, Police Executive Research Forum, Center for Strategic and International Studies.

——. 2006. *Changing the Guard: Developing Democratic Policing Abroad.* New York: Oxford University Press.

Bittner, Egon. 1975. *The Functions of the Police in Modern Society: A Review of Background Factors, Current Practices, and Possible Role Models.* Seattle, Washington: University of Washington Press.

Brogden, M. 1999. "Community Policing as Apple Pie." In *Policing Across the World*, ed. R. I. Mawby. London: University College London Press.

Caparini, Marina and Marenin, Otwin. 2004. *Transforming Police in Central and Eastern Europe—Process and Progress.* Geneva: DCAF—Geneva Centre for the Democratic Control of Armed Forces

Carothers, Thomas. 1999. *Aiding Democracy Abroad: The Learning Curve.* Washington, DC: Carnegie Endowment for International Peace.

——. 2007. "The Sequencing Fallacy." *Journal of Democracy* 18, no. 1: 12–27.

Chevigny, Paul. 1995. *Edge of the Knife: Police Violence in the Americas.* New York: The New Press.

Cohen, Stanley. 1972. *Folk Devils and Moral Panics.* London: MacGibbon and Kee.

Dahl, Robert. 1971. *Polyarchy: Participation and Opposition.* New Haven, CT: Yale University Press.

European Sourcebook of Crime and Criminal Justice Statistics. *European Sourcebook of Crime and Criminal Justice Statistics 2006.* 3rd ed. Den Haag: Boom Juridische Uitgevers. Available at http://www.europeansourcebook.org/.

Federal Bureau of Investigation (FBI). 2006. "Crime in the United States: Murder and Non-negligent Manslaughter Rate." Table 16. Available at http://www.fbi.gov/ucr/ucr.htm.

Frayer, Lauren. 2007. "Iraqi Police Train for Future but Struggle in Violent Present." Associated Press, April 28.

Freedom House. 2007. *Freedom in the World 2007*. New York: Rowman and Littlefield.

Gearty, C. 2007. *Civil Liberties*. Oxford: Oxford University Press.

Gettleman, Jeffrey. 2008. "Kenya, Known for Its Stability, Topples into Post-election Chaos." *New York Times*, January 3.

Goldstein, Herman. 1977. *Policing a Free Society*. Cambridge, MA: Ballinger.

Hinton, Mercedes S. 2006. *The State on the Streets: Police and Politics in Argentina and Brazil*. Boulder, CO: Lynne Rienner.

Hobbes, Thomas. 1991 [1651]. *Leviathan*. Cambridge: Cambridge University Press.

Huntington, Samuel P. 1991. *The Third Wave: Democratization in the Late Twentieth Century*. Norman: University of Oklahoma Press.

Independent Commission on the Security Forces of Iraq. 2007. *The Report of the Independent Commission on the Security Forces of Iraq, September 2007*. Available at www.cfr.org.

Jones, T., T. Newburn, and D. J. Smith. 1994. "Policing and the Idea of Democracy." *British Journal of Criminology* 36, no. 2: 182–98.

Karl, Terry Lynn. 2000. "Economic Inequality and Democratic Instability." *Journal of Democracy* 11, no. 1: 149–56.

Lipset, Seymour Martin. 1981. *Political Man: The Social Bases of Politics*. Baltimore: Johns Hopkins University Press.

Marenin, Otwin. 1996. "Policing Change, Changing Police: Some Thematic Questions." In *Policing Change, Changing Police: International Perspectives*, ed. Otwin Marenin. New York: Garland.

Mawby, R. I. 1990. *Comparative Policing Issues*. London: Routledge.

O'Donnell, Guillermo. 1998. "Horizontal Accountability in New Democracies." *Journal of Democracy* 9: 112–26.

Reiner, R. 1993. "Police Accountability: Principles, Patterns, and Practices." In *Accountable Policing: Effectiveness, Empowerment, and Equity*, ed. R. Reiner and S. Spencer. London: Institute for Public Policy Research.

Schedler, Andreas. 2002. "The Menu of Manipulation: Elections without Democracy." *Journal of Democracy* 13, no. 2: 36–50.

Sheptycki, James and Wardak, Ali. 2005. *Transnational and comparative criminology*. London: Glass House.

Skolnick, Jerome H. 1966. *Justice without Trial: Law Enforcement in a Democratic Society*. New York: Wiley.

Skolnick, Jerome H., and David Bayley. 1988. *Community Policing: Issues and Practices around the World*. Washington, DC: National Institute of Justice.

Statistics Canada. 2007. "Homicide Rate by Province and Territory: CANSIM." Table 253–0001. Available at http://www40.statcan.ca/l01/cst01/legal12b.htm.

Stenning, Philip. 2006. "Review of Hinton (2006) and Bayley (2006)." *British Journal of Criminology* 47, no. 2: 346–50.

Transparency International. 2007. *Corruption Perceptions Index*. Berlin: Transparency International.

Tyler, Tom. 1990. *Why People Obey the Law*. New Haven: Yale University Press.

United Kingdom Home Office, Research Development and Statistics. 2007. *Crime in England and Wales 2006–7: Summary of Recorded Crime Statistics*. Available at http://www.homeoffice.gov.uk/rds/recordedcrime1.html.

United Nations Office on Drugs and Crime (UNODC). 2005. *Eighth United Nations Survey of Crime Trends and Operations of Criminal Justice Systems, Covering the Period*

*2001–2002*. March. Available at http://www.unodc.org/unodc/en/data-and-analysis/Eighth-United-Nations-Survey-on-Crime-Trends-and-the-Operations-of-Criminal-Justice-Systems.html.

———. 2007a. Data for Africa Programme Description. Available at http://www.unodc.org/unodc/en/data-and-analysis/Data-for-Africa.html.

———. 2007b. *Ninth United Nations Survey of Crime Trends and Operations of Criminal Justice Systems, Covering the Period 2003–2004*. November. Available at http://www.unodc.org/unodc/en/data-and-analysis/Ninth-United-Nations-Survey-on-Crime-Trends-and-the-Operations-of-Criminal-Justice-Systems.html.

U.S. House of Representatives Committee on Armed Services, Subcommittee on Oversight and Investigations. 2007. *Stand Up and Be Counted: The Continuing Challenge of Building the Iraqi Security Forces*, 110th Congress, 1st sess., July.

World Bank. 2007. *World Development Indicators 2007*. CD-ROM. Washington, DC: World Bank.

Zakaria, Fareed. 1997. "The Rise of Illiberal Democracy." *Foreign Affairs* 76 (November–December): 22–43.

# Part I

# Europe

# 2 Turkey

## Progress towards democratic policing?

*Andrew Goldsmith*

## Introduction

As Turkey began its journey down the path to formal accession to the European Union in October 2005, a number of issues were clearly on the agenda for further significant change if Turkey, a country of nearly 72 million persons, was to satisfy the EU entry criteria. One of these issues was the strengthening of civilian authority and democratic control over Turkey's security forces. Another was the incidence of the use of torture and other arbitrary punishments by police and other members of security forces. In its 2007 report, Human Rights Watch reported on a "sharp increase in indiscriminate and disproportionate use of lethal force by security forces in dealing with protestors, as well as during normal policing" during the preceding year (Human Rights Watch 2007). Achieving change in Turkish policing, it will be shown, has been, and continues to be, a slow process, due partly to some unique internal characteristics as well as to its geographical location adjacent to one of the world's most volatile political regions. As recent events continue to suggest, the nature of modern Turkey, the directions it is taking in terms of political and social reform, and the role and significance of the Turkish military establishment, present the outsider with a confusing, even contradictory, sense of how much and how quickly the EU accession agenda will be realized in the coming years.

The Turkish security sector is as complex as it is substantial (Bilgin 2005), as will become more evident shortly. The largest component, the Turkish Armed Forces (TAF), account for nearly 520,000 uniformed personnel, leaving aside the gendarmerie component which also falls organically under the TAF. Policing is undertaken under normal (that is, non-emergency) conditions by two institutions, the Turkish National Police (TNP) and the Jandarma (gendarmerie). The latter has been and remains essentially military in character, tradition, and command, wherein lies one of the key challenges facing civilian police reformers today. Looking to their past public record, the police and security forces have long held a reputation for widespread, even systemic, disregard for human rights including the practice of torture of criminal suspects and political dissidents, disappearances, and unlawful killings (Amnesty International 2007a). This alarming situation has been compounded by the lack of accountability of security force personnel for their actions. Not only have the judicial authorities failed to deal adequately with allegations of abuse, but also civilian authorities have exercised at best an incomplete, ad hoc, and unsatisfactory degree of control and influence over the actions of security personnel. While Turkish civilian authority over military personnel has long been, and remains, problematic for reasons of constitutional authority as well as longstanding *realpolitik*, the shortcomings of oversight in respect of the TNP and the Jandarma have arisen as clear problems despite the availability of formal civilian jurisdiction over their policing and law-enforcement functions. Matching the practice with the existing theory of democratic policing in Turkey, as I shall explore in greater detail below, is part of the challenge facing reformers going into the future.

Analysing the state of Turkish policing in the context of emerging democracies requires the distinctiveness in many respects of Turkey's position to be recognized. Unlike many other emerging democracies, it is not a 'fragile' or 'weak' state—it has operated independently since 1923, and is militarily speaking, very strong, with nearly one million personnel currently serving in its armed forces and police. However, it does rank as a developing country with 'medium' human development, ranking number 94 of 177 countries assessed by the United Nations Development Programme (UNDP 2005).[1] It does not share with many other countries in this category the recent experience of emerging from a long period of authoritarian rule nor that of typical post-conflict societies. The country's experience with democratic government dates back to 1945, albeit admittedly not with periods of significant military-dominated interruption. It therefore must be seen as an "old democracy among developing countries" (Shambayati 2004: 253). However it is also widely conceded among political observers and scholars that despite its relatively long period of experimentation with and experience of democratic institutions, Turkey's model of democracy "remains unconsolidated" (Shambayati 2004: 253). Ongoing uncertainties regarding freedom of expression and freedom of association, as well as the unresolved issue of civilian authority over the military, are three prominent areas in which this lack of consolidation is evident.

A number of factors need to be considered in making sense of this position. As noted already, the influence of the Turkish military upon political affairs has been longstanding and profound in the history of the republic (Jenkins 2002). Founded by an avowedly secular military leader, Ataturk, in 1923, the country has long operated upon the principle of the indivisibility of the Turkish military and the Turkish state. This principle has been deeply ingrained in the majority of the population over subsequent generations through public memorials, national days, public education and practical demonstrations of elite military influence over the polity through the execution of a series of military interventions in 1960, 1971, 1980, and 1997. The geo-strategic significance of Turkey has also played a part. Sharing borders, inter alia, with Iraq, Syria, Iran and parts of the former USSR has long given the country's military a pre-eminence in international security agendas and justified a robust domestic stance on matters of state security. The threat posed by Kurdish separatists over several decades, especially in the country's south-eastern provinces, but also through political actions and terrorist attacks in metropolitan centres including Istanbul and Ankara, has lent a sense of urgency to security considerations, reinforcing the importance of the military in Turkish daily life as well as political affairs. It is worth noting that one of the country's two policing and law-enforcement bodies, the Jandarma, is also engaged in border protection and taking action against Kurdish terror-ist groups in war-like operations, thus reinforcing the significance of military, as opposed to civilian, authority in terms of what it does, and also blurring in a tactical sense the traditional distinction within civilian policing models between policing and military functions.

Another factor of growing significance for the security agenda is the influ-ence of Islam upon politics. Symbols such as head scarves have generated noisy debates and worse as pressures for acceptance of more overt expressions of religious faith within this overwhelmingly Muslim nation encounter the resistance of those seeking to uphold the secular traditions of Kemalism and the Turkish state.[2] Here, the predicament for both the TNP and Jandarma has become trickier. For the TNP, growing internal migration from poorer, rural areas to the peripheries of major cities has meant that it has had to confront a rising number of fundamentalist believers mainly from the east and south-east of the country moving to live within areas traditionally under its control and dominated by more educated and secular populations. The TNP has had to deal with regular political demonstrations on such issues, bringing into focus once again the longstanding difficulties faced by the Turkish state in accommodating freedom of expression and association. For the Jandarma, the urbanization of the fringes of major centres, due largely to large-scale internal migration from the Kurdish regions in the south-east, has meant a higher concentration of persons living in what had been once relatively unpopulated areas under their control and responsibility. This movement has brought with it concerns about the presence of Kurdish separatists in larger numbers in or close to urban centres, and the developments at the periphery of many Turkish cities has also produced a blurring and indeed overlap of jurisdictional responsibilities between the TNP and the Jandarma (Cerrah 2007). Indeed, in such areas, the TNP stations can sometimes be found alongside or located in the same street as the Jandarma post.

## Crime in Turkey

Three changes in particular in the last twenty-five years have had an adverse impact upon the crime and security picture. Each reflects Turkey's unique geographical and demographic circumstances. The first is the internal migra-tion already mentioned. The second is the pivotal geographical significance of

Turkey in terms of transnational trafficking, eastwards and westwards, of humans, weapons and illicit drugs, and related money-laundering activities. Turkey shares borders with various European and Middle-eastern countries, making it a cross-roads for all sorts of commerce, licit and illicit. The third is the significance of 'home-grown' terrorism, in particular the terrorist activities of the Kurdish nationalist PKK. While there are limits in terms of the crime statistics kept at a national level, it would seem that the decade from 1994 to 2004 saw a significant increase (more than 50 percent) in almost all crime categories, from 200,000 crimes (excluding terrorist offences) to 322,000 crimes (Cerrah 2007). Comparatively, Turkey's homicide levels are higher (3.83 per 100,000) than countries such as Australia (1.28), Canada (1.93) and England and Wales (1.62), but lower than many other countries, e.g. Georgia: 6.22; Ukraine: 7.42; and Ecuador: 18.33 (UNODC 2005).

The growth of shanty-type migrant settlements on the edges of major Turkish cities has produced the predictable calls for greater public order policing and preventive patrols with respect to these communities. The significant numbers of Kurdish citizens living in these places, often under the jurisdiction of the militarized Jandarma, creates ongoing tensions. Political demonstrations are not uncommon in the major cities of Turkey, but persons participating are vulnerable to both prosecution for public order and political offences, and to more summary forms of treatment (Amnesty International 2007b). Certain regional groups active in major cities located mainly in the western part of the country are associated with organized crime activity, especially groups from the Black Sea and Kurdish regions (Cerrah 2007).

## Turkey's policing model

As should be clear from the discussion so far, there is no single, uncontested policing model in Turkey. The history of public administration, including civilian policing, derives from the Ottoman period in the nineteenth century in which the French *prefecture* model was formally adopted. Over time, in reflection of its provenance, the civilian administration has tended to be highly bureaucratized and centralized in nature. One consequence has been to effectively preclude any local democratic input into policing as well as other public services. Decisions about policing priorities have tended to come from central edicts in Ankara, either from the Ministry of Interior or the General Directorate of Security, the headquarters of the TNP. On this basis, the TNP has largely reflected the ideal of bureaucratic, professional policing—consistent with other police forces of this nature, the TNP has developed a high degree of institutional autonomy not just from the society in which it operates but also from the civilian administration under which it is formally subjugated by law. The lack of effective internal civilian controls over the TNP, as well as the Jandarma, has recently been noted in reviews undertaken by the Ministry of Interior and the United Nations Development Program and the EU (Goldsmith 2005).

In light of such reviews and EU-related accession pressures, there are reform activities within the TNP geared to implementing, at least to some degree, features of policing practised elsewhere in the developed world. One current initiative is the establishment of an independent police complaints body, supported by the EU. Within the TNP itself, various community policing type programs can be found, at least superficially emulating programs of a similar nature in Britain and Western Europe. However, gestures of this kind have not yet produced profound changes in the nature of policing provided. Public order policing is still very present on the streets of Turkish cities as a model of what the police do. Turkish policing scholars still note the failure to shift philosophically from the ideal of 'force' to one of 'service' (e.g. Cerrah 2006).

The TNP is a large force by world standards. It has approximately 175,000 sworn police, supported by almost 18,000 clerical/assistant positions, a total of nearly 193,000 persons. As a ratio, those numbers alone in a country of more than 67 million persons deliver one police officer per 382 citizens. Then, the Jandarma numbers must be considered. Estimates of their number vary from 280,000 to 300,000. When added to the number of TNP personnel (plus the Coast Guard numbers of 2,200), the ratio reduces considerably to one police/law-enforcement official per 146 citizens (Cerrah 2006: 88). This figure is very high by world standards, albeit one can tell little about the nature of policing from these figures themselves. In terms of gender, 5.4 percent of the TNP is female, with very few in senior positions.[3]

One of the key features of the Jandarma, in contrast to the TNP, is the high reliance it places upon national service conscripts to make up its numbers—in the vicinity of 80 percent. These conscripts are typically young men who undergo a short training program of around six weeks that is separate from other law-enforcement officials. Normally, their period of service is fifteen months. Needless to say, there are limitations in terms of their operational competence given such short periods of preparation and length of service (Sariibrahimoglu 2006). The TNP, by contrast, is a career police service that does not rely upon conscripts and offers basic police training over a two year program (Cerrah 2006). In addition to the national service component of the Jandarma, it must also be remembered that its principal law-enforcement responsibility lies in the rural areas of Turkey—across 91 percent of Turkey's land area, and that it is formally under the Ministry of Defence for training and all non-law-enforcement purposes. Hence, it is a militaristic law-enforcement body in nature, but one relatively unprofessional in law-enforcement terms as measured in terms of the level of relevant skills among the vast majority of its personnel. As will be noted below, it has a tendency to remain more aloof from civilian authorities than the TNP, rendering it less subject to civilian control.

## Police-military sector relations

The Turkish military has been widely viewed by many Turks as superior in competence and ethics to all other Turkish institutions, including the police. It is also very large by comparison—excluding the Jandarma, the Turkish Armed Forces number more than 500,000 (Sariibrahimoglu 2006). Hence, it has been observed, the military has tended to act disdainfully towards the police, often because of the police's poor record, comparatively speaking, in terms of discipline, use of force, and corruption (Jenkins 2002). During the 1990s in south-eastern Turkey, the police formed 'Special Teams' to deal with the PKK (Kurdish Workers' Party—Partiya Karkaren Kurdistan) threat. Apparently, their methods were all too often brutal, disrupting intelligence networks established by the military among the local Kurdish populations. In addition, according to Jenkins (2002: 88), "the military complained that the police's widespread use of torture in predominantly Kurdish cities was alienating local people and swelling the flow of recruits for PKK units in the mountains." However, such joint operations are relatively unusual, so that for the most part, the TNP and the military have little to do with each other. The case is somewhat different in relation to the Jandarma, whose officers may have attended military training schools, have been equipped with military-style weapons, and be drawn into more paramilitary-style activities in the rural areas with the other armed forces.

The civilian character of the TNP is established in large measure by its location under the Ministry of the Interior, to which it must look for its budget and from which it receives its directions and instructions. This is reinforced by the separate and quite elaborate system of police education now to be found in Turkey (Cerrah 2006). In law-enforcement terms, the separate training and the variations between them, present a problem of consistency of approach. Where the geographical boundaries between urban and rural zones are clear and undisputed, it poses relatively few problems in that the two law-enforcement bodies can get on with their tasks without reference to each other. However, urbanization on the once-rural fringes of large cities has meant that the jurisdictional distinctions have become blurred, with the result that in some places both the TNP and the Jandarma claim to be the relevant law-enforcement authority. While overlaps can produce confusion and potential doubling-up of resources, another problem in such circumstances can be the vacuum of law enforcement created, as each agency takes the view that it is the other's responsibility, resulting on occasions with neither responding to the situation in question. In the light of these ongoing difficulties, there is a clear need for this situation to be clarified as a matter of law as well as in practice as quickly as possible (Cerrah 2006).

The potential conflicts become more acute at times as between the Jandarma acting in their law-enforcement capacity and in their role as part of the Turkish military establishment. This potential clash is structured into the very laws that define the Jandarma's obligations, to the Ministry of Interior in times of peace and under the command of the Turkish Armed Forces in times of war and national emergency (Sariibrahimoglu 2006). One consequence of these mixed allegiances is that on occasions, in response to public order situations in which the Jandarma have sought assistance from other security forces, they have turned to the Armed Forces in preference to the nearest TNP station for that assistance.[4] From a law-enforcement perspective, the irregular involvement of non-law enforcement personnel in policing duties is clearly undesirable.

Another outcome of this unusual arrangement is that on occasion Jandarma personnel will undertake law-enforcement operations in urban areas without notification of the local TNP commander or the relevant civilian authority. It is generally indicative of a lack of trust and coordination between the two law-enforcement bodies, one that in part can be attributed to the military allegiances and traditions of the Jandarma. Most disturbingly of all, in March 2006, it was revealed that in 1997 the General Staff of the TAF and the Ministry of Interior had signed a secret protocol on Security, Public Order, and Assistant Units (known as EMAYSA which "allows for military operations to be carried out for internal security matters under certain conditions without request from the civilian authorities," including the collection of intelligence (European Commission 2006: 8). Such a failure to establish clear divisions between police and law enforcement, and military functions during peace-time continues to be a matter of concern for the European Commission.

## Other aspects of the criminal justice system

The criminal justice system, like the system of public administration, owes its origins to the European (principally French) system of justice. Unlike many other unconsolidated democracies, particularly those emerging from periods of internal conflict, Turkey has a longstanding set of justice and correctional institutions that complement in formal terms the law-enforcement agencies. In short, there are penal codes, prosecution departments, military as well as civilian courts, and detention and correctional centres, which can be used to process suspects brought to court by the police. However, police and gendarmerie confidence in the effectiveness of the other elements of the justice system has often been quite low (Jenkins 2002). In many emerging (and indeed relatively 'emerged') democracies, such a situation often has given rise to summary 'police justice'. Indeed, it would seem, many of the conditions that can precipitate arbitrary, extra-legal actions are present in Turkey as well, as the following discussion shall show.

Many components of Turkey's justice system have been subjected to criticism over the years. These include procedural inefficiencies as well as out and out abuses of individual rights, including torture. While some of these problems took place during the various periods of military government in Turkey's modern history, allegations of torture and abuse within the detention centres and prisons have long been a complaint of human rights NGOS, both domestic and internal. Such concerns at least in some measure continue to the present day (Amnesty International 2007a), though it is conceded that the levels of abuse of detainees including use of torture has diminished significantly over recent decades in response to visits and reports by bodies such as the European Committee for the Prevention of Torture (CPT) (CPT 2006) and the UN Special Rapporteur on Torture. Other complaints have arisen in terms of lengthy and unfair trials, as well as political (and possibly military) interference in the administration of justice (Amnesty International 2007a, 2007b).

The failure of prosecutors and courts to successfully bring to account perpetrators of abuses from within the security forces (impunity) has been another regular charge leveled by NGOs and other observers against the effectiveness and equity of the criminal justice system (Amnesty International 2007b; Caglar 2003). Such shortcomings are particularly apparent in cases of use of lethal force. When they occur, and they are followed by official denials or lack of investigation, they often provoke public disquiet and even major demonstrations. The shooting of a father and son in Mardin (south-east Turkey) by members of a police anti-terrorist unit in November 2004 (the "Kiziltepe Case") resulted in official denials and cross-allegations, which was then followed by a public protest by approximately 5,000 persons (Bese 2007; Amnesty International 2007b). The operation of Turkey's inquisitorial court system has been associated even in ordinary criminal cases with long delays, hearings months apart, and an apparent lack of judicial preparedness given the delays and volumes of cases to be heard (Jenkins 2002). The systems' reliance on testimony, rather than evidence given orally in open court, it has been argued, based on logic as well as experience in the Turkish case, has put pressure on police in criminal cases to generate testimonies implicating the persons in custody in particular crimes. "Almost certainly," Jenkins suggests, this state of affairs "increases the prevalence of torture and physical abuse during questioning" (2002: 88).

The nature of offences under the Turkish Penal Code and relevant anti-terrorist legislation also affect what police do and who gets brought to book for their actions. Not unlike many other countries, Turkey has expanded its anti-terrorist provisions in the last few years, partly at least to reflect the fact that it has itself been the victim of several serious bombings in cities such as Istanbul and Ankara, causing significant death and injury in a number of instances. NGOs have expressed concerns about the level of lethal force that recent changes have authorized police personnel to use in anti-terrorist operations—"direct and unhesitating force" to "render the danger ineffective" in Article 16 of the revised Law to Fight Terrorism was singled out for concern in a recent Amnesty International report. In addition to specific anti-terrorist laws, the operation of specialist criminal courts in Turkey has led to criticism over a considerable period. The State Security Courts, abolished in 2004, have since been replaced by Heavy Penal Courts to hear charges under the anti-terrorist legislation. These courts have been challenged for the unfairness of their trial procedures and the prolonged nature of trials, during which time those charged are typically being detained in custody (Amnesty International 2007b).

Another criminal offence that has generated a lot of controversy recently, especially in light of the EU accession talks, is Article 301 of the Turkish Penal Code. This provision is directed against those who denigrate Turkishness, the Republic, or any of the state institutions. It is apparently quite widely used by police and prosecution authorities. A famous recent case of its use was that of Orhan Pamuk, the Turkish novelist and Nobel Prize winner, whose trial resulted in his acquittal. While many other such cases have ended similarly, the fact that policing, law enforcement and justice system resources are expended in such ways is not without significance. Even if some Turkish citizens support such prosecutions, as undoubtedly many do, the particular law-enforcement priorities on display scarcely escape foreign notice, especially within Europe where such events run the risk of confirming some of the fears held already about the wisdom of granting EU membership to Turkey. In this sense, it is the shortcomings of Turkey's criminal justice system as a whole, rather than the police in particular, that fall under foreign scrutiny for the existence and operation of such laws.

## Obstacles to democratic accountability

A number of the historical and structural characteristics of Turkish policing have been mentioned already, several of which carry with them difficulties in terms of rendering policing in Turkey more accountable, transparent, and professional in democratic, Rule of Law terms.

The legal frameworks governing policing and law enforcement in Turkey are labyrinthine in complexity and also generate much uncertainty and confusion about their practical significance. Such undesirable features of the law itself provide a pretext for those police and law-enforcement officials formally subject to it to ignore it and at times to act as if the law did not exist. Lacking clear lines of responsibility in these circumstances makes the exercise of accountability extremely difficult for civilian administrators and the courts alike (Goldsmith 2005). These problems arise with respect to both the TNP and the Jandarma. Sariibrahimoglu (2006) has noted that "approximately 600 laws and regulations define the gendarmerie's responsibilities and duties" (2006: 105). A similar situation with the TNP has been noted by Caglar, who stated, "neither police officers nor the public know what are the exact duties of the police." He went on to say, "There is no definitive police officer job description" (2003: 417).

There is a fundamental problem with respect to the Jandarma and its organic location under the Turkish Armed Forces. While its military discipline system, at least in theory, offers some protection against abuses of rights of various kinds, its value must be assessed in terms of its record in this regard. Unfortunately, the relative opaqueness of the institution scarcely assists its own claims to have adequate procedures of an internal nature to provide accountability. While the Jandarma has overhauled its internal complaints procedures in recent years, it is not clear to many observers that levels of impunity have been reduced or that the changes have provided an adequate substitute for more civilian-staffed or accountable mechanisms for investigation or oversight of complaints filed by members of the public or indeed by law-enforcement personnel. As noted earlier, the institutional autonomy of the Jandarma from civilian authorities, practised on a de facto basis (although less clearly warranted under the applicable laws), means that there is very little opportunity even for appointed civil servants responsible for their oversight, let alone ordinary citizens, to take issue with Jandarma actions. The fact that Jandarma operations are predominantly rural in nature and often paramilitary in character makes the weakness of such internal procedures and the absence of a viable alternative of graver concern.

One should not overstate the differences in this regard compared to the TNP. The TNP itself, as noted earlier, is highly centralized in nature, so that directions from Ankara are often sought by district commanders even in the face of requests or directions from local civilian authorities with formal authority over those district commanders. These civilian authorities are themselves appointed from Ankara to represent the central government in a range of areas, including internal security. However, particularly at the district level, their confidence and competence to act as a check and monitor upon policing and law-enforcement activities at the local level is limited and at least at times non-existent. Their capacity to act in this way is further undermined by the politicization of security matters that goes on within the TNP, the Ministry of Interior and the government. This can result in the appointment of TNP commanders without the consultation or approval of district-level civilian authorities, even without notice; similarly, the removal of police commanders can occur despite the fact that they enjoy wide support within the cities and towns they serve. The point here is that such changes without consultation or notice are widely seen to be on political, rather than merit, grounds. Hence the professionalism, as well as accountability, inherent in such actions falls into doubt.

Another consideration in looking at prospects for accountability is the state of police/community relations in Turkey, and in particular, the degree of public confidence in the police and law-enforcement agencies. What is agreed among commentators and observers is that there is a large gap between the police and Jandarma *and* the public at large. An ongoing feature of police-citizen relations at a personal level is the prevalence of various forms of corruption. Police officers in Turkey are not particularly well-paid and many work very long hours (Cerrah 2006). So ways of supplementing income through the selective enforcement (or non-enforcement) of the law are widely practised among the police ranks, although some observers believe the incidence may be dropping in recent years (Caglar 2003). Bribery is widely encountered in a range of other services sought by the public, so that the police are not unusual to the extent that they also seek bribes. Given the mixed motives likely to be associated with bribery (especially citizen-initiated cases), it remains unclear how this practice bears upon public attitudes towards the police. However it seems at least likely, drawing on recent European-based research around the issue of public trust in police, that such practices contribute to a lower level of public regard for the police, especially within the contexts of more generalized distrust and experiences of corruption and, interestingly, relatively high levels of public expenditure upon policing and security (Kaariainen 2007). While there is a need for more research specific to the Turkish case, both of these contextual factors would seem to apply in the present case (on widespread corruption in the Turkish public sector and judiciary, see European Commission 2006), reinforcing the risks to the standing of Turkish police and law-enforcement officials under present circumstances.

The existence of a gap between police and community bodes negatively for more democratic forms of accountability. While Cerrah has stated that the Turkish public is less supportive of efforts by police to fight crime than members of the public in most developed democratic states (Cerrah 2006), perhaps paradoxically, Cao and Burton (2006) have recently reported from their survey and found that the Turkish public rate their confidence in their police quite highly compared to member states of the EU, Turkey's neighbours and other Muslim countries (2006: 459). The authors of this study attribute an improvement in public attitudes to greater democratization of Turkish policing, involving in part an attempt by the police to appeal to the mainstream of Turkish society. Here, one of the ironies of 'democratic policing' emerges—Cao and Burton note that while Amnesty International recently criticized Turkish police for its record of abuses of individual rights, "the police in Turkey received a great deal of support for their tough action against Kurdish separatist demonstrations" (2006: 461) from the general public as well as from the political elite. Such generalized support may not however, as Cerrah (2006) seems to suggest, translate into positive, frequent exchanges between police personnel and citizens. Given the absence of real accountability mechanisms at the grassroots in Turkey for dialogue between citizens and police, it would seem useful in such settings to distinguish between 'real' democratic accountability in the sense just described on the one hand, and, on the other, a more diffuse 'populist' accountability in which a largely disengaged population expresses general support for particular law-enforcement policies, for example, taking tough action against pro-Kurdish demonstrators.

Cao and Burton find grounds for some optimism about future improvements in police–community relations in Turkey, in relation to the movement of many rural people, mostly Kurds, to the urban centres. They note: "Many rural residents (especially Kurdish people) have found urban police to be more civil than both the rural police and the military they encountered. As a result, even Kurdish confidence in the police has become higher over the years" (2006: 461). This finding is curious when measured against findings from other countries that rural populations generally enjoy greater trust in their police than urban residents (Kaariainen 2007). The explanation in the Turkish case may be that rural resident–police relations are not typical comparatively speaking with other countries, given the prominence of internally displaced persons (IDPs) and the significance of the Kurdish separatist issue in rural areas (especially in the south-east of the country), including a history of the use of martial law (Bese 2007).

Further impediments to accountability arise in terms of the functioning of the prosecutors and courts. Some of the difficulties faced with the courts have been mentioned already—these same problems contribute to the prevalence of impunity in cases against police and other security personnel (Caglar 2003; Cerrah 2006; Amnesty International 2007b). This is not to say that cases are never brought successfully against TNP or Jandarma officials (see Sariibrahimoglu 2006), but such cases appear to be very rare. While prosecutors have a responsibility to ensure that persons in custody are not abused and that they are well-treated, in the past, this responsibility has not been effectively exercised for the most part (European Commission 2006), as the ongoing, although diminishing, reports of torture in police and Jandarma facilities attest. Confidence in the ability of civilian authorities to effectively investigate allegations of abuse by law-enforcement officials is deservedly low in a system in which, according to Sariibrahimoglu (2006: 110), "the gendarmerie retains the right to withhold information from the public prosecutor." The existence of curious rights of this nature, as well as clear evidence of the unilateral exercise of de facto prerogatives by police and law-enforcement officials to resist civilian oversight, certainly lends support to those who still see a "deep state" at work within the Turkish establishment and society (Green and Ward 2004).

In addition to the possibility of Turkish courts, there exists the avenue of the European Court of Human Rights. Many cases are brought from Turkey on a variety of matters, not all related to policing or law-enforcement issues. In the past, much external scrutiny has focused on Turkey's prison system and the treatment of detainees. This interest in detention facilities continues. Many applications to the European Court relate to the right to fair trial, and significant numbers of matters deal with the prohibition against torture (142 cases in the twelve months to 31 August 2006) and the right to life (78 cases in the same period). Despite improvements in the procedures for executing these judgments in recent years, there remains a problem of delay in a significant number of these cases (European Commission 2006: 11).

Another potential mechanism for enhancing policing accountability are the Human Rights Boards, established relatively recently under the Turkish Presidency. They were intended to receive complaints of a human rights nature from citizens, including from those with complaints against police and law-enforcement officials. These are relatively new and poorly resourced bodies, and given their origins and sponsorship, dependent upon the Presidency rather than being strongly independent in nature. Further evaluation of these bodies is needed. The UNDP/Ministry of Interior assessment exercise, headed by the author (Goldsmith 2005), encountered little understanding among NGOs of their role and many persons interviewed expressed scepticism regarding their efficacy as an oversight mechanism for police and law enforcement. This lack of relevance to policing oversight is reflected in the recent statistics for the Board which show that the majority of matters filed relate to health, non-discrimination, rights to property, and social security (European Commission 2006).

A fundamental obstacle to improved accountability for state security operations lies in the existence of what many Turkish observers have come to call the 'deep state' (*derin devlet*). This refers to a shadowy power structure within the state apparatus with links to criminal groups and senior military figures. A car accident in 1996 in a small town called Susurluk, in which most of the car's occupants died, exposed the existence of connections between a prominent politician, a young female model, a well-known police chief involved in special anti-terrorist operations, and a wanted criminal. Subsequent inquiries into these connections did not progress far in terms of definitive conclusions or public accountability, but underlined for many Turkish observers the existence of such an entity in Turkish society and its corrupting influence upon proper political and legal conduct (Cerrah 2007).

## Policing and private security

Little has been written to date on the topic of private security firms in Turkey. There has been an attempt to regulate the sector through legislation in 2004. The need for such regulation has reflected the growing involvement of international private security providers in the Turkish market, as well as expanding local firm involvement. This law has attempted to codify the roles of the sector relative to those of public law-enforcement bodies. The norm has been set, for example, that there should be a presumption that such private personnel should be unarmed. It is also the case, as in many Western countries, that private police personnel carry only the authority of private personnel, rather than that of public law-enforcement officials (Eryilmaz 2006). One regulatory mechanism of note is the establishment under the 2004 law of Local Province Security Commissions, comprising members from both the public and private security sectors as well as members of the Chambers of Commerce and Industry. Such a coordinating mechanism in the security sector, especially with local involvement, is unusual for Turkey, given the absence of similar consultative mechanisms at the local level for bringing not just interest groups but ordinary citizens together with police and gendarmerie.

## Current reform programs

The European Union has been particularly active in promoting policing reform in Turkey, and continues to be so. The discussion here focuses upon those very recent, well-publicized activities in this area. The reform programs tend to focus upon either the TNP or the Jandarma, so it makes sense to discuss them separately. However, there are two shared reform goals that should be mentioned.

The first of these is in fact a project working with the Ministry of Interior to strengthen the authority and capacity of civilian administrators (governors, district governors) and prosecutors over the activities of the Jandarma and the TNP. One finding of the UNDP/Ministry assessment (Goldsmith 2005) was that the Jandarma operated particularly autonomously from civil authorities, and that the hand of civilian authorities needed to be strengthened in the interests of enhanced accountability. A similar situation was found with respect to the TNP, though less extreme. The current EU-funded, UNDP-administered reform project looks at overhauling the legislative foundations of the civil/policing relationship, clarifying lines of authority and responsibility as between civil authorities, the TNP and the Jandarma, and building capacity within the Ministry of Interior for the effective exercise of that authority.

While this program can be criticized for not being democratic, or at least sufficiently democratic (Cerrah 2006) in terms of bringing police authority under direct elected political control, if effective, it will significantly reduce the amount of unaccountable authority exercised by the principal policing and law-enforcement institutions in the country.

Another priority being driven by the EU Accession Partnership and the National Programme for the Adoption of the Acquis (NPAA) involves restructuring the capacity of both policing bodies to tackle organized crime, money laundering, drug trafficking and financial crime. These moves are also being complemented by programs intended to strengthen the forensic capacities of both bodies to undertake effective investigations (Cizre 2007: 18).

Two other projects affecting the TNP have been proposed. One is the establishment of an independent police complaints commission, a common feature in many European and English-speaking countries in the past decade or two. Work is proceeding at present under EU sponsorship on a twinning arrangement with the Independent Police Complaints Commission for England and Wales. Currently, putting to one side the largely ineffective role played by civilian administrators, local prosecutors and Human Rights Boards in this area (Goldsmith 2005), there is no place outside the TNP itself where citizens can file, and have dealt with relatively expeditiously and impartially, complaints about police or law-enforcement behaviour.

Another project, begun in 2005, was the Community Policing project, established under the wider EU sponsored program of Strengthening of the Responsibility, Productivity and Effectiveness of the TNP. According to

Cerrah (2006: 97), this project will last 24 months and provides "an important opportunity to match the existing structure of its police force to EU standards." It has two aspects, one related to better managerial practices and the other concerned with better service delivery and police education (Cerrah 2006). The project is being coordinated by Spain for the EU.

In the case of the Jandarma, in addition to the Ministry of Interior-led program on civilian oversight of both policing bodies mentioned above, two other initiatives can be mentioned. The first is one directed to a reduction in the number of conscripted members of the organization, with their replacement by greater use of professional personnel. This shift has been viewed as a means of improving transparency and professionalism and hence, accountability (Sariibrahimoglu 2006: 103). However, the project stalled in 2005 when the Jandarma withdrew its participation in this UK-partnered project on the grounds that it was expected to conform to the Turkish military personnel policies, which were being reformed independently. It would seem that the impasse remains unresolved. The second project is for the establishment of a Border Police Organization, as it has been stipulated by the EU that it does not want the Jandarma to play an active part in border policing once Turkey joins the EU on a full membership basis. Once again, there has been Jandarma and indeed TAF resistance to this project, reportedly on the basis that both are reluctant "to transfer authority to a border guard body consisting of civilian professionals" (Sariibrahimoglu 2006: 104)—under existing law, land border protection is the responsibility of the TAF.

## Prospects for reform

What factors will shape future policing reform in Turkey? Turkey's policing reform agenda reflects the consequences of a number of factors and influences. In addition to the 'atmospheric' agenda items raised by globalization (e.g. 'community policing,' or computer-assisted dispatch systems) that are commonplace and widespread among police forces in many quarters of the globe (Ellison 2007), there are the direct opportunities presented through increased contact between police officers and gendarmerie officials and police and law-enforcement officials in other countries to meet at conferences and regional training sessions, as well as through participation in United Nations police peace-keeping operations. Both Jandarma and TNP officers have served and are serving in various missions abroad, a relatively new trend but one likely to continue into the future, with opportunities for further contact and interaction with police from many other countries likely.

The other obvious source of reform ideas in policing is channelled through Turkey's attempt to achieve political and economic integration with the European Union. This prospect has added momentum for change across the Turkish security sector and within civil society, opening up new spaces for broader, and less state-centred concepts of security. As Bilgin notes (2005: 176):

Although Turkey has had to deal with 'strategic globality' for a long time, the process of joining the EU posed challenges that involved the adoption of international societal norms, which are perceived by some to threaten Turkey's 'national security.' Such norms weaken the grip of the state over political processes and introduces 'new' actors who challenge established approaches to issues (such as cultural pluralism, linguistic rights or gender relations) that are considered 'sensitive' by some.

However change in fundamental terms towards EU membership has been partial, with considerable difficulty and tardiness in respect of implementation of those changes agreed to formally. Michael Emerson (2004: 2) noted that if "the EU strictly followed its prior doctrine [for membership], the conclusion would have to be that Turkey does not yet fulfil the Copenhagen criteria," despite "huge progress with constitutional amendments and seven harmonization packages, since there are too many implementation shortcomings (e.g. penal system, judiciary)." In Turkey, there remains a considerable number of 'Euro-sceptics' within the security sector who are reluctant to give up traditional security sector practices and who are suspicious of human rights and community policing agendas. In any country, resistance to new, more open, security and policing ideas can sometimes take the form of 'indigenizing' those ideas in ways that render them incapable of achieving real change and thus threatening the status quo. In this regard, Turkey is unlikely to be different. In a discussion on Turkish community policing I held with one senior TNP official,[5] it became quickly clear that what he saw it to mean was that citizens would more willingly provide police with criminal intelligence than they had in the past—there was not a sense of genuine partnership and reciprocity between police and community in his account.

One of the interesting challenges will be the extent to which the Jandarma is able to embrace reform. This perhaps will depend upon the extent to which the Turkish Armed Forces more broadly undergoes change that renders it more transparent and subject to civilian authority and the Rule of Law. As noted earlier, Jandarma personnel are serving outside Turkey, so that some of the same processes at work with respect to civilian police, pushing along the development of a global police consciousness and professional identity, are also there for the Jandarma. However, there is not the same network of law-enforcement agencies and officials analogous to the Jandarma situation that there is for police. There are gendarmeries elsewhere with which some exchanges and relations are held, but it is a much smaller group that does not reach into countries such as Canada, the United Kingdom, or the United States, from which many of the key ideas for policing reform emanate (Goldsmith and Sheptycki 2007).

A far more significant, yet unlikely, reform would be the merger of the Jandarma with the TNP under the responsibility of the Ministry of Interior. The current division between the Ministries of Defence and Interior, reinforced by separate training and command structures, reduces the potential for coordination of resources and consistency of approach. While some senior police would welcome an amalgamation of this nature (Cizre 2007), it would be a huge political achievement against the gradient of traditional power relations within the Turkish state. While such an idea does not seem to have been advanced explicitly by the EU in Accession talks, its insistence however on separate, civilian border guards for Turkey in the future (thus removing the Jandarma from this role) and its involvement in the current project for establishing an independent complaints commission for the TNP and the Jandarma, indicates the importance in such an environment as Turkey presents of keeping a focus upon ensuring incremental steps in support of the further civilianization of policing and law enforcement.

Other areas recently announced as important objectives for pre-Accession progress include training of police for combating violence against women, independent monitoring of detention facilities, and advances in transnational cooperation in the fight against organized crime (European Commission 2007).

## Conclusion

Inevitably, policing reform in Turkey will largely be shaped by the ongoing shifts in the balance of civil–military relations. This balance will reflect the ability of Turkey as a nation to establish greater equilibrium socially and politically on questions such as the role of Islam in domestic politics and the threats faced by the nation as a whole. Hangii and Tanner recently observed:

> The problem of sustained reform is that the Turkish Army continues to use international crises such as Cyprus or the fight against Kurdish insurgents in south-east Turkey to reassert its standing in domestic politics. The Army's main argument against reform has been that national security and unity must take precedence over democratization.
>
> (2005: 66)

The direction in which national security discourse is developing, and hence policing reform is headed, is not simply charted. Globalization, professionalization, and EU accession requirements push more or less in one direction, towards the broadening of discussion to include citizen safety as well as state security, while unresolved tensions in the Middle East and the Kurdish question domestically continue to legitimate taking hard, militarized stances against perceived threats to state security. One encouraging, significant shift in recent years, Cizre has recently noted, is that civil society has become increasingly vocal on these matters. The critical problem of 'understanding' the security problem has passed; "precepts that shape national security policies are increasingly being debated by civilian bodies" (Cizre 2007: 21). Those debates will inevitably draw continuously and more deeply in the future on internal security and crime control debates going on in Europe and elsewhere. Generational change in the areas already identified, rather than short-term major reforms, therefore looks more likely. In the meantime, progress within policing in areas such as accountability and professionalism moves along somewhat erratically and tentatively.

## Acknowledgements

I would like to thank Professor Ibrahim Cerrah of the Turkish Police Academy, Ankara, Turkey for sharing information with me during the writing of this chapter, and for commenting on an earlier draft.

## Notes

1   By way of comparison, Sri Lanka is no. 93, and the Dominican Republic no. 95 on the UNDP's Human Development Index (HDI).
2   The founder of the modern Turkish state was Mustafa Kemal Ataturk, who died in 1938. The secular philosophy he established during his lifetime has been maintained through key public institutions, not least the Turkish Armed Forces. This secular, modernizing standpoint, often accompanied by public celebration of the life of Ataturk, is often referred to as 'Kemalism' after its founder.
3   No figures for gender in the Jandarma could be located during the research undertaken for this chapter.
4   Interview with a provincial governor, Turkey, September 2005.
5   This interview occurred in May 2005.

## References

Amnesty International (AI) (2007a) *Report 2007: Turkey* (London: AI).
Amnesty International (AI) (2007b) *Turkey: The Entrenched Culture of Impunity Must End* (London: AI).
Bese, Ertan (2007) "Office of Special Operations" in Umit Cizre, ed., *Almanac Turkey 2005: Security Sector and Democratic Oversight* (Istanbul: TESEV/Geneva Centre for the Democratic Control of Armed Forces).
Bilgin, Pinar (2005) "Turkey's changing security discourses: The challenge of globalization" *European Journal of Political Research*, 44, 175–201.
Caglar, Ali (2003) "Policing Problems in Turkey: Processes, Issues and the Future" in Stan Einstein and Menachem Amir, eds, *Police Corruption: Paradigms, Models and Concepts—Challenges for Developing Countries* (Hunstville, TX: Office of International Criminal Justice).
Cao, Liqun and Burton, Velmer (2006) "Spanning the continents: assessing the Turkish public confidence in the police" *Policing: An International Journal of Police Strategies and Management*, 29, 451–463.
Cerrah, Ibrahim (2006) "Police" in Umit Cizre, ed., *Almanac Turkey 2005: Security Sector and Democratic Oversight* (Istanbul: TESEV/Geneva Centre for the Democratic Control of Armed Forces).
Cerrah, Ibrahim (2007) "Democratization of Policing: The Case of the Turkish Police" in M. R. Haberfeld and Ibrahim Cerrah, eds, *Comparative Policing: The Struggle for Democratization* (Los Angeles: Sage).

Cizre, Umit (2007) *Prime Movers, Specific Features and Challenges of Security Sector Reform in a 'Guardian State': The Case of Turkey*, Policy paper no. 17 (Geneva: Geneva Centre for the Democratic Control of Armed Forces).

Committee for the Prevention of Torture (CPT) (2006) *Report to the Turkish Government on the visit to Turkey from 7 to 14 December 2005* (Strasbourg: CPT).

Ellison, Graham (2007) "Fostering a Dependency Culture: The Commodification of Community Policing in a Global Marketplace" in Andrew Goldsmith and James Sheptycki, eds, *Crafting Transnational Policing: Police Capacity-building and Global Policing Reform* (Oxford: Hart Publishing).

Emerson, Michael (2004) *Has Turkey Fulfilled the Copenhagen Political Criteria?* (Brussels: Centre for European Policy Studies).

Eryilmaz, Mesut (2006) "Private Security" in Umit Cizre, ed., *Almanac Turkey 2005: Security Sector and Democratic Oversight* (Istanbul: TESEV/Geneva Centre for the Democratic Control of Armed Forces).

European Commission (2006) *Commission Staff Working Document: Turkey 2006 Progress Report* (Brussels: Commission of the EC).

European Commission (2007) *Decision of the European Commission, 30 April, Multi-annual Indicative Planning Document (MIPD) for Turkey 2007–09* [http://ec.europa.eu/enlargement].

Goldsmith, Andrew (2005) *Final Report: Preparatory Assistance for Civilian Oversight of Policing and Law Enforcement* (Ankara: UNDP/Ministry of Interior).

Goldsmith, Andrew and Sheptycki, James (2007), eds, *Crafting Transnational Policing: Police Capacity-building and Global Policing Reform* (Oxford: Hart Publishing).

Green, Penny and Ward, Tony (2004) *State Crime: Governments, Violence and Corruption* (London: Pluto Press).

Hangii, Heiner and Tanner, Fred (2005) *Promoting security sector governance in the EU's neighbourhood*, Chaillot Paper no. 80 (Paris: Institute for Security Studies).

Human Rights Watch (2007) *Country Summary: Turkey* (January 2007).

Jenkins, Gareth (2002) "Power and unaccountability in the Turkish security forces" *Conflict, Security and Development*, 1, 83–91.

Kaariainen, Juha (2007) "Trust in the Police in Sixteen European Countries: A Multilevel Analysis" *European Journal of Criminology* 4, 409–435.

Sariibrahimoglu, Lale (2006) "Gendarmerie" in Umit Cizre, ed., *Almanac Turkey 2005: Security Sector and Democratic Oversight* (Istanbul: TESEV/Geneva Centre for the Democratic Control of Armed Forces).

Sariibrahimoglu, Lale (2006) "The Turkish Armed Forces" in Umit Cizre, ed., *Almanac Turkey 2005: Security Sector and Democratic Oversight* (Istanbul: TESEV/Geneva Centre for the Democratic Control of Armed Forces).

Shambayati, Hootan (2004) "A Tale of Two Mayors: Courts and Politics in Iran and Turkey" *International Journal of Middle Eastern Studies*, 36, 253–275.

United Nations Development Programme (UNDP) (2005) *Human Development Report* (New York: United Nations).

United Nations Office on Drugs and Crime (UNODC) (2005) *Ninth United Nations Survey of Crime Trends and Operations of Criminal Justice Systems* (New York: United Nations).

# 3 Policing in the 'new' Russia

*Adrian Beck and Annette Robertson*

## Introduction

Like most of the independent states that were created following the disintegration of the Soviet Union in 1991, the Russian Federation is often described as a 'country in transition', referring to the move from a socialist-based society to one rooted in the principles of capitalism. This transition, however, is much broader than merely changing the economic system insofar as it entails a radical shift from totalitarianism to democracy, which requires an overhaul of the previously-existing system and all of its institutions, including the criminal justice system and the police. This process could never be anything but monumental, tortuous and painful, particularly given the economic, social, and political instability that characterises many countries going through a process of transition.

This chapter reviews the development of police reform in Russia since the collapse of the Soviet Union. In doing so it touches upon other relevant issues, including the historical, political and cultural context in which policing in Russia has been defined and implemented. The main focus, however, is on the theory and practice of police reform, which will be discussed within a critical framework that seeks to evaluate the success – or otherwise – of the process thus far. The chapter concludes by arguing that, although a great deal of change has been introduced over the last 10 to 15 years in the sphere of criminal justice, as the country has attempted to introduce principles more in keeping with democratic ideals, much of the police reform has in fact been superficial or involved the continuation – and even the reinforcement – of Soviet trends and traditions, rather than a break from past practices and principles. As such the prospects for the evolution of the Russian police into a trusted, transparent and accountable police service are not encouraging.

## The general background to police reform

The collapse of the Soviet Union left 15 newly-independent states with criminal justice systems characterised by a legal, cultural and organisational framework that firmly bore the mark of totalitarian regimes (Shelley, 1996).

This was clearly not in keeping with the underlying principles of democratic states, where the rule of law is firmly established and upheld. In the chaos that followed the disintegration of the Soviet Union many countries faced the unenviable challenge of overhauling their criminal justice systems at the same time as the economic, social and political infrastructure crumbled. In Russia this abrupt transition was accompanied by soaring crime rates, caused by factors such as increased social inequality (poverty and unemployment), as well as weakening social control (Gilinskiy, 2006). All types of crime increased from the late 1980s, including huge increases in violent crime.[1] The crime situation has also been adversely affected by secessionist struggles – in the Caucasus in particular – putting added strain on the country's security and police services.[2]

In the aftermath of the collapse some agencies, such as the K.G.B. (The Committee for State Security), which was reorganised and renamed the F.S.B. (The Federal Security Service) and the Ministry of Justice were in many respects quicker to respond to the challenge than the Ministry of Internal Affairs (the MVD – *Ministertsvo Vnutrennykh Del*), which is responsible for policing and the police – or the *militsiya* (the militia), as they are known in Russia. Although extensive attempts have been made to reform the militia since the early 1990s, they continue to be seen as part of the problem of the lack of law and order in the country, rather than the solution, for many reasons – including endemic corrupt practices – as elucidated below.

## The historical context of police reform in Russia

Russia has been striving to overcome the legacy of communism, including highly centralised, militaristic, politicised and authoritarian law-enforcement agencies since the collapse of the Soviet Union in 1991 (Galeotti, 1993; Shelley, 1996; Mawby, 1999). The collapse resulted in a profound crisis in the sphere of law and order, leaving the MVD, which is responsible for policing the huge Russian Federation, in a very weak and disorganised position (Handelman, 1995). It lost power and authority as a result of many internal and external factors, including the decline of central control and anti-government protests, alongside escalating crime rates – especially of a more serious nature, for example, organised, violent and drug-related crime (Dashkov, 1992; Galeotti, 1993; Lotspeich, 1995; Kudriavtsev, 1999; Gilinskiy, 2006). This had implications for levels of fear and insecurity amongst the public (Favarel-Garrigues and Le Huerou, 2004), and also resulted in less public confidence in the militia (Morozov and Sergevnin, 1996; Zvekic, 1996; Timoshenko, 1998).

It was against such a critical background that reform of the militia was first mooted and during the early 1990s measures were undertaken to introduce changes to policing, guided by the principles of guaranteeing human rights and freedoms, providing a more determined fight against crime, and maintaining public order and safety. Consequently, much new legislation was introduced and many changes made to the organisation and functions of the militia (see Beck and Robertson, 2005 for details). It soon became clear, however, that the reform of such a key ministry as internal affairs had to be developed and implemented much more systematically to include every aspect of its work.

## Police reform in Russia: 1996–2005

In 1996 a steering group of academics and practitioners drafted a 'Concept (Paper) for the Development of the Internal Affairs Agencies and Internal Troops of Russia' (MVD, 1996), which summarised the short, medium and long-term development plans for the MVD over the decade 1996–2005. Recognising the changes that had occurred to Russia's economic, political and social circumstances, as well as its deteriorating crime situation, which had resulted in increased public and media demands being made on the MVD, particularly the militia, the Concept Paper defined the impetus for reform as a means of facilitating the development of a democratic and legal state, with the overarching aim being 'to make the MVD capable of guaranteeing the unfailing protection of individuals, society and the state from criminal encroachment' (MVD, 1996).

In addition to the general theoretical basis for reform, the Concept Paper outlined the practical changes envisaged in order to achieve its broader aims, which included improving accountability and performance to 'socially acceptable levels', ultimately in the hope of restoring and maintaining public respect in the militia. The key tasks placed before the militia were to achieve a turning point in the fight against crime; adopt a maximum public-oriented approach; and to mobilise all social resources to counteract criminal expansion. It was envisaged that the major part of the reform process would be implemented by the end of 2005, including the creation of a new legal, organisational, financial and technical framework for the MVD; the introduction of a new system for selecting, training and appointing militia personnel; the technical re-equipping of the militia and internal troops (the Russian 'gendarmerie'); and the provision of legal and social guarantees and improved working conditions for MVD personnel (MVD, 1996).

Given that this timeframe has elapsed, the extent to which these aims were achieved can now be evaluated against the criteria set by the MVD in the Concept Paper. In this respect a decade may seen like a relatively short period in the history of a country seeking to introduce democratic principles, but given that certain key objectives were established in the document to this deadline, it should be possible to draw some conclusions about the success or otherwise of the reform programme as a whole, as well as the prospects for further reform. The following sections review and evaluate the key changes that have been made to the theory and practice of policing in Russia, as well as the results of reforms implemented to organisational structures, operational policies and practices, and performance and accountability measures.

## The theory and practice of militia reform in Russia

### Early changes to policing principles and laws

When the Soviet Union collapsed, the newly-created Russian Federation inherited more than 4,000 pieces of Soviet legislation, most of which had never been made available to the public[3] and many of which directly breached civil rights. The 1991 Law 'On the Militia'[4] was a landmark in some respects, publicly defining for the first time the role and duties of the militia, and thus welcomed by some as a genuine break with the Soviet past, but less positively by others as merely a public endorsement of the same powers secretly provided for under Soviet rule (Handelman, 1995). Nevertheless, the law clearly defined the legal status and organisational structure of the militia, as well as its role in the country's executive power structure.

The law established the militia's guiding values as legitimacy, humanism, social justice, political neutrality, impartiality and respect for and observance of human rights. Consequently, the militia are expected to protect every citizen irrespective of their nationality, political convictions or other circumstances. Importantly, from the perspective of establishing democratic values, the law states that militia personnel must uphold the law and prohibits the formation of political parties or organisations with political aspirations.

The Law 'On the Militia' therefore encompasses many of the key principles required for the development of democratic policing in Russia and should have released the population from the wide-reaching police control that had characterised Soviet society (Shelley, 1996). However, as was the case under Soviet rule, when official declarations and legally-determined principles often failed to translate into practice, even when it came to administering justice and law enforcement (Gilinskiy, 2000), many of this law's provisions are routinely ignored or flouted, as outlined below.

### Human rights and the militia

The militia's record in terms of observing and respecting the rights of the Russian public is very poor. Abuses of power are widespread in their treatment of suspects, as reported by the Russian media and human rights organisations such as Amnesty International (2007, 2003, 2002) and Human Rights' Watch (2006). Depending on the source of information, between one-third (*Ekho Moskvy Radio*, 2005) and one-half (Coalson, 2004) of all complaints received by the Office of Russia's Human Rights' Ombudsman concern the activity of the militia. Complaints include allegations of torture, beatings, unlawful detention, planting evidence and illegal searches, leading the Ombudsman to state that 'the most important and urgent questions are the state of human rights in the law-enforcement agencies' (*Nezavisimaya Gazeta*, 2004). Russian citizens increasingly turn to the European Court of Human Rights (ECHR) for assistance, and the latter regularly issue edicts against Russia for breaches of its citizens' human rights, including the militia's continued use of torture and other illegal methods to secure confessions (Amnesty International, 2006).[5] It is likely that Russian citizens, frustrated by the lack of perceived justice obtained from their national judiciary, which is not always seen to act impartially, will continue to turn to the ECHR to protect and uphold their rights.

## *Impartiality*

Particularly problematic is the prevailing attitudes of some members of the militia towards certain ethnic minority groups, particularly those from the Caucasus and former-Soviet Asian republics, who are often labelled as 'drug dealers' and more recently as 'terrorists' (Shelley, 1999; Amnesty International, 2003; Human Rights Watch, 2003). This demonstrates the militia's failure to adhere to another of the law's guiding principles – to treat everyone impartially and without discrimination, and it extends to how the militia police other groups in society – including, for example, political opponents of the regime and gay rights activists, who have found themselves on the receiving end of the heavy hand of the law, whilst according to Gilinskiy (2006) nationalist, anti-Semitic, neo-fascist and skinhead groups act with impunity.

Moreover, the militia are not always as impartial as they should be in respect of protecting individuals and businesses from 'criminal encroachments'. This is particularly evident in their involvement in commercial disputes (Solomon, 2005; Favarel-Garrigues and Le Huerou, 2004), whereby the militia support whichever side pays them to do so. Calls are habitually made for an end to militia involvement in commercial disputes – including by the president (Feifer, 2003) as this is seen to be closely related to militia corruption and clearly calls their impartiality into question.

## *Politically-neutral?*

The lack of neutrality extends to politics: again in keeping with the Soviet tradition of acting as 'instruments of the Communist regime' (Conquest, 1968: 30), the Russian militia remain far from apolitical (Timoshenko, 1997) and political affiliation appears as strong as it was during Soviet times. To a significant extent this is dictated by political structures and allegiances, since the Minister of Interior is appointed by the president. From 2001–2004 militia reform was spearheaded by Boris Gryzlov, one of the leaders of the United Russia (*Yedinaya Rossiya*) political party, which supports President Putin. Whilst in post as Minister of the Interior Gryzlov faced criticism about his political affiliation and reliance on the MVD at all ranks to support him and the president – for example, campaigning during elections – given that the militia are expected to be politically-neutral (Latynina, 2003).

This type of political allegiance continues down through the ranks as regional militia chiefs are directly responsible to the president, whilst local militia units are largely dependent upon the local authorities for resources such as office buildings and their upkeep, as well as housing for militia personnel. At grassroots' level officers (and also militia cadets/students) are subservient to their superior officers (who, in turn, are under the control of the local, regional or national authorities), facilitating a type of political association and interference, which directly contravenes the law on the militia, forbidding engagement in political activity, including campaigning, and which is certainly not in keeping with democratic ideals.

To a great extent, therefore, on every level the militia remain 'objects of political manipulation' (Gilinskiy, 2000: 177), a situation that has only been exacerbated by subsequent political developments such as the transfer of control over local MVD branches from regional governors (previously elected, but now appointed by the president) to presidential envoys appointed in each of Russia's seven federal regions.[6] Moreover, the creation of regional security councils, comprising the regional heads of law-enforcement, military and intelligence agencies not only deprived regional elites of a serious support base (Kryshtanovskaya, 2003), it also strengthened the role of the president's office in the regions, further embedding the militia in contemporary political structures. Given such underlying continuity and indeed strengthening of certain aspects of Soviet-style policing, (the lack of observance of human and civil rights, discriminatory approaches and political patronage described above), many key provisions of the Law 'On the Militia' appear to have been largely undermined.

## Structural and organisational reform

In addition to a new approach to the ethos of policing, which resulted in the legislative changes outlined above, more practical reforms to the organisational structure and operational policies were also implemented in order to facilitate the militia's law-enforcement work. It is worth noting that these modifications were an attempt to consolidate changes that had been occurring since 1991, as mentioned previously, and were intended to have a positive impact on management efficiency, co-operation with other law-enforcement agencies and NGOs, international relations, the financial and technical base of the militia, legal and social protection for employees, levels of professionalism, and internal control/discipline (MVD, 1996), the last two of which in particular had implications for the development of democratic policing in Russia.

However, although on the surface a great deal of organisational reform has been planned and/or implemented in the Russian militia during the last 10–15 years, this has occurred with apparently little real impact on the efficiency or effectiveness of policing, as detailed later. Landmarks in organisational change include: in 2000 the penitentiary system was transferred from the MVD to the Ministry of Justice, and in 2001 the fire department was transferred to the Ministry of Civil Defence, Emergencies and Disaster Relief. These transfers of responsibility were seen as a means of enabling the MVD to rid itself of significant logistical burdens, enabling it to focus on core law-enforcement duties, but these measures were in fact required under the membership terms laid down by the Council of Europe.

A further round of restructuring in 2001 led to the streamlining of the many departments within the MVD into only three key departments: the Criminal Militia, the Public Security Militia and the Logistics Service, which are headed by the Minister of Internal Affairs' deputies. These services include most of the main directorates (police command units) and independent directorates within the Ministry's Headquarters, but main directorates were also created in each of Russia's seven federal regions, to be overseen by presidential envoys, as mentioned above.

In 2002 plans were announced for the decentralisation of certain elements of policing with the creation of new municipal or local public security units, funded by regional governments and controlled by the local authorities: these were to maintain the name 'militia'. This was to be accompanied by the reorganization of criminal investigation departments (CID), which were to be funded and controlled by the MVD at the federal level, and renamed 'the police'. These two organisations were to be complemented by a third, a National Guard type organisation that encompassed the MVD's special units and internal troops (Favarel-Garrigues and Le Huerou, 2004).

Whilst the 2001 restructuring can be seen as a means of tightening presidential control over regional authorities, the 2002 plans, had they been implemented, could have resulted in a measure of decentralisation of public policing that would have both weakened the centre's control over local policing – a positive step in terms of democratic models of policing (Solomon, 2005) – whilst also lessening its financial burden to the localities. Despite assurances that the new structure would be in place by 2004, this never materialised. Why these plans were not implemented is unclear: much criticism was levelled at the proposals from many quarters, including the MVD, which highlighted the lack of preparation by local authorities to assume such responsibilities, but perhaps the main problem relates to the probable undermining of government control that could have resulted from such decentralisation, potentially also – apparently – to the benefit of local criminal groups, which can play an important role in local politics (Gurov 2004, cited in Solomon 2005). The end result, however, is that policing in Russia remains highly centralised, with decision-making lying at the top of a pyramid system of control, which ensures that, although responsibility is devolved throughout the federation to regional, city, district and local policing units, it is organised on the basis of a strict hierarchy. Unfortunately, such a highly-centralised police system is less likely to be conducive to a public-service orientation, whereby resources are targeted at the local level to address local needs on the basis of local priorities, rather than centrally-determined targets enforced to national dictates.

*Evaluating structural and organisational reform*

Although the militia have undergone a great deal of organisational and structural change over the past 10–15 years, many commentators argue that this has tended to be more superficial than substantive (Gilinskiy, 2000), to the extent that there has been a significant degree of continuity in structure, personnel, and policies (Beck and Robertson, 2005). Most significantly, perhaps, is the fact the post-Soviet police force essentially remains a 'militia', with more than just echoes of its militaristic past. Along with the federal security services and armed forces, the militia form one of Russia's armed power structures. Its personnel are routinely armed and entitled to use their weapons to defend both themselves and members of the public, but whilst figures are available on the number of deaths and injuries sustained by militia officers on the job, there are no figures to indicate the level of gun use by militia officers whilst on duty.[7]

Although a more superficial indicator of militarisation (Wright, 2002), it is perhaps also significant – at least symbolically – that MVD personnel wear uniforms and have, since the 1930s, used a ranking system very similar to that of the armed forces, whereby all officers grades are ranked from private to general of the militia. More than a decade of reform has failed to have any impact on this system, with anecdotal evidence suggesting that the overall number of those holding senior ranks rose significantly during the late 1990s and early 2000s. Given that rank determines pay rates and members of the militia can only improve their level of remuneration via promotion, this preference to maintain the status quo is understandable. Moreover, many previously-designated civilian posts, including some academic and logistic posts at the MVD's educational facilities, were in the late 1990s subsumed into the ranking system, conferring additional benefits which people are now reluctant to lose. Whilst this is logical from the point of view of militia personnel, such militaristic overtones and values are not in keeping with a democratic policing organisation.

## Reforms to operational policies and practices

In Russia the militia are responsible for many functions traditionally carried out by police forces in other countries, such as the maintenance of public order, crime prevention and investigation, and traffic control, but their remit extends to additional areas, not generally associated with policing in advanced democracies, for example vehicle registration, transportation security, issuing visas, internal passports and residence permits, as well as licences for printing presses. The militia – in the form of local or beat officers – also act as a probation service for millions of ex-prisoners (Nurgaliev, 2005). Most of the latter functions are, again, largely a legacy of the Soviet era, whereby the militia were part of the system of totalitarian control and supervision over the population as a whole, primarily through the use of internal passports and residence permits.

*Internal passports and residence permits*

The issuing of internal passports – used as a type of national identity card – began in 1932 as a means of controlling the movements of the Soviet population, and in particular to regulate the urban and rural populations (Conquest, 1968). As such they were deemed to be one of a series of 'quasi-political controls' that also included the licensing system and the police ancillary and informer networks (see below), all of which were used to enforce the system on which the Communist dictatorship depended for its existence (Conquest, 1968). Given this background, it is hugely significant that, despite the collapse of the Soviet regime, much of this system continues to exist in one guise or another, which highlights a lack of reform in this area.

The internal passport system worked hand in hand with the '*propiska*' (permit) system, whereby in order to secure work in the cities, everyone was required to have a valid residence permit provided by the militia. Although acknowledged as being anti-constitutional (Shelley, 1999), the *propiska* system is still widely used in Russia's larger cities and still closely administered by the militia. As well as regulating population movements, the *propiska* and internal passports systems provide ample opportunity for abuse, for example the militia use the regulation to extort bribes from those found not to be in possession of one or the other. Likewise, for some people not eligible for residence permits in cities such as Moscow, offering a bribe to a militia officer is perhaps the only way to remain in the city.

*Traffic control and inspection*

Another area that allows huge scope for corruption is the traffic control system. The Traffic Police (known by the Russian acronym GIBBD, which stands for 'Government Inspection of Road Safety') are well-known as being amongst the most corrupt militia units – perhaps because the nature of their duties and the amount of contact they have with the public facilitate this. In recent years plans have been mooted to try to reduce the opportunities for corruption in the traffic militia by, for example, introducing a different system for administering fines, which does not involve the militia collecting them on the spot. Whilst this may help reduce the problem, it does not preclude drivers from offering bribes informally so as not to have to pay the formal fine.

*Police auxiliaries*

Although the secret informer networks of the Soviet period no longer exist, echoes of police ancillary groups are apparent in the 'voluntary patrols' still championed to one extent or another by the MVD and other interested parties, particularly city mayors such as Moscow's Yuri Luzhkov. Although far removed in a political sense from the supposedly 'Voluntary Societies', which became the 'Brigades for Assisting the Militia' (created in the 1930s) and subsequently the People's Squads of the 1950s under Krushchev (Conquest, 1968: 63–64), the new voluntary groups are also tasked with assisting the militia to fulfil their duties by patrolling local streets and housing estates. To what extent this represents a cost-cutting exercise and/or is really representative of a genuine interest in developing police/public relations is difficult to discern, but it is nonetheless interesting that these old forms of community policing are being revived – at least amongst older generations, to whom, anecdotally, this mostly seems to appeal. This has at least partly come about as a result of a major policy initiative developed in the early 2000s aimed at bringing the public and police closer together, which complemented the task set before the militia in the 1996 Concept Paper of 'mobilising all social resources to counteract criminal expansion', as discussed in more detail below.

## Police practice and performance reforms

A key aim of reform was to restore public trust and confidence in the militia by refocusing the latter's activity towards the former, which involved two elements: working with the public in preventing and controlling crime and involving the public in evaluating police performance.

### Work with the public

As mentioned above, it was expected that the Soviet public would be involved in crime prevention and control by taking part in 'voluntary' groups (*druzhiny* [8]) organised within work-places and educational establishments to patrol local streets and housing blocks (Mawby, 1990). These groups worked closely alongside the regular militia, although their loyalties lay with the Communist Party (Mawby, 1990). Efforts to involve the community in law and order peaked under Krushchev in the early 1960s, but subsequently declined – probably because of the apathy of many 'volunteers' and the 'over-assertiveness of undesirable (careerists or even criminal) elements who used the squads as a cover for their activities' (Conquest, 1968: 64).

During the late 1980s, perhaps in response to a growing fear of crime (partly provoked by the glasnost-inspired increased access to crime data and their use by politicians and the media, as well as genuine rises in crime), attempts were made to restore public involvement in crime control. Favarel-Garrigues and Le Huerou (2004: 18) see the resulting 'Workers' Detachments for Cooperation with the Militia' as precursors to the private security services that subsequently flourished in commercial enterprises. It is interesting to note that these organisations have become one of the state militia's main competitors for private protection (alongside the 'mafia', see Varese, 2001), since the latter is also offered by the militia through its 'Extra-Departmental Security Service' (*Nevyedomstvennaya Okhrana*).

In 1999, following the deaths of around 300 residents of Moscow and

Volgodonsk, neighbourhood-watch type groups spontaneously appeared in the capital and other cities, reviving a form of community participation in crime control.[9] This perhaps served as a catalyst for the drafting and implementation in 2002 of new legislation by the Moscow city administration on public involvement in crime prevention. Although media coverage was not particularly favourable, tending to focus on the more negative potential of 'supervision' and 'snooping' of the Soviet system and even anticipating the establishment of an additional security force to serve the purposes of the city authorities (Paton Walsh, 2003), which echoed the Soviet tradition of Party control, this has not deterred the proliferation of such activities throughout the country. In fact, according to the MVD by the end of 2005 around 300,000 members of the public were involved in around 35,000 such organisations, which may be far below the 6 million enrolled in 1964 (Conquest, 1968), but whereas the latter's involvement was probably not voluntary, that of the former is. According to the MVD, during 2004 such volunteers helped to solve more than 4,000 criminal cases and to prevent half a million minor offences (*Shchit i mech*, 2005). They were also involved in maintaining order and security at 150 major events and during regional elections. This clearly is an approach that the MVD is keen to promote to continue to 'keep getting closer to the public' (*Shchit i mech*, 2005).

### *The extra-departmental guard service (EDGS)*

Another legacy of the Soviet system is this semi-independent police service, which provides private individuals, groups of residents and businesses with security-guard services on a commercial basis. Created in 1952 the EDGS has expanded in recent years in response to the demand for the protection of goods and services, which has also seen the private security industry flourish in Russia – often involving both former and serving police officers seeking more lucrative earnings (Favarel-Garrigues and Le Huerou, 2004). In some respects the EDGS is a hybrid organisation: working on a commercial basis (and thus enjoying far better resources than the regular militia, including cars and equipment, but paradoxically having to subsidise the regular militia), but still under state control and expected to respond to everyday calls for police assistance. In terms of democratic principles, the development of a fee-paying militia 'service', as opposed to a free public 'force' is interesting and raises issues related to discrimination, social justice and two-speed policing for those who can or cannot afford it.

### *Improving performance and accountability*

The 1996 Concept Paper outlined the practical changes envisaged in order to achieve its broader aims, which included improving the militia's accountability and performance to 'socially-acceptable levels', ultimately in the hope of restoring and maintaining public respect, which has long been absent

(Shelley, 1996; Zvekic, 1996). In keeping with this overall aim, significant reforms were developed and introduced to try to improve militia performance and accountability.

A positive outcome of the collapse of the Soviet system was increased access to information, including crime statistics, which prior to 1989 had been subject to secrecy laws. The release of statistics resulted in rising levels of fear of crime amongst the Russian public (Favarel-Garrigues and Le Huerou, 2004), but also suggested that they were being manipulated, if not falsified to understate the true crime situation (Favarel-Garrigues, 2000). Such manipulation and falsification by the militia was, in some respects, understandable given the way in which performance bonuses were allocated (on the basis of detection and clear-up rates), which made it attractive to the militia not to register the more obviously unsolvable crimes reported by members of the public. Moreover, militia units have to meet certain minimum and maximum quotas (for example, arrest rates for particular offences) to demonstrate overall success in crime control, management and prevention. This led to a huge 'dark figure' of crime and allowed the Russian militia to make spurious claims about high clear-up rates (Goryainov *et al.*, 2001), which only served to further alienate the public and lower their confidence in the militia.

In an attempt to address these shortcomings two interlinking initiatives were introduced: the militia were ordered to register every incident reported to them by the public, and the criteria by which militia performance is measured were widened to include factors such as national and regional reporting levels, local conditions, and – most significantly – public opinion of militia performance. The compulsory registration of all reported crime was piloted in the early 2000s, accompanied by ominous forecasts of huge increases in recorded crime[10] and also clear warnings that any concealment of crimes would be taken very seriously and result in disciplinary measures. Despite the forecasts and forewarnings, the anticipated spike in recorded crime rates never materialised: rather official rates over the next year fell by 17 per cent (MVD, 2003). Although this huge decrease was later explained by legislative changes that reclassified some minor crimes as administrative offences, the incumbent MVD chief still relied on this data to sing the praises of the militia in controlling crime.[11]

However, more recent statistics suggest that this 'Soviet mythology of success' (Beck and Robertson, 2005: 255) may be losing its hold and that these measures may be having more of an impact on recording practices. During 2005, for example, the Russian militia recorded just over 3.5 million crimes, a rise of almost 23 per cent on the previous year's figure (MVD, 2006). Most of the additional crimes recorded were reported by the Minister of the Interior as being of 'minor or medium severity, precisely the latent crimes that used to be ignored by local militia offices', which he suggested showed that Russia's crime map had become more objective (*Nezavisimaya Gazeta*, 2006). These initiatives were further consolidated by additional regulations issued in 2005 on receiving, recording and approving crime reports and on evaluating militia performance.

*Improving accountability and oversight*

Throughout the Soviet era, the militia were subject to the dual control of the Ministry of Internal Affairs and the Communist Party. Under this system there was little scope for public oversight, although it probably existed to some extent, particularly given the public involvement in crime control previously outlined (Favarel-Garrigues, 2000). Since the collapse of the USSR and the demise of the Communist Party, oversight is conducted both officially (internally and externally) and unofficially. Internal oversight and control is enforced by the Minister of Internal Affairs and the MVD's Internal Security Service (*Sluzhba sobstvennoi bezopastnosti*), whilst external oversight is applied by the Prosecutors' Office and the president. Although legislative control exists in theory, in practice it is very unlikely to be applied, given the overall concentration of power in Russia in the president. The media and human rights group are largely responsible for ensuring informal oversight, since there is no legal provision for public oversight, apart from on an individual (complaints') basis. On this last point it is worth noting that informal oversight may become more problematic as a result of restrictions placed on both the media and NGOs as part of an apparent crack-down on government critics.[12]

The militia are thus largely responsible for policing their own house, with the remit of the Internal Security Service, (the status of which was changed to a full main directorate in 2001, perhaps indicating the increasing importance attached to this unit), being to detect and prevent illegal behaviour within the militia. In 2001 10,000 officers were called to account and more than one thousand faced criminal proceedings for abusing their power.[13] In 2002, in response to more than 63,000 complaints from the public, more than 21,000 police officers were censured for criminal and other offences, and 17,000 were sacked (Kosals, 2002). In 2004 a further 18,400 officers faced punishment of one type or another, and 28,000 officials were punished for violating the complaints' procedures, 583 of them under the Criminal Code (Nurgaliev, 2005). These figures suggest that at least some effort is going into curbing militia deviancy, including corruption, whilst simultaneously suggesting that the scale of the problem is huge. In this respect it should be noted that corruption is a society-wide problem that requires both greater and more generalised efforts if it is to be addressed in any real and lasting way.

## Evaluating reform

Having outlined some of the key reforms introduced since the adoption of the Concept Paper in 1996, it is possible to evaluate the extent to which the reform has been successful or otherwise in terms of achieving its key objectives, and also the prospects for future reform.

## Upholding the rule of law?

From the Concept Paper it is clear that the reform of the MVD, and in particular the militia, was first and foremost conceptualised as a means of facilitating the development of a democratic and legal state in Russia, which infers the establishment of the rule of law. Unfortunately, this has yet to be achieved and in this respect the Russian militia are often seen as being part of the problem, rather than the solution to establishing the rule of law. One of the main reasons for this state of affairs is the expansion, rather than decline of corruption in comparison with its scale during the Soviet era. Thus, according to Gilinskiy (2006: 280), organised crime has widened its sphere of influence since the collapse of the Soviet Union and has caused 'the total corruption of government, administrative and law-enforcement bodies at all levels'. Statistics show that thousands of militia personnel are sacked annually for breaking the law – primarily for engaging in corrupt practices – but this is likely to represent only the tip of the iceberg (Kosals, 2002; Nurgaliev, 2005).

However, corruption within the militia takes diverse forms and needs to be understood within the Russian/Soviet context, rather than using purely western definitions and terms of reference. Whilst not wishing to underplay or excuse the small-scale rule-breaking and bribe-taking that occurs throughout Russian society (as well as in other former Soviet and Eastern European societies; see Lovell *et al.*, 2000; and Miller *et al.*, 2001) of much greater seriousness is the large-scale corruption within the militia that sees law enforcement cooperating with criminal groups and individuals, including those involved in organised crime (Handelman, 1995). This large-scale collusion between law-enforcement and criminal groups, which takes many forms, developed during the early years of post-Soviet Russia when the collapse of the great socialist experiment and the rapid and largely uncontrolled development of capitalist structures resulted in ample scope for such criminal co-operation. For example, it was during this period that the militia set up their own protection rackets, which were widespread by the mid-1990s, rendering extortion a regular occurrence – by the very organisations supposedly responsible for upholding law and order (*Argumenty i fakty*, no date).

Of course there is another side to corruption and there are many factors that have to be taken into account when examining the low-level militia corruption that some argue is seen by many participants as 'acceptable and normal' (Gilinskiy, 2006: 281). These factors include low salaries and a poor level of legal consciousness, as well as a lack of respect for the law (Shelley, 1999). Its breadth – not just within the militia, but throughout society, including government circles – means that it is a perennial problem and not one likely to be solved in the short – or even longer term without serious efforts on the part of the government and its ministries.

Anti-corruption drives are habitually given prominence by the MVD and mentioned in presidential dispatches, and periodic campaigns result in thousands of – largely, but not exclusively – low-ranking officers being sacked annually for corrupt practices. Occasionally those in the higher ranks of the militia – the so-called 'werewolves in epaulettes' (as they have been designated in the Russian media and by politicians) do come under investigation and can end up in prison (Latynina, 2003). Whilst this may suggest the government is serious – at least to some extent – about rooting out corruption in the militia, this reactive approach primarily addresses the symptoms of corrupt practices, rather than the underlying causes of the problem, for example the lack of transparency and accountability as well as the lack of decent salaries for militia employees. However, not even higher salaries would necessarily improve the situation, given that this does not deal with the underlying culture of corruption, which may have the effect of normalising small-scale abuses in the thought processes and practices of the police (Bayley, 2001).

Whilst the scale, scope and acceptance of corruption in Russian society remains a huge obstacle to democratic police reform, small initiatives, such as removing the militia from involvement in the payment of fines, may help to prevent both the militia and members of the public from abusing the system in this way. This does not necessarily combat the culture of corruption, but it could make it more difficult to sustain. More important, however, is the development and introduction of some type of external, including public, oversight, which would be an additional means of controlling and disciplining the militia. Without such independent external oversight it is difficult to envisage how the Russian militia can break out of the cycle of corruption that afflicts this public institution, as well as many others (Gilinskiy, 2006) and thus promote the rule of law.

### *Winning the fight against crime?*

As previously mentioned crime rates soared after the collapse of the Soviet Union, and statistics suggest that the Russian militia have largely been unable to 'achieve a turning point in the fight against crime' as planned in the 1996 Concept Paper. For example, according to MVD's figures (cited in Gilinskiy, 2006) recorded crimes reached just over 3.5 million in 2005 – almost one million more crimes than recorded in 1996. This equated to an increase in the rate of recorded crimes per 100,000 of the population from 1,778 in 1996 to 2,500 in 2005, a rise of 40 percent in one decade. In fact these rates of recorded crime understate the true crime rates in Russia for two inter-related reasons: the lack of reporting by victims of crime and the militia's failure to record many crimes reported to them, which amounts to a 'cover-up', as evidenced by the 'impossibly high clear-up rates' still claimed by the militia (Gilinskiy, 2006: 272). In contrast it should also be borne in mind that some of the increase may be explained by changes to legislation, which can have the effect of creating the impression of more crime, when in actual fact only the classification and recording of crimes has changed. It seems likely, however, that the lack of reporting and recording continues to outweigh any such considerations, as evidenced by Gilinskiy (2006).

It is interesting to note that the rising crime levels witnessed in Russia have been accompanied by a decline in the number of offenders detected by the police (from 1.6 million in 1996 to 1.3 million in 2005) as well as in the number of people convicted (from just over 1 million in 1996 to 767,000 in 2003; later figures not available) (Gilinskiy, 2006: 263), again suggesting that no turning-point has been reached in respect of the fight against crime in Russia over the last decade. However, in this respect the MVD perhaps set itself an unrealistic task: can any police service or force hope ever to win the fight against crime, rather than to manage the crime problems they face by working with the broader policing family – including the general public? This aim itself is evocative of a Soviet approach, but there are nonetheless factors that may play a part in understanding the militia's inability to fulfil the task of fighting crime more generally in recent years, including high rates of staff turnover and lower rates of professionalism brought about by a general lack of resources and adequate funding levels (Solomon, 2005).

*Staff turnover*

Since the collapse of the Soviet Union the MVD has experienced a high degree of organisational instability (Gilinskiy, 2000), the impact of which has been felt at different levels and within different services within the militia.[14] High turnover rates amongst the rank-and-file members of the militia have been attributed to the low morale produced by the lack of status and prospects, and more generally by poor working conditions, especially low pay. Also significant is the perceived appeal of benefits available in the private sector, which has resulted in huge numbers leaving for more well-paid jobs (Favarel-Garrigues and Le Huerou, 2004). The end result is a huge loss of experienced staff, and a corresponding decline in the collective institutional experience and expertise of the remaining complement of staff. Cumulatively, this could not fail to have an adverse impact on the militia's ability to do their job, however this is defined and redefined by the MVD hierarchy.

*Resource issues*

The situation regarding the financing of the militia is difficult to determine, given that access to information is restricted, however, just as the lack of funding for policing was the norm during the Soviet era (Conquest, 1968), the Russian militia appear to have experienced a similar lack of financial support. Shortages of the most basic equipment are well documented (Shelley, 1999) – and apparent to any visitor to a Russian police station – although it is unclear to what extent this may be the result of financial mismanagement in addition to a general lack of funding. Some cities and towns evidently fare better than others, with larger cities tending to be much better equipped than smaller and more rural towns and areas. Also significant in this regard is the relative profitability of the private militia service previously mentioned, which is used to a great extent to subsidise the regular militia divisions (Favarel-Garrigues and Le Huerou, 2004). The next phase of reform, envisaged for 2006–2016 includes plans for the introduction of a new computer system (with the technical assistance of the European Union), whereby equipment is to be provided in ready form, rather than money allocated for the purchase of the necessary equipment, again seemingly with the aim of preventing corruption (*Nezavisimaya Gazeta*, 2006).

## Overall evaluation

From the evidence presented above it is clear that Russia still has a long way to go before it can be considered to have introduced a democratic policing system, taking into account that this should be based on the principles of accountability, the defence of human rights, transparency and professionalism (Kratcoski and Cebulak, 2000; Marenin, 2000; Bayley, 2001). Whilst it is evident that policy and lawmakers alike are familiar with the guiding principles of democratic policing, and that various elements have been introduced to the laws and policies that should govern the practice of policing in Russia, in spite of various attempts to change practices, the overall assessment of reform is 'could do better' and serious doubts remain about the MVD's ability to implement genuine democratic policing.

This negative assessment, however, deserves some qualification: for example, the fact that police reform in any country – and even more so in countries in transition – is a complex subject should not be ignored. In this respect Russia perhaps deserves to be given credit for recognising the need for change and seeking to reform the militia in pursuit of democratic principles and ideals. It would be naïve and unrealistic to expect in such a relatively short period of time a total shift from a model of policing based on defending the political regime to one that offers a public service that protects the rights and freedoms of all citizens.

Moreover, no model of policing can be transposed directly into a country, but rather different aspects of democratic policing must be adapted and adopted according to the experiences, expectations and culture of any given country (Beck and Chistyakova, 2002; Robertson, 2005). It is possible that the refraction of democratic policing principles and ideals through Russian experiences and culture has resulted in some distortion of what types of activity are required. For example, much has been made in Russia of turning the police towards the public – an admirable aim – but the process by which this is being attempted – largely it seems by trying to involve the public in policing, rather than consulting communities about their policing concerns and needs – is questionable. This throwback to the Soviet era demonstrates a fundamental misunderstanding of the rationale behind engaging the public in issues related to their safety and security. It also suggests that the 'Soviet' mindset of the militia remains strong.

In this respect the Russian militia have not moved into the realms of offering a service to the public and remains essentially a force – with the exception of those who can afford to pay for the additional services offered by the Extra-Departmental Guard Service. The latter organisation most certainly views its clients as customers, to whom it must provide a quality service, unlike the regular militia, who are more likely to see the public as little more than a source of information (or bribes). This in itself is interesting as it demonstrates that militia attitudes towards the public can be changed: for the regular militia the challenge is to do so in the absence of additional financial reward. The overriding aim of police reform in Russia should perhaps therefore be to change the militia from defenders of the political regime into a public service that defends human rights and freedoms, as well as the lives and property of all of the country's people, not just the select few who can afford it.

In practical terms police reform requires large-scale changes not only to what the militia do, but also how they do it. Perhaps, as Solomon (2005) has suggested, too much attention is being paid in Russia to the process of reorganisation rather than the content of policing and how this is implemented. Of course some elements of democratic policing – such as developing a professional service – require reforms to be undertaken in both areas, that is, improvements to what the police do (reduce/prevent crime; maintain public order etc.) and how they do it (in relation to the public). In countries such as Russia it is perhaps easier to focus on the former than deal with the latter, which would require substantial changes to the culture and mindset of the militia. Paradoxically, although the former is also important, in many transitional states there is arguably a far greater need for reform of the way that the police do their jobs – particularly in relation to their relationship with the public. In this respect, despite efforts to make improvements in Russian society, the end result would appear negligible as illustrated by continued low rates of public trust and confidence in the militia. As the police cannot operate effectively without the support and trust of the public (Bayley, 2001), it is crucial that this continuing problem be addressed.

In this respect it is important to note the MVD does not operate in a vacuum and that policing in Russia takes place within the national and local contexts, which are shaped by many conflicting pressures and opportunities: the militia are therefore not solely to blame for the lack of genuine change and continued reliance on Soviet-style attitudes and methods. The public must also take responsibility, for example, for its complicity in corrupt practices (e.g. offering bribes to traffic police to avoid higher fines or the annoyance of having to go to a bank to pay them). In contrast public opinion is also affected by experiences of dealing with the police and any complaints and discipline procedure must therefore also win their confidence and trust, or else police legitimacy will always be in question.

In many respects the Russian MVD has performed well in terms of establishing the strategic direction of reform – that is the type of legislative, organisational and practical changes required to facilitate policing based more on democratic ideals, but it appears their scope and depth, as well as the results achieved are not in keeping with what is required in a democratic society. This seems particularly true in key areas such as accountability and legitimacy.

The absence of accountability – perhaps the first principle of democratic policing – is a key issue where Russia is found wanting. Modern policing in a democratic country demands that police officers respect the law and the basic rights and freedoms of all members of society. They must uphold and apply the law, but they must also be subject to it themselves too. They should set the example in terms of discipline, and where they fail in this regard they should be subject to independent oversight. Without this, it is difficult to see how genuine democratic policing can be achieved in Russia.

Of course there are no quick fixes when it comes to police reform. What is needed is a long-term strategy that – most importantly – benefits from the political will to both initiate and sustain it. Russian society has changed and so must the militia and their practices. Previously we have argued that police legitimacy cannot be legislated into existence but must be achieved on the basis of positive interaction with the police (Beck and Robertson, 2005). The same can be said for the development of democratic reform: whilst legislation can provide the legal framework to introduce democratic change, the rule of law must be enforced to ensure any measure of success. Currently this is lacking in Russia, and although genuine enforcement cannot be ruled out completely, it is difficult to see how large-scale and deep-seated corruption can be overcome in the near future in order to facilitate the creation of democratic policing in a democratic state. It could be argued, therefore, that corruption itself is undermining the development of democratic policing.

It is also the case that the absence of any kind of lustration law – as introduced in some of the other former Soviet states and Eastern European countries – is perhaps significant, since this seems to have allowed Russia to roll back some democratic reforms and liberties, such as press freedom, won since the end of the Soviet Union (Elster, 2006). Finally, it is clear that police reform does not happen in a vacuum, and in this respect it has to be understood within an increasingly complex political process, where the pressure on police to impose the will of the government may always be at odds with improving police-public relations. It is doubtful, therefore, the extent to which Russia will achieve a genuinely democratic policing model in the near future.

## Notes

1  General crime increased from 1,000 per 100,000 of the population in 1985 to 2,500 in 2005; homicide rates from 6.3 in 1987 to 22.1 in 2004; GBH from

14.7 in 1986 to 40.7 in 2005; and assaults with robbery from 5.8 in 1986 to 44.8 in 2005 (Gilinskiy, 2006).

2 Security issues remain acute in Dagestan, Ingushetia and Chechnya, where policemen often come under attack by 'terrorists' seeking secession.

3 For example the Regulation 'On the Soviet Militia' was authorised in 1973, but only published in 1985.

4 Zakon RSFSR 'O militsii', 1991: http://zakon.kuban.ru/sayt/ (accessed 07/03/03) (Translation: Law 'On the Militia').

5 For example a landmark judgement was passed by the ECHR in the case of Mikheyev v Russia (27th January 2006). The complainant, Mikheyev, was a traffic police office who was detained in 1998 and tortured by the police in order to make him confess to a crime that not only did he not commit, but had never taken place (the missing girl whom he was accused of raping and murdering subsequently turned up safe and well). To escape further threats of torture, Mikheyev jumped out of the police station window, breaking his spine in the fall. Criminal cases related to his torture and general ill-treatment were stopped more than 20 times before three officers were eventually found guilty of mistreatment in 2005 (Amnesty International, 2006).

6 These federal regions, each with its own presidential envoy, were created in 2000.

7 759 cases of deaths and injuries were caused by militia use of firearms in 2001, and during 2002 more than 250 regular militia officers were killed while on duty (*Moscow Times*, 2003). In 2005 322 officers died and more than 4,000 sustained injuries on the job (From interview with First Deputy Minister of the Interior, Alexandr Chakalin (*Shchit I Mech*, 30/11/05). Whilst the former Minister of the Interior, Boris Gryzlov, equated high numbers of fatalities with the sense of responsibility that prevailed amongst militia officers, others have attributed this – at least partly – to a lack of education amongst militia personnel.

8 From the Russian *drug* or friend, this diminutive form of the noun means 'little friend' so the volunteers were the 'little friends' of the police.

9 Three blocks of flats were destroyed by bombs placed in their basements. The government blamed Chechen rebels and launched its second war in the Republic. Two Chechen nationals were eventually found guilty of the bombings, but doubt was cast on the veracity of the investigations, amongst others by Alexander Litvinenko, who wrote a book alleging that the Russian security forces may have been behind the bombings as a means of justifying the repression that followed in Chechnya.

10 The MVD were possibly concerned as a result of a prior attempt to improve registration in 1989. The campaign floundered when some regional police chiefs failed to act as instructed, whilst others did, resulting in an increase of 20 per cent in recorded crime, which earned the Minister of Internal Affairs a reprimand from President Boris Yeltsin (Saradzhyan, 2001).

11 According to the minister, even by adhering to the strict requirement to register all citizens' complaints, fewer than 3 million crimes were registered in 2002 (*Komsomolskaya Pravda*, 2003).

12 Very few sources of independent media remain in Russia, and threats and attacks on journalists critical of the government are well-documented, including some very high profile deaths such as Anna Politkovskaya in October 2006. The handling of the investigation into her murder has been so mismanaged by the Prosecutors' Office as to make a trial, never mind a conviction, virtually impossible.

13 From a report by the Deputy Minister of Interior given to the international conference, 'Preventing Police (Militia) Corruption', Moscow, 11–12 February 2002.

14   Data from the MVD show that length of service figures vary for different units within the militia. For example, in the criminal militia around 60 per cent of staff average between three and ten years of service, whilst 15 per cent have less than three years' experience and 20 per cent between 10 and 20 years. In the public security militia around half of all staff have between three and ten years' experience, compared with 27 per cent with less than three years and 17 per cent with between 10 and 20 years (MVD, 2001).

# References

Amnesty International (2002) *The Russian Federation: Denial of Justice*, Oxford: Amnesty International Publications.

Amnesty International (2003) *'Dokumenty!' Discrimination on the Grounds of Race in the Russian Federation*, Oxford: Amnesty International Publications.

Amnesty International (2006) 'Russian Federation: European Court of Human Rights found Russian police guilty of torture and ill-treatment of detainee', *AI Public Statement*, 30th January.

Amnesty International (2007) *Amnesty International Report 2007: Russian Federation* (accessed 01/06/07: http://thereport.amnesty.org/eng/Regions/Europe-and-Central-Asia/Russian-Federation).

*Argumenty i fakty* (no date) Interview with Lieutenant-General of the Militia Konstantin Romodanovsky, Head of the Main Directorate for Internal Security, MVD Russia (cited on MVD website: http://www.mvdrf.ru/).

Bayley, D. (2001) *Democratizing the Police Abroad: What to Do and How to Do It*, Washington: US Department of Justice.

Beck, A. and Chistyakova, Y. (2002) 'Crime and Policing in Post-Soviet Societies: Bridging the Police/Public Divide', *Policing & Society*, 12 (2): 123–137.

Beck, A. and Robertson, A. (2005) 'Policing in Post-Soviet Russia', in W. Pridemore (ed.) *Law, Crime, and Justice in Transitional Russia*, US: Rowan and Littlefield, pp. 247–260.

Coalson, R. (2004) 'Analysis: Russia's Ombudsman Speaks Out', *Radio Free Europe/ Radio Liberty* (accessed 25/09/07: http://www.rferl.org/featuresarticle/2004/06/00d97e5f-dc14-4a35-ae9b-a791f9106124.html).

Conquest, R. (1968) *The Soviet Police System*, London: The Bodley Head.

Dashkov, G.V. (1992) 'Quantitative and Qualitative Changes in Crime in the USSR', *British Journal of Criminology*, 32 (2): 160–166.

*Ekho Moskvy Radio* (2005) Interview with Russia's Human Rights' Ombudsman, Vladimir Lukin (accessed 25/09/07: http://www.eng.yabloko.ru/Publ/2004/radio/040213_ekho.html).

Elster, J. (2006) *Retribution and Reparation in the Transition to Democracy*, New York: Cambridge University Press.

Favarel-Garrigues, G. (2000) 'Implementing Struggle Against Economic Crime in Russia: Bureaucratic Constraints and Police Practices', in M. Pagon (ed.) *Policing in Central and Eastern Europe: Ethics, Integrity, and Human Rights*, Ljubljana: College of Police and Security Studies, pp. 269–288.

Favarel-Garrigues, G. and Le Huerou, A. (2004) 'State and the Multilateralization of Policing in Post-Soviet Russia, *Policing & Society*, 14 (1): 13–30.

Feifer, G. (2003) 'Police Corruption Chokes Progress', *Johnson's Russia List* (accessed 20/03/03: http://www.cdi.org/russai/johnson/7070–12.cfm).

Galeotti, M. (1993) 'Perestroika, Perestrelka, Pereborka: Policing Russia in a Time of Change', *Europe-Asia Studies*, 45 (5): 769–786.

Gilinskiy, Y. (2000) 'Challenges of Policing Democracies: the Russian Experience', in D. Das and O. Marenin (eds) *Challenges of Policing Democracies: A World Perspective*, Amsterdam: Gordon and Breach Publishers, pp. 173–194.

Gilinskiy, Y. (2006) 'Crime in Contemporary Russia', *European Journal of Criminology*, 3 (3): 259–292.

Goryainov, K.K., Ovchinskiy, V.S. and Kondratyuk, L.V. (2001) *Ulusheniye vzaimootnosheniya grazhdan i militsia: dostup k pravosudniyu i sistema viyavleniya, registratsiya i ucheta prestuplenii*, Moscow: INDEM Fund (Translation: Improving the relationship between the public and the police: access to justice and the system of detecting, registering and recording crimes.).

Handelman, S. (1995) *Comrade Criminal*, London: Yale University Press.

Human Rights Watch (2003) Briefing Paper on the situation of Ethnic Chechens in Moscow, (accessed 04/04/03: http://www.hrw.org/backgrounder/eca/;russia032003.htm).

Human Rights Watch (2006) *Overview of human rights issues in Russia* (accessed 01/06/07: http://hrw.org/english/docs/2006/01/18/russia12218_txt.htm).

*Komsomolskaya Pravda* (2003) 'Inter'vyu Ministra vnutrennykh del Rossii, Borisa Grylova', *Komsomolskaya Pravda*, Moscow, 8 May (Translation: Interview with the Minister of Internal Affairs, Boris Gryzlov).

Kosals, L. (2002) *Informal Economic Activities of the Police in Russia: Sociological Analysis*, Unpublished report, Moscow: Institute of Population Studies.

Kratcoski, P. and Cebulak, W. (2000) 'Policing in Democratic Societies: A Historical Overview', in D. Das and O. Marenin (eds) *Challenges of Policing Democracies: A World Perspective*, The Netherlands: Gordon and Breach Publishers, pp. 23–44.

Kryshtanovskaya, O. (2003) 'Putin's Dangerous Personnel Preferences', *Moscow Times*, 2 July.

Kudriavtsev, V.N. (1999) 'Sovremenniye problemy borb'y c prestupnost'iu v Rossii', *Vestnik Rossiiskoj Akademii Nauk*, 69 (9): 790–797 (Translation: The contemporary problems of fighting crime in Russia).

Latynina, Y. (2003) 'Arresting PR and Electoral Intrigue', *Moscow Times*, 2 July.

Lotspeich, R. (1995) 'Crime in the Transition Countries', *Europe–Asia Studies*, 47 (4): 555–589.

Lovell, S., Ledeneva, A. and Rogachevskii, A. (2000) *Bribery and Blat in Russia: Negotiating Reciprocity from the Middle Ages to the 1990s*, London: Macmillan Press Ltd.

Marenin, O. (2000) 'Democracy, Democratization, Democratic Policing', in D. Das and O. Marenin (eds) *Challenges of Policing Democracies: A World Perspective*, The Netherlands: Gordon and Breach Publishers, pp. 311–334.

Mawby, R.I. (1990) *Comparative Policing Issues: The British and American Experience in International Perspective*, London: Allen & Unwin.

Mawby, R.I. (1999) 'The changing face of policing in Central and Eastern Europe', *International Journal of Police Science and Management*, 2 (3): 199–216.

Miller, W.L., Grodeland, A.B. and Koshechkina, T.Y. (2001) *A Culture of Corruption: Coping with Government in Post-communist Europe*, Hungary: CEU Press.

Morozov, V.M. and Sergevnin, V.A. (1996) 'Utilization of the International Experience of the Police Recruiting, Selection and Training in the Russian Federation', in M. Pagon (ed.) *Policing in Central and Eastern Europe: Comparing Firsthand Knowledge with Experience from the West.* Slovenia: College of Police and Security Studies, pp. 99–102.

*Moscow Times* (2003) '250 Policemen Killed', *Moscow Times*, 14 January.

MVD (1996) *Kontseptsiya razvitiya organov vnutrennykh del i vnutrennykh voisk MVD Rossii*, Moscow: MVD (Translation: the Concept of Development for the Internal Affairs Agencies and Internal Troops of Russia).

MVD (2001) *Spravka po rabote s lichnyn sostavom*, Moscow: MVD (Translation: Personnel Information Booklet).

MVD (2006) *Kratkii analiz Sostoyaniya Prestupnosti*, Moscow: MVD (Translation: Summary of Crime Situation).

MVD Research Institute (2003) *Izucheniye obshchestvennogo mneniya o sostyanii kriminogennoi obstanovki i otsenki deyatel'nosti organov vnutrennikh del*, Moscow: MVD (Translation: A study of public opinion on the crime situation and evaluation of the activity by law-enforcement bodies).

*Nezavisimaya Gazeta* (2004) *Lukin becomes a dissident*, Nezavisimaya Gazeta, 17 June.

*Nezavisimaya Gazeta* (2006) Interview with the Minister of the Interior of the Russian Federation, Army General Rashid Nurgaliyev, Nezavisimaya Gazeta, 9th March.

Nurgaliev, R. (2005) Speech of the Minister of the Interior of the Russian Federation at the Extended Ministerial Session, Moscow: MVD.

Paton Walsh, N. (2003) 'Moscow seeks spies in suburbs', *Guardian* (accessed 16/07/03: http://www.guardian.co.uk/russia/article/0,2763,998986,00.html).

Robertson, A. (2005) 'Criminal Justice Policy Transfer to Post Soviet States: Reviewing the Impact of Two Research Projects', *European Journal of Criminal Justice Policy and Research*, 11 (1): 1–28.

Saradzhyan, S. (2001) 'Gryzlov to Overhaul Lagging Police Force', *Moscow Times*, 3 July.

*Shchit i Mech* (2005) Interview with Aleksandr Chekalin, First Deputy Minister of the MVD, *Shchit i Mech*, 11 May.

Shelley, L. (1996) *Policing Soviet Society: The Evolution of State Control*, London: Routledge.

Shelley, L. (1999) 'Post-Socialist Policing: Limitations on Institutional Change', in R.I. Mawby (ed.) *Policing Across the World: Issues for the Twenty-first Century*, London: UCL Press, pp. 75–87.

Solomon, P. (2005) 'The Reform of Policing in the Russian Federation', *Australian and New Zealand Journal of Criminology*, 38 (2): 230–241.

Timoshenko, S. (1997) 'Prospects for Reform of the Russian Militia', *Policing and Society*, 8: 117–124.

Timoshenko, S. (1998) 'The International Crime Victim Survey in Moscow (Russia) 1996', in N. Hatalak, A. Alvazzi del Frate and U. Zvekic (eds) *The International Crime Victim Survey in Countries in Transition: National Reports*, Publication No. 62, Rome: UNICRI, pp. 459–476.

Varese, (2001) *Russian mafia: private protection in a new market economy*, Oxford: Oxford University Press.

Wright, A. (2002) *Policing*, Cullompton: Willan Publishing.

Zvekic, U. (1996) 'Policing and Attitudes Towards Police in Countries in Transition: Preliminary Results of the International Crime (Victim) Survey', in M. Pagon (ed.) *Policing in Central and Eastern Europe: Comparing Firsthand Knowledge with Experience from the West*, Ljubljana: College of Police and Security Studies, pp. 45–59.

# 4 Policing in Serbia

## Negotiating the transition between rhetoric and reform

*Sonja Stojanovic and Mark Downes*

## Introduction

Serbia has witnessed dramatic change over the past two decades, from the end of communism, to the rise of nationalism, the Balkan conflicts and finally the wave of democratic transition that culminated in the ousting of the Milošević regime in October 2000. Like all emerging democracies, one of Serbia's main challenges is overcoming the legacy of its past. The transition from a central-ised, politicised and militarised police force to a 'service' that views its role as being a guarantor of the rule of law and a public service, is a long and painful journey. The role that a (un)reformed police and justice sector plays in the process of democratisation cannot be underestimated; similarly a process of democratisation has a direct impact on the trajectory of reform within the police. Understanding this symbiotic relationship in the case of Serbia is one of the main objectives of this chapter.

It has been seven years since the inception of police reforms in Serbia as part of the democratic transition, even after this time the question remains whether the reforms have reached their tipping point, the point of no return when it comes to creating a democratic, effective and service-oriented police. While the tide of change within the Serbian police is evident, in some areas the political will to support the radical reform required has receded under the current government. While many reforms have taken place, most have occurred at a formal, structural level, and have not been followed-up or consolidated through the reform of management practices, a change in police culture and the day-to-day substance of police work.

To understand how best to tackle the challenges facing today's police service in Serbia, it is necessary to understand its historical legacy. The period since the end of communism can be divided into three distinct phases: first, the period of authoritarian policing under the government of Slobodan Milošević (1990s); second, the period of early democratisation which lasted from the fall of Milošević's regime until the assassination of the first demo-cratic Prime Minister, Zoran Djindjic (2000–2003) and third; the period after the assassination of Djindjic until the present day (2003 to today). The challenge for the Serbian police service in the period since the transition to democracy has been to overcome the legacy from the Milošević era. In October 2000 the new government inherited a militarised police force, which lacked democratic accountability and a public administration that was under the destabilising influence of the nexus of organised crime and remnants of the former regime.

This chapter will chart the recent history of police reform in Serbia; detail the evolution from a socialist model of policing to a democratic police that merges western influences with Serbian police and administrative culture. The main drivers of change within the Serbian police service will be analysed, together with the challenges that remain in areas such as police accountability and the fight against organised crime. Finally, the reform process will be placed into its system-wide and regional context before conclusions are presented on the product and the future prospect of the reform process.

## Understanding the legacy of the past

### *Institutional inheritance from the Socialist Federal Republic of Yugoslavia (SFRY)*[1]

The legacy of socialism in Yugoslavia has similarities with other communist states, but it also has some unique features attributable to the brand of socialism that emerged in the SFRY. Compared to the Warsaw Pact countries,[2] the Yugoslav regime was perceived as 'soft communism' – less repressive, with a more open political system, which from the early 1970s provided a much better standard of living than in other parts of eastern Europe. As in other communist states, the name of the force charged with providing public security, *milicija* (militia), highlights the militarised nature of policing. The *milicija* developed from the post-Second World War militias, responsible for the suppression of the political opposition, into a more representative law-enforcement body in late 1960s whose objectives were to protect the state and its citizens from crime. However, when forced to choose between protecting the state and protecting its citizens – the former took priority. The authoritarian and highly politicised nature of the police in this period can be understood from its legislative foundation, which included the obligation of ensuring 'protection of the constitutional order',[3] a role that in practice was exercised to legally target political dissidents.[4]

A second component inherited from the socialist era related to the management and function of the police. This legacy included a decision-making structure that was highly centralised, with one of the central roles of the police being an administrative hub for the state, which included its role of registering citizen's associations and public meetings, issuance of passports and identification cards, maintenance of a citizenship directory and the public registry (Kutnjak-Ivkovic in Caparini and Marenin, 2004: 197). As in most communist era public administrations, the dominant organisational culture in Yugoslavia was highly bureaucratised, centralised and functioned with a high level of supervision of day-to-day decision-making at all levels. The centralisation of decision-making and subordination to politics prevented the delegation of both operational and administrative authority amongst the rank and file, which hindered the development of the capacity for personal judgement and discretion by individual police officers.

While the centralisation of decision-making and absence of a culture of delegated authority and individual discretion were challenged after the fall of communism, the second set of broad administrative competencies maintained its 'logic of appropriateness' (March and Olsen, 2005) long after the democratic transition in most of the Yugoslav successor countries. This could be explained by the corporatist nature of emerging polities and the incumbent expectation on the part of the public that the police, as the most effective part of the central state, should deliver administrative services in a uniform way, instead of decentralising such services to the municipal level. The Yugoslav police structure and division of competencies between federal and republican levels was set up in accordance with the model of the West German Federal Police. The dominant legal legacy was from the French legal system, while the public administration draws its 'logic of appropriateness' from the Austro-Hungarian tradition. All three legacies have in common the expectation of acquiring 'legitimacy from above', i.e. by central government (Koci, 1996). This is a key characteristic of the continental style of policing and remains a dominant feature of Serbian policing today.

The third component inherited from the old Yugoslav system was the primacy of the intelligence service over public security authorities. The Yugoslav police was organised into two sectors based on the function they performed: *Public Security Service* (regular police) and *the State Security Service*. The State Security Service (RDB – *Resor državne bezbednosti*) performed the role of both intelligence and counter-intelligence services. Both the public security and the state security components existed at a federal level ('the Federal Secretariat of Interior') and oversaw Secretariats of Interior in all six constitutive republics (Bosnia and Herzegovina, Croatia, Serbia, Macedonia, Montenegro and Slovenia). While in theory the two components of the police – Public Security Service and the State Security Service – were equal, in practice the State Security Service were better resourced, in terms of financial and human resources. Moreover, the State Security Service was afforded far more discretion and influence in setting security policy. This resulted in the development of a culture of impunity, a lack of accountability and openness towards the public. The authoritarian system of governance was based on the fear of informants and covert surveillance and not on consent as in democratic societies. This was justified as crime rates in communist parts of the world were much lower than in the Western countries, due to tight state control over civil life.

At that corporate level, subordination to politics (and party officials) prevented the creation of a capacity for policy development within the state executive. During the transition and consolidation of democracy, this weakness of state capacity across the entire public administration turned into a major obstacle to the efficiency and coherence of police reform initiatives and featured prominently in public opinion polls which cited the over 'politicisation of public administration'.[5]

## The 1970s liberalisation and its impact on the Yugoslav policing model

The late 1960s and early 1970s saw the increasing liberalisation of political life in Yugoslavia, with the move towards comparatively greater autonomy in civic life and greater diversity within the public administration. This change was based on trends towards the institutionalisation of the self-management system[6] in all spheres of public life and greater decentralisation of power within the federation. In this period the constitutional changes allowed Yugoslavia's constitutive republics to acquire competency over almost all aspects of public policy except defence and foreign policy. Such an institutional framework allocated the main agenda-setting role to the republican communist elites. The republican police were put almost under the sole supervision of the republican communist party. This period witnessed the transfer of authority from the federal level *militia* to the constituent republics of SFRY. The authority to provide public safety in the territories of the republics was transferred to the republican Secretariats of Interiors, with an exception of so-called 'state security' (the political intelligence service). All of the Secretariats of the Interior at a republic level had a state security component, but its chain of command remained under the auspices of the federal level police.

The requirements for greater ethnic representation within the public service were promoted as part of the ideology of 'unity and brotherhood'.[7] The self-management principles were practised through, for example, the freedom of local communities to appoint their local police chief (albeit in practice still partially influenced by the local branch of the Communist Party) (Gorenak, 1996: 2). The fostering of closer relationships between police officers and the local community was initiated through the application of the Yugoslav form of 'sector policing' (Bakic and Gajic, 2006: 20). This included the face-to-face contact with the people they served in a clearly defined beat area (sector). In recent years when the Serbian police service (re)introduced the concept of community policing, the experience of 'sector policing' was one of the main points of reference for both police officers and citizens. In ethnically diverse regions of Serbia, this led to a greater visibility of ethnic minorities both within rank-and-file positions and particularly in command positions, the latter often filled in accordance with the principle of positive discrimination and quotas for minority groups set by the Communist Party.

The liberalisation of political life during the 1970s was accompanied by a greater orientation towards Western norms and standards, both in terms of police cooperation and the introduction of Western police experiences and techniques into Yugoslav policing. Dvorsek (1996) explains that the Yugoslav police established cooperation with all major Western police services

(American DEA, FBI, Scotland Yard, etc.) from the 1950s. The scope of this cooperation and emulation of foreign models increased gradually over the years. The emulation of foreign models started first with technical, non-political areas of policing (equipment, forensics, IT and telecommunications etc.), and progressed towards the cooperation in areas such as the fight against trafficking of drugs and anti-terrorism in the 1970s. The slowest progress was made with regard to the introduction of new management techniques from the policing sector in Western countries. However, even this modest progress with regard to management techniques was more progressive than in other socialist countries.

Simultaneously, greater efforts were paid to the professionalisation of the police in all of the republics in line with their Western counterparts. For example, all police services introduced open competition for management posts. Professionalisation also included a move towards demilitarisation and a more service-oriented provision of public security, as seen through the adoption of civilian job titles instead of military ranks and new insignia in 1976 (Koren, 2003). Greater representation of ethnic minorities, coupled with the opportunity for local communities to provide input to policing policy, increased the legitimacy of the police in the eyes of the public.

One of the main long-term influences from this period was the general lack of civilian expertise with regard to policing policy and practice. Most police were recruited at a very early age, through a cadet-type high-school system, which was followed by further education at the Police College for the managerial cadre. This insular type of education led to a high level of socialisation and homogeneity developing among police officers. All police-related research was carried out by specialised research institutes which were the part of the intelligence services. The result was a general lack of capacity within civil society and the public that could analyse and question policing policy and practice. This later proved to be one of main obstacles to the establishment of democratic parliamentary oversight following the democratic transition in 2000. The security sector was comparatively weak in this regard in comparison to other policy sectors where some civilian expertise existed outside of state structures even during communism.

### The Milošević era and the Balkan wars of the 1990s

The effects of the semi-liberalising policies of the 1970s were curtailed at the end of the 1980s when Slobodan Milošević took over power within the Communist Party in Serbia. His policies, justified with nationalistic rhetoric of the need to protect Serbs from the effects of minority self-rule and the separatist movements in other republics, led to a return to centralisation. The right to control policing within their territory was abolished for Serbia's two Autonomous Provinces of Vojvodina and Kosovo (Bakic and Gajic, 2006: 1). As a consequence, soon afterwards the representatives of ethnic minority populations started leaving their jobs within the police, eventually leading to a massive boycott of all public office by ethnic Albanians in Kosovo, which spilled over to the three municipalities in the south-eastern Serbia,[8] and also included the Muslim population of Bosniaks in Sandzak and to a lesser extent ethnic Hungarians in Vojvodina. The effectiveness of policing and its legitimacy deteriorated as Serbia exited from communism and as it moved in the direction of an illiberal democracy[9] (Vachudova, 2005).

Although Serbia moved from a one-party political system to a multi-party system, and made an incremental transformation from a planned to a market economy, the authoritarian nature of Milošević's reign overshadowed substantively the nature of these reforms. The formal precondition of free elections for democratisation initially existed in Serbia, but once Milošević was elected to office he limited the fairness of future competitions through the control of the media, frequent changes in the legislative framework and the intimidation of a weak and disintegrated opposition. There is not enough space in this chapter to analyse all aspects of this type of authoritarian regime, however it is important to highlight that the police was transformed into the main tool of repression of the Milošević regime. The result was the extreme militarisation and politicisation of the security services, resulting in the public holding strong anti-state attitudes and the privatisation of security as a response to the loss of authority by the police.

Since he never completely trusted the Yugoslav Military, Milošević militarised the police 'in an attempt to create his own praetorian paramilitary' (Bakic and Gajic, 2006: 1). Weber (in Kadar, 2001: 45) provides an additional reason for this trend in the obligations taken under the Dayton Peace Agreement, which required reducing the number of staff in the armed forces. Milošević interpreted this as reducing the number of personnel in the army, while boosting the numbers and power of the police. In 1993, as a part of Milošević's attempts to create the command cadre for his praetorian paramilitary, the Police Academy was created based on the model and curricula of the Military Academy (e.g. including subjects such as military tactics and theory of military operations). Militarisation was further reflected symbolically in the reintroduction of ranks in 1995, combat-style uniforms were worn as regular everyday uniforms on the streets of Serbia, investment in military equipment and weaponry[10] and the introduction of a privileged status for the police among all public administration bodies. This was reflected in regular and higher compensation for their work in comparison to other parts of the public administration.

Furthermore, in the early 1990s the conflict among different ethnic groups in SFRY resulted in civil wars which ended with the dissolution of the federal state into initially five new independent states. The Serbian police, almost completely devoid of representatives from ethnic minorities, was mobilised by Milošević and used on the side of ethnic Serbs in the hostilities in Croatia, Bosnia and Kosovo. The majority of the most serious operations were carried out by special police units made up of criminals who returned from the West and were put under the direct command of intelligence components of the police. By the late 1990s the whole police force became engaged in full combat operations in Kosovo upon the emergence of an armed insurgency movement (Kosovo Liberation Army-UÇK). The common experience of participation in the Yugoslav conflicts and the obligation to serve in Kosovo during the ten-year long state of emergency, led to the socialisation of literally the whole police force into the military style of command and control. Due to the high levels of stress experienced together, police officers developed bonds of loyalty that reinforced their dislocation from the public and created an occupational culture of secrecy. This was especially evident in relation to the participation of Serbian police paramilitary units in war crimes which was put into the public domain by the investigators of the International War Crimes Tribunal (ICTY) in The Hague and a few NGOs in the aftermath of the fall of Milošević's regime. A mass grave of 980 ethnic Albanians from Kosovo was discovered in 2001 on the police service's Special Antiterrorist Unit (SAJ) premises in a Belgrade suburb (Monk, 2001: 13, Caparini and Day, 2002: 6; Amnesty International, 1999; Human Rights Watch, 1999). The ICTY indicted Vlastimir Djordjević, Milošević's Police Chief during the armed conflicts in Kosovo, and Sreten Lukić, the chief of the police forces in Kosovo at that time (and later the national Chief of Police during the first democratic government). A number of lower ranking police officers have also been indicted by the Serbian courts. Some have been processed and convicted.

The experience of a typical police officer during the Milošević regime is eloquently described in the immediate aftermath of the fall of the Milošević regime by Colonel Manojlovic, then Deputy Chief of Belgrade Criminal Police and leader of a pilot community policing project:

> As early as the beginning of 2000 I was very much aware of the situation created in ten years of Miloševic's regime. I mean: you can't have a police officer carrying his pistol in the street for two weeks and then carrying an automatic rifle for another three weeks in the field in Kosovo as a simple infantryman, scared to death; then he's back in the street, in the middle of Belgrade, loaded as he is by his post-traumatic stress syndrome; of course they started to crack ... Miloševic's police was a repression machine, a civil war army, an immense riot squad. No wonder the citizenry was alienated: the cops were either beating them up – or sneering behind the administration counters.[11]

The primary role of the police during the Milošević era was to protect the regime through suppressing the opposition and reinforcing the 'the oligarchic power cliques that embraced different political and economic institutions' (Pridham, 2001: 16). Since most of his rule was based on this informal hierarchy, which linked state institutions and organised crime, as well as different types of paramilitary groups, the aim was not to preserve the efficiency and legality of the police, but rather to ensure indisputable loyalty to the regime. This was achieved through the increased politicisation of the police service, with all top managerial posts now being allocated based on political, if not personal loyalty, while the principle of open competition for managerial posts was abolished (Bakic and Gajic, 2006: 1).

The lack of professionalism or interest in the suppression of crime, as well as a repressive attitude towards the public and a record of human rights violations, led to increasing distrust of, and loss of legitimacy in, the police. Examples of police intimidation and human rights abuses included the frequent requests for proof of identity on the streets to the beating of the opposition members during major anti-regime demonstrations (1991, 1992, 1996–1997, 1999 and 2000) and ethnic minorities in Sandzak and three municipalities in the south of Serbia and Kosovo. The intimidation of political opponents included the contract killing of some of the most prominent opposition figures in the latter part of the Milošević regime. The police were perceived as serving the interests of the state or their own private interests, rather then those of the public. Along with other quasi-democracies such as Croatia, Georgia, Russia and Slovakia, the Serbian public at the end of the 1990s perceived police as the most corrupt public officials (Zvekic, 1998: 77 and Fatic, 2000).

A perceived, and real, increase was also witnessed in criminality[12] due to the spill-over effects of the Balkans wars (which meant that weapons were readily available and opportunities for illegal activities increased, in many cases being seen as patriotic acts). State sponsored smuggling and other illegal activities which could bring profit to the regime in contravention of the UN sanctions were encouraged. This as a consequence led to a greater tolerance in society for a whole spectrum of 'grey' market activities, including tax evasion as a standard and the transformation of criminals into role models in a rapidly impoverishing society (Shentov *et al.*, 2004; Corpora, 2004). This was exacerbated by the reduction of private incomes and the rapid impoverishment of a significant portion of the population coupled with weak economic regulation, and a political environment that actively encouraged organised crime under the supervision of the state security apparatus (Shentov *et al.*, 2004; Jamieson, 2001).

During the 1990s, personal incomes in Serbia declined considerably. A 'middle class' ceased to exist, while the number of people living on or below the poverty line doubled and GDP figures plummeted. At the end of 2000 overall GDP was 45 per cent of its 1989 equivalent, whereas GDP per capita was 40 per cent lower than in 1989, which is the largest drop in GDP in Central and Southeast Europe.[13] Over the same period the crime rate also increased and the type of crime turned more violent. This is illustrated in the Figure 4.1 below[14] which illustrates the trends in general crime in the period of 1991 to 2005.

The beginning of the 1990s saw a visible increase in the rate of serious violent crimes (crimes of murder, armed robbery, etc). While there has been a decline in these figures over the last number of years, violent crime levels have not returned to their pre 1990s levels and is a lasting legacy of this

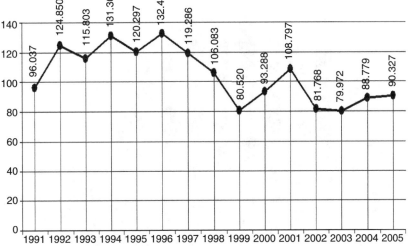

*Figure 4.1* Overall crime rates in Serbia 1991–2005.

*Source:* Taken from *The Initial Framework of the National Crime Prevention Strategy*

period (Simeunović-Patić, 2003). Another negative trend that survived democratisation is the increased number of unresolved murders, approximately between 25 and 30 per cent of total reported murders (ibid.). Figures 4.2 and 4.3 highlight this trend, taking the number of murders committed during the period 1990 to 2004.[15] It is worth noting the difficulty that exists in obtaining accurate data on crime figures in Serbia.

In the course of research for this chapter, the authors found that crime statistics, including homicide statistics were not published regularly and that they were different standards of monitoring crime trends. For example, police classified/registered as homicide only the cases which were reported as intended murders, while the cases of deaths caused by serious bodily injuries were classified in a separate category. The Public Prosecutor's Office registered only those cases which were prosecuted, while the Statistical Office of the Republic of Serbia registered all deaths caused by intentional action whether or not the intention was to murder or to harm someone severely. For example Table 4.1 below illustrates the difference in figures acquired from police and from the Statistical Office. It is also important to note that the figures presented in Figures 4.2 and 4.3 and Table 4.1 do not report adequately the situation in Kosovo since the beginning of the 1990s when police–ethnic Albanian relations significantly deteriorated culminating with armed conflict in 1998 and 1999. The figures for these two years do not report the casualties that occurred on both sides during the conflict.

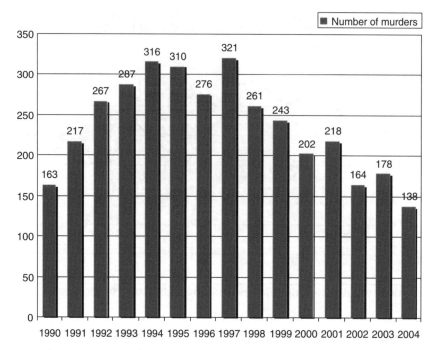

*Figure 4.2* The number of murders as recorded by the Statistical Office of the Republic of Serbia.

The spread of violence and institution corruption throughout the 1990s created a sense of collective insecurity which in turn led to the increase in the provision of security by non-state actors, whether by local gangs or a booming private security market. This deficit in the legitimacy and capacity of the state to provide public security perpetuated a vicious circle in which citizens were not willing to cooperate with the police, thereby further weakening the efficacy of police to provide basic security.

## The first generation of reforms: following the political transition

The relatively bloodless[16] transition of power that resulted from the storming of the Yugoslav Federal Parliament on 5 October 2000 occurred not only because of people power on the streets of Belgrade, but also because of the pacts made between some of the opposition leaders and a few key people in Milošević's security apparatus. The latter promised not to violently suppress the demonstrations in exchange for immunity. After the transition and under significant international pressure, early parliamentary elections were called for in December 2000. In the meantime, the interim government composed of opposition representatives from the broad coalition of the Democratic Opposition of Serbia (DOS[17]), the Serbian Renewal Movement (SPO) and

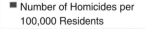

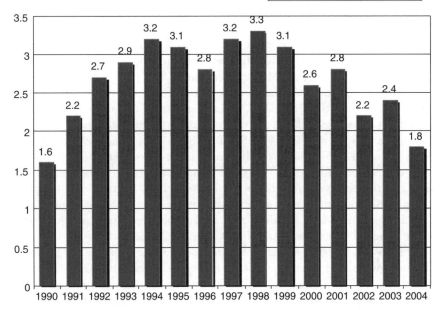

*Figure 4.3* The number of homicides per 100,000 inhabitants as recorded by the Statistical Office of the Republic of Serbia.

*Table 4.1* Total number of homicides reported by the Ministry of Interior and the Statistical Office in the Republic of Serbia

|      | *Ministry of Interior* | *The Statistical Office of the Republic of Serbia* |
| ---- | ---- | ---- |
| 2000 | 201 | 202 |
| 2001 | 205 | 218 |
| 2002 | 166 | 164 |
| 2003 | 148 | 178 |
| 2004 | 133 | 138 |

representatives from Milošević's party, the Socialist Party of Serbia (SPS), was established after three weeks of negotiations.

The pacted nature of the transition 'from within' (negotiated first among members of the opposition coalition) and 'from below' (initiated by the opposition), curtailed many of the options of the newly elected government after the first free and fair elections in December 2000. A section of the Serbian polity today claims that the diversity of political ideologies and a clash of egos within the DOS blocked opposition leaders[18] from reaching consensus on a follow-up to the peaceful revolution. This part of the Serbian polity highlights the lack of a decisive and systematic purging of public administration from the remnants of undemocratic and criminalised elite after the fall of Milošević's regime (the lack of a so-called '6 October revolution') as the major stumbling block in breaking with the past. Nine out of 13 police generals as well as hundreds of other senior police officers across the service were sent into 'honourable retirement'.[19] While this may have been politically expedient, a dissatisfaction remains with the lack of a review of the role of the police during the Milošević era. Some think that the lustration was curtailed due to the pacts made with parts of old security apparatus (by Djindic's Democratic Party (DS)), and the insistence on legality rather than legitimacy in ruling with the old regime within the interim government (by Kostunica's Democratic Party of Serbia (DSS)), justified at the time by the perceived need to avoid the 'revolutionary justice' experienced immediately after the Second World War.[20] A third explanation relies on the need of the new government to acquire the loyalty of the security forces in order to calm the simultaneous mutinies that broke out in prisons across the country and the insurgency of ethnic Albanian militants in the three municipalities in the south of Serbia which commenced in November 2000.

The private security sector created under Milošević continued to blossom in the unregulated environment following the transition. There remains today a lack of regulation/legislation for the registration and functioning of private security companies (PSCs). In the immediate aftermath of the transition PSCs provided employment for many of the police and intelligence officers who 'voluntarily' left the service following the 5 October handover. Many officers who were still part of the service also looked for an additional source of income in the private sector after their salaries were decreased under pressures from the IMF for a reduction in public spending and an end to the privileged status the security service had previously enjoyed. Bearing in mind that many of these companies served as a conduit for money laundering and extortion by the nexus of organised crime and extreme nationalistic forces, and that the estimates of their human and financial capacity exceed those of the national police service, it is clear why the private security sector presented a latent threat to the authority of the state. While accurate official data on the number of people and companies operating in the Serbian private security sector does not exist, it is estimated that PSCs currently employ 47–50,000 people, most of them carrying firearms (SEESAC, 2005). At the same time, the Ministry of Interior reportedly employs about 45–46,000 staff, out of whom 35,000 are sworn officers, while the Serbian Armed Forces provide work for 28,000 personnel (Milosavljević, 2006).

Civil society in Serbia emerged and matured during the 1990s and played a significant role in mobilising the public towards greater democratisation. However, at the beginning of the transition, with the exception of human rights organisations, civil society lacked an in-depth understanding of policing issues to be able to effectively scrutinise the functioning of the Ministry of Interior or to provide input into the policy development process in the broader security sector (including military, customs and intelligence services). The lack of capacity within civil society and the media, along with the politicians' preference for employing staff with party affiliation, allowed the police bureaucracy to profit from their unique experience and acquire the agenda-setting role. As in the case of other post-communist countries, civil society's lack of capacity to scrutinise the work of the police, as well as the supremacy of the executive over the parliament in the transition period, did not allow for the development of effective external or parliamentary oversight of the police. All legislation that was put forward for adoption during this period, together with the priority areas requiring external funding were proposed by the police service itself. The government failed to build a broad constituency for the reform process and did little to involve civil society groups, think-tanks or the public.

The immediate period after the 5 October transition, until the assassination of late Prime Minister Zoran Djindjic (12 March 2003), was marked by the unsystematic introduction of reforms across the police service. Initially, 'reforms' were symbolically important but still cosmetic, changes such as the replacement of combat uniforms with police uniforms, the change of the name from militia (*milicija*) into police (*policija*) and return to the international security community through re-admission to Interpol and the establishment of cooperation with a number of international actors (international organisations, bilateral assistance, etc.).[21] New political leadership opened up the Ministry of Interior and encouraged greater cooperation with civil society and the media. Community policing pilot programmes were initiated and efforts were made to improve the representation of women and different ethnic groups within the police.[22] Although visible, these reforms were introduced without a coherent strategy and without the required structural changes needed to make the reforms sustainable, and were primarily driven by recommendations coming from the international community. The deep polarisation and in-fighting amongst the political leadership regarding the conditionality exercised by the international community in respect of cooperation with the International War Crimes Tribunal for the former Yugoslavia (ICTY), resulted in constant accusations between the two biggest parties in the democratic government about corruption and links with the former regime and did little to increase the authority of the first post-transition government. Due to the lack of electoral incentives and trustworthy allies in the security sector, the first democratic government did not prioritise what would have been painful security sector reforms in favour of more visible economic reforms.[23]

## The second generation of police reforms: from cosmetic to consolidation?

The enthusiasm for police reform – visible during the Djindjic government – did not manage to compensate for the extreme political volatility of the period. The results of reforms from today's perspective appear modest in scope. The only reform that managed to pass the test of time – the separation of state security from the Ministry of Interior into a separate agency, the Security Intelligence Agency (BIA) in 2002 – seems not to have been sufficient for breaking the parallel governing structures surviving from the former regime. This cost Prime Minister Djindjic his life. He was assassinated on 12 March 2003, a victim of a conspiracy that involved elements of security apparatus and organised crime. The immediate assassin was Deputy Commander of the Special Operations Unit (JSO), a paramilitary unit which was at that time still part of the Ministry of the Interior. The members of that unit played a key role in organised crime activities across the Western Balkans for the Milošević regime and were notorious for their participation in war crimes in the conflicts of the 1990s, as well as for the political assassinations against opposition leaders in the 1990s.

The government attempted to reclaim the initiative on security by instituting a state of emergency and created 'a window of opportunity' for a determined police response to the assassination and the investigation of organised crime. The massive police operation, codenamed 'Sabre', took place during the 40-day long state of emergency, it led to the arrest of more than 11,665 people and detention of 2,697 – including a number of senior and mid-level MoI and BIA officials (Bakic and Gajic, 2006: 36). For the first time in decades, the public image of the police and support for their actions increased dramatically. This was explained by the public revulsion at the penetration of organised crime into the state administration and the apparent efficiency of Operation 'Sabre' (e.g. it is said that the price of heroin on Belgrade streets tripled during Operation Sabre). However, the public approval for the police action was reversed following accusations by Amnesty International of the political misuse of Operation Sabre and human rights violations as well as the emergence of details of contacts between Djindjic's cabinet and the 'Zemun Gang' which sponsored the JSO action. Public confidence in the police returned to its usual level of cynicism and apathy.

An important consequence of the public discourse after Djindjic's assassination was the institutionalisation of the belief of the need to overhaul the police service, due to the widespread penetration of organised crime within the public administration, a belief held by both the Serbian public and the international donor community (Downes, 2004). This belief was not diminished even after the Special Court for Organised Crime found a group of 12 men guilty of the assassination of Serbia's reformist Prime Minister Zoran Djindjic (May 2007 after a trial lasting over three years). Due to the multitude of contradictory conspiracy theories presented in the media and inconsistent statements given by the main political protagonists, the Serbian public remained confused and polarised over the circumstances surrounding the Djindjic assassination and related involvement of major political groups. The prosecution portrayed the accused as part of a conspiracy whose purpose, by killing Prime Minister Djindjic, was to halt cooperation with the ICTY and to prevent a crackdown on Belgrade's organised crime network, which was prepared by the Djindjic government. Above all, the trial did not provide any answer to the question of whether there was a wider political conspiracy behind the Djindjic murder plot.

In the follow-up to Djindjic's assassination, as a consequence of several high-profile corruption scandals, early parliamentary elections were held in December 2003. While successful elections helped to further institutionalise democracy, the politicisation of the police service continued with more than 700 police managers being replaced by staff loyal to the new government (Bakic and Gajic, 2006). On the positive side, during more than three uninterrupted years in office, the police have started implementing some of the structural changes aimed at providing more of the mid-term framework for development and preparations for EU accession. Piecemeal successes have been achieved such as decreasing the number of incidents of police brutality though the establishment of the Inspector's General's Office tasked with internal affairs investigations and significantly upgrading crime scene investigation capacity and procedures. Major efforts were made to enhance the institutional set-up for the fight against organised crime through the establishment of a central criminal intelligence unit and the development of targeted organised crime strategies. The most important changes include the adoption of a new Law on Police that *de jure* separates the professional operational (police) from policy/political (Ministry) component of policing, the development of a strategy for the reform of police education, and the development of an integrated border management system and the demilitarisation of the border. However, a deeper examination of the adopted measures reveals a continued concentration of decision-making in the hands of the Minister, thus ensuring that the structural conditions remain for the future politicisation of the service. For example, according to the new law 'the minister, in consultation with the Director General of Police, appoints and dismisses regional police chiefs', Article 24 of the Serbian Law on Police.[24] Also the Minister has discretion to refuse to delegate autonomy to the internal affairs unit in its investigation of their colleagues and to decide on confidential procurement of resources for the Ministry if she/he deems that any of these actions could endanger the national security.

The formal operational autonomy of the police is further hampered by a dominant management style featuring over-centralisation of decision-making and micro-management of everyday tasks.[25] The lack of transparency and inclusiveness with regard to the reform process has weakened police morale and the level of trust between the political and professional decision-makers, which is a pre-requisite to move reforms forward. The focus on vertical accountability to a few political decision-makers hampers horizontal communication and coordination among different organisational units within the Ministry and especially with other entities across the public administration. This is a general weakness of the Serbian public administration, probably stemming from lack of national consensus on key priorities and weak management capacity. The representatives of other parts of the criminal justice system have praised the police for its openness in comparison to the Milošević era, but they have also criticised the police for acting only on their request and not proactively seeking partnerships with the rest of public administration or civil society. Most police managers interviewed suggested that after seven years (since the inception of reforms), it is time to develop a corporate-level strategy which will decrease uncertainty and provide common ground from which to move the reforms forward. In order to ensure the consolidation of democracy and the sustainability of reforms, there is a great need for building structural capacity[26] for strategic planning, human resources management and better coordination among the branches of the police in the Ministry of Interior and interagency cooperation across the criminal justice sector in Serbia. The increased efficiency of the police service in dealing with organised crime has to be linked with work on structural integrity – increasing the capacity for both internal control and parliamentary and external oversight.

## The role of the EU and international community in shaping Serbia's policing model

After the ten years of political isolation, democratisation opened the Serbian police not only towards the Serbian public, but also towards international cooperation. This was a new experience for the management of the Serbian police, as until 2000 all international cooperation was channelled through the Federal Ministry of Interior. Only after the peaceful restructuring of the Federation into the loose union of Serbia and Montenegro in April 2003 did all competencies for both operational[27] and political police cooperation[28] transfer to the republican level. Meanwhile, the Serbian police had accepted assistance from the international community which triggered an intensive process of knowledge transfer and capacity development.

The first phase of international cooperation overlaps with the first phase of the reform process. With the objective of compensating for the years lost under Milošević with regards to EU accession, and with the incentive of sharing the financial burden of reconstruction, the new elites were more susceptible to policy ideas and models conditioned with support offered by the international community. Much of the property and equipment of the Ministry of Interior was destroyed during the NATO bombing campaign in 1999. More than 100 buildings and other facilities were destroyed and the damage was estimated at US$ 781,248,000 (Dordević in Janković, 2003: 175). In the early stages of the transition, the international community showed great interest in supporting democratisation within the police service, focusing its assistance on 'soft' reforms such as police education and training, the introduction of community policing, human rights standards and especially making the service more representative. The EU did not play an important role at this stage, since Serbian political elites were preoccupied with solving domestic political disputes and security problems, while the EU was more oriented towards preparing for the big Eastern enlargement of 2004. The OSCE's role as a guarantor of the peace process in south Serbia, and the role it played in the establishment of a multi-ethnic policing element (MEPE), enabled the OSCE to bring to the table alternatives from other policing models. The six priority areas for police reform recommended by the OSCE in the *Study on Policing in the Federal Republic of Yugoslavia* (Monk, 2001) were adopted as part of the official reform agenda: police education and development, accountability (both internal and external oversight), organised crime, forensics, community policing and border police reform.[29] These reforms were further expanded and operationalised in project proposals with the assistance of the Danish Institute for Human Rights during the development of the Ministry of Interior's *Vision Document for Police Reform*. This process exposed almost all units from the Ministry to foreign models of policing and the basic principles of democratic policing, but failed to involve 'users' of police services, civil society or politicians in defining the core priorities for the Ministry.[30] Moreover, the lack of coordination among donors and lack of capacity for strategic planning and analysis in the Ministry led to the unsystematic introduction of reforms.

The inappropriateness of importing whole- or piece-meal solutions from foreign policing models usually became evident during the implementation stage where either a lack of material and human resources or uncodified rules and police culture proved to be major obstacles to reform. For example, the suggestion to establish a 'neighbourhood watch' scheme as a part of the pilot projects aimed to introduce Western models of community policing, was rejected by the public interviewed as part of a public perception survey (Partner, 2002). The reason for the public's reluctance to report crime and cooperate with the police was their memory of similar behaviour in the recent communist past when they were systematically spied on or feared of being spied on by their neighbours, as a means of political control by the undemocratic regime. The problems arose even with the institutionally closer continental examples[31] because of the lack of understanding on the part of the international community that the police reform process was as much a political as a technical process, and that the assumptions made regarding the implementation of reforms were part of the strategic competition between the political elites. Attempts to influence the Serbian reform process with concepts from other policing models rarely included any deliberation on the 'triggers of change' or mistakes made in previous reform attempts in the countries of origin.

The second period of engagement by the international community was triggered by the assassination of Prime Minister Djindjic when the focus of the international community shifted towards the 'control paradigm of policing' such as the fight against organised crime. However, donors were reluctant to invest in 'hardware' or equipment that will increase police efficiency without assurance or the necessary accountability structures in place to prevent its misuse.[32] Therefore, the assistance given was in the form of policy advice and guidance for the development of a police strategy for the fight against organised crime, an integrated border management strategy and the establishment of a system of criminal intelligence. During this period, the prospect of EU membership within the Stabilisation and Association framework was re-confirmed for all Western Balkan states at the EU Summit in Thessalonica in 2003 and greater EU funds became available to the Serbian police. However, early elections and the slow administration of EU funds postponed more intensive cooperation with the EU with regard to the police reform process.

The third period of international engagement commenced with the election of the government led by Prime Minister Kostunica in the beginning of 2004. During this time, international cooperation became centralised and more institutionalised through the newly established Bureau for International Cooperation. Despite almost a year-long blockade of decision-making due to the early elections and subsequent replacement of a great number of senior and mid-level managers, slowly a new wave of reforms[33] was initiated after the *Feasibility Study for Serbia and Montenegro's Accession to the EU* was adopted in April 2005. One of the major breakthroughs in police reform was the adoption of a new Police Law which was listed as a key priority in the Feasibility Study.

## Prospects for the police reform process

When understanding the trajectory of change, the police should not be viewed in isolation; it is necessary to understand security and justice as a system of interconnected parts. Within emerging democracies, specific problems that may relate to the policing sector include: indiscipline, violence, or racketeering on the part of security services; a general lack of accountability; insufficient police presence, the prioritisation of local public safety needs; discrimination in the provision of police services to different regions, localities, or demographic groups; continuing conflict and a confusion regarding the differing roles and functions of a police and military style formations that are not attuned to public safety issues; and/or a security void that may need to be filled through some form of community action or co-production. Within the justice sector, the lack of an adequate legal framework, lack of an independent judiciary, of willingness to uphold the rule of law, politicisation and selective implementation of the law, all erode confidence in state structures and undermine the public sense of security. Linking reform of the police to a broader reform of the justice and security system is necessary if police reforms are to have their desired impact.

Similarly, reform of the police has to be understood as both a political and technical process. Unless the issue of statehood and loss of Kosovo undermines domestic politics, it is feasible to expect that the main dynamics of police reform in Serbia will soon become oriented towards the prospects of

Serbia's accession to the EU. Therefore, it is important to have in mind the nature of the Stabilisation and Association process. Due to its recent past mired by conflict, the focus of the Stabilisation and Accession Framework for whole Western Balkans is not only focused on developing individual state capacity on security, but also on developing interdependent regional networks to help further pacify the region. As a result political conditionality in relation to war crimes and the establishment of regional cooperation are likely to remain pre-conditions for support in the coming years. Due to the perception of Serbia and its neighbours as primarily weak states with a problematic security sector, it is likely that there will be greater conditionality in the area of Home Affairs during the accession negotiation than was the case of enlargement to Central European states. The conditionality will most likely manifest itself in the prioritisation of security related matters earlier in the negotiation process as a precondition for the economic development. More importantly, EU officials predict greater involvement of the European Commission and more prescriptions in the area of 'soft Acquis', conditions for membership which are not developed in detail or standardised among member states, such as police accountability.

This brings us to the second major challenge ahead of Serbian police in that it is improving planning and management capacity in the Ministry of Interior. The Ministry lacks transparent budgetary procedures, cost accounting, human resources planning and management and career development. The entire organisation, structure and culture of the police remains highly centralised and committed to outdated management techniques (Downes, 2004). Authority is rarely delegated from senior management within the Ministry to district commanders, let alone local station chiefs, resulting in even the most basic decisions reaching the desk of the minister. This top-down approach not only perpetuates the legacy of communism and the Milošević regime, but also demoralises police personnel, stifling the belief that serving in the police is a viable career option for talented recruits. While the new police law creates a legal distinction between the Ministry of Interior and the police service, decisions on the appointment of operational staff and the centralisation of decision-making means that the police service remains highly politicised with little distinction between control and accountability. The continuing politicisation of police by both democratic governments has done little to enhance either legitimacy or effectiveness and only emphasises the need to disentangle control and accountability and decentralise the operations and activities of the Ministry and police.

Third, it is important to keep in mind institutional and political legacies, because they provide *the unwritten context* in which both the police service and the population are socialised. Thus, the heritage of a reactive, repressive standard of behaviour is more likely to persist in time through informal socialisation in such a police culture despite the introduction of new formal regulations for the police profession. This can be overcome only through a long-term change-management process that looks to change police culture through updating police training but also, even more importantly, the readiness of management to consistently apply these new values in practice, demonstrating the appreciation of both human rights and creative initiative by their subordinates (Pagon, 2004). In reality, this might require a change of generations among the management cadre in the Ministry. It seems that the path from autocracy has also defined the actors and constraints to manoeuvre their ability in the initial stage of police reforms. Due to the 'pacted' nature of the transition and the weak governance of the security sector, as well as environmental challenges of inter-ethnic conflict, it seems that the new democratic leaders postponed the process of lustration and vetting of security personnel. A heavy price has been paid for this inaction, politically but also in terms of police accountability.

Because of Serbia's level of political flux, the process of police reform over the past seven years was never certain. While it is clear that some elements within government are committed to the process and progress has been made in a number of areas, much work remains ahead to ensure that reform goes beyond rhetoric and towards the creation of an effective and accountable police service.

## Notes

1 For an overview of the official history of Serbian police; see further the website of the Serbian Ministry of Interior http://www.mup.sr.gov.yu.
2 The Warsaw Pact is the name commonly given to the treaty between Albania, Bulgaria, Czechoslovakia, East Germany, Hungary, Poland, Romania, and the Soviet Union, which was signed in Poland in 1955 and was officially called 'The Treaty of Friendship, Co-operation and Mutual Assistance'. Nominally the Warsaw Pact was a response to a similar treaty made by the Western Allies in 1949 (the North Atlantic Treaty Organisation, or NATO) as well as the re-militarisation of West Germany in 1954. The Pact quickly became a powerful political tool for the Soviet Union to hold sway over its allies and harness the powers of the combined military of eastern bloc countries. All the communist states of Central and Eastern Europe were signatories except Yugoslavia.
3 See the text of the oath taken by each member of the militia before beginning work in the service from 1946, as defined in Article 45 of the National Militia oath (Koren, 2003: 16–17).
4 Although the Yugoslav system was much more liberal than other communist systems, the early post-war years were marked by equally fierce suppression of opposition, including members of the Communist Party who dared to question Tito's breaking of the alliance with Stalin in 1948, as well as Yugoslav citizens who were of the same ethnic origin as aggressors in the Second World War (e.g. Vojvodina's Germans, Italians in Istra).
5 See interpretation of quantitative and qualitative research done or *Politics and Everyday Life: Serbia* by Cvetkovic *et al.* (2003), Gredelj (2005).
6 Workers' Self-management (WSM) was the official doctrine of Yugoslav socialist regime between 1950 and the break-up of the Yugoslav Federation. It started by giving freedom to direct producers to control their firms and was later implemented in all spheres of social life. An example of participatory democracy

in practice were the self-managed meetings of workers at which literally all employees in one company or institution (from those responsible for cleaning to the CEO) would discuss strategic guidelines issued by the Party, plans for work, disciplinary measures against employees, etc. In line with the concept of self-management 'working people' were to decide how their organisation was run and managed. The Yugoslav WSM was, however, always limited by the fact that the state remained in the hands of the Communist Party which limited the extent of WSM to the local or sectoral level, and thus created a dual system of power between the bureaucratic state and the WSM movement.

7  Precise figures for this period are unavailable, but this conclusion is based on interviews undertaken by the authors with leaders of ethnic minority parties during their work with the OSCE from 2002–4.

8  Bujanovac, Medvedja and Presevo are municipalities with a significant Albanian population situated at the cross-roads with Kosovo and Macedonia.

9  An illiberal democracy as defined by Vachudova is an elective democracy in which most of the democratic institutions exist formally, but in practice, the newly-elected leaders curtail political rights in order to remain in power.

10 Including heavy weaponry such as mortars, mines and rocket launchers (Weber, in Kadar, 2001: 44).

11 Interview by Flindt Pedersen and Vasic as a part of assessment of reform prospects carried out by the Danish Institute of Human Rights in 2001. See further http://www.humanrights.dk/news/featureuk/Serbia_DIHR_UK/.

12 Although police statistics for this period are largely unreliable due to the heritage of the socialist system of measuring crime rates which discouraged officers from registering all reported crimes, because they were awarded only for those crimes that were solved. The lack of trust in police efficiency and impartiality meant that citizens were and still are reluctant to report crimes.

13 The site of Government's Team for Implementation of Poverty Reduction Strategy http://www.prsp.sr.gov.yu/engleski/kolikoje2003.jsp

14 Figure 4.1 is taken from the draft of *The Initial Framework of the National Crime Prevention Strategy* presented at the roundtable organised by the Ministry of Interior on 23 April 2007.

15 The data for Figures 4.2 and 4.3 and Table 4.1 was acquired after submission of a freedom of information request for access to information of public importance. The data was received on 5 December 2007 by e-mail.

16 One demonstrator was run over by a truck that carried demonstrators coming from the countryside, while another died of a heart attack, possibly due to nerve gas used by riot police during the storming of National TV (RTS), a symbol of Milošević's regime.

17 DOS – Democratic Opposition of Serbia, the coalition of pro-democratic parties that toppled the Milošević regime.

18 Especially between the now late Zoran Djindjic, president of the Democratic Party (DS) and Vojislav Kostunica, the president of the Democratic Party of Serbia (DSS) who took two key posts in the country after the regime change: the first as PM in Serbia, the second as president of the Federal Republic of Yugoslavia.

19 The interview with Gendarmerie commander Goran Radosavljević to the Daily Glas Javnosti on 15 November 2001, www.glas-javnosti.co.yu cited in Bakic and Gajic (2006: 5).

20 Marina Trivunovic, 'Police Reform in Serbia' in Caparini and Otwin (eds) (2004: 266).

21 This was listed in all interviews in Serbian Ministry of Interior as one of the greatest positive changes since the fall of Milošević's regime. This did not, however, stop interviewed police officers from being critical about the attitude of international actors.

22  In 2001 Serbian uniform police employed only 21 female police officers, 118 Albanians, 496 Hungarians, 380 Bosniaks. Five years later, in the six-monthly report to Serbian parliament, the Ministry reported that it employed 2,726 female officers, out of whom 124 took command posts; 296 Albanians, 487 Hungarians, 453 Bosniaks, 40 Romas (www.parlament.sr.gov.yu).

23  For example the special undercover task group *Poskok* in charge of mapping organised crime gangs or the newly envisaged Office of Inspector General tasked with internal affairs in the Ministry of Interior did not get adequate material support and political authority to be effective in tackling organised crime and police corruption.

24  See further: http://www.parlament.sr.gov.yu/content/at/akta/akta_detalji.asp? Id= 296&t=Z

25  This goes to as far as the Minister of Interior having to approve each travel application for all of 40,000 employees, including attendance on training courses or participation at a conference.

26  The model on balancing support for structural capacity with that of structural integrity is taken from Monk *et al.* (2001) *OHR Report on a Police Follow-On Mission to UNMBIH and the UN International Police Task Force.*

27  For example, the function of the national Interpol Office.

28  For example, responsibility for negotiations with the EU police experts in the Stabilisation and Association Process (SAP) designed to facilitate the Western Balkans' (Albania, Croatia, Bosnia and Herzegovina, Montenegro, Macedonia, Serbia) integration into the EU.

29  For the progress achieved in each of the priority areas see Bakic and Gajic, 2006.

30  For more information on the vision process see Downes (2004: 39–40).

31  The most often copied were the German and Austrian models, probably due to the greater geographical and cultural proximity, but also because Germans were the biggest investors and donors in the CEE region. In policing the most emulated was the German police model since the federal police in former Yugoslavia was based on the Western German model (Dvorsek, 1996).

32  This was specially related to the police dependence on surveillance equipment of the BIA, formally separated intelligence service. This information is based on interviews with the managers of MoI's Service for the Fight against Organised Crime, July 2006.

33  Some of the reforms are adoptions of Police Education and Training Strategy, Integrated Border Management Strategy, improving the management of chain of evidence and forensic capacity and promotion of the Inspector General's Office in charge of internal affairs. This last-named was possible only because the head of that office was a political appointee from a coalition member party with a strong agenda in investigating wrongdoing of security services and self-promotion.

## Bibliography

Alvazzi del Frate, Zvekic, U. and M. van Dijk, J. (eds.) (1993) *Understanding Crime Experiences of Crime and Crime Control*, Publication No. 49. (Rome: United Nations Interregional Crime and Justice Research Institute).

Amnesty International (1999) *Annual Report on Yugoslavia (Federal Republic Of).* Available from: http://www.amnestyusa.org/annualreport.php?id= 2F71BA53F1F0C2FA80256A0F005C1BC4&c=YUG.

Bakic, B. and Gajic, N. (2006) 'Police Reform in Serbia – Five Years Later' (The British Defence Academy's Conflict Research Study Centre). Available from: www.defac.ac.uk/colleges/csrc/document-listings/balkan/06(21)BB.pdf.

Brunhart, R. and Gajić N. (2005) *Policing the Economic Transition in Serbia: Assessment of the Serbian Police Service's Capacities to Fight Economic Crime* [online]. (Belgrade: OSCE Mission to Serbia and Montenegro) pp. 6–8. Available from: http://www.osce.org/serbia/item_11_18263.html.

Caparini, Marina and Graham Day (2002) 'Democratic Control of the Police and Police Reform in the Federal Republic of Yugoslavia and Serbia' (Geneva: Geneva Centre for the Democratic Control of Armed Forces (DCAF), *Working Paper Series* – No. 2).

Caparini, M. and Marenin, O. (eds.) (2004) *Transforming Police in Central and Eastern Europe*. (London: Transaction Publishers, on behalf of the Geneva Centre for Democratic Control of Armed Forces).

Caparini, M. and Marenin, O. (2005) 'Crime, Insecurity and Police Reform in Post-Socialist CEE.' *The Journal of Power Institutions In Post-Soviet Societies*, Pipss.org: Issue 2 – Reflections on Policing in Post-Communist Europe [online]. Available from: http://www.pipss.org/document330.html.

Caparini, M. and Otwin, M. (eds.) (2004) 'Security Sector Reform and Post-Conflict Stabilisation: The Case of the Western Balkans' in Bryden, A. and Hänggi, H. (eds.) *Reform and Reconstruction of the Security Sector* (Munster: LIT Verlag).

Corpora, C. (2004) 'The Untouchables: Former Yugoslavia's Clandestine Political Economy.' *Problems of Post-Communism*, 51 (3), pp. 61–68.

Cvetković, V.N, Jakšić, B., Popov, N., Savić, M. and Stupar, M. (eds) (2003) *Politika i svakodnevni život-Srbija 1999–2002 (Politics and Everyday Life: Serbia: 1999–2002)*. (Beograd: Institut za filozofiju i društvenu teoriju; Belgrade: Institute for Philosophy and Social Sciences).

Danish Institute of Human Rights, 'Vision Process for the Reform of the Ministry of Interior of Serbia', Available from: http://humanrights.dk/themes/systems+in-+transition/from+force+to+service. www.humanrights.dk/departments/international/partnercountries/thebalkans/balkanother/Serbia_DIHR [Accessed Nov. 2005].

Djordjević, I. (2003) 'Overview of the process of reform of the Ministry of Interior of the Republic of Serbia', in Jankovic P. (ed.) *Druga škola reforme sektora bezbednosti* (The Second School of Security Sector Reform). (Belgrade: G17 Institute).

Downes, M. (2004) *Police Reform in Serbia: Towards the Creation of a Modern and Accountable Police Service*. Belgrade: Law Enforcement Department, OSCE Mission to Serbia and Montenegro. Available from: http://www.osce.org/serbia/item_11_18263.html [Accessed 06 February 2006].

Downes, M and Keane, R. (2006) 'OSCE Approaches to Security Sector Reform.' In G. Peake, E. Scheye and A. Hills (eds), *Arresting Insecurity*, (London: Taylor and Francis).

Dvorsek, A. (1996) 'Applicability of Western Police Experiences – Desires And Possibilities From The Viewpoint of Slovenian Police.' In *Policing in Central and Eastern Europe: Comparing Firsthand Knowledge with the Experience from the West* [online]. (Ljubljana: College of Police and Security Studies). Available from http://www.ncjrs.gov/policing/app85.htm [Accessed 19 March 2006].

Fatic, A. (2000) *Corruption in Serbia*. (Belgrade: the Management Centre).

Flindt Peterson, S. (2003) 'Vision Process for the Reform of the Serbian Ministry of Interior' [online]. Available from: http://humanrights.dk/themes/systems+in-+transition/from+force+to+service

Gorenak, V. (1996) 'Organizational Changes In Slovenian Police In the Period

Between 1989 and 1996', in *Policing in Central and Eastern Europe: Comparing Firsthand Knowledge with the Experience from the West* [online] (Ljubljana: College of Police and Security Studies). Available from http://www.ncjrs.gov/policing/org229.htm [Accessed 15 July 2006].

Gredelj, S. (ed.) (2005) 'Politika i svakodnevni život tri godine posle (Politics and Every-Day Life- Three Years Later)', *Filozofija i društvo (Philosophy and Society)*, 2 (27) [special issue].

Human Rights Watch (1999) *World Report 1999. Federal Republic of Yugoslavia. Human Rights Developments*. Available from: www.hrw.org/worldreport99/europe/yugoslavia.html.

Jamieson, A. (2001) 'Transnational Organised Crime: A European Perspective.' *Studies in Conflict and Terrorism*, 24, pp. 377–387.

Janković, P. (ed.) (2003) *Druga škola reforme sektora bezbednosti – zbornik predavanja* (The Second School of Security Sector Reform, The Collection of Lectures). (Belgrade: G17 Institute, Centar za proučavanje odbrane i bezbednosti).

Kadar, A. (2001) 'Police in Transition.' Budapest: on behalf of Hungarian Helsinki Committee, *CEU Press*.

Kešetović, Ž. and Davidović, D. (2006) 'Policing in Serbia – Challenges and Developments', in G. Meško, and B. Dobovšek, (eds.) *Policing in Central and Eastern Europe – Past, Present, Future* (Conference Proceedings). (Maribor: The Faculty of Criminal Justice and Security) [online]. Available from: http://www.fpvv.uni-mb.si/conf2006/Film-Policing.pdf [Accessed 4 May 2007].

Kešetović, Ž., Bajagić, M. and Korajlić, N. (2006) 'Police-Media Relations in the Transition from Autocratic Regime to Democracy', in G. Meško, and B. Dobovšek, (eds.) *Policing in Central and Eastern Europe – Past, Present, Future* (Conference Proceedings). (Maribor: The Faculty of Criminal Justice and Security) [online]. Available from: http://www.fpvv.uni-mb.si/conf2006/Film-Policing.pdf [Accessed 4 May 2007].

Koci, A. (1996) 'Legitimation and culturalism: towards policing changes in the European "post-socialist" countries', in *Policing In Central And Eastern Europe: Comparing Firsthand Knowledge with Experience from the West* (Ljubljana: College of Police and Security Studies) [online]. Available from: http://www.ncjrs.gov/policing/leg219.htm [Accessed 4 May 2007].

Koren, M. (2003) *The Slovene Police*. (Ljubljana: The Ministry of the Interior of the Republic Slovenia, Police, General Police Directorate).

March, G.J. and Olsen, P.J. (2005) 'Elaborating the "new institutionalism" ' [online]. *Arena Working Papers*, 11/2005. Available from: http://www.arena.uio.no/publications/working-papers2005/papers/05_11.xml [Accessed on 27 June 2006].

Markovic, Dragana (2002) 'The Police Reform in Yugoslavia. New Age for the "Blues"? New Visions, New Missions', in Gordan Kaljdziev (ed.), *Yearbook of the Balkan Human Rights Network*, 2002, Part II, pp. 287–301.

Milosavljević, B. (1997) *Nauka o policiji (Police Science)*. (Belgrade: Police Academy).

Milosavljević, B. (2003) 'Dvogodisnje bilans i perspektive reformi policije u Srbiji' (Two-year Police Reform in Serbia: Stocktaking and Forecasting) in P. Janković (ed.) *Reforma sektora bezbednosti:zbornik predavanja* (Security Sector Reform, The Collection of Lectures). (Belgrade: G17 Institute, Centar za proučavanje odbrane i bezbednosti), pp.79–93.

Milosavljević, B. (2004a) *Ljudska prava i policija* (Human Rights and the Police), Centar za antiratnu akciju, Beograd (signatura I 133).

Milosavljević, B. (2004b) 'Reform of the police and security services in Serbia and Montenegro: attained results or betrayed expectations.' P. Fluri, and M. Hadžić (eds) *Sourcebook on Security Sector Reform*. (Geneva and Belgrade: Geneva Centre for the Democratic Control of Armed Forces and Centre for Civil–Military Relations).

Milosavljević, B. (2006) 'Model of Law on Private Security Companies.' *Western Balkans Security Observer* (No.1), pp. 20–21.

Monk, R. (2001) *Study on Policing in the Federal Republic of Yugoslavia*. (Belgrade: OSCE Mission to the Federal Republic of Yugoslavia).

Monk, R., Tor, T.H. and Rumin, S. (2001) *OHR Report on a Police Follow-On Mission to UNMBIH and the UN International Police Task Force*. (Belgrade: OSCE).

OSCE (2005) *Improvement of Communication between Media and Police – Final report of the first phase of the project*. (Belgrade: OSCE Mission to Serbia and Montenegro) [online]. Available from: http://www.osce.org/documents/fry/2005/12/17386_en.pdf [Accessed 4 June 2006].

Pagon, M. (2004) 'A Study of Police Reform in Slovenia' in M. Caparini and O. Marenin (eds) *Transforming Police in Central and Eastern Europe*. (London: Transaction Publishers, on behalf of the Geneva Centre for Democratic Control of Armed Forces).

Partner Marketing Research Agency (2002) *Public Perception of the Police in Serbia*, Survey conducted on behalf of the OSCE Mission to the FRY and the Serbian Ministry of Internal Affairs, Belgrade.

Peake, G. (2004) *Policing the Peace: Police Reform Experiences in Kosovo, Southern Serbia and Macedonia*, Saferwold report, Available from: http://www.saferworld.org.uk/publications.php/46/policing_the_peace. www.saferworld.org.uk/publications/Policing%20PA2.pdf [Accessed 4 June 2006].

Peers, S. (2000) *The EU Justice and Home Affairs Law*. (Harlow: Longman).

Pridham, G. (2001) 'Uneasy Democratizations – Pariah Regimes, Political Conditionality and Reborn Transitions in Central and Eastern Europe', *Democratization*, 8 (4), Winter 2001, pp. 65–94.

Ryan, B. (2002) *Police Perception Survey in Serbia*, Survey conducted on behalf of the OSCE Mission to the FRY and the Serbian Ministry of Internal Affairs, Belgrade.

SEESAC (UNDP) (August 2005) 'SALW and Private Security Companies in South Eastern Europe: a Cause or Effect of insecurity?' (Belgrade: UNDP).

Shentov, O., Todorov, B. and Stoyanov, A. (2004) *Partners in Crime – The Risks of Symbiosis between the Security Sector and Organised Crime in Southeast Europe*. (Sofia: Centre for the Study of Democracy).

Simeunović-Patić, M.B. (2003) 'Ubistva u Srbiji u kontekstu tranzicije i rata.' Temida br.4. Žrtve i globalizacija: 12.

South Eastern Europe Clearinghouse for the Control of Small Arms and Light Weapons (2004) *Public Perception of Small Arms and Security in South Serbia*. (Belgrade: UNDP).

Stodiek, T. (2006) 'The OSCE and the Creation of Multi-Ethnic Police Forces in the Balkans', *CORE Working Paper 14*. (Hamburg: CORE, University of Hamburg).

Trivunovic, M. (2004a) 'Police reform in Serbia.' In M. Caparini and O. Marenin (eds) *Transforming Police in Central and Eastern Europe: Process and Progress*. (Münster, LIT Verlag), pp. 265–285.

Trivunovic, M. (2004b) 'Status of police reform after four years of democratic transition in Serbia.' *Helsinki Monitor*, 3, pp. 172–186.

Vachudova, M.A. (2005) *Europe Undivided*. (Oxford: Oxford University Press).

*Vision Document for Police Reform, The* (2003) Belgrade: Ministry of Interior of the Republic of Serbia.

Zvekic, U. (1998) *Criminal Victimisation in Countries in Transition.* (Rome: United Nations Interregional Crime and Justice Research Institute).

Zvekic, U. and Stankov, B. (1998) *Victims of Crime in the Balkan Region.* (Rome: United Nations Interregional Crime and Justice Research Institute).

## *Website*

www.mup.sr.gov.yu Official website of Serbian Ministry of Interior.

# Part II
# Asia

# 5 Policing in South Korea

## Struggle, challenge, and reform

*Byongook Moon and Merry Morash*

## Introduction

Since its establishment in 1894, the Korean police force has experienced significant challenges and struggles, mainly because of the colonization of the Korean Peninsula by Japan (1901–1945), the Korean War (1950–1953), and subsequent political instability. As in other politically unstable countries, the authority and power of the police in South Korea has frequently been abused as a political instrument to suppress political opponents and restrain citizens (Hoffman, 1982; Moon, 2004). During several periods, military personnel were heavily involved in national political matters and with the criminal justice system, including the police. Various torture techniques and harsh maltreatment against political opponents and citizens were used, resulting in pervasive human right violations, and police brutality and corruption (Heo, 1998; Nahm, 1988; Pyo, 2001a; Vreeland *et al.*, 1975). Unfortunately but expectedly, the legitimate role of the police to enforce the law and protect peace and public order was largely neglected in some periods. Serious questions about police political neutrality, fairness, and professionalism led to public–police antagonism and compromised police authority (Heo, 1998; Moon and Zager, 2007; Nahm, 1988; Vreeland *et al.*, 1975).

During recent decades marked by rapid industrialization and democratization, policing has experienced both structural and functional transformations. In 1991, the Police Act was enacted to bring about political neutrality and structural autonomy of the police (Heo, 1998; Pyo, 2001a). In 2000, the Korean National Police Agency (KNPA) implemented a major reform to emphasize a cooperative and collaborative relationship with the public, police professionalism, elimination of corruption, and the creation of a police image as fair and trustworthy (Pyo, 2001b). Despite the progression and structural reforms, the police in South Korea still face numerous political and institutional challenges to become a fully democratic police force.

This chapter examines the history of modern policing in the historical and political context of South Korea and issues and contemporary challenges faced by the Korean police. First, the chapter briefly presents information on South Korean politics, culture, economy, and crime. Second, it examines the history of modern Korean policing, specifically focusing on colonial policing during the Imperial Japanese occupation, military dictatorship policing, and reform-oriented democratic policing. Third, the chapter examines the organizational structure and functions of Korean policing. Following this is a discussion of several critical issues facing the Korean police, including corruption, excessive use of force, police stress, recruitment of women, and a negative relationship with the public. The final section of the chapter describes the goals and objectives of a recent reform movement the South Korean police have implemented.

## Cultural, political, and economic conditions in South Korea

Once known as the land of morning calm, Korea has a five-thousand-year dynamic and distinct cultural history. Koreans have maintained a strong national identity, and developed a unique language (called "Hangeul"). Korea is a very ethnically homogeneous country and has historically preserved a vertical social structure emphasizing harmony among group members, a strong work-ethic, duty, and respect toward elders and government authority (Lee, 1990).

The Korean peninsula is located in North East Asia, surrounded by China, Russia, and Japan and is about the size of Britain (Korean Overseas Information Service, 2007). Because of its unique geographical location and strategic military importance, throughout its history Korea has suffered numerous invasions and periods of foreign occupation, notably by China and Japan (Macdonald, 1988). During the twentieth century, Korea endured considerable turbulence and violence: Japan annexed Korea in 1910 and ruled and suppressed Korean people and society until 1945; at the start of the cold war, the Korean peninsula was divided into South and North Korea by the world superpowers, the United States and the Soviet Union; and during the Korean War (1950–1953), there was considerable destruction of the Korean peninsula and its people.

After the war, the political system in South Korea was for many years unstable and military personnel were deeply involved in political events, including successful military coups in 1961 and 1979. Ree Syng Man, the First President of the Republic of Korea (1948–1960), was forced to resign due to corruption and manipulation of election results. In 1961, Major General Park Chung Hee seized power from a civilian government in a military coup and held tight control over political and social aspects of Korean life until his assassination in 1979. Taking advantage of political instability caused by the assassination of President Park, General Chun Doo Hwan led another successful military coup in 1979. In succession, the illegitimate governments were heavily dependent on military power and the criminal justice system to suppress anti-government demonstrations and restrain citizens and political opponents. Using the citizens' fear of communism and potential military conflict with North Korea, the regimes also frequently fabricated spy (espionage) incidents in order to maintain their political power, especially during times of political turmoil or national elections. Consequently, human rights abuses, brutality, and torture-related cases of death perpetrated by the military and the criminal justice system were pervasive.

Numerous demonstrations for political democratization and against illegitimate regimes were staged during the 1980s and early 1990s. Particularly massive demonstrations in 1987 by students, religious leaders, and the general public were a turning point, paving the way to transition to a democratic Korean society. The Constitution was amended, allowing a direct presidential election by the full electorate (West and Baker, 1991). Political and social democratization of the Korean society progressed steadily, and civilian presidents with no military backgrounds were consecutively elected and made peaceful transitions into office. The Truth Commission was established and there were numerous parliamentary investigations of bloody military crackdowns on pro-democratic movements and numerous suspicious deaths of civilians who participated in anti-government movements. Two former dictators were found guilty of playing major roles in the 1979 military coup and were sentenced to long prison terms. After serving two years in prison, they were pardoned by President Kim Dae Jung in an attempt to reconcile disagreements in the nation. With a steady progression and achievement of political and civil liberties, South Korea is currently ranked as one of the most politically liberated nations in Asia (Freedom House, 2006).

Despite considerable political turmoil until the early 1990s, South Korea had achieved an unprecedented economic success, called "the Miracle of Han River," rapidly transforming a rural and agricultural society into an urbanized and industrialized society. Between 1965 and 1979, with a state-centered and export-driven economic system, South Korea maintained an average annual growth rate of 9 percent (Collins, 1990) and developed into the eleventh largest economy in the world. Also, South Korea's gross national product (GNP) per capita rose dramatically from $79 in 1960 to over $10,000 in 1995. However, a financial crisis that began in 1997 led to social unrest, bankruptcies, layoffs, suicides, and family disruptions. Through massive financial reforms, South Korea was able to overcome the financial crisis, and its economy has rapidly recovered and improved.

Rapid industrialization and urbanization in Korean society has resulted in a significant rise of both violent and non-violent crime rates. According to the 2006 Crime White Paper by the Judicial Research and Training Institute, the overall number of crimes more than tripled between 1976 and 2005. For violent crime such as murder, robbery, arson, and rape, around 5,300 offenses were reported in 1976, but almost 20,000 felony offenses were reported in 2005. Similarly, property crime (e.g., theft, fraud) increased approximately 300 percent during this period.

## History of modern policing in Korea

Prior to the fourteenth century, there was no formal police organization in Korea, and military personnel were responsible for maintaining social order and peace (Hoffman, 1982; Pyo, 2001a). In 1471, a well-organized special semi-military police agency, called "Po Do Chung," was formally established in each province and county to address a rising crime problem of rampant thievery (Hoffman, 1982; Myong, 1959; Pyo, 2001a). The chief of Po Do Chung was an army general, and an estimated 64 officials (called "Po Do Ri") were stationed in particular Po Do Chung jurisdictions (Myong, 1959). The pre-modern police agency was an authoritarian force with enormous power; even local governors had to follow the orders of the chief of Po Do Chung (Lee, 1990). The police agency evolved from its original emphasis on controlling crime and took on increased actions as a military army (Hoffman, 1982).

As part of the Japanese-initiated reform movement to colonize the Korean peninsula, in 1894, Po Do Chung was abolished and replaced by a modernized national police force, called "Kyomg Mu Kum" (Bureau of Police Affairs). The centralized and paramilitary Bureau of Police Affairs replicated the Japanese police system, which was modeled on a continental European policing style (Pyo, 2001a). Provincial police bureaus, police stations, and mini-police stations were established throughout the country. A new rank system (director, superintendent, captain, lieutenant, and policeman) was implemented (Myong, 1959). Physical examinations and written tests were used in the selection of police, and before they were assigned to a field unit, cadets received formal, two-month long training, focusing on laws, first aid, and Japanese language (Myong, 1959). The modernized police were separated from the military and its main roles were to maintain order and prevent and detect crime (Hoffman, 1982; Myong, 1959).

After the 1894 reforms, Japanese personnel were deeply involved as advisors and officers, and had substantial effects on both policing and the judiciary (Pyo, 2001a; Heo, 1998). Japanese military police personnel were stationed in major cities to investigate any anti-Japanese movements. In addition, a law was passed to allow Japanese personnel to be hired as police officers working for the Korean government, and by 1908, almost 40 percent of police officers (1,863 out of total 4,991 police officers in Korea) were Japanese (Heo, 1998).

In 1910, Japan formally annexed Korea and placed the Korean police under the direct control of the Japanese Governor General. Using the centralized national police, Japan brutally and violently suppressed and ruled Korean citizens until the end of the Second World War in 1945. Between 1910 and 1919, the Japanese military police performed both civilian police work and other duties, including gathering intelligence and promoting the use of the Japanese language (Pyo, 2001a). Military police stations were set up throughout the country, especially in rural areas, and the number of military police officers steadily increased up to 12,423 in 1917 (Heo, 1998).

Also, more police stations and mini-police stations were established, and Japanese personnel held important and high-ranking positions (Hoffman, 1982; Myong, 1959; Nahm, 1988). There were 481 police and mini-police stations in 1910, and then an additional 250 stations were added within three years (Heo, 1998).

After the "Samil Independence Movement" (March First Independence Movement), when there were massive non-violent demonstrations of Koreans against Japanese occupation of the Korean peninsula, the Japanese colonial government began to implement appeasement and assimilation policies. Notably, separate from the military police, a civilian police force was responsible for controlling crime and maintaining peace and order (Myone, 1959). However, similar to the military force, the Japanese-led civilian police force used unlimited power to brutally control and suppress the Korean people, torturing and killing numerous Koreans.

The period of Imperial Japanese occupation from 1910 to 1945 is viewed as the darkest era for the Korean people (Nahm, 1988). Unbounded police power infiltrated and permeated every aspect of the Korean people's lives. As Meade (1951: 119) wrote, legislation "granted the police surveillance over the public's every thought, word, and private action." The 30 years of brutality and suppression that Koreans experienced from the Japanese-led police created a deep hostility of Koreans toward the police, and this hostility was passed from generation to generation. Scholars and practitioners trace contemporary problems with legitimacy, corruption, and brutality to Korea's history of Japanese Imperial domination (Lee, 2002; Pyo, 2001a).

The Japanese government's unconditional surrender to the Allies in 1945 ended Japan's 35-year colonial occupation and liberated the Korean peninsula. The United States occupied the South, and the Soviet Union controlled the North. Initially, the American Military Command was unaware of the extent of Japanese employment within the Korean police and of the police-related needs of the country, but once the situation became apparent, American Army planners diverted a team of U.S. police specialists to Korea (Hoffman, 2005). The United States Army Government in South Korea (USAMGIK) established the Korean Police on February 16, 1946 (Hoffman, 2005), implemented a series of structural and functional policing reforms, and followed up on civilian U.S. advisors' recommendations to remove the Japanese from police positions and replace them with trained Koreans. Police duties were limited to controlling crime, preserving social order and peace, and collecting intelligence information on communist and anarchist activities (Pyo, 2001a). Militia organizations were banned, police officers' summary punishment was abolished, a national police board was created, and female police officers were hired. Beginning in 1946, police personnel from the Detroit Police Department and the State Police of Michigan worked in Korea to set up specific police operations, and subsequently high-ranking Korean police officers began coming to the United States to attend conferences focused on democratizing police organizations (Hoffman, 2005). U.S. police advisors worked with the Korean police up until the 1960s, but to adequately address the challenges, the Korean people drove the actual changes and reforms to the police force (Hoffman, 2005).

Numerous Koreans had been hired as police officers in order to fill the void left by Japanese personnel. However, without proper background investigations and no specified criteria, many unqualified personnel and criminals were employed (Pyo, 2001a). Moreover, facing the manpower shortage, USAMGIK decided to utilize former Korean police officers who worked for the Imperial Japanese Government as high-ranking officers in the newly established Korean police force (Myong, 1959). Many of these police officers were involved in corruption, human rights abuses, and excessive use of force, causing further antagonism between the public and the police.

In 1948, the Republic of Korea was established and the national police were reorganized under the direct control of the Ministry of Home Affairs (Myong, 1959). Two years later, North Korea invaded South Korea, and the resulting Korean War saw the loss of life of millions of Koreans and the destruction of the Korean peninsula. In addition to ordinary police duties, the Korean National Police actively participated in military operations such as guarding key supply areas, fighting against enemy guerrilla forces, and protecting national network systems (Myong, 1959). During three years of the Korean War, more than 10,000 police officers were killed while on duty and many more were injured (Myong, 1959). Some scholars have argued that as a result of the police involvement in the war, which did ultimately save the country, the police were socialized toward a military style of operation (Hoffman, 2005).

The political system after the war was unstable, and military personnel were deeply involved in politics for sustained periods of time. During the First to Sixth Republics (1948 to 1992), Korean government varied but was essentially dictatorial and authoritative (Moon, 2004). Lacking legitimacy to govern, government depended heavily on the police to suppress demonstrations, control citizens, and hinder political opponents. As a result, throughout the period, the Korean police engaged in repeated reorganization to promote modernization, and reform plans were proposed to insure structural and political autonomy of the police.

Still, the police were heavily entangled in domestic politics and were used as an effective political tool to sustain the political power of illegitimate regimes (Moon, 2004). After successful military coups by Park Chung Hee in 1961 and Chun Doo Hwan in 1979 and the consecutive establishments of military governments (1961–1993), military personnel who had played dominant roles were assigned to high-ranking police and other governmental posts. For example, retired or ex-military officers were hired to fill high police positions, and many police were mobilized to collect information about political dissent, labor movements, and anti-government student movements (Hoffman, 1982; Heo, 1998). In addition to putting the Korean police under the direct control of the military government, the government established the

Korean Counterintelligence Agency (KCIA), which was given unrestricted police power (investigating/interrogating, arresting, and detaining political opponents and citizens) in the name of national security.

As public demonstrations against authoritarian governments increased dramatically, numerous police personnel were deployed to break up the demonstrators. Tear gassings and aggressive police tactics against demonstrators led to deaths of both citizens and police. These incidents deeply ingrained the public's views of police as tools of authoritarian and illegitimate governments (Lee, 1990; Lee, 2002).

Police abuse of human rights and acts of brutality, at their extreme culminating in torture related deaths, were common (Cohen and Baker, 1991; Pyo, 2001a). During a 1987 police interrogation of an anti-government student organization, a 21-year old Seoul National University student, Pak Chong Chol, died after being held under the water and forced to swallow it. Though few police were charged or disciplined for such actions (Macdonald, 1988), in this case there was a public outcry regarding human rights abuses (Cohen and Baker, 1991).

As Korean society was rapidly democratized, opposition parties' political pressure to prevent the political manipulation of the police by a ruling government and insure the structural autonomy of the police was intensified. Consequently, the Police Act was enacted in 1991, significantly modifying the structure of the Korean police. The current Korean National Police Agency (KNPA) was established as an independent agency, out of the direct control from the Ministry of Interior who is responsible for administering various political elections.

The National Police Board (NPB), consisting of seven civilians, was created to provide advice on police-related budget, equipment, and personnel administration policy. Although the Police Act was criticized by scholars for failing to fully insure political neutrality of the Korean police, it has been considered as a first step to developing a politically independent Korean police (Heo, 1998).

Even though reform-oriented civilian leaders were consecutively elected as presidents beginning in 1992, massive public demonstrations (i.e., anti-government movements, capital–labor conflicts, and social unrest—especially during the financial crisis between 1997 and 1998) continued to occur. As a result, the Korean police continued to focus on controlling social unrest rather than crime, and this focus led to violent confrontations between demonstrators and the police (Pyo, 2001a). The result was open public questioning of police fairness and legitimacy. In the face of this crisis of legitimacy, the Korean police implemented a major reform in 1999, partially influenced by the nationwide reform movements initiated by the President Kim Dae Jung and partly by the popularity of the community policing model in the United States (Moon, 2004; Pyo, 2001b). Korean police administrators adopted an operational theme emphasizing the service roles of the police (citizen-oriented policing), and the importance of public–police partnerships characterized by cooperation and collaboration. The reform led to programs designed to improve public–police relationships and to prevent crime through police partnerships with the community (see Pyo, 2001b).

## Structure of the police in South Korea

Since the establishment of the modern Korean police in 1894, South Korea has maintained a highly centralized national police system. The national police headquarters is located in Seoul, the capital of South Korea, and is headed by a Commissioner General. The national police headquarters is organized into seven bureaus (Administration and Planning, Safety, Affairs, Security, Intelligence, National Security, and Foreign Affairs) and five affiliated institutions (National Police University, Police Comprehensive Academy, National Central Police Academy, National Police Hospital, and Driver's License Agency).

As of 2006, the number of sworn police officers was 95,613 and the ratio of police officers to the population was one to 510. The majority of police officers are male (approximately 95 percent) and non-ranking officers (approximately 86 percent). Consistent with broader societal values, Korean police at the supervisory level are highly educated.

Fourteen provincial police headquarters are under the direct control and supervision of the national police headquarters. Each provincial police headquarters, having an organizational structure similar to that of the national police headquarters, is in charge of administering police departments and mini-police stations in its geographic district. There are 235 police departments around the country and, depending on the number of citizens within the jurisdiction, each is categorized as a first, second, or third level. A police department is considered as first level when the number of residents within its jurisdiction is more than 250,000. The second level police department is responsible for a medium-sized city with a population between 150,000 and 250,000. The third level police department is responsible for a rural area with fewer than 150,000 residents. Most police departments belong in the first level category, since more than two-thirds of Koreans reside in metropolitan areas. A police station is headed by a senior superintendent and has varying numbers of mini-police stations, depending on the number of residents in the jurisdiction.

A unique characteristic of the Korean police is that a sub- (or mini-) police station, popularized quite recently in Western countries by decentralized, neighborhood-based community policing, has existed as the core division since the establishment of the modern Korean police. Unfortunately, the sub-police station system in Korea was originally developed by Imperial Japan to effectively suppress Korean people, rather than to better serve the needs of citizens. Thus even though the sub-police stations are geographically decentralized, they are administratively centralized, and remain under the direct and tight control of a supervising police station (for more information about the history of a sub-police station system in South Korea, see Moon *et al.*, 2005).

In 2006, there were 825 regional patrol stations and 529 mini-police stations throughout the country and more than 40 percent of total police personnel were assigned to sub-police stations. Each sub-police station operates twenty-four hours a day on a three-shift system, and an inspector or senior inspector is responsible for operations and management. New police officers are typically assigned to a sub-police station for approximately two years.

A sub-police station in South Korea performs four general roles (Rho, 2000). First, a mini-police station acts as a site for maintaining public order, preventing crime, and responding to criminal activities in its beat areas. Police officers in sub-police stations regularly patrol their beat areas on foot or by patrol cars around the clock. Second, a sub-police station is a central place for establishing and managing public–police cooperation programs in order to receive residents' voluntary assistance in maintaining order and preventing crime. As of 2002, there were approximately 3,400 Voluntary Patrol Organizations, with 92,000 citizens involved. Among numerous such programs, the "Voluntary Patrol Organization" and "Crime Reporting Agents Program" are the most popular and successful (Rho, 2000). Third, sub-stations function as outposts that have direct contact with residents and provide various services to community members. Patrol officers frequently visit and contact residents in their beat areas in order to understand their concerns and needs. They also provide road directions, lost and found information, and establish an emergency system for contact with hospitals, drug stores, or car repair shops so that residents can easily use them without difficulty during a holiday or at night (Korean National Police Agency, 2002). Fourth, a sub-police station performs on a small scale the same tasks a police station performs. Every police officer in a sub-police station is assigned to one of a number of major duties such as investigation, crime prevention, traffic, or security. For example, officers who are assigned to traffic are expected to arrive at the scene of a traffic accident. Officers who are assigned to criminal investigation fill out reports of criminal arrest and investigate the whereabouts of those who have failed to pay penalties. Though empirical research examining the effectiveness of police sub-stations is rare, the sub-police station system is known to play critical roles in preventing crime and maintaining a low crime rate in South Korea. Sub-police stations increase face-to-face interaction with residents and improve citizen satisfaction. A study by Moon *et al.* (2005) examined police officers' attitudes toward the effectiveness of the mini-police station system. A majority of officers in the sample reported that the system prevented crime and improved the relationship and mutual understanding between citizens and police.

The other unique characteristic of policing in South Korea is a combat police system that includes military combat police units and auxiliary police units. The military combat police system was established in 1967 to guard and combat against military infiltration by North Korean spies and armies (Song, 2006). Military combat police officers are selected involuntarily from drafts of mandatory military conscripts. They receive basic military training for five weeks and additional basic policing training at the National Central Police Academy (NCPA) for two weeks. After training, military combat police are assigned to each provincial police headquarters, where they serve for 24 months under the supervision of a Senior Inspector in the police force. There were 18,174 military combat police officers in 2004. The auxiliary police system was established in 1982. Auxiliary police are selected from people who voluntarily apply for this alternative to their mandatory military service. Similar to military combat police officers, they receive basic military training for four weeks and a basic policing training for three weeks. As of 2004, there were 32,435 auxiliary police officers (Song, 2006).

Inconsistent with their intended purpose, a majority of military combat and auxiliary police officers, especially military combat police officers, have been deployed to confront and break up demonstrations. Violent confrontations between military combat officers and demonstrators have involved thousands of tear gassings and the use of aggressive tactics by the police (using long batons and metal shields), resulting in numerous injuries and even deaths for both sides. In a widely publicized incident, two farmers demonstrating against a government plan to open the domestic rice market to foreign countries were killed during a confrontation between demonstrators and military combat units in 2005, resulting in the resignation of the Commissioner General. Critics argue against deploying military combat police officers to break up demonstrations because they lack professionalism and are emotional and violent (Song, 2006). Recognizing the potential problems, the Korean National Police Agency announced several plans to prevent officers' aggressive and violent responses to demonstrators, such as the creation of combat police units consisting of only sworn police officers, to control a demonstration, and minimization of physical contacts between the police and demonstrators through the use of a water cannon.

## Critical issues in Korean policing

With a remarkable achievement of democracy, political freedom, and nationwide reform movements in recent decades, there has also been considerable progress in improving the structure and function of the Korean National Police. A major police initiated reform has been implemented to establish a positive relationship with the public, to create a fair and trustworthy police image, and to address police corruption and excessive use of power. Despite the progress, the Korean police still face serious problems with political neutrality, antagonism between the public and the police, corruption, excessive use of force, recruiting and retaining women officers, and high levels of job stress and dissatisfaction among officers. This section explores these critical issues.

*Political neutrality and structural autonomy*

Historically, political neutrality and structural autonomy of the modern Korean police have not been ensured. In many periods, police were heavily involved in domestic politics, manipulating presidential/parliamentary elections, and spying on political dissent and anti-government labor/student movements (Hoffman, 1982). Moreover, the highly centralized police structure, with a concentration of police power among a few high-ranked officers has made possible the ruling regimes' use of the police as an effective political tool. Promotions and assignments to important positions have been based on officers' relationships with ruling parties and their loyalty to regimes in power (Moon, 2004; Pyo, 2001a). For example, without a fixed period of tenure, the Commissioner General has frequently been changed at the will of the ruling regime. The average tenure has been less than a year, which has significantly diminished the political neutrality of the police (Pyo, 2001a). Consequently, high-ranked police officers become more concerned with the interests of parties in power than of the citizenry, and police are deeply involved in political matters.

In order to prevent the political manipulation of the police and bring about structural autonomy from the Ministry of Interior, reform plans (i.e., 1955, 1960, 1972, 1980, 1985, and 1989) were proposed several times but never implemented (Heo, 1998; Kim, 2000). The key aspects of these reform plans were: 1) the creation of the National Police Board comprised of civilians to become a superior office of the police independently operating the Korean police and 2) the stipulation of the political neutrality of the police in the Constitution.

The 1991 Police Act did establish the National Police Board, which is an advisory committee, under the Minster of Interior. It advises on issues like budget, equipment, and personnel administration. The Board falls short in producing the political neutrality of the Korean police (Heo, 1998; Pyo, 2001b). It has no power to supervise the police or affect the promotion of high-ranking officers. In 2003, a two-year fixed tenure system for the Commissioner General was implemented to further promote the political neutrality of the police. However, the first Commissioner General, Choi, under the fixed tenure system resigned two months before the completion of his tenure over the conflicts of police personnel changes with the government.

The second Commissioner General, Heo, also resigned in the midst of his tenure under the political and public pressure for farmers' deaths during the confrontations between demonstrators and the police. The benefits of at least two-year terms for the Commissioner General have yet to be realized.

*The negative relationship between citizens and the police*

Police-community relations that have been historically hostile (Hoffman, 1982; Pyo, 2001b) continue to be problematic in South Korea. Not only are there deeply rooted negative feelings that go back generations, but also rapid political democratization and individualism have led to challenges to police authority (Moon, 2004). Some citizens challenge the legitimacy and authority of the police, question police officers' fairness in handling both criminal and non-criminal cases, and openly reveal disrespect of the police. Police officers' orders and directions are frequently ignored, and officers have been often kicked and injured by drunken citizens.

Research on the relationship between the public and the police from both the public's and the officers' perspectives (Han and Bu, 2000; Lee, 1984; Lee, 2002; Moon and Zager, 2007; Park, 1999) shows a widespread distrust and mutual suspicion. For example, Park (1999) concluded from data from 134 citizens that 38 percent of respondents reported negative perception toward the police, and only 20 percent indicated that they saw the police as trustworthy. For an open-ended question regarding the image of the police, many respondents described the police as engaged in the suppression of demonstrations, authoritarian, repressive, and using their authority excessively. In a sample of around 250 citizens, Han and Bu (2000) examined citizens' trust toward government organizations (i.e. military, prosecutors, firefighters, and the police) and found that the police were ranked at the bottom among seven government organizations. While 67 percent of respondents reported that firefighters were the group that had the most positive image, less than 1 percent of respondents indicated that the police had the most positive image. In a cross-national comparative study of police in South Korea and the United States, Lee (2002) examined police officers' perceptions of citizens' trust. Ninety-one percent of Korean officers reported citizens' distrust of the police, and 71 percent of them report a negative relationship with the public. One study (Lee, 2003: 338) found that between 1982 and 1995, distrust of the police and a proclivity to protest against them grew from characterizing 27 percent of the population to characterizing 53 percent. In a recent study, Moon and Zager (2007) examined officers' attitudes toward citizen support for a sample of 434 Korean police officers. Consistent with previous findings (Lee, 1984; Lee, 2002), the study found that a majority of Korean police officers perceived that citizens do not support and trust the police. Overall, these findings suggest that distrust and antagonism between the police and citizens is deep-rooted in the minds of the public and police, despite recent reform efforts to improve the image of the police.

### Police brutality and corruption

Though there is no empirical research on the prevalence of police corruption and abuse of power in South Korea, there is knowledge of some recent cases of torture, and it is generally known that police corruption is widespread. Mentioned above are the deaths of two farmers during violent clashes between demonstrators and the military police units in 2005. The farmers died as a result of police officers' excessive force and brutality, and the Commissioner General was forced to resign.

Officers frequently take bribes, especially from entertainment-related business owners. Some officers receive or demand bribes from suspects in return for releasing them without further investigation or for manipulating the cases in favor of suspects (Chang, 2002).

In response to widespread police corruption, the Korean police have instituted a series of counteractions. Harsh penalties including dismissal and even criminal charges for officers and citizens involved in bribery have been used. A financial reward system for reporting police corruption was implemented in 2004. Citizens reporting police bribery could receive up to approximately $10,000, depending on the validity of the report, seriousness of the case, and its contribution to the bribery prevention effort. Though the level of officers' involvement in corruption, especially bribery during traffic violation stops, has been reduced by the reform and prevention efforts, police corruption and bribery scandals continue to be reported in news media. Moreover, few police officers have been harshly disciplined or criminally charged for their involvement in corruption and bribery cases (Moon, 2004).

### Recruitment of women police

A woman who had been a former U.S. police officer and lawyer in Detroit was included in the advisors initially sent to Korea at the end of the Second World War. Following the practice in the United States at that time, she developed a 500-woman female police division that worked primarily in prisons for women and providing crime-related social work services to women and juveniles who perpetrated or were victimized by crime. Despite the early involvement of women on the police force, their numbers remain very small.

Although contemporary South Korean women have begun to enter the workforce in increasing numbers, compared to other OECD (Organization for Economic Co-operation and Development) countries, which share a commitment to democracy and a market economy, South Korea is low in women in the workforce (60 percent) (Jaumotte, 2003), and very low in the proportion of police who are women. In 1995, the Korean police set a goal to increase the proportion of police women to 10 percent by 2014 (Kim *et al.*, 1995). By 2000, women comprised 2.4 percent of the Korean National Police (Natarajan, 2005), and by 2006 they were approximately 5 percent. Police women hold positions in specialized work, for example with juveniles, and are not fully integrated into the police force either by similar training or by common work experiences. A recent survey by Kim (2006) revealed that male officers were negative about increasing the number of policewomen and expanding their duties. However, female police officers did not agree that their access to different positions should be denied.

*Work related stress*

Work-related stress is of general concern because of negative effects on health, and for police, because it results in problems with job satisfaction and retention in the occupation (Jung, 1999; Kim *et al.*, 2002; Lee, 1995; Lee, 2002; Park, 2002). A 2004 survey of 686 South Korean police showed that three types of workplace problems—being ridiculed by coworkers when they asked questions or being allowed to make mistakes, harassment by other officers, and perceived public disrespect of police were predictive of stress (Morash *et al.*, 2007). Support from superiors was associated with a low level of stress. The importance of ridicule as a stressor is consistent with the seriousness of "loss of face," that is being seen as worthless and being disregarded (Kim and Nam, 1998), in a collectivist culture (Hwang *et al.*, 2003). Stress from perceived public disrespect is not unexpected, given the historically negative relations between police and the public. The importance of superior officers in preventing or alleviating stress is consistent with the East Asian emphasis on management in a paternalistic role (Aycan *et al.*, 2000; Tang *et al.*, 2000), including the managers' detecting and addressing their subordinates' hidden feelings of discontent (Song and Meek, 1998). Thus, relations among coworkers and with superiors and relations with the public would seem to be critical to reducing stress among South Korean police.

## The Korean national police reform efforts

In 1999–2000, the Korean national police implemented "Operation Grand Reform 100 Days" in response to the crisis of police legitimacy and negative relationship with the public. This reform was heavily influenced both by President Kim Dae Jung's massive national reform movement emphasizing the importance of democracy and human rights and by the popularity of community policing in the United States. The Korean police reform centered on transforming the existing police culture, creating partnerships between the public and the police, and improving the public image of and attitudes toward the police. Numerous efforts and programs were initiated. For example, the philosophy of citizen-oriented policing and the importance of pro-active crime prevention were emphasized. In order to prevent violent clashes with demonstrators, a policy of non-use of CS gas in response to peaceful demonstrations was introduced. The police have also implemented several programs such as a citizen police academy and a volunteer community patrol program to provide citizens with an opportunity to better understand police work. To learn about residents' concerns and suggestions about crime prevention, a crime prevention recall system was created, and crime prevention seminars were held locally. Furthermore, the police have established a separate unit at every police station to receive and investigate complaints of police malpractice and corruption. Efforts were also made to modernize police equipment and improve the police working environment (i.e., increasing police salaries and the introduction of a three-shift system). The massive reform that was initiated by top police administrators was intensive and widespread, and has been well received by rank-and-file officers and the general public. An initial police report showed that the number of police malpractices significantly decreased and citizens' attitudes toward the police had improved.

The intensity of the reform spirit and efforts slowly decreased, especially after the resignation of the reform-oriented Commissioner General Lee in 2002. Yet, police reform continues to be a top priority of the police, since it is consistent with a broader government effort to reform the political, economic, and cultural environments, to combat corruption, and to create a transparent society (Pyo, 2004). Each new Commissioner General has emphasized the importance of police reform and has implemented various new programs for the Korean police to be reborn as a democratic and respected police force (Pyo, 2004). In 2003, a police reform committee was established under the Korean National Police Agency to provide a blueprint for police reform. Consisting of 18 professional civilians in various fields, the committee advises on the overall direction of reform, especially focusing on police performance reform and the implementation of decentralized policing. The enhancement of police professionalism and the successful implementation of community policing continue to be emphasized as a means to improve the police image and regain police legitimacy.

## Conclusion

Policing in South Korea has changed markedly since the modern police force was instituted. Many of the changes were influenced by Japan, and then later the United States, but ultimately the contemporary police force was heavily affected by the rapid shift to a booming industrialized economy and democratization of the country. In recent decades, there have been continuous structural and functional changes, ensuring political neutrality, separating military operations from policing, improving job environments, handling public demonstrations properly, recruiting more female officers, and preventing police corruption and brutality.

Additionally, the police face the challenges of decentralizing the police force in the era of local autonomy in South Korea, resolving the problems associated with a difficult relationship with the public prosecutor's office, and addressing the internal conflict and tension between administrators and line officers caused by the current recruiting system. The decentralized police system—the creation of local police agencies, in addition to the current centralized police—has been exemplarily implemented in several cities to prevent the concentration of police power and to better serve the needs of local citizens. Uniquely, the prosecutor's office in South Korea has extensive power over the police; for example, a prosecutor has a legal right and responsibility for directly supervising every phase of a police officer's criminal investigation, including the initiation of the criminal investigation of a case (Lee, 2002). The poor relationship with the prosecutor's office has been known to be a significant source of stress among police officers. In recent decades, the police have made a great effort, but without much success, to normalize the relationship with the prosecutor's office, gaining the legal right to initiate criminal investigations independently and without the prosecutor's direct supervision. The South Korean police also faces the unique challenges of threats from North Korea, as they try to ensure a democratic and free society, in part through the structure and the functions of police officers.

The Korean National Police Agency (KNPA) is in transition to be reconstituted as a democratic and professional police force, overcoming a traditionally-held oppressive and corrupted image among the general public. Long-term effects of contemporary reform movements need to be examined; however, several recent studies continue to show deep-rooted distrust and antagonism toward the police in the minds of citizens, indicating the necessity of continued and intensive reforms for the Korean police to improve their relationship with citizens and to achieve the status of a fully democratic force.

## References

Aycan, Z., Kanungo, R., Mendonca, M., Yu, K., Deller, J., Stahl, G. and Kurshid, A. (2000). 'Impact of culture on human resource management practices: a ten-country comparison,' *Applied Psychology: An International Review*, 49: 192–221.

Chang, D. (2002). 'A study on corruption of the public officials,' unpublished master thesis, Chosun University.

Cohen, J. and Baker, E. (1991). 'U.S. foreign policy and human rights in South Korea', in W. Shaw (ed.) *Human Rights in Korea: Historical and Policy Perspective*, Harvard, MA: Harvard University Press.

Collins, M.S. (1990). 'Lessons from Korean economic growth,' *The American Economic Review*, 80: 104–7.

Freedom House (2006). Freedom in the world. http://www.freedomhouse.org/template.cfm?page=15. Accessed March 23, 2007.

Han, J. and Bu, K. (2000). 'A study on the improvement of police image,' *Police Science Collection of Treatise*, 16: 3–113 (in Korean).

Hoffman, V. (1982). 'The development of modern police agencies in the Republic of Korea and Japan: A paradox,' *Police Studies*, 5: 3–16.

Hoffman, V. (2005). 'Development of the Korean Police after World War II: Information from Korean and American Scholars,' paper presented at the Korean National Police Conference. Seoul, Korea, November 23, 2005.

Heo, N. (1998). *History of Korean Police Administration*. Seoul: Dongdowon (in Korean).

Hwang, A., Francesco, A.M. and Kessler, E. (2003). 'The relationship between individual-collectivism, face, and feedback and learning processes in Hong Kong, Singapore, and the United States,' *Journal of Cross-Cultural Psychology*, 34: 72–91.

Jaumotte, F. (2003). 'Labour force participation of women: Empirical evidence on the role of policy and other determinants in OECD countries,' *OECD Economic Studies*, 37: 51–108.

Jung, H.W. (1999). 'Coping strategies on police stress: A micro approach,' paper presented at the Annual Conference of Korean Sociological Association. Seoul, Korea.

Kim, J. (2000). 'Analysis of change of Korean police organization,' *Korea Police Journal*, 2: 45–66 (in Korean).

Kim, J.Y. and Nam, S.H. (1998). 'The concept and dynamics of face: Implications for organizational behavior in Asia,' *Organizational Science*, 9: 522–34.

Kim, S. (2006). 'Police activities and gender differences: Empirical research on police sub-culture and female officers' role stress,' *Criminal Justice Research*, 17 (in Korean).

Kim, S., Yoon, D., Kim, M. and Im, B. (1995). 'The task of personnel administration for equal employment of women civil servants,' *Women's Studies Forum*, 12. http://www2.kwdi.re.kr/. Accessed December 15, 2006 (in Korean).

Kim, S.Y., Ku, J.T. and Yoon, K.C. (2002). 'Street-level police officer's job stress: the degree and determinants of job stress,' *Korean Journal of Public Administration*, 40: 123–47.

Korean National Police Agency (2002). *Korean Police Annual Report 2002*. Seoul: Korean National Police Agency.

Korean Overseas Information Service (2007). 'Geographic location.' http://korea.net/korea/kor_loca.asp?code=A0101. Accessed March 10, 2007.

Lee, A. (2003). 'Down and down we go: Trust and compliance in South Korea,' *Social Science Quarterly*, 84: 329–43.

Lee, S. (1990). 'Morning calm, rising sun: National character and policing in South Korea and in Japan,' *Police Studies*, 13: 91–110.

Lee, S. (2002). 'A study of Korean police sergeants' stress,' *International Journal of Comparative and Applied Criminal Justice*, 26: 85–99.

Lee, W. (1984). 'Police and community relations in the Republic of Korea,' unpublished policy paper for masters degree, E. Lansing, MI: Michigan State University.

Lee, W.G. (1995). 'Problems caused by police job stress and its countermeasures,' *Korean Association of Public Safety and Criminal Justice*, 4: 193–223 (in Korean).

Lee, Y. (2002). 'A cross-national comparative study of police: Criminal Investigative policies and practices in the U.S. and South Korea,' unpublished doctoral dissertation, E. Lansing, MI: Michigan State University.

Macdonald, D.S. (1988). *The Koreans: Contemporary Politics and Society*, San Francisco: Westview Press.

Meade, E. (1951). *American Military Government in Korea*. New York: King's Crown Press.

Moon, B. (2004). 'The politicization of police in South Korea: A critical review,' *Policing: An International Journal of Police Strategies & Management*, 27: 128–36.

Moon, B. and Zager, L. (2007). 'Police officers' attitudes toward citizen support: focus on individual, organizational and neighborhood characteristic factors,' *Policing: An International Journal of Police Strategies & Management*, 30: 484–97.

Moon, B., McCluskey, J. and Lee, S. (2005). 'The patrol officers' perception toward efficacy of mini-police stations in South Korea,' *Journal of Criminal Justice*, 33: 441–49.

Morash, M., Kwak, D. H., Hoffman, V., Lee, C.H., Cho, S.H., and Moon, B. (2007). *Stressors, Coping Resources and Strategies, and Police Stress in South Korea*. E. Lansing, MI: Michigan State University.

Myong, C. (1959). 'The police system of the Republic of Korea,' unpublished master thesis, E. Lansing, MI: Michigan State University.

Nahm, A. (1988). *Korea: Tradition and transformation—A history of the Korean people.* Elizabeth, NJ: Hollym International Corporation.

Natarajan, M. (2005). 'Status of women police in Asia: An agenda for future research,' Fourth Australasian women and policing conference : Improving policing for women in the Asia Pacific region. Darwin, August 21–24, 2005. http://www.aic.gov.au/conferences/2005-policewomen/natarajan.html.

Park, G. (1999). 'A study on the police image marketing,' unpublished masters thesis, Yonsei University (in Korean).

Park, S.S. (2002). 'A study on the effect of stress on the turnover of police,' *Korean Association of Public Safety and Criminal Justice*, 13: 99–135 (in Korean).

Pyo, C. (2001a). 'Policing: the past,' *Crime & Justice International*, 17: 5–6.

Pyo, C. (2001b). 'Policing: the present and future,' *Crime & Justice International*, 17: 7–8.

Pyo, C. (2004). 'Korean policing and reforms' http://www.cwpyo.com/bbs/data/Police4/KoreanPolice(DrPyo).hwp. Accessed March 20, 2007.

Rho, H. (2000). 'Efficient management of a mini-police station,' *Journal of Korean Association of Public Safety and Criminal Justice*, 10: 37–74 (in Korean).

Song, K. (2006). 'Abolishment of a combat police system,' *Democracy Law*, 30: 131–60 (in Korean).

Song, Y.H. and Meek, C.B. (1998). 'The impact of culture on the management values and beliefs of Korean,' *Journal of Comparative International Management*, 1. http://www.lib.unb.ca/Texts/JCIM/bin/get.cgi?directory=vol1_1/&filename=Song.html. Accessed December 15, 2006.

Tang, T.L.P., Kim, J.K. and O'Donald, D.A. (2000). 'Perceptions of Japanese organizational culture—employees in non-unionized Japanese-owned and unionized US-owned automobile plants,' *Journal of Managerial Psychology*, 15: 535–59.

Vreeland, N., Just, P., Martindale, K., Moeller, P. and Shinn, R. (1975). *Area Handbook for South Korea*, Washington, DC: Foreign Area Studies.

West, J.M. and Baker, E.J. (1991). 'The 1987 constitutional reforms in South Korea: Electoral process and judicial independence,' in W. Shaw (ed.) *Human Rights in Korea: Historical and Policy Perspectives*, Harvard, MA: Harvard University Press.

# 6   Democratic policing in India

## Issues and concerns

*Arvind Verma*

## Introduction and country profile

India symbolizes unity in diversity despite considerable geographic, cultural, linguistic, religious and ethnic divisions. Even though Hinduism is the religion of 80 percent of the people, Islam, Christianity, Sikhism, Jainism, Buddhism, Zoroastrianism and even Judaism all have significant followings. Apart from 23 officially recognized major languages, English being one of them, Indians speak in more than 1,600 dialects. India is a liberal, parliamentary form of democracy with more than 600 million registered voters. Moreover, despite a history of colonial rule and exploitation India at present has an economy which is growing at an enviable annual rate of 9 percent. India's business and especially the information technology sectors are recognized around the world. Yet, despite such positive developments India remains ranked fifty-fifth amongst 102 developing countries on the Human Poverty Index mark, and has an adult literacy rate of 39 percent (UNDP 2006). The democratic polity and regular elections have failed to involve people being marginalized by new economic policies, a situation that is causing serious challenges of order maintenance to the police. The crime situation, particularly violent incidents, also remains alarming in some parts of the country, particularly in India's mega-cities such as Mumbai, Calcutta, and Delhi. While the National Crime Records Bureau does not publish disaggregated statistics for these cities, making public only provincial (state) and national-level statistics, the following table provides some indication of the scale of violent crime. It is important, however, to read these figures with caution. Crime minimization by authorities, technical recording problems, and under-reporting of crimes (particularly those which carry a social stigma) due to the bureaucratic delays that can be involved, lack of confidence in authorities, and fear of reprisals all contribute to under-representation of the extent of the problem.

India attracted traders, adventurers and conquerors from its earliest history. However, most of the invaders like the Greeks, Persians, Mongols, Kushans, Afghans and the Arabs settled down, intermingling with the local population, thereby enriching the culture, language and art of the country.

*Table 6.1* Levels and rates of selected violent crimes in India, 2006

| Type of crime | Cases reported | Rate per 100,000 inhabitants |
| --- | --- | --- |
| Murder | 32,481 | 2.9 |
| Attempted Murder | 27,230 | 2.4 |
| Dowry Deaths | 7,618 | 0.7 |
| Kidnapping and Abductions | 23,991 | 2.1 |
| Rape | 19,348 | 1.7 |

*Source:* National Crime Records Bureau (2007)

Over the years this helped develop a composite culture symbolized by the Taj Mahal, an Indo-Persian architectural marvel. Despite the rise and fall of kingdoms most of the country retained its local practices and absorbed the characteristics of the ruling classes. Trade and movement of people remained unrestricted over the vast geographical land and this helped to create a diverse society that would emerge as a salad bowl, each constituent retaining its flavor and yet be an essential part of the whole. This heterogeneity helped strengthen democratic traditions teaching different groups to come together for the common good.

The British arrived late but by the beginning of nineteenth century they controlled major parts of the country. They assumed formal power in 1857 throwing off the last Mughal Emperor Bahadur Shah Zafar and the cloak of the East India Trading Company. The British introduced the system of modern administration in India creating districts, courts, bureaucracy and a formal police organization. Most of these administrative structures have continued largely unchanged even after independence and many of the present day problems of corruption, misuse of force and unaccountability appear to be related to their basic design. Hence it is useful to describe them in some detail here.

## The colonial model

The British created a system of bureaucracy after their victory at Plassey in 1757 when they won administrative control over Bengal. Even after emerging as the de facto dominant political power in the country the British kept their interests limited primarily to trade and commerce. The biggest challenge was the general disorder where weak and indolent rulers did little to provide safety and security to the people. Besides the general lawlessness, a quasi-religious cult called "Thugs" (literally, swindlers) had spread terror across the country. The thugs would befriend travelers on the road and gain their confidence. Once their guards were lowered they would strangle and loot their goods. The thugs formed a secret society and operated over long distances across the heartland. Colonel Sleeman, a senior police official is credited with dealing with this group effectively. His tracking of the members of this group and ending of the thuggery is part of the lore of Indian policing (Giriraj Shah 2002).

In the main, the British focused on commercial activities that supported an expanding capitalism in search of new markets and resources. Despite the success of Robert Peel's reforms introduced for the London Metropolitan Police, the system in India remained primitive and had the limited objective of controlling the subjects. Sir Charles Napier is credited for designing the colonial police model around 1845 which was based upon the Royal Irish Constabulary. The main objectives were to deal effectively with order maintenance problems and establish the writ of the East India Company in the region. Furthermore, the Mughal system of police stations administered by officials called Kotwals, Thanedar and Darogas developed in the seventeenth century was also retained. "The British not only borrowed this structure but also took over the feeling and tone of the Mughal administration—a mixture of great pomp and show combined with benevolent and despotic intervention" (Cohn 1961: 8). The police were to be the bulwark of the Raj in India.

Such a police system was clearly an embarrassment to the imperial power for it was an organization that was ineffective in relation to both order maintenance and crime control. It also reflected a corrupt, brutal and inefficient picture of the ruling power since it reflected poorly upon the legitimacy of British administration that was touted as one based on law and fair dealing. The need to remold and strengthen the administrative and legal systems developed by the East India Company had become imperative by the middle of the nineteenth century. Nevertheless, after a real threat of losing power from the first war of independence in 1857, the outlook of British officials changed completely. The Police Commission set up to recommend reforms was clearly told that "functions of a police are either protective and repressive or detective" and that "the line which separates the protective and repressive functions of a civil force from functions purely military, may not always, in India be very clear" (Imperial Gazetteer of India, Part IV, reprint 1909: 380). Accordingly, a police force was designed that could "develop a sense of fear of authority in the entire population" and "could serve as the first line of defense" (Gupta 1979: 7).

The British efforts to streamline the administration finally led to the Police Act V of 1861 that still governs the Indian police of the twenty-first century. The Act created a new leadership cadre (the Indian Police Service) designed to supervise and check the subordinate police formations and make it more professional. The police departments were organized provincially and placed under the chief of police called the Inspector General (IG), assisted by Deputy Inspector General (DIG) in charge of ranges comprising three to four districts. A Superintendent of Police (SP) was in charge of the police department at the district level and was entrusted to supervise the functioning of police stations. The SP exercised complete control over the lower-ranking native officers serving in the police stations and was responsible for all the police functions including the discipline and internal management of the force under his control. In this scheme, the senior police officers, though playing only a supervisory role exercised extraordinary powers and developed elaborate procedures to keep control over the subordinate officers. Up until 1921 no Indian was admitted to this elite service and even by 1947, the number of Indian officers in the service was proportionately small.

Under the new system, the police station was run by a sub-inspector who would have one to three junior sub-inspectors or assistant sub-inspectors and eight to ten constables to assist him in his various duties. The police station remained the established symbol of the police department and the place for citizens to go for any police services. Over a fixed jurisdiction it was responsible for all police duties, like patrolling, crime control, information gathering and assisting local authorities during periods of calamities. The police station was inspected frequently by the senior officers and was, in theory, under constant supervision. This mode of control was taken to be the best way to ensure that the police department was functioning properly and efficiently.

Many British officials thought themselves to be "guardians" (Woodruff 1954) and argued that the colonial administration made life "secure for ordinary citizens" and that the police system was a "reliable instrument for the maintenance of law and order" (Griffiths 1971). However, for the Indian people the experience was often quite different from this picture. The organizational culture of the Indian police was assiduously built to convey an impression of subjugation and to ensure that the subjects never dared look into the eyes of their rulers. Accordingly, the organizational ethos, the style of administration and its purposeful separation from communities were deliberate practices within the police department, designed to maintain their lofty position. The system perpetuated the façade of guardianship, although the British senior officers rarely disciplined and controlled the more extreme behavior of native subordinate personnel. The organizational culture further enabled a small number of senior officials to wield complete control over the organization and their grandeur was deliberately built to create an obvious form of authority. "The morning parade and salute to the commanding officer, the armed sentry at the Superintendent's gate and armed escort on their tours were symbols that placed the officers on a high pedestal" (Verma 1999: 272). This paternalistic style of governance provided limited avenues for the citizens to seek redress for their grievances and the archaic departmental rules further prevented efforts to discipline the corrupt and abusive subordinates. Furthermore, British officers on official tours utilized the local personnel to take care of personal needs, food and entertainment. The legend of tiger hunts and lavish parties was largely built upon the shoulders of native police station officers who had to make these arrangements for their superiors (Verma 1999). The local feudal lords also vied with one another to show their subservience to touring officials especially in rural areas. This was encouraged by the colonial power as the British Raj was largely symbolic and had to co-opt native landlords and rulers to support the system of governance (Yang 1989).

Such practices aligned the police with the ruling elite and the department appeared to function at their behest to suppress discontent. No wonder the venality, corruption, brutality and indifference made Indian police personnel the hated symbols of British imperialism (Verma 2002).

Unfortunately, the Police Act V of 1861 is still applicable[1] and the organizational structure, culture, ethos and even most of the rules and regulations continue unchanged (Arnold 1992). Despite independence and the establishment of a democratic government and considering the bitter and protracted struggle against the British rule in which the police were used ruthlessly to deal with freedom fighters, Indian leaders still choose to continue this British-made machinery without fundamental changes. Bayley (1969: 45) comments that no further structural reforms in police administration in India have been made except for some "tidying up, tinkering with and elaborating upon the existing arrangements," a remark true even today. The police and the justice system remains fundamentally the same as designed in 1861.

## Police and the military

The need for armed force has been a constant feature of India since the task of order maintenance is considerable (Seminar 1999). The skewed economic development generates feelings of neglect, exclusion and injustice which frequently bring the population onto the streets to protest against the government. The democratic system still "does not necessarily bring significant changes in the nature of politics, relationship between the ruling class and the ruled, power relationship amongst the various segments of society, the institutional mechanism for resolving conflict" (Ghanshyam Shah 2002: 18). The daily street protests, demonstrations against government policies, rallies and violent opposition against development projects and the frequent intragroup, inter-caste and communal riots create frequent situations leading to confrontation with the police (Verma 2007). Kohli (1990) has categorized this as a crisis of "governability" of the Indian state where the reliance and emphasis on the armed wing of the police continues to grow. For example, in 2005, there were 56,235 riots reported to the police and riotous mobs were responsible for killing 15 and injuring 1,415 police officers in the country (National Crime Record Bureau (NCRB) 2006: 471). The seriousness of law and order problems may be understood from the use of deadly force against the citizens. In 2005, there were 92 incidents of police firing to control riotous mobs in which 44 civilians were killed and 198 persons sustained injuries (ibid. 2006: 463).

The Indian police were structured as a paramilitary force for the exercise of coercive powers. However, there are clear guidelines and legal requirements that separate the military from the police forces in the country. The army cannot be deployed without the express order of the District Magistrate who is a civilian authority. The deployment of the army is usually to assist in emergencies such as floods, earthquakes and other natural disasters. Nevertheless, the army has been engaged to operate against militant groups in Jammu-Kashmir (J&K) and the North Eastern States.

In India, a large number of armed units have also been created that are police forces but limited in their roles for order maintenance and security duties. Both the central and state governments have funded a large number of these battalions for specialized problems confronting the country. Moreover, every state also maintains its separate armed units that are also exclusively meant for order maintenance and security purposes and cannot be used for normal investigation and policing work. These armed battalions are drilled and trained almost like military regiments. They do not carry heavy weapons but are equipped with automatic rifles and have better arms than the local police forces. They live in barracks, and have no direct contact with the citizens.

Nevertheless, there are several concerns about this emphasis on armed policing at the expense of civil policing in the country. Indian police have become notorious for "false encounters and extra judicial killings" (Ahmed 2004; Amnesty International 2007). The National Human Rights Commission has started following these complaints seriously and 122 intimations were received from the various state governments about killings in encounters during the year 2004–2005. Separately, the Commission also received complaints in another 84 cases (NHRC 2006). No information is available about the final outcome of these inquiries. Over the years the numbers of armed police personnel have grown considerably while the proportion of crime investigators and those working in the local police departments has been decreasing. Moreover, there is considerable evidence to show that armed police exercise considerable discretion and their deployment leads to serious political and social repercussions (Verma 1997). In particular, elections, communal harmony and political conflicts are all affected by resort to armed policing methods. Furthermore, in the Indian Constitution, the central government has been given major administrative and economic powers and slowly, the center has also encroached upon the additional areas of local authority. For example, the central government has taken powers to deploy central forces anywhere in the country without the consent of the state governments and to declare some areas as 'disturbed'. The deployment of central forces in the North Eastern States and the application of the 'Disturbed Area Act' have led to bitter opposition and conflict in these regions. On a number of occasions the central government has dismissed elected state governments on charges of failing to maintain order. The unfortunate result of these political decisions has been the dominance of order maintenance considerations over crime control and service functions of the police. "The ideal of a civilian police force has not materialized in practice" in the country (Das and Verma 1998: 365).

# The criminal justice system

## *The courts*

The judicial system in India is established as a unitary body with the Supreme Court at the apex, High Courts at the state level and Lower Courts at the district level. Articles 124–151 of the constitution define the status of the judiciary in the country in which the Supreme Court with 25 judges and one chief justice has been established as the highest court under Article 124(1). The president appoints the justices after consultation with the chief justice of the Supreme Court and High Courts. The judges hold office until they are 65 years of age and a judge of the Supreme Court can only be removed after an extraordinary session of the parliament in which two thirds of the majority of the house have to vote in an impeachment proceeding (Sharma 1966). The Supreme Court has been invested with three kinds of powers: original, appellate and consultative or advisory jurisdiction. The Supreme Court is the final court of appeal and Article 134 of the constitution specify the provisions under which an appeal can be made about a judgment of any subordinate court of India. The courts have the power of judicial review and "there is no question that the Supreme Court has immense power, and exercises it often" (Gadbois 1987: 127).

However, the colonial model has continued in the administration of courts and prisons too. Most of the legal statutes and regulations enacted during the British rule remain on the book. Although the judiciary has been given an independent status and has become an extremely powerful institution, its internal administration is of poor quality. Trials take an abominably long period to complete and even important criminal cases continue for more than a decade. At the end of 2005, there were 105,11,497 criminal cases pending at the trial stage (NCRB 2006: Tables 4.9 and 4.13) and every year the pendency is growing. Consequently, getting justice from this system is an uphill challenge that deters most citizens from approaching the courts.

Nevertheless, the Indian Supreme Court has redeemed itself by adopting an extremely innovative and forceful process of judicial activism. Beginning in the 1970s some judges began the process of admitting Public Interest Litigation (PIL) brought by concerned citizens. An important and unique provision is spelled out by Article 32 (1) of the Indian constitution. This section empowers a citizen directly to approach the Supreme Court for enforcement of the fundamental rights guaranteed under Part III, Article 14–32 of the document. The Supreme Court and the High Courts are authorized to take cognizance of any such complaint and issue orders as a writ. It is this provision that has provided the means for extended judicial action.

Justice Bhagwati and Krishna Iyer, who are credited with this innovation, argued that it is virtually impossible for a poor person to seek judicial relief due to procedural and financial problems. The poor cannot afford a lawyer and generally, being illiterate, they do not understand the legal procedures. They stipulated that if a person's fundamental rights are violated then *any* concerned citizen can bring this to the attention of courts for speedy redressal. Justice Bhagwati asserted, "in a country like India where issues of poverty, exploitation and differentialism are regularly coming before the courts, the judges cannot turn away pleading legal formalism or lack of capacity from deciding such issues and still claim that courts stand for all the citizens" (cited in Sharma 1994, pp. 55–56).

In the case of SP Gupta vs. Union of India (AIR 1982 SC 149) a seven-judge constitution bench further clarified that any member of the public, acting in a bona fide manner and having sufficient interest in redressing a public wrong, can bring the matter to the attention of the court. This form of judicial activism not only empowered the human rights activists working amongst the people but also put considerable pressure upon the government agencies to pay attention to due process and rights of the population. The courts intervened in a wide variety of matters brought to their attention by special interest groups, public-spirited lawyers and social activists. Police and prison officials, civilian bureaucrats and government employees, were all taken to task for their callousness and inefficiency through simple letters addressed to the courts. PIL has continued with vigor and has been used to address issues ranging from the liberation of bonded laborers, emancipation of women and children from their exploiters, custodial deaths, torture of suspects, environmental degradation, political corruption, accountability in governance even to the deterioration of the Taj Mahal. The recent enactment of the Right to Information Act, again coming at the behest of the courts, has further strengthened the citizens. PIL has touched every field of social, economic, political and sectarian concern and has emerged "as the most powerful mechanism for ordinary citizens to correct a wrong and force the callous officials to honor their fundamental rights" (Verma 2001a: 153–154).

*The prison system*

The Indian Prisons Act, 1894 and the Indian Prisoners Act, 1905 still form the basis of archaic prison administration in India (Biswas 2007). The duties, responsibilities and functions of the prison staff continue to be guided by the colonial ethos developed during the British period. Not surprisingly, the prison system is characterized by sub-human conditions, over-crowding, lack of sensitivity, poor training and rampant corruption of the personnel (Biswas 2007). An all-India Committee on Jail Reforms (1980–1983), known as the Mulla Committee, drew attention to the horrible conditions of the jails and made many recommendations regarding reclassification of prisoners, vocational training and problems of under-trial prisoners. Unfortunately, recommendations of this committee, National Human Rights Commission, National Police Commission and even one from a National Commission for Women have been ignored. Prison administration continues unchanged and over-crowding makes any reform efforts difficult to achieve. In Tihar prison, the largest in the country and situated in the capital, Delhi, at present [May 2008] there are 11,174 prisoners currently held in accommodation designed to house a maximum of 6,250. The problem arises from the large number of remand prisoners who are incarcerated awaiting trial. In Tihar at present there are 8,913 prisoners waiting trial that sometimes take as much as 1–5 years to complete (Tihar Prisons 2008). The vast majority are poor and, unable to hire competent lawyers, have found themselves languishing in prisons for years (Dhagambar 1992).

The Indian judiciary, scathing in their criticism of the government have time and again drawn attention towards the plight of prisoners. The courts have attempted to improve the situation through a number of judgments. *Hussainara Khatoon* created the rights to a speedy trial. In the *Sunil Batra* case the Supreme Court asserted that a prisoner does not lose all the rights when in custody and cannot be deprived of rights beyond those stipulated by the courts. The justices laid down that the court has a continuing responsibility to ensure that jail administrators do not exceed the sentence passed in the case. The judgment listed excesses such as solitary confinement, degrading or forced labor, denial of essential amenities or meetings with relatives and friends as clear violations of prisoners' rights (Verma 2001a). The judgment in *Sanjay Suri vs. Delhi Administration* led to the creation of a separate facility for the children housed in jails. These and other actions by the courts subsequently led to a reformed Juvenile Justice Act passed in 1988 which has banned the practice of incarcerating children with adult offenders and ensuring other forms of humane treatment of young offenders. In *Rudal Sah vs. State of Bihar* the court laid down the principle of state liability for the action of its officials and directed that this money be paid immediately to the victim, a practice that has compensated a large number of victims of state indifference. In another remarkable case of *Shiela Barse vs. State of Maharastra* the courts inquired into the ill-treatment and torture of female prisoners and using this case as a basis, laid down several procedures for the safety of women when taken into police custody. What is interesting is the assertion by the Supreme Court that convicted persons go to prison *as* punishment and not *for* punishment (Charles Shobraj vs. Superintendent, Tihar jail, AIR 1978, SC 1514).

Constant criticism and media publicity has prompted the government to address some of the glaring problems of prison facilities that comes from improper sanitation, untidy lockups, and inadequate number of cells. The government has embarked upon a "Modernization of Prisons" scheme which is being implemented over a period of five years (2002–07) in 27 states with an outlay of Rs.1800 crores or 450 million US dollars (Biswas 2007). There is greater emphasis upon training of prison personnel and the Regional Institute of Correctional Administration established at Vellore seeks to cooperate with other approved bodies to facilitate training of prison officials. The National Human Rights Commission not only monitors prison statistics but investigates complaints against prison conditions. The Commission has proposed two model prison bills for consideration by state governments: the Indian Prison Bill of 1996 and The Prisons (Administration and Treatment of Prisoners) Bill of 1998 respectively. The Ministry of Home Affairs which is responsible for administration of prisons in India has, however, yet to act.

There have been many interesting in-house reforms that have been initiated by determined administrators. Perhaps the biggest name here is that of Kiran Bedi who in her capacity as Inspector General of Prisons, Tihar Jail brought remarkable changes in the administration and introduced several innovative practices. Her advocacy of Vipassana, a meditation practice, received wide appreciation and also won for her the prestigious Magsaysay award from the Philippines government. She also mobilized citizen support who came out in large numbers to run special programs for rehabilitation and re-integration of prisoners back into society. Further, many states have established "open prisons" where inmates live with their family in especially ear-marked villages. They are allowed to seek employment in nearby areas but have to be back home by evening. Almost no prisoner has ever gone missing.

## Police accountability and community relations

### Politicization of the police

The Indian police were designed as the ruler's police and have no provision for local accountability. The 1861 Act created a centralized police organization with command, control and decision making concentrated at the top. Furthermore, the colonial government, unsure about the loyalty of native subordinates, also developed a policy wherein no government functionary could be posted in his or her "home district" and every three years must be transferred to another post. This system continues unchanged today. Such a provision prevents the police officers from developing local links and effectively creates a situation where an officer has no stake in the local community. It also prevents any form of local accountability to the people. The only option for an aggrieved citizen who has a complaint against an officer is to go for an internal inquiry to the police headquarters or to approach the courts for civil damages. There is no system of local monitoring by some kind of citizen body and no input from the citizens to determine the nature of policing for their area.

This three-year tenure policy has played havoc with the organization. First, it has provided the politicians with a powerful mechanism to interfere in organizational matters. The transfer-postings are controlled by the politicians who do not follow any administrative guidelines. They use these powers to place "their" officers in crucial positions. "The police are unable to discharge their duties properly because politicians impede their functioning" (Verma 2000: 19). The police leadership has lost much control over their subordinates and police chiefs are facing enormous difficulties in operating their department being generally unable to discipline officers who are politically connected

(Raj Kumar 2000). Since police are organized at the state level all organizations are large units with thousands of personnel. Thus, almost at any given time several hundred personnel are being transferred from one unit to another. Politicians can exercise considerable power through threats of transfer or to make attractive offers of alternative postings. The politicization of the Indian police has therefore become a serious problem.

Incidentally, this problem was vividly highlighted by the Shah Commission appointed to look into the atrocities committed during the "emergency" period of 1975–77, when Indira Gandhi suspended the Parliament and assumed dictatorial powers. The entire police force became captive to the small coterie wielding power within the Gandhi household. Despite strong recommendations of the National Police Commission, appointed in 1978, political control over the police has not been reduced but in fact has increased substantially. The police have become a useful instrument in political battles too. Thus, the destruction of the mosque by Hindu zealots at Ayodhya (1992) and the killing of Sikhs in Delhi (1984) or Muslims in Gujarat (2002) was enabled by shackling and preventing timely police action. The nature of political order in the country affects policing (Reiner 1992) and in India, police action is invariably guided by the politics of the country.

Control over the police department provides a means for harassing political opponents through intimidation, arrests and even threats to their supporters (Verma 2000). Furthermore, this control also enables the anti-social elements aligned to the ruling party who are useful in "capturing" the election booths and in serving as demonstrators and frenzied supporters during political rallies (Verma 2005). The police are also used for gathering political intelligence used in countering the strategies of the opposition parties (Seminar 1977; Raman 2002). A separate "special branch" has been created within the organization ostensibly to collect political intelligence that has security implications. However, the unit is now directly controlled by the Chief Minister for seeking intelligence on the opponents both inside and outside the party establishments. In many states the special branch is even utilized to shortlist candidates from the ruling party for the Assembly elections.

The Indian system does not prohibit a criminal from contesting elections unless he or she has been convicted by a judicial court. Since criminal trials linger for a considerable period of time many criminals have taken advantage of this to make a transition from the underworld to the political arena. The politicians approach them for muscle power to intimidate opponents and to fight election battles. The criminals in return seek protection from law enforcement agencies by the intervention of politicians. The two have formed an unholy alliance and a politician, Kapil Deo Singh, even confessed on the floor of Bihar Assembly that he patronized and would continue to patronize gangsters and criminals to fight and win elections as long as the existing system of electoral competition is not changed (GOI 1980). It did not take long for the criminals to realize that instead of relying upon politicians they could become one by "booth capturing" and aligning directly with political bosses. Many criminals have won and even become ministers wielding power over the officers investigating and prosecuting their cases. At present there are reportedly 125 elected members in the parliament who have a criminal background (Kashyap 2007). The Vohra committee, appointed to look into this phenomenon, reported a strong nexus between the politicians and criminals and that "all over India, crime syndicates have become a law unto themselves" (cited in Kashyap 2007). This "criminalization of politics" is perhaps the most dangerous trend seen in India in the past three decades (Tharoor 1997).

### Resource constraints

The salary and perks for public servants are largely inadequate. Historically, the Indian police personnel have been paid low wages and have traditionally "lived off the office". Free meals, drinks, supplies, entertainment, free transport and special treatment, are brazenly extorted from the people without fear of disciplinary action. Despite frequent and widespread charges of corruption against the Station house officer (Arnold 1986), the British, and now the Indian leadership, have not made any serious attempt to reform the system (Gupta 1979; Verma 2005).

Further, the economically strapped governments have failed to provide adequate resources to the police department. Police lack buildings, vehicles, communication equipment and even basic protective gear. Rural areas in particular lack the basic infrastructure of roads and communications and consequently are thinly policed. Inaccessible areas have therefore been affected by extremism where militants operate largely free from police surveillance (Mitra 2007). The police–citizen ratio in most parts of the country also remains low (122 per hundred thousand) (NCRB 2006) and is a major concern. Moreover, constables constituting almost 80 percent of the force cannot take up investigative responsibilities and can only be engaged in guard duties, for serving summons and as helping hands. Consequently, the workload on investigating officers and supervisors is considerable. This is further aggravated by the lack of modern communication technology, data storage and processing systems which impacts adversely upon police performance.

### Generalized weakness in the rule of law and police discretion

The ancient civilization of India had developed a variety of institutional mechanisms to handle social conflict and deviance. The most important of these was the Panchayat system, a council of local village elders that resolved problems on a mutual basis of understanding and accommodation. It was cost effective, swift and generally worked to bring victim and offender together. Such a peacemaking, restorative justice format (Sullivan and Tifft 2006) had worked for hundreds of years and was acceptable to the majority of the people.

However, the British could not leave such powers to the local people and transplanted their own system of judicial processes, rules of evidence and prosecution by the state. The decisions of Panchayat were not accepted by British authorities and the people were forced to take their complaints to the courts for resolution. Unfortunately, poor communications, alien rules of engagement and emphasis upon written words and use of English as the medium of judicial transactions meant that a new body of intermediaries, lawyers and translators had to be created that functioned from the premises of courts rather than from the village itself. For the illiterate masses this was a nightmare: the costs were unbearable, the proceedings were incomprehensible and time consuming, and, further, they were forced to operate through lawyers who were exploitative.

Additionally, laws invariably provide considerable discretion to police officers. The power to register crimes, for example, enables the police to act as gatekeepers to the criminal justice system. The Indian police are known not to record thousands of such complaints made by citizens and artificially keep the crime statistics down. This so-called minimization of crime is a serious and widespread problem across the country. Indian lawmakers have also have enacted several new offences to deal with social problems peculiar to Indian society. For example, the Untouchability Abolition Act of 1956, the Bonded Labor Abolition Act of 1976 and the Dowry Prohibition Act 1961 have criminalized a number of social practices that were inconsistent with a modern state where everyone has equal rights. Nevertheless, the caste system, the labor practices and the system of dowry for marriage of daughters are norms that have evolved over hundreds of years. Despite criminalizing such practices these continue unabated throughout the country and the police do not commonly enforce such laws. This further reinforces the image of the police as exercising extraordinary discretion and being unaccountable for its actions. Unfettered discretion and corruption reinforce the image that the police are there to serve only the rich and the powerful segments of society, thus alienating a majority of the citizenry.

## External impact on policing issues

The terrorist attacks in India, especially in Jammu and Kashmir, waged by Islamist extremist groups based in and supported by Pakistan and the growing and disruptive influence of pan-Islamist extremist and terrorist outfits, is one of the biggest threats to the security of this country (Sahni 2007). There is considerable evidence to suggest the involvement and manipulation of Islamist groups operating in and out of India by Pakistan's Inter Services Intelligence (ISI) agency (South Asia Terrorism Portal 2007). More than 35,000 people have lost their lives in the conflict since 1989 and, even at present, an average of over 200 lives are lost each month in Jammu and Kashmir (Sahni 2007). A recent report suggests that outside Iraq India records the highest number of terrorist attacks and killings (Raghuraman 2007).

On the eastern front, Bangladesh too has been slipping into chaos, and the rise of militant Islamic fundamentalists is becoming a growing concern. Various extremist groups operating in India's Northeast States of Assam, Mizoram, Tripura, Nagaland and Manipur find shelter and support from Bangladesh. Groups like the United Liberation Front of Asom, one of the most active terrorist groups, was courted by the Government of Begum Khalida Zia whose Bangladesh National Party is backed by the fundamentalist Jamaat-e-Islami party. Begum Zia's rule was synonymous with rising communal tension and Islamist extremist mobilization in Bangladesh. Her regime provided many of these groups operating in India with training camps, bank accounts, arms purchases, and so on.

Another neighbor, Nepal, has witnessed a major upheaval with the overthrow of the King and participation in the government by the so-called Maoist party. This leftwing group staged a large number of murderous attacks on the Nepalese army and had been waging a bitter war with the government. Now, under a deal the group has come out into the open and is participating in the governance of the country. The problem for India is the link of this group with many leftwing extremists groups like the Maoist Communist Center and the People's War Group operating in central India. Indeed, the corridor from Nepal to Andhra Pradesh has been described as a "liberated" zone (South Asia Terrorism Portal 2007) and is posing one of the biggest threats to the stability of the region. To compound the problems, the island nation of Sri Lanka is engaged in its own civil war with the Liberation Tamil Tigers Eelan (LTTE), a formidable terrorist organization that killed the former Prime Minister Rajiv Gandhi in a suicide attack in 1991. LTTE finds support in the state of Tamil Nadu across the sea and the ruling DMK party is sympathetic due to its Tamil ethnicity. This continues to pose problems for the Indian police in the southern states that face threat but cannot operate freely as the politicians prevent the police from operating against LTTE operatives active on Indian soil. Finally, many mafia-type groups operating in the underworld of Mumbai find shelter in the Middle-East nations of Dubai, Kuwait and United Arab Emirates which have a large number of migrants from the sub-continent. The governments of these countries have generally moved slowly to take action against organized criminal syndicates operating from their border which continues to create problems for the Indian authorities. The rapid growth of the Indian economy is also providing opportunities to legitimize illegal money controlled by smuggling cartels. India is at the periphery of major drug-producing regions of the world and the dynamics of organized crime, narco-terrorism, and religious fundamentalism are all creating a dangerous mix of challenges for the Indian police.

## The agenda for police reform

The Indian political system, besieged by divisions based on caste, religion, region and special interests, is unable to form consensus over major policies especially in such a crucial area as criminal justice. All policies are assessed in terms of gain and loss for each party or intra-party factions and the "political will" to take hard decisions is currently lacking. A window of opportunity opened in 1978 with the appointment of a National Police Commission to examine the problems of policing and to suggest a mechanism to deal with citizen grievances. Unfortunately, before the Commission could complete its work the government fell and the recommendations, particularly the one to shield the police from political control, were rejected by the new government (Verma 1998). Terrorism, beginning in the Punjab in the 1980s, followed by a rise of extremism in Jammu and Kashmir, both supported by Pakistan, also implied that in the name of dealing with exigencies police reform was put on the back burner. The growing threat of terrorism has created an environment where successive governments, whether from the right or left, are reluctant to 'hand-cuff' police use of force. The creation of a humane, law-abiding and locally accountable police system is still not on the agenda of any political party.

Nevertheless, a variety of secondary factors are coalescing to force changes in the system. As democracy is taking firmer roots in the country, corruption, development and security are becoming election issues. The recent Assembly election in Uttar Pradesh was "lost" by the ruling Samajwadi party on the issue of growing lawlessness in the region (Gupta 2007). Consequently, elected governments are being forced to address these public concerns. The Election Commission, too, has asserted independence from the government and has evolved several mechanisms to ensure free and fair elections. Innovations like electronic voting machines and efforts to shield election officials from political influence have helped clean up the election process. Further, forcing all candidates to file affidavits describing their family assets and criminal cases filed against them is at least helping educate the voters to make an informed choice. In the last decade very few ruling parties have been able to retain their power and with the frequent changes in governments the issue of accountability and good governance are becoming increasingly important.

A major catalyst for reform has been the higher judiciary that has been engaged in innovative activism to enforce progressive policies. The courts have pursued human rights violations and have brought both the senior officers and political leaders into its ambit in several cases. Several large scandals like the Hawala[2] and the Fodder[3] cases were initiated by the persistence of judges (Verma 2001a). These led to the conviction of not only several corrupt bureaucrats but also important political figures, thus enhancing the faith of citizens in the judicial process. The Supreme Court, acting on PILs filed by public spirited citizens, has also forced the government to initiate several administrative reforms.

One such effort has had a major impact and deserves to be mentioned here. A retired police officer filed a public interest petition (Writ Petition (Civil) No. 310 of 1996) requesting the Supreme Court to ask the government to explain what action had been taken on the recommendations of the National

Police Commission (NPC) of 1978. The National Human Rights Commission (NHRC) was also admitted as one of the interested parties and this Commission too endorsed the substantive recommendations of the NPC. The Supreme Court directed the Government of India to constitute a high-powered committee to review action taken on the recommendations of the National Police Commission, Law Commission, National Human Rights Commission and Vohra Committee, and suggest ways and means for implementing the pending recommendations of the above Commissions/Committee. The government dragged its feet and the matter lingered for several years. Finally, in September 2006, almost ten years after the filing of the first petition, the Supreme Court ordered the government to:

- Establish a State Security Commission to protect police from political pressure and to ensure that police act according to the laws of the land.
- Select the chief of police by a transparent process on the basis of good service and range of experience and to give a minimum tenure of at least two years.
- Separate the investigating wing from the law and order police to ensure speedier investigation, better expertise and improved rapport with the people.
- Establish a Police Complaints Authority to look into complaints against police officers.

At the behest of the Supreme Court several States have begun instituting Complaints Authorities and Security Commissions, and promising to give fixed tenure of at least two years to chiefs of police. It is still uncertain how the changes are going to affect the performance of police and how to make it accountable to the people. Nevertheless, the agenda of some kind of reform of the Indian police has been set in motion.

A more promising reform is the new generation of leaders, technologically-aware and innovative, who are taking control of the Indian police. This new breed emerged after the system of examination was changed in 1980 by the Union Public Service Commission. The new format added subjects from professional disciplines like engineering, management and law and gave the option to take the examinations in vernacular languages. This has opened the doors to a large set of students from professional institutions like the Indian Institutes of Technology and Management and to those coming from non-English medium schools. At present the number of engineers serving in the Indian Police Service for example is around 500 of a total of 2,000 or so officers. The senior police service retains its attraction and top university graduates compete for these limited posts. This service provides the benefits of subsidized housing, job security and health insurance but the main attraction largely stems from the high status, power and prestige enjoyed by the service from the British period. Approximately 200,000 graduates take the examination from which only the top fifty to sixty candidates are selected.

Not surprisingly, the Indian police boasts of the most educated and qualified students joining its leadership ranks. These new entrants have brought a welcome change in the workplace and have introduced a variety of technological applications in the field of management and supervision.

A new development is the growth of the private security industry in the country (Nalla 1998). The rapid growth in the economy and growing threat of kidnapping for ransom has encouraged many retired police and army officers to start their own security agencies providing guards, couriers, surveillance and even limited investigations for a fee. The large numbers of new housing complexes, shopping malls and industrial parks have further created the demand for security guards and security apparatus. A number of media channels have also begun the trend of staging sting operations to expose corruption, nepotism and bribery (Srivastava 2005). Furthermore, new companies providing services in data management, cyber security and applications of technology are building associations with the police, military and security agencies. Their growth is likely to spur demand for more professional services from the police organization. The Bureau of Police Research and Development (BPR&D) (2007) is promoting private sector management practices upon police training, management and performance evaluation.

The real strength of democracy is to empower citizens and get them involved in their own affairs. The failures of the political class to address important citizen issues and the growing criminalization of politics have led to a number of citizen initiatives that have mushroomed in the form of nongovernmental organizations. There are now hundreds of thousands of such organizations that are engaged in matters ranging from education, legal aid, environment protection, women's issues, trafficking, combating superstition, development issues, health and political reforms. Indian democracy is witnessing a vibrant phase with the direct involvement of people forging partnerships for special interests. Many human rights groups have vigorously pursued specific cases which have led to the punishment of guilty police officers. In major incidents like the anti-Sikh riots in 1984 in Delhi, the role of the state in communal riots in Gujarat in 2002 and the misuse of force in the North East and Jammu-Kashmir by the army, these citizen groups have worked hard to ensure justice to the victims of state apathy or direct involvement. These groups have forced the police to be more accountable, transparent and respectful of due process. These citizen initiatives are bringing real reform of the criminal justice system.

The demand for the government to be transparent and provide information to citizens about its actions and decision-making processes is the hallmark of democratic governance. It was in 1975 that the Supreme Court in *Raj Narain vs. State of UP* (AIR 1975 SC 865) laid down that the citizens have a right to know every public act, and what is done by the public functionaries in a public manner. It still took another thirty years of intense public pressure before the Indian Parliament passed the Right to Information (RTI) Act 2005 to establish a procedure to seek information from the government. This Act has empowered the citizens with a law, which can be "an instrument to curtail the direct fallout of opaque administration—corruption, inefficiency and the arbitrary use of power" (Infochangeindia.org 2007). The Act has become a catalyst for opening the government to the citizens. In the first year of enactment almost 42,876 petitions were filed by the citizens utilizing this new mechanism for redressing their grievances. The most remarkable achievement was that of one Arvind Kejriwal, a former bureaucrat who single-handedly launched a social revolution through his organization called "Parivartan" (Transformation). He worked with common people to utilize the act and helped expose the public distribution system that was siphoning off almost 90 percent of the grain procured for the poor.

The Act has been used by the citizens to push corrupt bureaucrats to follow the rules and address the needs of the people. In the Naraini block of Banda in UP's Bundelkhand, a historically backward and neglected region, the villagers periodically protested against lack of civic amenities, bad roads and sub-human living conditions but no one listened. After the passage of the RTI Act some villagers filed a petition to know how funds earmarked for this village have been spent. "Within a month, they got what they wanted . . . work on a 7.8 km approach road and a bridge" (Pande 2006). A national helpline has been set up where citizens can get information and help in filing petitions for their problems with Indian bureaucracy. For example, a fruit vendor called to know how he could complain against the denial of a ration card by the local official. Another house owner sought information to get the neighborhood development plan so that he could initiate action against people encroaching on public land (Venkatraman 2007). The RTI Act is beginning to force democratic accountability of the government agencies including the police.

## Conclusion: the prospects for police reform

Manning (2005) argues that democratic police are publicly accountable, subject to the rule of law, respectful of human dignity and that they can intervene in the life of citizens only under limited and carefully controlled circumstances. In theory, the Indian police function under a well-defined legal framework where the supremacy of the courts exists in principle and strongly in practice too. Police actions are guided by laws and organizational regulations and in principle every police action has to be publicly accountable. However, in practice the design and organizational ethos is such that police officers operate beyond the principles of law and are generally not accountable to local citizens. The Indian police are directly controlled by ruling party leaders and are used for political objectives. Despite one of the most qualified and well-trained police leadership cadres in the world the organization continues to suffer from internal problems and external influences. The independence of police leadership is heavily compromised and they are not only ineffective in maintaining discipline over their personnel but also unable to prevent politicians from using the organization for partisan purposes. These are having dangerous consequences for the organization and the democratic functioning of the nation.

Furthermore, the protests of dissatisfied citizens quickly turn to violence. The growing internal conflict and a perception that matters are to be settled outside the arena of the justice system is a major danger to the country. Most citizens have little faith in the ability of the police to conduct an impartial investigation and bring offenders to justice. Indian society is becoming difficult to govern and the inability or unwillingness of elected leaders to implement progressive policies are creating obstacles that have long-term implications. Terrorism remains a distinct and serious threat to the stability of the country and the deliberate violence fanned by neighboring countries, particularly Pakistan and Bangladesh, continues to flame tensions. The unfortunate aspect of these internal and external threats is that the government is unlikely to prioritize reform of the police and reduce its political shadow. Reform is a political process and unless the pressure to change comes it is unlikely that the politicians are going to hand over control or modify a mechanism that benefits them handsomely. Political developments will continue to affect the functioning of the police department and this will limit its ability to develop as a democratic force in the society.

Nevertheless, there are positive signals and reasons to remain optimist. Young Indians are more confident of themselves and the economic growth is forcing rapid transformation of the society. Indian companies and managers are competing in the world market and adding a forceful voice of change in the governance of the country. The citizenry is beginning to apply new technologies to make government more accountable and transparent. The young police leaders are also introducing new technologies in their work and are eager to compete with their counterparts in the private sector. Even though fundamental changes in the police system are difficult, the efforts are getting stronger. It is certain that the police of the twenty-first century will be different from the model created in 1861.

## Notes

1 Under a directive by the Supreme Court this Act is being revised; this is discussed later in the chapter.
2 Many Cabinet ministers were suspected of receiving bribes from a business person.
3 A Chief Minister was accused of siphoning public funds on fictitious bills.

## References

Ahmed, Zubair. 2004. Bombay's crack 'encounter' police, *BBC News*, June 9.
Amnesty International. 2007. *India. A Pattern of Unlawful Killings by the Gujarat Police: Urgent Need for Effective Investigations*, May 24, available online at http://www.web.amnesty.org/library/Index/ENGASA200112007.

Arnold, David. 1986. *Police Power and Colonial Rule, Madras 1859–1947*. Delhi: Oxford University Press.

Arnold, David. 1992. Police Power and the Demise of British Rule in India 1930–47. In David M. Anderson and David Killingray (eds), *Policing and Decolonisation*. Manchester: Manchester University Press, pp. 42–61.

Bayley, David H. 1969. *Police and Political Development in India*. Princeton: University Press.

Biswas, Mrityunjay. 2007. *Reforms in prison administration* <http://news.indlaw.com/guest/columns/default.asp?mrityunjay April 28>.

Bureau of Police Research & Development 2007. 'Articles on Police Leadership' <http;//www.bprd.gov.in/index 1.asp?linkid=402>.

Cohn, Bernard S. 1961. *The Development and Impact of British Administration in India*. New Delhi: Indian Institute of Public Administration.

Das, Dilip K. and Verma, Arvind. 1998. The Armed Police in the British Colonial Tradition: The Indian Perspective. *Police Studies: The International Review of Police Development and Management* 21 (2): 354–367.

Davis, K.C. 1969. *Discretionary Justice: A Preliminary Inquiry*. Baton Rouge: Louisiana State University Press.

Dhagambar, Vasudha. 1992. *Law, Power and Justice: Protection of Personal Rights Under the IPC*. New Delhi: Sage.

Gadbois, George H. Jr. 1987. The Institutionalization of the Supreme Court in India, in John R. Schmidhauser (ed.), *Comparative Judicial Systems: Changing Frontiers in Conceptual and Empirical Analysis*. Boston: Butterworths.

Government of India (GOI). 1980. *Second Report of the National Police Commission*. Ministry of Home Affairs, Faridabad: Government of India Press, Chapter XV, section 15.5.

Griffiths, Percival, Sir. 1971. *To Guard My People: The History of the Indian Police*. London: Ernest Benn Limited.

Gupta, Anandswarup. 1979. *The Police in British India: 1861–1947*. New Delhi: Concept Publishing Company.

Gupta, Shekhar. 2007. Don't take me for granted, don't peddle your past, talk of my future. *Indian Express* (editorial), 13 May.

Imperial Gazetteer of India. 1907–1909. *Part IV (Administrative)*, reprint 1909. Oxford: Clarendon Press.

Infochangeindia.org. 2007. *One Year After: State Report Card on RTI*, available at http://infochangeindia.org/features388.jsp.

Kashyap, Subhash C. 2007. India at Sixty: Criminal Politician Nexus Getting Stronger, *The Tribune*, 15 August.

Kohli, Atul. 1990. *Democracy and Discontent: India's Growing Crisis of Governability*. New York: Cambridge University Press.

Lobo, John. 1992. *Leaves from a Policeman's Diary*. New Delhi: Allied Publishers.

Manning, Peter K. 2005. The Study of Policing. *Police Quarterly* 8 (1): 23–43.

Mitra, Deputy Inspector General Durga Madhab (John). 2007. Understanding Indian Insurgencies: Implications for Counterinsurgency Operations in the Third World. Monograph, *Strategic Studies Institute*, 20 February, available at http://www.strategicstudiesinstitute.army.mil/pdffiles/PUB751.pdf.

Nalla, Mahesh, 1998. Opportunities in an Emerging Market. *Security Journal* 10: 15–21.

National Crime Records Bureau (NCRB). 2007. *Annual Crime in India 2006*. Government of India, available at http://ncrb.nic.in/home.htm.

National Human Rights Commission (NHRC). 2006. *Annual Report 2004–2005*, pp. 15–16, available at http://nhrc.nic.in.

Pande, Alka S. 2006. After sixty years of neglect, Information Act changes UP village. *Indian Express*, 25 December.

Raghuraman, Shankar. 2007. India loses maximum lives to terror except Iraq. *Times of India*, 27 August.

Raj Kumar. 2000. Lallo keeps 'uniformed friend' happy. *Times of India*, 22 June.

Raman, B. 2002. *Intelligence: Past, Present and Future*. New Delhi: Lancer Publishers and Distributors.

Reiner, Robert. 1992. *The Politics of the Police*. Toronto: University of Toronto Press.

Sahni, Ajai. 2007. *South Asia Overview*, available at http://www.satp.org.

Seminar. 1977. *The Police: A Symposium on the problems of Law and Order in a Democracy*, No. 218, October. Bombay: R. Thapar, pp. 10–34.

Seminar. 1999. *Policespeak: A Symposium on the Role of the Police in Our Society*, No. 483, November. New Delhi: R. Thapar.

Shah, Ghanshyam. 2002. Introduction. In Ghanshyam Shah (ed.) *Social Movements and the State*. New Delhi: Sage, pp. 13–31.

Shah, Giriraj. 2002. *The Life and Times of Maj. General William Sleeman: Elimination of Thuggeries in India*. Delhi: Eastern Book Corporation.

Sharma, B.M. 1966. *The Republic of India: Constitution and Government*. New York: Asia Publishing House.

Sharma, Moolchand. 1994. *Justice PN Bhagwati: Court, Constitution and Human Rights*. New Delhi: Universal Press.

South Asia Terrorism Portal. 2007. *Maoist Assessment Year 2006*, available at http://www.satp.org.

Srivastava, Siddharth. 2005. A Stinging Exposure of India's Corrupt *Asia Times* (Online) Dec. 23 <www.atimes.com>.

Sullivan, Dennis and Tifft, Larry (eds). 2006. *Handbook of Restorative Justice: A Global Perspective*. London and New York: Routledge.

Tharoor, Shashi. 1997. *India: From Midnight to the Millennium*. New York: Arcade Publishing.

Tihar Prisons. 2008. *Prisoners' Profile*, available at http://tiharprisons.nic.in.

United Nations Development Project (UNDP) 2006. Human Development Report 2006. Table 3—Human and Income Poverty: Developing Countries, page 293; <http://hdr.undp.org/en/media/hdr_tables_2006.pdf>.

Venkatraman, Shilpa. 2007. Hello RTI, I am a fruit seller, I have a ration card problem. *Indian Express*, 26 January.

Verma, Arvind. 1997. Maintaining Law and Order in India: An Exercise in Discretion. *International Criminal Justice Review* 7: 65–80.

Verma, Arvind. 1998. National Police Commission in India: Analysis of the Policy Failures. *The Police Journal* LXXI (3): 226–244.

Verma, Arvind. 1999. Police Corruption in India: Roots in Organizational Culture *Police Studies: The International Review of Police Development and Management* 22 (3): 264–278.

Verma, Arvind. 2000. Politicization of the Police in India: Where lies the Blame? *Indian Police Journal* XLVII (4): 19–37.

Verma, Arvind. 2001a. Taking Justice outside the Courts: Judicial Activism in India. *The Howard Journal of Criminal Justice* 20 (2): 148–165.

Verma, Arvind. 2001b. Policing of Public Order in India. *International Journal of Police Science & Management* 3 (3): 213–225.

Verma, Arvind. 2002. Consolidation of the Raj: Notes from a Police Station 1865–1928. *Criminal Justice History* 17: 109–132.

Verma, Arvind. 2005. *The Indian Police: A Critical Review*. Delhi: Regency Publications.

Verma, Arvind. 2007. The Anatomy of Riots: A Situational Crime Prevention Approach. *Crime Prevention & Community Safety: An International Journal* 9(3): 201–221.

Woodruff, Philip. 1954. *The Men Who Ruled India: The Guardians*. New York: Schocken Books.

Yang, Anand A. 1989. *The Limited Raj: Agrarian Relations in Colonial India, Saran District, 1793–1920*. Berkeley: University of California Press.

# 7 Police reform and reconstruction in Timor-Leste

## A difficult do-over

*Gordon Peake*[1]

In early 2006 the United Nations' presence in Timor-Leste was winding down with a sense of job well done. Peacekeepers and police had withdrawn already and the UN Office in Timor-Leste (UNOTIL), a small political mission, was scheduled to end in May 2006. Although not without its critics, the UN appeared to have successfully laid strong foundations for sustainable peace in the recently established state. Among the cherished successes was the National Police of Timor-Leste (Polícia Nacional de Timor-Leste, PNTL), the national police institution created from scratch in 1999 and midwifed subsequently by United Nations police (Jones *et. al* 2005). Although it was a new institution, many of its senior officers brought experience in policing, having served as Timorese members of the Indonesian police service (POLRI) during that country's twenty-four year occupation.

The plaudits proved premature. Instead of packing their bags, a severe public order downturn in mid-2006 compelled the United Nations to return in greater number and for international police to reassume executive policing tasks. Responding to two months of riots, shootings and the disintegration of state security forces, the Timorese government invited military and police assistance from Australia, New Zealand, Malaysia and Portugal. While they restored a workaday sense of calm, more concerted work to restore state institutions was needed. And so, in August 2006, the UN Security Council established the multidimensional UN Integrated Mission in Timor-Leste (UNMIT), the fifth UN mission on the half-island since 1999, and the third since independence in May 2002.

Secretary-General Kofi Annan observed that the magnitude of the tasks facing UNMIT meant it was 'likely to stay for many years'.[2] Although all elements of the mission are interconnected, its success will be measured largely by its effectiveness in helping reform the police.

It is a large police-building mission, the second largest of all UN mandated peacekeeping missions. There are over 1,600 members of the United Nations police mandated with officers drawn from at least forty countries. United Nations police have re-assumed primacy for policing, making Timor-Leste the only sovereign state in which a non-national is in charge of a police service.

In many respects, the police re-building process is something of a 'do-over' opportunity for the UN police, a chance to prove that they have addressed the deficiencies that arose in the creation of the PNTL (Hood 2007). Although the PNTL was operationally effective in certain basic respects, it was often feeble as an institution. Policies in the fields of discipline, recruitment and promotion were largely absent and planning capacity was poor. The institution was deeply politicized and fragmented with the country's first interior minister using elements of the police in a manner close to a political militia.

The question now is whether the 'blue berets' will be any better this time at creating an effective police institution than their predecessors were during the transitional administration. Although there is perhaps not enough distance from the events of 2006 to make an accurate judgement, the results are not encouraging. Many of the previously identified mistakes of approach, style and strategy are being repeated once more (Rees 2004; Hood 2007). It leaves open the question of whether the UN 'model' of importing a technicolour array of uniforms drawn from all points of the globe can ever be effective in carrying out a complex, dynamic and multi-faceted reform process.[3] This question holds true not just for the UN mission in Timor-Leste but the sixteen other peacekeeping missions in which United Nations police are engaging in reform. Most are taking place in even less permissive environments than Timor-Leste. As one senior UNMIT official commented: 'if we cannot do state-building and police reform here, in a small country with a comparatively benign political environment, then how can we even contemplate working in somewhere like the [Democratic Republic of] Congo?'[4]

Developing 'capacity' in the PNTL has proved difficult. The international police are confronting both a sceptical and resistant national police institution and a public seared by memories of recent past practice that is reluctant to invest trust and legitimacy in it. Achieving adequate training and equipment for police officers, establishing an accountable and rights-respecting institution complete with functioning managerial structures and systems, and operating as part of a wider rule of law fabric, remains a work in progress. Their grousing about making little headway is mirrored – albeit in less florid language – in evaluation reports.

To some extent, these above observations almost write themselves. They further reinforce the dominant perception captured in the large policy literature about the police. These lessons could be summarized thus: reform is an extremely difficult task that requires cutting through gnarls of management, leadership, political will, set attitudes, established behaviours and negative public perceptions. Reforming and rebuilding a police system demands the condensing of diverse training skills in a very short period and fast-forwarding the development of skills that are ideally built up over generations. This daunting task is compounded by the manner in which reform is organized and finding officers of sufficient quality, finding them in sufficient quantity, and doing so in a timely way is difficult. In short, these conclusions pertain as much to Timor-Leste as they do to any post-conflict or recovering state. They sound eerily familiar.

But, taking these observations to its logical conclusion leads to a wider question as to feasibility that is often dodged by the policy literature and ducked by policy makers. Is this model of 'police-building', whether through the UN or bilateral donors, really tenable in the longer term? Continued relative failure requires thinking about the core assumptions underpinning the reform model, and its attempts to replicate a formal model of policing that is fashioned in developed, or donor, countries and which, oddly, privileges the 'formal' in a way dissonant to the actual plurality of policing service provision.

Although critiques of international police reform efforts are often scathing, the solution is often to instrumentally make the 'means of doing business' better, rather than evaluating the core assumptions of the business proposal itself (Neild 2001; Hansen 2002; Greene *et al.* 2004; Marenin 2005; Goldsmith and Dinnen 2007). Such a re-hatting of the basic old idea has occurred in UNMIT.[5]

The continuingly poor yield needs to encourage and instigate a re-evaluation of the 'universal' notions of how a police force should work, in conditions where state institutions are feeble and where alternative, sub-state methods have both deeper roots and proven capabilities. The experience also suggests that the current delivery model – using mostly police to change police – may need to be broadened to include wider skill sets. This may cause donors and international organizations to put police reform in perspective. The importance of policing should not be overestimated. While police reform is a vital task, it needs to be rooted in a larger state-building strategy. It also speaks to how dilemmas in state-building are to be managed. UNTAET had to get things going quickly and put a local face on law enforcement. The dilemma was that in providing a façade of local ownership they probably hobbled building a long-term institution.

Focusing solely on the UN and donors' role in building the police in this young democracy would be skewed, however. It would ignore the cadences and rhythms of national politics and disregard the extent to which, *pace* Bayley, the police institution is barometric of wider political developments (Bayley 2001). Focusing on the national scene shows a police force still trying to instantiate popular legitimacy in a difficult environment. Although Timor-Leste emerged from Indonesia in 1999, the occupation cast long shadows on all new institutions but especially the police. This holds in three respects. First, there is insufficient materiel for building new institutions. In 1999, and even in independence in 2002, the would-be nation had few formal accoutrements of sovereignty upon which to build a state: no ministries, no institutions, no police and just a handful of courts. Moreover, the human materiel to animate these institutions was limited in number. Second, the new state has limited resources upon which to assert its power, which has implications for all state institutions including the police. Beyond the capital, Dili, relatively few police are stationed; those that are work devoid of such workaday essentials as a functioning car and an adequate communications system. Third, there is an absence of social trust and capital, eroded substantially in an internecine and compromising twenty-four year occupation that pitted family against family and friend against friend. The fact that PNTL was lead by ex-POLRI officers who were the perceived lackeys of the occupier also undermines the legitimacy of the force in the eyes of the people. When allied to a relatively small population – despite large growth, Timor-Leste's population is still under a million people –, the result is that police officers – and related justice institutions – are not considered impartial and apolitical functionaries. Instead, the decision to trust an officer is mediated and negotiated through a complex web of family, region and perception and trust in the police as an institution remains weak. As a result, the majority of everyday disputes are, for reasons of both convenience, swiftness and legitimacy, carried out without direct reference to the state system. What constitutes a crime is derived from local-based understandings rather than legal texts; what steps need to be taken to resolve a conflict are similarly derived on local- and regional-based notions. In this respect, Timor-Leste, five years into statehood, still has 'many of the features of a stateless society' (Hohe and Nixon 2003: 37). For the vast majority, justice – including crimes as serious as sexual assault and larceny – is accessed and provided through a tapestry of regionally diverse kinship systems, cosmological understandings and what political scientists would call dispute resolution systems. In turn, it seems that the PNTL meshes with these systems, officers often being present as witnesses and final authorities. This meshing and fusion of the formal and the informal helps explain the startling statistics of 'no crime this month or last' which are recorded in official station logs.[6]

An analysis of the development of PNTL in a young democracy with weak institutions poses challenging questions about police institutional development in a young, small democracy: how can the police be insulated from political interference; how can walls be constructed so as to protect accountability? Delving into police reform from the two separate viewpoints of the international and the national turns up a gulf of difference on what reform to do, what reform to prioritize and how reform should be managed. The differences between what is intended for the police of Timor and how Timor is *policed* is further evidence as to the flaws in the international 'police-building' model approach.

This chapter divides into four sections. The first examines the historical and current political background, detailing the relative newness of state structures in Timor-Leste, and the even newer phenomenon of a democratic, community-focused, policing model. The two sections that follow examine international and national processes and details the problems, responses and continuing challenges of instantiating authority for the police. A brief conclusion assesses the prospects for future reform in Timor.

## Historical background: long colonialism, short-lived state and long occupation

In 1999, after twenty-four years of Indonesian occupation, the people of the former Portuguese colony of East Timor voted for independence. Following three years of United Nations transitional administration, the Democratic Republic of Timor-Leste came into being on 20 May 2002. It was the first new nation of the twenty-first century and one of the smallest, with a population of less than a million people.

Throughout the Indonesian occupation, the East Timorese resistance led an armed struggle against the Indonesian army for national independence. An estimated 45,000 living individuals who fought in and/or clandestinely supported the resistance campaign claim the title of a 'veteran', which accords them continued residual social legitimacy and authority (McCarthy 2002; Peake 2008). This makes them approximately 5 per cent of the current population. The struggle for independence was a twinned effort that combined the gun with the soap box. As well as in the forests of Timor-Leste, Timorese in the diaspora waged a diplomatic campaign to force the international community to restore Timor-Leste's short-lived independence.

In constructing a broad front to oppose the Indonesian occupation, Timor's politicians and fighters found a unity of purpose lacking in 1975 as Portugal hastily and chaotically withdrew from its former colony. Despite the threat of the former colony being swallowed up by its larger neighbour, Timor's political elite remained fractured. Several political parties emerged during that period with opposing visions for the future. The Frente Revolucionária de Timor-Leste Independente (FRETILIN) party argued for immediate independence from Portugal, backed up by its Forcas Armadas de Libertacao Nacional de Timor-Leste (FALANTIL) militia while other parties, most notably the União Democrática Timorense (UDT), were significantly more cautious.

Their differences turned violent as a civil war between UDT and FRETLIN began in August 1975. By November, FRETILIN was in the ascendancy and declared unilateral independence.[7] It would be a short-lived 'state'. Two weeks after the national flag was raised, and with the tacit consent of Australia and the United States who feared a FRETILIN-run Timor-Leste would become a communist outpost in the South Pacific, Indonesia invaded and duly annexed the territory.

Many members of Timor's small Portuegeuse-speaking political elite fled the territory, most relocating to Portugal or lusophone Africa. During the early years of the occupation, FALINTIL controlled a significant portion of the country. As Indonesian control strengthened, the fighters were eventually pushed east, and their activities underground. Their tactics changed to that of a 'hit-and-run' guerrilla force.

Some of the internal conflict that characterized post-colonial politics endured, both within Fretlin, and between Fretlin and other groups. Its effects still inflect post-independence Timor-Leste's political dynamics. However, the trend was towards unifying the resistance and presenting a broad, non-partisan front. The driving force behind this unity is often credited to resistance leader, 'Xanana' Gusmão. Part of the invigoration meant removing FALANTIL from a direct political association with FRETLIN and placing it under the framework of a broad resistance movement. Timor-Leste is thus somewhat remarkable as the normal chronology of a political movement in reverse: split, then unity.

All historical narratives risk being inflected with teleology and Timor's is no exception. Although the above paragraphs may have conveyed the sense of a unfied national struggle, this was not always the case. Behind the rubric of national liberation were a series of small conflicts and family-based disputes, which accented regional and linguistic differences still further as well as eroding social trust. Testimony collected by the Timor-Leste Truth and Reconciliation Commission during 2002–4 records a series of micro-conflicts, and micro-attempts to 'police' their resolution.

It was to be a protracted and bloody twenty-four year conflict. The Timor-Leste Truth and Reconciliation Commission determined that some 102,000 Timorese suffered conflict-related deaths during the occupation; their report records a brutal Indonesian occupation with large incidences of arbitrary detention, torture, forced displacement and gender-based violence (CAVR 2004: 44–47).

During the occupation, policing was conducted by the Indonesian police (POLRI). The dominant style was colonial with the police auxiliary to the Indonesian army and complementary to a large intelligence service. Timor was always regarded as Daearh Operasi Militer (DOM) or a Military Operations Area and therefore POLRI were always the subordinate to the military commander.

Although the leadership of the police hailed from outside the island, a substantial number of the organization's members were drawn from Timor itself. Characterizing how this force behaved – and the motivations and approach of Timor officers – is difficult. Testimony collected by the Commission for Reception, Truth and Reconciliation (CAVR) is varied and insusceptible to analytically meaningful generalization – some Timorese were supportive of the occupation, others used membership of the police as a 'trojan horse' to funnel information to the resistance; others still were actual members of the clandestine movement. In a feature that would define post-independence politics, family affiliation and networks often determined either opinions of officers and/or officers' perceptions of the population.

In such an atmosphere, communities policed themselves. In the early years of the occupation – when FRETLIN still controlled large portions of the territory – the guerrilla group carried out 'popular policing' functions (Walsh 1999; Ospina and Hohe 2001). As the occupation tightened, this 'formal informal' policing receded, although membership of the forest resistance continued to bequeath legitimacy to individuals carrying out policing functions.

In the main, though, the majority of everyday disputes and crimes were dealt with through a diverse amalgam of customary and village structures. Not only were they more physically, linguistically and cultural accessible, and in accord with long-standing traditions, they also obviated the need to go through the state system. Dealing with the POLRI carried a Janus-faced risk: intrusion by the occupying power and earning the opprobrium of community members and the resistance.

The occupation ended through a combination of diligent lobbying but also old-fashioned luck. A series of circumstances meant the question of Timor was 'ripe' for resolution in the late 1990s (Zartman 2001). Within the context of a national reform movement occasioned by the Asian economic crisis, in January 1999 Indonesia proposed a referendum to offer the people of East Timor a choice between autonomy or independence.

The UN conducted the 'popular consultation' on 30 August 1999, with 78.5 per cent of voters choosing independence. Pro-Indonesian militias immediately launched a campaign of violence upon announcement of the result, which was not contained by the Indonesian authorities. The POLRI stood by. Many of the Timorese members of the force simply left their posts.

In addition to large-scale casualties (estimated to be 1,000), in just a few weeks the territory was physically devastated. Over half the population fled their houses in fear.

Under intense pressure, Indonesian president B. J. Habibie agreed to an international security presence to quell the violence and restore order. On 15 September 1999, the United Nations Security Council authorized the Australian-led International Force for East Timor (INTERFET) to restore peace and security under Chapter VII of the United Nations Charter. In October, the UN Transitional Administration in East Timor (UNTAET) was established to administer the territory for a transitional period. UNTAET was endowed with state-like powers and, along with Kosovo, enjoyed the most comprehensive mandate in the history of UN peacekeeping.

Following military intervention by Australia, the UN Transitional Administration in East Timor (UNTAET) was established in October 1999 to run the territory for an intermediary period and help shepherd it to independence.

### Incomplete statebuilding

Although a relatively small territory as compared to other UN peacekeeping missions, UNTAET's mandate was colossal: to lay the foundations for building a new state. A mass exodus of Indonesian civil servants prior to and immediately following the territory-wide violence and destruction left an enormous capacity vacuum.

This held true of the police. The POLRI component simply withered away. Public order policing was being conducted by peacekeeping troops and there was no dedicated 'community-focused' police (not that there really had been one before).

The UN transitional administration faced a complete vacuum of formal policing when it assumed responsibility for the territory in 1999 and created two new forces to fill it. Under UNTAET, an international police force assumed primary responsibility for actual policing, while an accelerated plan was made for founding and developing a professional, impartial and politically neutral indigenous police service to take over that responsibility. The UNTAET force was composed of police officers of more than fifty nationalities with experience of policing but not of Timor-Leste; many of the Timorese politicians and police would have local knowledge and linguistic advantage but little policing experience.

As noted, the preponderance of Timor-Leste's lusophone elite had fled following the invasion, returning to the homeland nearly a quarter of a century later. It was a strange homecoming. Although the elite, many were not familiar with the basics of their own land. Language was one issue: while they spoke Portuguese (and were to make it the official language alongside Tetum) only a small number of the general population did so. They spoke their own regional language – Timor-Leste has fifteen – as well as the national patois, Tetun, and Bahasa Indonesia. The result is linguistic confusion: official police paperwork and the courts work in Portuguese which the vast preponderance of Timorese – around 90 per cent do not speak fluently. Interacting with the police and the courts – an already stressful experience – becomes more so. The linguistic gulf was symptomatic of wider differences in politics, approach and knowledge (Mydans 2007).

## Creating a new police

Amidst an uncertain wider political context, this approach of creating two new police forces has been to a large extent a novel experiment. Only in Kosovo, a mission that started at the same time, was this approach attempted.

There was little prior guidance in how to go about enacting this ambitious mandate. Previous blueprints for the Timor – drafted during attempts by Timorese in 1997 and 1998 to devise a blueprint for governing – mentioned policing sparingly. Far more attention alighted on 'non-security' institutions such as health and education. However, all of those plans envisaged the process taking place in the aftermath of a negotiated political agreement, not a scorched earth policy. No plans had foreseen executive authority for policing coming from the international community. But in the absence of a viable local police force following the conflict there was no practical alternative to a direct takeover of civilian policing: responsibility for civilian policing fell in a somewhat ad hoc fashion to the international community for the first time in a generation. (The last mandate with policing responsibilities was Congo.)

UNTAET's mandate involved two important innovations. For the first time, international police would be directly responsible for law enforcement operations. And while previous mandates had provided for training, mentoring and oversight of local police forces, the Timor mandate tasked international organizations with building a new force from the ground up. Once that force was able to stand on its own, authority would be transferred in stages from the international force, whose role would then revert to one of monitoring and oversight.

There were very few specifics about the new local police force contained in the legal instrument that created it. Resolution 1272 did not specify the ethnic makeup of the new force, its structure or its specific tasks. The shape of the force was only to become clear in the months after the arrival of UNTAET, when international police officers began planning the police. The lack of preparation was reflected in the multiple names and appellations this new institution had in its first years: first East Timor Police Force, then East Timor Police Service and, in 2002, the Portuguese language National Police of Timor-Leste (PNTL)

It was somehow decided that the PNTL force would number 3,000, a number seemingly plucked from the air (King's College 2002). The intended composition was multi-ethnic, with a 20 per cent quota for women officers, above the Western European average for female participation, which stands at 10 per cent. The force would be trained in the ethos of 'democratic policing'. For a 'democratic' police, there was very little democratic scaffolding around it. A police regulatory framework didn't come into place until mid-2001, two years into the mission.

The aims of the force's creators were as ambitious as the obstacles facing them were large:

> Our aim was a combined model of North American and Western European policing traditions – a collective version of those countries that have a history of providing democratic policing, that is, policing where the rights of the citizen are meant to come before protecting the interests of an ethnic group or the state. It's was an alien model and one that few of these new officers will have had exposure to.[8]

The officers who make up the UN's police force are startlingly diverse. During UNTAET, Timor's police stations contained a mixture of uniforms and languages from more than fifty countries. The quality of officers in terms of skills, range of experience, standards and previous training is equally diverse. Given the large number of donor countries and their geographical spread, it is hardly surprising that the mission combines such a wide array of policing styles and practice. Nor are the different approaches to policing restricted to inter-country variation; officers from different departments in the same country display different attitudes to the same problems. How to stop traffic – e.g. whether to stand in the front, or at the side or the back of the motorist – was but one of the many workaday policing tasks in which there was contradictory practices.

Oddly for a mission in which police institution building was to be the primary task, very few officers had experience in actually building an institution. In 2002, an observer noted that just two of the 1,500-strong international police force had experience in this area, 'and one was politically compromised' (Hood 2007: 143).

Oral history testimony of officers who served in the transitional administration recounts chronic disorganization. Commanders were of variable quality; too many seemed to have been appointed because of their early arrival or because of previous mission experience, rather than on their ability. Standards varied with little apparent formal supervision or direction and officers could choose whether to work hard or not. Different nationalities have different lengths of mission, and different arrival and departure dates. This means that personnel are changing regularly and few people remain in a job for more than a few months at a time. Formal hand-over procedure when an officer leaves the mission was missing. This has often created problems with contacts being lost, information being mislaid, etc. There is little evidence of work continuity or long-term strategy; everything functions on a short-term basis. Officers had a patchy knowledge of wider mission activities. One observed that there were always at least two police development plans being written, often in blissful ignorance of the other.[9] But with no regulation in the early days it shows that the SRSG was not involved, and the Timorese leadership, who were all in the National Council, were not involved. There was gap in the framework from the Mandate to the law to the plan.

The other half of the uniformed policing equation, the indigenous, long-term inheritors of the entire policing set-up in Timor-Leste, are just as diverse as their international counterparts which vary widely in terms of age, background, fitness and aptitude. Some of the new recruits barely reach the minimum age requirement; others are over 50 and span the range of educational and professional backgrounds.

While it was symbolically and practically imperative that locally trained officers get out onto the streets as quickly as possible, two early decisions helped shape perception and effectiveness.

The first was to not start completely from scratch. In a decision that would have wide reverberations, UNTAET decided that the backbone of the new Timor police would be Timorese officers who served in POLRI. The first commander of the PNTL, Paulo Fatema de Martens, had previously been the highest ranking Timorese in the POLRI. While it was understandable, the risk with this strategy was that it would mean that the new police would be indelibly associated with the older, Indonesian model. Did UNPOL see the dilemma of fast implementation versus tainted force? Probably not. With little familiarity with the local context, they privileged experience over the past, with little thought as to how the past would impact on future legitimacy.

The second was to abbreviate the training programme to such an extent that little was imparted. Early Timorese officers went through six weeks of training, to be then followed by mentorship by international personnel. The abbreviated training course is enough to introduce the basics of policing but little more. The worry is that one is trading away long-term competence in order to deploy a symbolically significant police presence out onto the streets.

Both decisions blighted police development with many of the risks flagged up proving all too prescient. Whether real or imagined, there was a strong perception from the outset that this 'new beginning to policing' was anything but, because of so many of the old (for some compromised) faces involved.

Such was the lack of faith in the new police that, despite independence, the UN retained authority over the police. In May 2002 a new mission was created to reflect the new political reality. The prime tasks of the United Nations Mission of Support for East Timor (UNMISET) were police related (executive policing and continued reform). Full policing authority was handed over in 2005 and UNMISET was replaced by the United Nations Office in Timor-Leste (UNOTIL), a much smaller mission than its predecessors, and conceived as a bridging operation to transition from peacekeeping to coordinated development assistance. UNOTIL was scheduled to end in May 2006, a decision compelled by member states' reluctance to fund it further.

## Defence reform

As the PNTL was developing so, too, was a national defence force. It was to be tensions and unresolved roles between these groups that led to the crisis of 2006. The force is the inheritor of the liberation movement. Six hundred and fifty FALINTIL joined the new defence force, the Falintil–Forças de Defesa de Timor-Leste (F-FDTL). Since its inception, the F-FDTL has been an institution searching for a role. According to the constitution, their function is to 'provide military defence for the . . . republic' (Rees 2004: 8). But in a small half-island state with low risks of external attack, what exactly is a defence force defending against? The risk that Indonesia would re-invade is negligible. The question of what the defence force is meant to do on a workaday basis, and what the state can afford remains very much a live one.[10]

Compared to the police, F-FDTL was relatively neglected by the international community including UNTAET and UNMISET, poorly funded by donors, and sidelined by the Timorese prime minister (Forman 2007). Its unclear status and minimal tasking stoked discontent and was a factor in Timor's political crisis in 2006. As many of its everyday functions were assumed by the PNTL, alleged unfair treatment ignited discontent. In February 2006, 594 F-FDTL officers, noncoms and soldiers went on strike over discrimination and promotions. The decision of the chief of the defence force to sack them in March 2006 prompted demonstrations by soldiers that took on a violent character and became intertwined with a range of other grievances and cleavages (United Nations Independent Commission of Inquiry 2006).

The relationship between and within the defence and police was always vinegary, the differences based on personality clashes, perceptions of role under the occupation, ancient differences of ideology and various forms of allegiance.

The acrimony escalated in the following months and increasingly acquired an ethnic character, as armed groups from Timor's eastern and western provinces clashed. The police split along similar lines. Thirty-seven people died and many houses were destroyed. Amid the violence 150,000 Timorese – 15 per cent of the entire population and mostly all from Dili – left their homes. Tellingly, this political rift rippled little into the rural areas where the PNTL and F-FDTL presence was weak or non-existent, a testament to the strength and continuing influence of social bonds.

Within the space of a few months, many of the institutions established by the UN and handed over to the government appeared to be rapidly unravelling. The tensions laid bare cracks between and within the political elite, the police and the security forces. The government seemed paralysed, with a split between Prime Minister Mari Alkatiri and President Gusmão. The PNTL and F-FDTL were at best incapable and at worst complicit in crime and lawlessness. The small UNOTIL mission could do little in such circumstances, and themselves were targets of getting fired on. In one of the most tragic stories in a harrowing time for the UN, the police chief of the UNPOL mission was fired at as he attempted to negotiate safe passage for PNTL officers hemmed in their headquarters by F-FDTL soldiers. Eight unarmed PNTL were shot dead in the attack.[11] By that point, most of the police leadership had taken to the hills. (Paolo Martins, the then police chief, never returned. He was elected to membership of the National Parliament in 2007.)

By late May, security in Dili and some surrounding towns had collapsed so completely that then-foreign minister José Ramos-Horta went on Australian TV to ask for help. Over 2,000 troops and police from these countries began to deploy as the Australian-led Operation Astute. Security Council Resolution 1704 was passed on 25 August 2006, paving the way for a new UN mission, the fifth in seven years. Restoring public security is a mission priority of the United Nations Integrated Mission in Timor-Leste (UNMIT) and UN civilian police its most visible face. The international officers are tasked with providing interim executive policing support, while simultaneously reconstituting the deeply politicized, institutionally weak PNTL. Echoing the relative neglect of the transitional administration, UNMIT's mandated responsibilities alight little on the F-FDTL. Most cooperation with the defence forces is handled bilaterally through programmes with Australia and New Zealand.

## *Incomplete statebuilding and the 2006 crisis*

In the grand scale of things, six-and-a-half years seems insufficient to liven and instantiate new state institutions. And so it proved. Judged with the benefit of hindsight, many of the institutions created by the UN and bequeathed to the new state were simply not fit for purpose. The short timeframe was not the only factor: the manner in which the UN approached state-building in Timor-Leste can be faulted in other respects. During the UN interregnum, Timorese participation in the process was frequently side-lined by a merry-go-round of advisers that stayed for short periods and insensitively imported 'off the shelf' models and ideas with little consideration as to either their appropriateness or utility (Chopra 2000).

The need for foreign troops a year after the departure of the last international peacekeepers raised doubts about the long-term prospects of one of the world's youngest nations. Beyond insecurity, Timor-Leste must cope with deep-seated social, economic and governance problems: high unemployment, rapid population growth, inadequate infrastructure, a weak public sector with limited service capacity, poor governance and fragile state institutions. Unemployment is running at about 40 per cent and is higher among the youth, per capita gross domestic product is $350 a year, few industries exist apart from coffee and the birthrate is 7.8 per woman, among the world's highest. Half the population still has no access to safe drinking water. Revenue from oil and gas in the Timor Sea has yet to fill government coffers.

And insecurity remains, especially in the major cities where there is a potent mix of unemployment, hopelessness, youth bulge and gang culture. Almost twice as many people have been killed in Dili in the September 2006 to February 2007 period than were killed during the course of the violence that marked the April to May 2006 crisis. The vast majority of those killed are young men. The formal system remains inadequate. There are three func-tioning courts and one ramshackle prison.

Encouraged to do so by the Timorese government, the UN made plans for a long-term operation to rebuild what had been regarded as a peacekeeping success. This will be a second test of the ability of UN peace operations to effectively build state institutions. The UN arrived better prepared this time, as the UN system was less integrated to handle complex peacekeeping in 1999. With UNMIT there has been a greater lead-in time and rigorous planning. Many of the senior personnel in the mission have prior experience in Timor-Leste.

### Police reform redux

As the UN assessment team discovered, the PNTL was without legal frame-works, mechanisms for control and well-functioning managerial systems. The force was politicized: a large number of former Indonesian police officers were recruited into the PNTL and placed in leadership positions. This contributed to growing mistrust of the PNTL among some sectors of Timorese society.

It also raised implicit questions about whether the 'executive policing and simultaneous democratic police-building' model can ever work. Police reform is a complex and difficult task in many peace operations. It requires overcoming profound political, cultural and logistical obstacles. It also demands the condensing of skills into short periods. Much turns on the manner in which policing is organized. It remains difficult for peace operations to find officers of sufficient quality, in sufficient quantity and in a timely manner, and fuse those individuals into coherent and well managed unit. Smith's characterization of the United Nations police as an endemic *ad hocracy* remains apt (Smith 2003).

The intentions are very well but are there enough individuals with these skill sets and moreover, if there are, can UNMIT recruit them in sufficient numbers? In both cases the answer is a broad 'no'. Despite the increasing attention devoted to police reform in discourse and recognition that many tasks in a police organization do not need to be carried out by sworn police officers, UN police remain almost exclusively made up of uniforms. The personnel system is also at fault. Defective thinking-through of what the mandated task would require was reflected in the posting of job descriptions that did not match individuals sought with actual task. This leaves the police reform process in a deeply injurious position from the outset.[12]

Often, the mission has little choice on who arrives and their aptitude and capability to take on the task assigned. Moreover, the manner in which reform is being approached carries uncomfortable echoes of the old style that proved so tragically ineffective.

## Mission tasks

The centrepiece of the UNMIIT police reform programme is known as the 'triple R' plan, mission shorthand for its three main aims of the reform process: reform, restructuring and rebuilding.

Built around the three main police functions of governance, administration and operations, the plan aims to develop the operational and administrative capacities of the PNTL; strengthen its operational independence, internal accountability structures and procedures, and external oversight mechanisms and structures; build an effective, independent and transparent internal disciplinary system; and establish effective institutional means for coordination between the PNTL and the defence sector.

The plan also intends to complement and support the phased approach of the UNMIT support to the PNTL in the restoration and maintenance of public security. The phased approach consists of the initial phase, which is characterized by the United Nations Police (UNPOL) having the primary responsibility in the conduct of police operations; the consolidation phase, which is characterized by the progressive handover of the responsibility for the conduct of police operations within districts or by units to the PNTL; and the full reconstitution phase, which is characterized by the final handover to the PNTL of the responsibility for the conduct and the command and control of all police operations in Timor-Leste. According to an early (rather immodest) draft of the plan 'the knowledge, skills and the professional attitude of the UNPOL officers are shared, imparted, and transferred to the PNTL officers giving them the privilege of developing their individual and group skills'.

In some respects this looks worryingly like previous faulted efforts: a plan developed in haste and in a harum-scarum implementation with a range of officers collectively picking up from the previous incumbents and, almost like a magpie, picking elements from reform processes that he or she knows about, or has access to. One observer attributed the different typefaces in early drafts of the document as illustrative of the multiple source texts it was drawn from. It also bears the mark of many 'commentators'. As each supervisor rotates in and out, they seek to put their own imprimatur on the document, reflecting their suggested interpretation of what the document should look like. As a result, the original 100-page draft now runs to over 500 pages.

This old familiar way of doing business was clear from the outset. Although the UN admitted itself that early plans were deficient because of rushed assessments, the assessment of the PNTL was (again) swift. An extensive, in-depth analysis of at least 45 distinct areas of policing was meant to take place in just 90 days, mostly by officers that themselves had little linguistic or contextual familiarity with the institution.

Given the comprehensive scale of the review, ninety days was insufficient to fulfil its tasks in anything other than a cursory way. Most of the raft of issues identified as worthy of examination are dealt with in a just a few paragraphs each.[13]

The assessment of the PNTL, completed in January 2007, was based upon the information collected pertinent to the organizational, administrative, managerial, logistical, budgetary and financial levels, the PNTL's internal accountability mechanisms, its external oversight and support structure, its human-resources management systems and procedures, its internal discipline system and its institutional arrangements for coordination with the defence sector.

Two structural problems remain. The first is that the UN's own way of doing business sounds worryingly like the problems identified in the assessment of the PNTL. Take for example, the assessment of PNTL's strategic planning capacity and institutional knowledge. 'These documents are not apparent in the offices. Access by staff in the Districts to these materials is generally poor. Manuals are badly maintained, not updated and in many cases missing. Manuals being used relate to previous missions'.[14] This injunction could apply to UNMIT itself. In an internal staff seminar, incoming UN police grumbled that there were few historical 'base' documents that they could access to familiarize themselves with previous UNMIT work, never mind the activity of previous missions.[15] Those that are there were found through internet searches like Google.

The second is that this 'old way of doing business' frustrates governments and influential donors. Previous plans under the transitional administration took place amidst the context of a transitional administration or a situation after independence in which the UN had reserved powers for security. Under UNMIT, their interlocutors are a young government understandably anxious to assert their sovereignty. The reform plan has taken little cognizance of this. Timorese complain, understandably, that 'plans are being devised up in Obrigado [UN HQ] without ministries knowing about it'. The Australians – the lead donor in Timor-Leste – complain of being cut out, despite their investment of time and effort. In part this complaint is understandable but it may also see a conspiracy theory when in fact there is none. It is simply characteristic of poor organization.

These are compounded by two operational issues. No matter how good the plan, two elements are required to implement it: trained staff and trusted officers. In both, UNMIT are lacking. The question now is whether the 'blue berets' will be any better at creating an effective police institution than their predecessors were during the transitional administration. The UN police do not provide their officers – who are often in country that they are not linguistically or culturally familiar with – with training about how to transfer knowledge. Despite the prominence given to the goal of capacity building, how one actually goes about transferring learning and experience remains thinly understood. Incoming officers receive little guidance to assist, leaving them to default back to learning – good and bad – gleaned from their home countries. The multiple ways of doing a traffic stop syndrome is alive and well again.

Their assignment is made doubly challenging because the PNTL seems stubbornly resistant to reform. According to a trusted human rights monitor 'many PNTL members do not report for their training courses or not turn up for duty at the designated place'.[16] Public trust in the PNTL remains low. And insecurity remains, especially in the major cities where there is a flammable mix of unemployment, hopelessness, youth bulge and gang culture. Most of the internally replaced remain in camps owing to personal fears of returning home.

Moreover, the UN's policing reform process only goes so far. Although the commission of inquiry identified *institutional* failings in the PNTL, the mandate is interpreted to deal only with *individual officers*. Thus, reform is necessarily an incomplete process as areas such as recruitment, training, promotion and command are beyond UNPOL's remit.

## *Informal policing*

The reach of the PNTL is also limited beyond the capital, Dili, and major conurbations. Six years after independence, the majority of everyday disputes in the country are still dealt with largely by informal means rather than through an under-resourced formal justice system. (There are just three functioning courts in the entire country.) In Timor allegiances to non-formal mechanisms for conflict resolution and restorative justice are stronger than fealty to the state. There are good reasons for this effectiveness. For the 80 per cent of the population who live in rural areas, accessing the nearest police post, magistrate, or even telephone might involve a lengthy and difficult journey. In any case, reliance on a formal police force may not be financially feasible, especially when funding ends and foreign personnel are withdrawn.

Despite this evident discrepancy in attention showered on a state police when most 'policing' goes on in a more subterranean fashion, the non-state sector is largely ignored by police reformers. The formal sector is privileged on almost every occasion.

Aside from the cost of such a venture and its financial sustainability, the UNMIT paid too little attention to the credibility, durability, legitimacy and salience of non-state spheres in Timor-Leste where 'policing' is already being conducted.

Like in other 'weak' and never-built states power and authority is exercised through informal structures and mechanisms that vary in their shape and organization, and which occupy a more central and accepted role over the lives of individuals. Trying to assert the formal authority in a state police service rubs against ingrained allegiances to mechanisms for conflict resolution and restorative justice that are specific to individual villages and regions and which involve a dynamic mix of rituals, taboos, protocols and social relationships (Mearns 2002).

While it is vital in state-building to strengthen the state's formal legal mechanisms, and while some of the worst offences should be dealt with through proper administration of the formal justice system, these efforts will only be successful if they acknowledge, and work with, far more established informal mechanisms aimed at restorative justice and dispute resolution. The formal is privileged because no one in UNMIT stays long enough to understand the informal. The experience evinces the difficulties of trying to create a new model with an ever-changing roster of staff. An officer's time in theatre is relatively short – mostly under a year – and many officers will rotate through at least two to three posts when they are there.

Understanding such a layered and ever-moving process is much more difficult than devising a means of reconstructing the institutions of a formal service. A detailed and nuanced understanding of the local culture, history and norms is difficult enough for anthropologists, let alone foreign police officers schooled in an entirely different background, and with little prior exposure to local languages and processes and little time to gain familiarity with them. In trying to re-assert the formal system of policing, UNMIT has adopted large-scale cognitive dissonance as to the extensive and central role that these non-state or sub-national actors play in Timor-Leste.

The same privileging of the formal can also be seen with other institutions of criminal justice. Courts and correctional institutions are emphasized, but customary methods of reconciliation, justice and community punishment tend to be ignored. Although the possibility of some hybrid third culture of policing and criminal justice that blends and meshes the formal and informal is increasingly raised in the academic/policy literature on policing, little percolates into mission planning (Baker 2006; Baker and Seheye 2007).

## The weak reach of Timor-Leste government and police institutions

Beyond Dili and some of the larger conurbations, the imprint of the state is faint. Despite Timor-Leste being of small size, communications beyond the capital is not easy and information frequently gets either mis-communicated or not communicated at all. Moreover, the administrative architecture to enact policy is simply not present. District administrative offices – the main arm of the state – have very little accoutrements.

This observation holds true for the police also. Although the police are present in the largish towns, their ability to do the job is hobbled by insufficient resources. Much of what equipment there is – donated during the transitional administration – shows signs of wear and tear. For example, in the district of Oecussi – about the size of Manhattan – there is just one functioning patrol car. Although it is by now almost a reflex to note that international statebuilding can bequeath institutions of shaky financial sustenance, the absence of basic sustainment is stark.

The same goes for the police governance architecture. Although a number of structures have been set up to provide both horizontal and vertical accountability, their upkeep is too much for the young state to afford. But another reason is the simple modalities of a small office (of uncertain capacity) dealing with various large issues without the human capital to animate them. Moreover, fulfilling the bureaucratic requirements required to help manage the various programmes proffered by international donors and humanitarian organizations also slows down the office considerably.

Another difficulty in instantiating the frequently advertised necessities of democratic policing is the smallness of the state itself, and the smallness of the political elite in particular. Jobs in Dili are a revolving door with figures involved in oversight and think tanks moving into parliament. Moreover, in a small country with strong regional and family ties, it is difficult to create information barriers within institutions to structures to separate and isolate the people who make accountability and oversight decisions from those who are the subject of those decisions. For example, the former defence minister used to share a house with the armed forces chief. The current secretary of state for defence is the nephew of the armed forces chief.

The pragmatic reality of politics and 'moving on' in a small place can also conflict with 'good practice' principles. The fall-out from the events of 2006 as they relate to the PNTL are a case in point. Although many senior ranking politicians and officials were censured in the The Independent Special

Commission of Inquiry for Timor-Leste into the events that occurred in April and May, the ramifications are slight for many. Only the former Minister of Interior has been jailed for his involvement.[17]

## Conclusion

The goal of reforming policing systems in transitional, conflict-torn and failed states has become a major focus of donor assistance projects, for without effective, efficient, equitable and accountable policing, wider social, economic and political development is not likely to be sustained. Although a large reform literature, written by members of a global police policy community, has been generated, few long-range improvements can be pointed out. In the case of Timor, previously identified poor practice risks are being replicated one more time.

This observation does not in any way denigrate those working on reform nor diminish their commitment. All have strong backgrounds in operations and implementation. And all generalized statements by their nature leaven out the nuances of the situation, and present the situation in starker terms than is the case. However, it is clear that the current model of police rebuilding needs re-thinking in terms of its contextual appropriateness and actual feasibility. In countries like Timor-Leste, geography, resources and contextual realities will conspire to restrict the reach of the police. Synonymizing the 'police' with 'policing' is not a tenable approach. The do-over may not work.

## Notes

1 The author would like to thank Jim Della-Giacoma for extremely helpful comments on an earlier draft. The opinions are the author's own.
2 Kofi Annan went on to say, 'Would it have made a difference if the U.N. had stayed longer, if we had not drawn down our forces too quickly? This is something that I must assess' (Paddock, 2006).
3 This is a challenge not just for the United Nations but for other bilateral donors, most particularly Australia, which has invested heavily in the police reform process. Australia is one of the largest police contributing countries to the UN missions as well as significant bilateral programming. Since 2004 – in an initiative developed in response to a perceived failure of UN police building – the Australian development agency, AusAid, has funded extensive reforms in the policing and justice sector. To some extent, the Australians' task should be easier. Officers and consultants share the same common language and, broadly, policing style. Yet, difficulties remain.
4 Interview, Dili, 2 October 2007.
5 When the UNMIT mission was designed in mid 2006, there was a tension between members of the assessment team. They were divided on whether UNMIT should be a 'boutique' policing operation, with a relatively small number of dedicated expert staff, or a larger mission with officers drawn from the larger UN national-based recruitment pool. The Civilian police division, which advocated the second approach, won out. The comparative failure of UNPOL in

Timor-Leste is frequently used in headquarters discussions as an argument against further large-scale police missions elsewhere.

6  Interview, Dili, August 2007.

7  The independence of the self-proclaimed Democratic Republic of Timor-Leste was recognized only by the former Portuguese colonies of Angola, Cape Verde, Guinea-Bissau, Mozambique and Sao Tome e Principe.

8  Interview with international police officer who served in Timor 1999–2000. Belfast, 2 December 2006

9  Walkingshaw Interview.

10  Writing in 2004, Rees argued that that 'Timor-Leste's defence policy is devoid of any calculations that cross-reference the capabilities of the defence forces with the commitment of the government' (Rees: 18).

11  Independent Special Commission of Enquiry for Timor-Leste 'Report of the United Nations Independent Special Commission of Enquiry on Timor Leste' Paragraphs 77–85.

12  Deficiencies in the hiring mechanisms of UN peacekeeping are often aired in internal UN reviews, called 'after-action reports'. Often these criticisms are so caustic that they very rarely wend their way into official UN documents on hiring (Smith, 2003).

13  To give some indication of the task, among the headline issues that were included in the terms of reference for the assessment were: PNTL Vision, Mission, Values and Goals; Government Reporting Requirements; Structure and Lines of Reporting; Strategic, Medium and Short Term Planning Capabilities; Policing Philosophy; Internal Control Practice and Procedures; Administrative Policies Including Media; Standardization Templates; Service Provision and Performance; Measuring and Reporting Organizational Performance; Strategic Planning, Performance Measures and Success Indicators; Public Trust and Confidence; The Operating Environment and Police Response; Disciplinary Policy and the Internal Investigations Process; Coordination and Support for Judiciary and Pro-secutions, Managing; Relationships and Partnerships; Legal Barriers and Changes; PNTL Support and Coordination with Prisons and Penal Authorities; Prison Facilities and Human Rights. Operational issues included: Styles, Strengths and Weaknesses of PNTL Leadership and Management; The Human Resources Man-agement; Strategic Human Resources Practices; Adequacy of Staffing Levels; PNTL Rank System; Delegation, Decision Making and Decentralization Prac-tices; Background/Recruitment; Individual Performance Management; Promo-tion Process; Other Human Resource Policies; National Command of the PNTL; District Command; PNTL Business Unit Management; Support Structures for Logistical Support; Police Uniforms & Equipment Issue; General Equipment, Computers and Radio Communications; Transport, Fuel, Vehicles and their Maintenance; Logistics Budgets; Records, Crime Statistics and File Manage-ment; Asset Replacement and Building Maintenance Capabilities; Facilities and Infrastructure; Financial Control; Financial Practice; National PNTL Budget; District/Unit Financial Control, Delegations and Budgeting; Applicable Laws for PNTL Knowledge; Understanding of the National Laws of Timor Leste Rela-tive to Policing; Law Review and Reform. Under Training, the following were considered: Training Structure; Level of Education; Certification and Competen-cies of Trainers; Training Manuals, Training Aids, Equipment; Bilateral Training Opportunities.

14  RRR plan, p. 24.

15  I asked UNPOL in Dili and New York whether there was a central repository of information that I could draw upon for this chapter. There was not.

16  'Screening PNTL Back Into Service' *The La'o Hamutuk Bulletin* June 2007, p 5.

17  Rogerio Lobato was allowed to leave Timor-Leste in August 2007 in order to seek medical treatment in Malaysia.

## Bibliography

Baker, Bruce (2006) 'The African post-conflict policing agenda in Sierra Leone', *Conflict, Security & Development*, 6 (1): 25–50.

Baker, Bruce and Eric Scheye (2007) 'Multi-Layered Security and Justice Delivery in Fragile and Post-Conflict Environments' *Conflict, Security and Development* 7(4): 503–528.

Bayley, David 'Democratizing the Police Abroad: What to Do and How to Do It' Washington DC, National Institute of Justice 2001.

Bowes, Edith and Tanja Hohe (2008) 'East Timor' in Chuck Call and Vanessa Hawkins Wyeth (eds.) *Building States to Build Peace* Boulder, CO: Lynne Reiner.

Chopra, Jarat (2000) 'The UN's Kingdom of East Timor' *Survival* 42(3): 27–40.

Comissão de Acolhimento, Verdade e Reconciliação (CAVR) (Commission for Reception, Truth and Reconciliation) (2004)

Forman, Shepard (1980) 'Descent, Alliance and Exchange Ideology among the Makassae of East Timor' in Jim Fox (ed.) *Flow of Life Essays on Eastern Indonesia* Cambridge: Harvard University Press.

Forman, Shepard (2007) 'The Failings of Security Sector Reform in Timor-Leste' in Center for International Co-operation *Annual Review of Global Peace Operations 2007* Boulder: Lynne Reiner.

Fox, James and Dionisio Babo Soares (2001) *East Timor: Out of the Ashes: The Destruction and Reconstruction of an Emerging State* London: Hurst & Co.

Fraenkel, Jon (2004) 'The Coming Anarchy in Oceania? A Critique of the "Africanisation of the South Pacific" Thesis' *Journal of Commonwealth & Comparative Politics* 42(1): 1–34.

Goldsmith, Andrew and Sinclair Dinnen (2007) 'Transnational Police Building: Critical Lessons from Timor-Leste and Solomon Islands' *Third World Quarterly* 28(6): 1091–1109.

Greene, Owen *et al.* (2004) *International Post-Conflict Policing: enhancing co-ordination and effectiveness*, Conference Report, Wilton Park.

Hansen, Annika S. (2002) *From Congo to Kosovo: International Police in Peace Operations* Oxford: Oxford University Press.

Hicks, David (1988) *Tetum Ghosts and Kin* Illinois: Waveland Press.

Hohe, Tanja and Rod Nixon (2003) 'Reconciling Justice: 'Traditional' Law and State Judiciary in Timor-Leste' Washington, DC: United States Institute of Peace.

Hood, Ludovic (2007) 'Missed Opportunities: The United Nations, Police Service and Defence Force Development in Timor-Leste, 1999–2004' in Gordon Peake, Eric Scheye and Alice Hills (eds.) *Managing Insecurity: Field Experience of Security Sector Reform* London: Taylor and Francis.

International Crisis Group (2006) 'Resolving Timor-Leste's Crisis' *Asia Report* No.120, 10 October.

Jones, Seth, Jeremy M Wilson, Andrew Rathmell, and K. Jack Riley (2005) *Establishing Law and Order After Conflict*, Pittsburgh, RAND Corporation.

Judicial System Monitoring Programme (2002) 'Findings and Recommendations: Workshop on Formal and Local Justice Systems in East Timor' Dili, East Timor, accessed at http://www.jsmp.minihub.org.

King's College London (2002) *A Review of Peace Operations: A Case for Change* London: King's College.

Linton, Suzannah (2001) 'Rising from the Ashes: The Creation of a Viable Criminal System in East Timor' *Melbourne University Law Review* 25(1): 122–180.

McCarthy, John (2002) 'FALANTIL Reinsertion Assistance Programme: Final Evaluation Report' Dili: International Organization for Migration.

Marenin, Otwin (2005) 'Reconstructing Policing Systems in Conflict-Torn Societies: Policies, Practices and Lessons Learned' *International Journal of Comparative Criminology* Geneva: Democratic Control of Armed Forces (DCAF).

Martin, Ian (2001) *Self-Determination in East Timor: The United Nations, the Ballot, and International Intervention* Boulder: Lynne Reiner.

Mearns, David (2002) 'Looking Both Ways: Models for Justice in East Timor', Canberra: Australian Legal Resources International.

Mydans, Seth (2007) 'A Babel for East Timor as Language Shifts to Portuguese' *International Herald Tribune*, 23 July.

Neild, Rachel (2001) 'Democratic Police Reforms in War-Torn Societies', *Conflict, Security, and Development* 1(1): 21–42.

Ospina Sofi and Tanja Hohe (2001) *Traditional Power Structures and the Community Empowerment and Local Governance Project (CEP) in East Timor.* Final Report, prepared for the World Bank/United Nations Transitional Administration in East Timor (UNTAET), Dili.

Paddock, Richard C. (2006) 'Bloodied East Timorese Hope the UN will Return' *Los Angeles Times*, 5 June.

Peake, Gordon (2008) 'Timor-Leste: A Challenge to the DDR Paradigm' in Robert Muggah (eds.) *Securing Protections: Assessing the Effectiveness of Disarmament, Demobilization and Reintegration in Post-Conflict Contexts* New York: Routledge.

Pinto, Julio (2002) *A More Secure Future: A Focus Group on Citizen Security in Timor-Leste* Dili: National Democratic Institute.

Rees, Edward (2004) 'Under Pressure: FALINTIL Forcas de Armadas de Timor-Leste–Three Decades of Defence Development in Timor-Leste' Geneva: Democratic Control of Armed Forces (DCAF).

Smith, Dennis (2003) 'Managing CIVPOL: The Potential of Performance Management in International Public Service' in D. Dijkzeul and Y. Beigbeder (eds.) *Rethinking International Organizations: Pathologies and Promise* London: Berghahn Books.

Traube, Elisabeth (1986) *Cosmology and Social Life: Ritual Exchange among the Mambai of East Timor* Chicago: University of Chicago Press.

United Nations, Report of the United Nations Independent Special Commission of Inquiry for Timor-Leste, Geneva 2006.

United Nations (2007) Report of the Security Council mission to Timor-Leste, 24 to 30 November 2007.

Walsh, Pat (1999) *From Opposition to Proposition: The National Council of Timorese Resistance in Transition* Canberra: Australian Council of Overseas Aid.

West, Ron (2007) 'Lawyers, Guns and Money: Justice and Security Reform in East Timor' in Charles T. Call (ed.) *Constructing Security and Justice After War* Washington, DC: United States Institute of Peace (USIP) Press.

Zartman, I. William (1991) 'Conflict and Resolution: Contest, Cost, and Change' *The ANNALS of the American Academy of Political and Social Science*, Vol. 518, No. 1, 11–22.

# Part III
# South America

# 8   Venezuela

## Policing as an exercise in authority

*Christopher Birkbeck and Luis Gerardo Gabaldón*

## Introduction

At approximately 10.30 p.m. on the evening of Monday 27 June 2005, six students (three men and three women) left the campus of a private university in Caracas to go home after taking an evening exam. Crammed into a small car, they began to traverse the city as the driver dropped off his friends at their homes. Their first destination was Caricuao, a lower-middle class neighbour-hood where two of the women lived. As they drove through the relatively deserted streets, they came upon a group of armed men and were told to stop. Apparently fearing that they were about to be robbed, the driver kept going and – aware of it or not – ran through a mobile checkpoint. Shots were fired at the vehicle, which finally came to a halt. The driver was killed in the car, while the other two men were killed (apparently execution-style) on the street. Each woman received one or more serious bullet wounds, but all survived. The group that was involved in the shooting was found to comprise 21 officers from military intelligence, four from the judicial investigation agency and one from the Caracas police. They were apparently looking for someone who had recently killed a police officer.

On 27 March 2006 a prosperous businessman in the city of Maracay, one hour west of Caracas, was kidnapped at a mobile checkpoint by individuals wearing police uniforms. Two days later his body was found in a neighbouring state. A former member of the National Guard (who later died in a shootout with judicial police) and two members of state police forces were implicated in this crime, along with several civilians. They had apparently been planning to 'sell' the kidnap victim to guerrilla groups in Colombia, but something obviously went wrong.

Just over a week later, on 4 April 2006, the bodies of three young boys from a wealthy Caracas family (together with their chauffeur) were found in undergrowth about an hour's drive from the city. They had been kidnapped at around 6.00 a.m. on the morning of 23 February 2006 when, on their way to school, they had been stopped at a mobile checkpoint manned by offi-cers from the Caracas Metropolitan Police. Active and retired officers from the Metropolitan Police together with members of the underworld were implicated in this high profile case, in which the kidnappers demanded ten billion *bolívares* (about 4.6 million US dollars) as a ransom. Numerous social groups and individuals had called for the release of the children, but to no avail.

The deaths of the three boys, aged 17, 14 and 12, caused a national outrage. Linked with the two previous cases, which had also received a great deal of media coverage, the general sentiment was that something was seriously wrong with the country's police forces. Democratic regimes are supposed to provide safety and security for their citizens, not kill them. Under strong pressure to do something, only a day after the boys' bodies had been found the government announced the creation of a National Commission for Police Reform (*El Universal* 16 April 2006). The Commission was composed of representatives from government, the universities and human rights organisations and was charged with producing a strategy for police reform by the end of the year. Funds were made available for the largest data collection exercise ever undertaken on the Venezuelan police and an extensive process of consultation with police officers and citizens was also undertaken (Gabaldón and Antillano 2007). There were high hopes that significant improvements in policing would result.

But the circumstances in which the commission had originated and the way in which its mission and objectives were framed meant that the chances of making meaningful changes were limited. To begin with, the incidents which led to the creation of the commission all involved middle- or upper-class citizens, but most victims of police use of force are drawn from the lower class. Thus, although the outrage seemed to be directed at police crime and violence, it was probably more strongly anchored in the feeling that such violence had transgressed class boundaries. There was therefore a very real possibility that if the officers involved in these crimes were punished, as some were, a sense of symbolic order would have been restored and the work of the Commission would lose its urgency and relevance.

In addition, it soon became obvious that the Commission's focus was, by accident or design, somewhat narrow. Data collection was most complete for the state and municipal police forces but much less so for the national policing agencies, some of which largely escaped attention. Indeed, it is interesting to note that some organisations, such as the judicial investigation branch and military intelligence, do not have the word 'police' in their names although they engage in activities that are typically considered as policing. Clearly some major definitional battles (who are 'the police'?; what is 'policing'?) needed to have been fought in order to bring national policing fully under review. Finally, the short time span allotted to the Commission for its work, combined with political uncertainties regarding the future of the country, represented a challenge for a long-term vision of the nature and problems of policing and the prospects for change.

The foregoing narrative conveys something of the magnitude of the problems affecting policing in Venezuela and of the difficulties in achieving meaningful change. In addition, it implies that a review of the democratically relevant dimensions of policing needs to include topics that were not directly considered as part of the reform agenda, such as the moral perceptions of crime and insecurity and the challenges of policing in an environment characterised by marked social inequality. Thus, we will leave the results of the Reform Commission until the conclusion to this chapter, although we will make considerable use of the data it collected.

Our focus will be on the problems with Venezuelan policing that are thrown into particular relief when seen through the lens of democratic principles. We identify and describe three such problems (inefficiency, corruption and punitive practices), seeking the institutional or cultural roots of each and examining any developments that have a bearing on their possible solution. Our analysis is prefaced by a description of the country and its police personnel, together with some brief considerations about Venezuelan policing as an exercise in authority. If democratic policing is primarily understood as a *service* to the *universal citizen*, based on a commitment to *human rights*, this authoritarian tradition is at odds with it on many counts. In the conclusion, we examine the results of the National Commission for Police Reform and assess the needs and prospects for positive change in the future.

## Background information

Venezuela is a country of 27.5 million inhabitants (INE 2007) that stretches from the Amazonian basin and Guiana Highlands in the south, across the Orinoco basin and the Andean or coastal mountain ranges to the Caribbean in the north. It attained formal independence from Spain in 1821, and was ruled mainly by autocrats until 1958 when democratic movements ousted Marcos Pérez Jiménez. For the next 40 years, two parties held an eventually declining dominance in national politics and were routed in the presidential election of 1998 when the leader of a failed 1992 military coup – Hugo Chávez – was swept into power with a huge margin of popular support. Chávez engineered a new constitution in 1999 and was re-elected in 2000 and 2006. Always a left-leaning politician, and a consummate media figure and political populist, Chávez has recently declared his intention of creating a 'Twenty-First Century Socialist Regime' in Venezuela. Much of his inspiration and the strategic support for this initiative appear to come from Cuba.[1]

Since the early twentieth century, the Venezuelan economy has been dominated by oil. Venezuela is the ninth largest oil producer in the world, and the fifth largest exporter (EIA 2007); oil accounts for about 30 per cent of the GDP, 50 per cent of government income (CIA 2007) and 85 per cent of the country's export earnings (ECLAC 2007). Following an unprecedented period of prosperity in the 1960s and 1970s, the economy went into sharp decline in the 1980s, with rising levels of poverty and inequality. However, the resurgence of oil prices during the first years of the new millennium, coupled with more social spending by the government, has done something to reverse this situation (Crespo 2006, WIDER 2007). Currently, Venezuela's gross domestic product (GDP) is slightly above the average for Latin American countries, but only about one seventh of the GDP of the wealthiest countries in the world (World Bank 2007). The prosperity of the 1960s and 1970s has never returned. Not only is the official unemployment rate quite high – 16.8 per cent in 2006 (World Bank 2007) – but about half of employed people are working in the informal sector (characterised by low wages, instability and a lack of welfare benefits) (INE 2006). Thus, despite the relatively abundant oil income, poverty is widespread: one third of the population is classified as poor (household income does not cover basic expenditures) and one tenth lives in 'extreme poverty' (income does not cover the cost of food) (INE 2006).

Over the last 20 years, reported crime rates have been broadly stable, with notable exceptions for certain kinds of violent crime (Gabaldón and Antillano 2007, Crespo 2006). During the 1990s, murder rates doubled from 13 to 25 per 100,000 inhabitants and then nearly doubled again to 44/100,000 by 2003, decreasing to 37/100,000 by 2005 (PROVEA 2006). These already high figures do not include deaths caused by *resistencia a la autoridad* (resisting authority, i.e., the police), which were equivalent to 5/100,000 in 2005 (and to which we return later in this chapter), or 'deaths being investigated' (16/100,000). Since 2000, kidnappings have also increased rapidly from 67 to 206. Not surprisingly, crime has recently become a significant cause of concern to citizens: according to an ongoing national opinion survey, by April 2006 personal insecurity was most frequently cited as the country's principal problem, overtaking unemployment which had previously held first place (PROVEA 2006). Part of this concern was fuelled by high profile murder cases in which the police were implicated, such as those described at the beginning of this chapter.

## The organisation of policing

If policing is understood as the defence of public order and the apprehension of wrongdoers by paid personnel, then there is a plethora of organisations and individuals engaged in that activity in Venezuela, some of which are called the police, but most of which are not. Some of them mainly undertake policing, but many are involved in other activities as well. Key divisions exist between public and private sector policing, and within the former, between different levels of government.

Historically, the organisation of public policing has been strongly linked to political developments, as governments have attempted to create or refashion police agencies to suit their own needs and the exigencies of the moment (Agudo Freites 1973, Birkbeck 1982). Currently, central government has a National Guard (*Guardia Nacional*), which dates from 1937 and is attached to the Ministry of Defence. Its 32,800 officers (Antillano 2007) are deployed throughout the country and are assigned to a variety of tasks: routine patrol work, public order, checkpoints, perimeter security for prisons, port security and environmental policing. Ranks, operational policies and organ-isational ethos are distinctly military. Central government also funds the Scientific, Penal and Forensic Investigation Corps (*Cuerpo de Investigaciones Científicas, Penales y Criminalísticas*, or CICPC), which can be traced back to 1958 and is charged with the primary responsibility for investigating crimes and preparing evidence for prosecution. Often called the 'judicial police', the CICPC is administratively attached to the Ministry of the Interior and Justice, but is functionally dependent on the Public Prosecutor's Office. Like the National Guard, its 8,200 officers (Antillano 2007) are deployed throughout the country.

Another central governmental police force is the Directorate of Intelligence and Prevention Services (*Dirección de Servicios de Inteligencia y Prevención*, or DISIP), which is attached to the Ministry of the Interior and Justice and can be traced back to 1969. The DISIP is primarily concerned with national security (crimes against the state) but also occasionally involves itself in the investigation of kidnappings or drug trafficking. It is so secretive that no published figures are available on its size, and little information is available about any other aspect of its activities. Somewhat similar is the Directorate of Military Intelligence (*Dirección de Inteligencia Militar*, or DIM), which is part of the armed forces. Although it deals mainly with crimes by or against the armed forces, it occasionally involves itself in special operations. More gener-ally, army personnel are often deployed in cases of serious urban disorder. Finally, 5,800 officers make up the Technical Corps for the Surveillance of Terrestrial Transit and Transport (*Cuerpo Técnico de Vigilancia del Tránsito y Transporte Terrestre*) (Antillano 2007). Apart from the general supervision of traffic and the investigation of accidents, they are responsible for surveillance, preliminary investigation and the occasional arrest of suspects in traffic offences that involve violations of the criminal law.[2]

Outside central government, each of the country's 23 states has a police force, as does the Capital District (centred on Caracas). Officers in these state police agencies, totalling about 58,000 members (Antillano 2007), are largely uniformed and have a variety of functions: public order policing, patrol, arrest of suspects, emergency response and community work. They are administratively attached to the state governor's office and nominally coordinated by the Ministry of the Interior and Justice. Starting in 1989, and following a new law on decentralisation, municipalities began to create their own police forces. There are currently 99 of them with a total of almost 11,000 officers (Antillano 2007). Their functions are generally the same as the state police agencies, although some of them are so small or lacking in infrastructure and resources that they can do little more than carry out specific tasks assigned by the mayor. Indeed, there is a definite impression that some of the municipal forces simply provide assistance (door-keeping, transport, protection, etc.) to the municipal authority.

The creation of municipal police forces has obviously increased the number of public police personnel over the last decade, but the increase has also been fuelled by the expansion of already existing forces. Notably, the number of state police officers has increased by about 50 per cent since 1990 (Antillano 2007; Rico *et al.* 1991). Overall, the expansion in the number of public police officers may only be a partial result of rising crime rates, increased concern about crime and the consequent public demand for greater protection. In their role as commanders of their respective forces, state governors and municipal mayors have usually been successful in controlling recruitment, promotion and many operational activities as part of their broader political and personal strategies (Antillano 2007). Thus, in a real sense these agencies are the patrimony of their political bosses and there has been a natural incentive to increase their size.[3]

Alongside the public police, private security personnel also engage in policing. This sector involves a wide variety of actors, ranging from international security companies, such as Brinks, to small-scale national companies with only a few employees, and the informal arrangements involving *vigilantes* (watchmen) in businesses, residences and neighbourhoods. There are even signs of dubiously legal self-help policing initiatives in some parts of the country. For example, the presence of protection rackets has been detected in western Venezuela, notably in the city of Maracaibo where car owners pay a monthly fee to avoid car theft (or to guarantee the return of a vehicle if stolen) (Parra 2004). It is not clear who runs these organisations or how they operate, but many would probably classify them as organised crime.

The sole study conducted to date on the formal security sector found that in 1997 there were 522 companies registered with the government, with a total of approximately 20,000 employees, although it acknowledged that there were an unknown number of 'pirate' companies (Morais 2006). At the informal level, most upper- and middle-class residential neighbourhoods have one or more watchmen, as do most construction sites and major road works. Along with target hardening, the employment of watchmen has been the commonest citizens' response to the perceived crisis in personal safety; thus, their number is not inconsiderable, although they are generally untrained and often provide little more than the illusion of protection (Romero Salazar *et al.* 2001). There are also some hybrid public–private initiatives in policing, such as the 'Neighbourhood Security Networks' set up by the Caracas Metropolitan Mayor, composed of residents who receive some basic training (including possibly in firearms, see PROVEA 2006), and who would work with the police in controlling neighbourhood disorder and problematic individuals. The cumulative result of all these developments is that the security guard and the watchman are encountered very frequently in daily life and are a standard feature of the social landscape. It seems as if everyone wants to have some kind of force that will provide security at their own bidding. However, because crime and disorder only rarely puncture the normality of daily life, even in 'high crime' areas, most security personnel find themselves doing a lot of other things, or nothing, most of the time (Gabaldón *et al.* 1990).

## Policing as an exercise in authority

Venezuelan academics have often commented on the military character of police agencies (e.g. Antillano 2006); however, this depiction is inexact. Obviously, there are some agencies that are quintessentially military, such as the Army, the National Guard and Military Intelligence. Additionally, other agencies have quasi-military structures and practices. For example, half of the state police forces are 'commanded' by a National Guardsman (Antillano 2007) and most employ a rigid distinction between the officers and the 'troops', as they are often referred to. Some of these agencies even drill their subordinate ranks at the start of the daily shift. However, the judicial police, the traffic police, the municipal police forces and private security agencies do not fit this model. They are neither military nor militarised institutions.

A better starting point for understanding the nature of police and policing in Venezuela can be found in the concept of *resistencia a la autoridad*, referred to earlier, which explicitly equates policing with authority. This notion of policing as an exercise in authority rather than, for example, a service to the public appears to underlie much of what goes on in police agencies (both public and private) and helps us understand many of the challenges to achieving democratic policing.

That the agencies engaged in policing are relatively authoritarian in nature is evident not only in the military and militarised organisations mentioned previously, but also in practices and routines that are much more widespread. For example, in all policing agencies, work is organised through orders (usually verbal) transmitted from higher to lower ranks, and subordinates almost never participate in decision making nor are granted discretion in carrying out their tasks. Authority is concentrated in persons, rather than roles, and bureaucracy is comparatively weakly developed. For example, three-quarters of state and municipal police forces lack a manual prescribing procedures and two-thirds do not have an organisational manual (Antillano 2007). Even in the agencies that have such guidelines, their existence may be irrelevant.[4] The general absence of documents and paperwork (Birkbeck and Gabaldón 2002) emphasises the personalised nature of control in these organisations, where the individual's gaze must be fixed upwards rather than downwards (or outwards). Paradoxically, although subordinates are granted no discretion they are rarely supervised.

Not only the police agencies but policing itself tends to be authoritarian in nature. This is revealed in the imperative tone that characterises many verbal interactions with citizens and in the unwillingness to explain what is going on. That these styles are second nature to policing is reflected in the attention garnered by alternative, service-oriented, modes of address (considered by all concerned to be 'politeness'), such as making requests and providing information. A national victim survey carried out in 2006 revealed that the largest category of respondents (22 per cent) found the police to be have been *prepotente* (overbearing, arrogant) in their most recent encounter with them, 18 per cent felt them to be negligent and 14 per cent found them to be violent.[5] Only 21 per cent felt them to have been professional, attentive or prompt (Gabaldón *et al.* 2007). As these results indicate, the authoritarian style also includes violence which may well reflect the disposition to use punishments when authority is challenged. Informal interviews with police officers reveal that beatings are not an uncommon response when citizens are hostile, disrespectful or recalcitrant (Monsalve 2006). Here we come full circle to the notion of resisting authority.

Authority, however, is not exercised in a social vacuum and the authoritarian style generates friction at all levels, which increases exponentially as one goes up the social scale. The authoritarian culture is not so strongly embedded in Venezuela that citizens will meekly take the role of subordinates in encounters with the police. Thus, there is an inherent tension in every encounter as the possibilities for authoritarian intervention are tested. New recruits, whether it be to the public police, private security companies or the small teams of watchmen in residential neighbourhoods, soon learn that they must be very careful with citizens who outrank them socially because complaints will be made to their superiors who (in a magnificent display of authority!) will sanction them for having acted inappropriately. Thus, the most important question that police personnel consciously or unconsciously ask themselves as they enter a situation is not 'What's going on here?' but 'Who am I dealing with?' (Birkbeck and Gabaldón 1996, Monsalve 2006). The authoritarian style only emerges fully when the police deal with citizens of low social status, because most police officers are themselves drawn from that segment.[6]

## Problems, responses and challenges

### *Inefficiency*

Inefficiency designates low levels of policing activity and is evidenced in several different ways. Paradoxically, while there are a comparatively large number of paid personnel who nominally engage in policing, the amount of active patrol work, and particularly intervention in situations involving crime or disorder, is quite low. One problem is the lack of mobility, evidenced in the 'checkpoint mentality' that pervades much street policing. The National Guard, the state and municipal police, security guards and watchmen spend an inordinate amount of time at locations where flows of vehicles or pedestrians can be monitored, to the comparative disadvantage of areas that are beyond their gaze. For example, data collected from state and municipal police agencies in 2006 reveal that they mounted more than 8,000 checkpoints during the previous week. Search and sweep operations, of which there were 4,270, are closely related activities and are usually carried out in low income neighbourhoods. These figures compare with 38,500 responses to calls from citizens (Antillano 2007). Much National Guard and traffic police work is also focused on checkpoints.

Checkpoints seem to work best only when the search is on for contraband or for known suspects; beyond that, they represent tiny islands of police presence in the far vaster spaces of public life. One factor that may encourage their use is that checkpoints are attractive strategies for the exercise of authority in a highly differentiated social universe. Thus, while symbolically announcing the presence of authority, the checkpoint arguably provides a relatively efficient mechanism for screening individuals and deciding whom to inconvenience. Mere visual cues aided by the occasional non-committal question are usually sufficient to measure the social status of the citizen and the likelihood of subsequent friction. Thus, the checkpoint conveys the *idea* of authority and the *potential* for intervention, but behind their usual laconic pose officers are always assessing the prospects for a successful exercise of their authority. Together with search and sweep operations, checkpoints raise important questions about the proper boundary between the public gaze and the right to privacy; in other words, about the extent to which a democracy should subject its citizens to routine surveillance and to the possibility of searches and identity checks. To date, this question has hardly been debated in Venezuela.

In some cases, the lack of resources contributes to the immobility of police personnel, as evidenced by the small municipal forces that may be without vehicles, but also in some more striking ways: in one state police force, officers are unwilling to go out on patrol unless they can locate a pair of handcuffs, because the latter are in extremely short supply within the agency (Birkbeck *et al.* 2005); in another, officers must get to work early to beat their colleagues to the available firearms (Monsalve 2006). Another impediment to routine patrol work and proactive policing springs from the organisational strategies used by the agency. For example, the recent study of state and municipal police forces found that, overall, 35 per cent of the officers were assigned to miscellaneous duties such as security for buildings, administrative tasks at HQ, official escort and so on. A further 7 per cent was assigned to special units, such as school patrol or the K-9 squad, while some agencies kept up to 10 per cent of officers in special 'emergency response groups'. Just over half of all officers (51 per cent) were assigned to patrol work (Antillano 2007).

In relation to crime reporting and criminal case investigation, the results from the recent national victim survey indicate that only 30 per cent of incidents were reported to the police. This figure may not be low compared to reporting rates elsewhere (UN 1999); however, the main reasons given for not reporting are quite striking: 38 per cent of respondents thought that the police would not have done anything about it, followed by 16 per cent who thought that the police would not even register the report (Gabaldón *et al.* 2007). Clearly, there is a considerable departure from the notion of the police as a service for victims of crime, a considerable loss of data on crimes committed, and some serious doubt about the reliability of official statistics on crime rates. The only detailed study of case processing, carried out on the judicial police, found that detectives were subject to rigid monthly quotas for

174 Christopher Birkbeck and Luis Gerardo Gabaldón

completing cases. In order to comply with them, cases were selected because of their ease of completion rather than their seriousness, and were often sent to the court without all the necessary paperwork in the file (Gabaldón *et al.*1996). Within this kind of administrative environment, it is easy to see why victims are often dissuaded or prevented from officially registering a crime. Although data from the CICPC indicate that the proportion of cases cleared has doubled from 41 per cent to 85 per cent since 1999, when the primary investigative responsibility was reallocated to the public prosecutor (PROVEA 2006), it is not clear what the official term *casos resueltos policialmente* (cases solved by the police) means in the context of these new legislative and administrative arrangements.[7]

A longstanding response to the problem of inefficiency has been the recourse to some notion of community. Thus, in the 1970s the judicial police opened neighbourhood offices in 'community service centres' in some of the larger cities (although by the early 1980s the institution had withdrawn to its traditional model of headquarters-based operations). In the 1990s, many state and municipal police forces developed community policing plans. Under one model, officers are deployed to specific neighbourhoods and work with local residents in identifying and responding to problems of crime and disorder. A second model involves the organisation of residents into neighbourhood security committees that are supposed to call in the police when problems arise (Aniyar de Castro 2003). Little is known about how these initiatives have worked, except for one early study of police deployment to residential neighbourhoods in the city of Mérida (Gabaldón *et al.* 1990). There, the researchers found that the officers sent to a high income neighbourhood established little rapport with householders and were timid in their responses to minor crimes and problem behaviours, fearing that the wealthy residents could create many problems for them back at HQ. Low income citizens passing through the neighbourhood were also left alone because the officers guessed that some of them would be working for the residents and therefore would be protected by them from police intervention. Things would have been very different had the police presence been requested by the neighbourhood residents (their deployment was an initiative of the police), but the officers would still have been unable to exercise authority, except against outsiders. They would have been treated as watchmen provided by the public purse. By contrast, in a low income neighbourhood, officers adopted a much more active and assertive stance, calling the residents to meetings, clamping down on neighbourhood nuisances and displacing crime and disorder to private domains or to times when they were not on duty. The police presence also exacerbated rifts within the neighbourhood, as some residents allied with the officers in their attempts to reduce disorder while others actively opposed them. Overall, not only was this an illuminating case study of the social dynamics surrounding authority, but it also revealed the problematic nature of 'community' and the widespread desire among citizens to treat the police as social capital for policing *others*.

Brief mention should also be made of a high profile attempt to improve police efficiency by recourse to a supposedly successful model of policing offered by William Bratton, the former police chief in New York. Bratton, George Kelling and other consultants were invited to Caracas by the then Metropolitan Mayor in September 2000 to discuss how 'zero tolerance' and 'broken windows' policing – the strategies that allegedly reduced crime rates in New York (but see Bowling 1999) – could be implemented in the capital city. Bratton proposed to create a pilot 'precinct' office for the police, a new system for reporting crimes, an anti-drugs unit and a mechanism for coordinating the municipal police forces (*El Universal* 3 March 2001). A second phase of this project was also envisaged, emphasising work with 'the community' (*El Universal* 21 August 2002). However, the intervention of the Metropolitan Police by the national government in November 2002,[8] together with the mayor's decision not to seek re-election in 2004, effectively ended the implementation of this project. No rigorous evaluation was ever made of its results, but the simple contrast between the institutional and social arrangements surrounding policing in New York and Caracas is sufficient to raise many doubts about the prospects for success.

Nevertheless, in seeking to develop a mechanism for coordinating municipal police forces, Bratton had hit on an idea which, with a broader sweep, has a long history in Venezuelan politics. A persistent theme in commentaries on the police concerns the multiplicity of agencies and the need to coordinate them. From this perspective, police inefficiency is considerably augmented by disparate training programmes, overlapping jurisdictions and the absence of legal or administrative mechanisms which might ensure that policing is coordinated in a reasonably rational manner.[9] For example, the Police Reform Commission's recent study found that among state and municipal police forces there is a wide variety of training arrangements. Forty-one agencies have their own permanent training centres, 35 put on courses as required, 37 send recruits to other training centres, while the rest use some combination of these methods (Antillano 2007). Although all training courses share common elements, the variations in content, length and quality undoubtedly lead to great diversity in subsequent styles of policing.

One response to the need for coordination has been to propose the fusion of agencies into a national police force, and legislative initiatives to this effect were mooted in 1974, 1976, 1987, 1990, 2001 and 2004 (Antillano 2007). All of these projects proposed the merger of state and (more recently) municipal forces into one national organisation, and some would have included other agencies with national jurisdiction. That these projects have stalled is undoubtedly explained in large part by the unwillingness of state governors and municipal mayors to relinquish control over 'their' police forces.

A second response to the plurality of agencies has been the attempt to achieve coordination by legislative fiat. For example, in 2001 the government issued a decree for coordinating public safety, which set out some very general guidelines for the resolution of overlapping jurisdictions. Thus, if two or more agencies are involved in a situation, the one with greater operational response capacity at the scene should assume control; or if an agency is unable to deal with a situation, it should call in an agency that has sufficient operational response capacity (Venezuela 2001). No study has been undertaken to determine whether this decree has had any measurable effect on police operations; however, the increasingly partisan political environment, particularly following the failed coup attempt against President Chávez in 2002, has permeated the police and now often pits 'government' and 'opposition' police agencies against each other (Gabaldón 2004, Ungar 2003).

### Corruption

Much anecdotal but little hard evidence is available regarding corruption in Venezuela. As elsewhere, it is a phenomenon that is extraordinarily difficult to measure, not only because of its potential complexity but also because there is little or no incentive for the parties involved to publicise what they have done. Thus, corruption usually emerges on the national scene only when it is used to create media-driven scandals that are designed to taint the reputation of political opponents. In turn, these scandals fuel the perception that corruption is quite widespread (e.g. Coronel 2006). For example, the 2006 Corruption Perceptions Index placed Venezuela in the 138th rank – the worst (along with Ecuador) for Latin American countries (Transparency International 2007).

With regard to the police, 'corruption' can be defined in a number of ways and may shade into other practices that are borderline legal activities. For example, how should we evaluate the use of subordinates to drive senior officers' children to and from school, the deployment of officers to guard particular stores or homes, or the selection of recruits through clientelist networks? Nevertheless, bribes are one activity which is clearly seen as corruption and for which recent and striking, albeit superficial, information exists. The national victim survey in 2006 found that bribes demanded by public officials were the third largest category of crime reported by respondents, affecting about 11 per cent of the population during the previous year. Eighty four percent of the bribery cases reported in the survey involved a member of the 'police or National Guard' (Gabaldón *et al.* 2007). Given the frequency of checkpoint policing, it is likely that much of this bribery was generated by citizens' desires to extricate themselves from identity checks and searches of personal property or merchandise as they went about their routine daily activities. Bribes are also congruent with the exercise of authority because they represent a material recognition of the officer's power to make problems for the citizen. Their acceptance, if engineered correctly, indicates discretion but not weakness. Bribes may frustrate the formal objectives of policing, but they could foster an emphasis on power in the encounter.

Another form of corruption is police involvement in drug trafficking. All sources agree that Venezuela is an important trans-shipment country for drugs, particularly cocaine produced in Colombia (e.g. BINLEA 2007, Carreño 2007, Webb-Vidal 2006); the disagreements arise concerning the amount of effort made by the Venezuelan government to combat this illegal trade and the level of involvement in it among government officials, the military and the police. Nevertheless, *some* involvement by police agencies is evident from isolated cases that come to light within the country, such as the mysterious 'loss' of five kilograms of heroin from CICPC offices in 2006 (*El Universal* 26 May 2006), and the detailed information unearthed by investigative reporting about links between the Venezuelan military (including the National Guard) and Colombian drug trafficking networks (Webb-Vidal 2006).[10] Despite the challenges to measurement, corruption is undoubtedly a problem in Venezuelan policing.[11]

### Punitive practices

The 1990s marked a paradigm shift for many police agencies. They entered the decade with relatively wide powers to detain individuals; they left it with none. Under the Vagrancy Law, enacted in 1939, the police could arrest and hold a broad category of vaguely defined social nuisances, deviants and petty offenders, and state governors had the power to imprison them for up to five years (Hernández 1977). Under the Criminal Procedure Law, dating from 1962, the police could detain most suspects for up to four days before releasing them, and if a reasonable case had been built up the suspect would be retained on preventive detention by the court and transferred to a prison while awaiting trial, often for a year or more (Venezuela 1962). These arrangements led to a large number of 'prisoners without trial' who were held in a prison system that is considered one of the worst in the region (Human Rights Watch 1997). Cumulatively, the Vagrancy Law and the Criminal Procedure Code meant that the police could use arrest as a short-term sanction and they could channel suspects to longer periods of distinctly unpleasant detention with relative ease.

However, the Vagrancy Law was struck down as unconstitutional in 1997. Then, in 1999 a new Criminal Procedure Code came into effect, which took away the police power to detain suspects, leaving them only with the power to arrest (Venezuela 1998). The new paradigm adopted for criminal procedure was the adversarial model which, among other things, shifted the primary responsibility for investigations from the police to the public prosecutor and limited the use of preventive detention to exceptional cases. Currently, apart from judicial arrest warrants executed by the police, suspects can only be arrested if they are 'caught in the act'; and in the latter case the public prosecutor must be informed within 12 hours. In turn, the public prosecutor has only a further 36 hours to put the case to the court for a decision on legal custody, and the guidelines for holding suspects on preventive detention have been made much stricter. As a result, the police cannot now use detention as a short-term sanction and even quite serious offenders are likely to be placed on conditional release pending trial, that is, 'back on the street' as the officers see it. There is no doubt that the police have lost power relative to the public prosecutor and that they have lost power over their traditional 'client population' (Monsalve 2007); in consequence, they have seen a reduction in the space for exercising authority. Ironically, this victory for individual liberty seems likely to have generated far greater levels of police violence as an alternative punitive strategy.

As reported previously, in 2005 civilian deaths through 'resisting authority' were 5/100,000 (a figure, which is higher than the murder rate for some of the world's most peaceful democracies, and represents 1,355 civilians killed). Of course, 'resisting authority' appears to legitimate the use of force by police agencies and would suggest that the population (or certain segments of it) is relatively hostile to them. However, that the balance of force appears to lie heavily on the side of the police, leading to excessive responses in the face of real or fictitious 'resistance', is indicated by the fact that between 2000 and 2005 the overall rate of civilian to police deaths in 'shoot outs' was 30 to 1, and that in 96 per cent of 'shoot outs' civilians were killed rather than merely injured (Antillano 2007). Thus, deaths through 'resisting authority' are a rightful category of concern in Venezuela. Following a relatively stable rate of about 2.5/100,000 (approximately 600 deaths per year) at the end of the 1990s, these cases increased dramatically after 1999 (by 50 per cent alone in 2000) to reach a high of 2,305 in 2003 (9/100,000) (PROVEA 2006). While the CICPC reported a total of 9,724 deaths through 'resisting authority' between 2000 and 2005, the Public Prosecutor found that 6,377 could probably be classified as police murders (61 per cent of them attributable to state police forces, 22 per cent to the CICPC and 13 per cent to municipal forces) (PROVEA 2006).

The timing of the increase in deaths at the hands of the police is what prompts our hypothesis that they may partly have been caused by the loss of police powers to detain citizens under the legislative changes of the 1990s. A second indicator of this type of adaptation can be found in the 'death squads' that have emerged during the new millennium in several parts of the country. Notable was the appearance of an 'Extermination Group' in Portuguesa State in 2000, composed of state police officers operating clandestinely who were estimated to have killed at least 68 victims by 2004. This group enjoyed quite a lot of popular support because it engaged in the 'cleansing' of 'antisocial elements' in poor neighbourhoods, and some members of the public were dismayed when police officers were arrested for their actions. The existence of similar groups has also been reported, or suspected, in at least seven other states. Crucially, the Ombudsman estimated that while only seven people were killed by this kind of action between 1997 and 1999, at least 1,409 were killed by these groups between 1999 and 2004 (Defensoría del Pueblo 2004).[12]

Declarations by the Ombudsman, the Public Prosecutor and various human rights organisations (e.g. PROVEA 2006) indicate that there is some serious concern about the extent of police violence; however, the efforts to hold police officers accountable for their actions are hampered by a number of factors. Principal among these is the punitive public attitude towards crime. Individuals and the media construct a Manichean world in which good and bad are sharply distinguished, and in which moral panics and moral indignation are easily triggered. In this normative universe, citizens demand decent treatment for themselves from the police but are willing to tolerate or even actively demand harsh treatment for wrongdoers (as evidenced by the support for death squads). In an opinion survey carried out in seven Latin American cities during the mid 1990s, 70 per cent of Caracas respondents felt that a person has the right to kill in order to defend the family and 61 per cent felt that a person has the right to kill in order to defend property, proportions that were considerably higher than elsewhere (Briceño-León *et al.* 2006). These attitudes undoubtedly underlie the public lynching of criminal 'nuisances' in lower income neighbourhoods, which have averaged about 115 per year over the last six years (16 per cent of them fatal) (PROVEA 2006). In a similar vein, 32 per cent of respondents in a Caracas survey agreed with the statement that 'The police have the right to kill criminals' (Briceño-León *et al.* 2003). In this moral climate, the police can exercise authority over deviant or otherwise socially powerless individuals (even to the point of killing them) with relative impunity.

It is only when the victims belong to the middle or upper classes (such as those involved in the events mentioned at the beginning of this chapter), or are killed in mass or spree shootings or in high profile situations, that the police are held accountable for their actions. But even here, there are considerable impediments to investigation and sanction. First, it is often difficult to reconstruct the events in order to determine responsibilities and decide on sanctions. In the embryonic bureaucratic environment that characterises police agencies, officers do not fill out incident or use-of-force reports (Birkbeck and Gabaldón 2002), and sites where citizens are killed are not treated as crime scenes. Forensic evidence is usually confined to an examination of the victim's wounds and to the firearms that were involved. Evidence from bystanders is hard to obtain because many people fear for their safety when providing evidence against the police. Under the high standards of evidence required for criminal convictions, many cases against the police may stall or be dismissed because of lack of information.

Second, procedures may be lengthy and unnecessarily complicated. For example, under the old Criminal Procedure Code, police officers accused of misconduct were subject to a preliminary inquiry, applied for by a prosecutor in a criminal court. If the court found evidence of probable wrongdoing it would refer the case back to the prosecutor and a normal criminal case would proceed. Such preliminary inquiries added months, in some cases years, to the case. The new Criminal Procedure Code of 1999 abolished the preliminary inquiry and any cases of alleged police misconduct are treated like all other criminal cases, although it is not known if the new arrangements have shortened case processing time. Third, rules for the use of force are usually so vague or incomplete that it is difficult to specify a clear situational standard for police behaviour against which to hold officers accountable (Birkbeck 2007). Fourth, judges have been notably favourable to police defendants and unwilling to convict them. For example, in a ruling on 25 July 2000, the Criminal Chamber of the Supreme Court held that shooting a driver in the back because he had failed to respond to a police order to halt (while a confusing exchange of shots was taking place nearby) was a 'justified homicide', and that the officer had 'done his duty' (Borrego *et al.* 2007: 191). Anecdotal reports indicate that this ruling has been posted in many police stations in the spirit of an official indication of how officers may deal with citizens who 'resist authority'.

Frustrated by judicial inactivity at national level, in the 1990s human rights organisations began to take cases involving police violence to the Inter-American system of human rights. The latter is essentially a civil justice framework that operates at international level. Standards of evidence are lower than in criminal courts and findings in favour of victims lead to financial and other sanctions for the government. So far, five different incidents have generated cases before the Inter-American Commission or Inter-American Court of Human Rights and several of these have now concluded with findings in favour of the victims. However, the successes achieved in this sphere are tempered by several drawbacks, notably the practice of making governments pay compensation for abuses rather than the police officers that committed them. Combined with the length of time that it takes to complete the proceedings (anywhere from eight to 14 years between the events themselves and the final outcome), this form of accountability has almost no consequences for police officers themselves (Birkbeck 2007).

## The prospects for police reform

If the foregoing analysis is correct, considerable changes are required in order to democratise policing in Venezuela. First is the need to move towards a conception of policing as a service rather than as the exercise of authority. Second is the need to recognise policing as a public rather than a private (or semi-private) good: the police should be accountable to society rather than to individuals or groups, and should work in terms of universal rather than particularist referents. Third is the need to reconstruct the moral lens through which citizens perceive crime and disorder; to embrace a more nuanced and empirically informed vision of the problem of 'personal insecurity' and remove the excesses generated by moral indignation. Fourth, there is a need to reduce social inequality, which provides the structural foundation for many current arrangements (and problems) in policing.

In stating the arguments this way, the previous paragraph reads much like a manifesto (a statement of desirable ends rather than plausible means), which is always the danger with this kind of exercise. In style, although not entirely in content, our conclusions read like those formulated by the National Commission for Police Reform in a short draft document on 'The Model for Venezuelan Police' presented in early 2007 (Gabaldón and Antillano 2007, vol 2: 237–250). There, the Commission set out the general principles of democratic policing, deriving from them a set of imperatives: policing in Venezuela should be public, non-military, efficient, universal, and respectful of human rights. It would be easy to dismiss those desiderata as a case of idealism unfettered by practical considerations, but to do so would be to ignore the need for a democratic discourse which should ultimately provide the framework for concrete changes (at least, that is the hope).

Additionally, in the same document the Commission formulated some brief proposals for organisational changes. Principal among these were the creation of a General Police Council, headed by the Minister of the Interior and Justice, which would coordinate all police activities; the design of a framework for organising the intervention by different police forces based mainly on the location, magnitude and complexity of the incident; the creation of a National Police which would sit above state and municipal forces; and the standardisation of training and promotion systems. With these proposals, the Commission was largely adopting a legislative approach to coordination and would even have added another agency – the National Police – to an already complicated institutional environment. The prospects for the success of these kinds of proposal, the danger that they might be hijacked for political purposes, and a careful consideration of alternative strategies for democratising policing all needed to be considered. But there would not be the opportunity to do so. The dramatic cases of police violence that had captured the nation's attention in 2006 had occurred in the run-up to a presidential election. In December 2006, Hugo Chávez was elected for a second six-year term and the pressure to respond to many pre-electoral concerns was now removed. In January 2007, the Minister of the Interior and Justice (who had presided over the National Commission for Police Reform) was replaced in a cabinet shuffle and the new minister soon made it clear that he was not interested in continuing the work of the Commission or implementing its proposals. That he could do this without any political backwash is explained by the fact that the country's attention during the post-electoral period has focused almost entirely on Chávez's manoeuvres for leading the country down the path to socialism. The first of these was the passage of an Enabling Law by the National Assembly in February 2007, granting the president legislative powers over a wide range of matters for a period of 18 months (*El Universal* 1 February 2007); the second was the announcement, in August 2007, of plans for constitutional reform, including the reorganisation of the country's administrative regions, the strengthening of popular power, and the removal of the barrier to presidential re-election (Chávez 2007). With such sweeping changes on the horizon, the matter of police reform has slipped from the public gaze. For now, the considerable body of empirical material and recommendations assembled by the Commission will continue to inform debates about policing, but its final proposals lie dormant.

But while the disappearance of the Commission means that police 'reform' has stalled (at least in the short term), our analysis of policing in Venezuela suggests that the panorama has been anything but static over the last 20 years and is unlikely to be so in the future. Some of those changes have had a positive impact, notably the attempt by some of the new municipal police forces to take the principles of democratic policing seriously. Thus, there is always the possibility that developments in the field of policing will prove beneficial, irrespective of whether they are billed as reform or not. However, an element of caution is also in order because other changes have had positive impacts in some ways but very negative side effects. We are thinking here of the removal of police powers of detention during the 1990s (an undoubted victory for civil liberties) and the (in our view) consequent increase in police violence.

In May 2007, President Chávez announced plans for creating a Community Police Force (*El Universal* 27 May 2007). In doing so, he made no mention of the Commission for Police Reform; indeed, a Community Police Force was not what the Commission had in mind. Thus, Chávez's apparent disregard of its work was clear evidence that the Commission's moment had passed. Its creation and functioning had been a product of a particular set of events and of a single government minister. Moreover, while a Community Police Force might appear to be the essence of democratic policing, there are real dangers that it could foster yet more authoritarian tactics, a greater lack of accountability, and even vigilantism, all of them incompatible with the objective of public safety and the principles of democracy.

## Notes

1  The current political scenario in Venezuela is well described by O'Donnell's (1992: 8) concept of a 'delegative' democracy: 'Delegative democracies are grounded on one basic premise: he . . . who wins a presidential election is enabled to govern the country as he sees fit, and to the extent that existing power relations allow, for the term to which he has been elected. The President is the embodiment of the nation. . . . In this view other institutions – such as Congress and the Judiciary – are nuisances that become attached to the domestic and international advantages of being a democratically elected President.'
2  There are other agencies attached to central government which have policing functions, such as the Maritime Police, the Airport Police, the Internal Revenue Inspectors and other investigatory branches in public administration, such as finance, banking, securities, communications and sanitation.
3  While international comparisons are fraught with definitional and methodological problems, compared to both Latin America and the wealthy nations Venezuela appears to have a relatively high number of police officers per unit of population (Antillano 2007). Counting the municipal and state police, the National Guard, CICPC and the traffic police, there are approximately 429 officers per 100,000 people.
4  While working on a research project in the late 1990s, our colleague Yoana

Monsalve was surprised to find that when she asked for a copy of the Caracas Metropolitan Police Operations Manual, it had to be searched for in the basement. Finally, a copy was produced and presented as 'the Department's copy'. This happened in an agency which at the time had 9,500 officers.

5 Although official crime statistics in Venezuela have been published on a regular basis since 1958, crime surveys provide more accurate information about levels of victimisation, particularly for non-conventional crime, reporting and perceptions of the criminal justice system. Victimisation surveys on a regional basis have been carried out since 1980 in Venezuela, and two national crime surveys were carried out in 2001 and 2006, the latter being the first to measure homicide, threats, extortion and kidnapping. For a detailed review see Gabaldón *et al.* 2007.

6 Recruits to supervisory level posts in the military and quasi-military police agencies are usually drawn from the lower middle class, but all line personnel in public agencies and security officers and watchmen in private networks are drawn from the lower class. Salaries are relatively low, somewhere between two and three times the minimum wage rate (Birkbeck 2003) for the public sector and at, or slightly above, the minimum wage in the private sector. Most police personnel remain firmly in the lower class throughout their working lives.

7 Figures from an independent source reveal that the clearance rate for homicides went down, from 88 per cent to 62 per cent between 1990 and 2000, although for vehicle theft it went up from 7 per cent a 14 per cent (Gabaldón 2006). Thus, the considerable increase in clearance rates reported by the CICPC since 1999 reflects either a dramatic change in institutional efficiency or a redefinition of 'clearance'.

8 The Metropolitan Police (MP) had shown itself to be largely on the side of the opposition during the demonstrations and clashes that led up to an attempted coup against Chávez in April 2002. Taking advantage of a (possibly engineered) strike by some of its officers, the government ordered military personnel into the MP in November 2002 and confiscated weaponry. Despite a ruling from the Supreme Court in December 2002 that annulled the government's action, at least 200 Army and National Guard officers were still deployed at MP police stations in August 2003 (PROVEA 2003).

9 In investigation and judicial work, the situation is somewhat better. Because the CICPC is considered to be the primary investigative agency, other police agencies will usually hand over arrestees and evidence early in the investigation.

10 Webb-Vidal's report also reveals that Colombian guerrilla and paramilitary groups have been operating across the very porous eastern frontier with Venezuela. The main guerrilla group, Fuerzas Armadas Revolucionarias de Colombia (FARC), has apparently counted on tacit, and occasionally explicit, support from the Venezuelan Army and National Guard. See also Robinson (2003).

11 In September 2006, and as part of the activities generated by the Police Reform Commission, the Minister of Justice issued a Code for Police Ethics, which contained 20 principles of police conduct, including honesty, integrity, equal treatment, moderation and the appropriate use of firearms. However, symbolic initiatives such as this amount more to a public acknowledgement of the problem than to an effective solution.

12 The Ombudsman's office (called *Defensoría del Pueblo*, literally, 'defence of the people') was created under the new Constitution in 1999. It is charged with the protection of both individual and collective rights of the population and, together with the Public Prosecutor and the General Accountant, forms part of a new 'Citizen Power' (Venezuela 1999).

184    *Christopher Birkbeck and Luis Gerardo Gabaldón*

# References

Agudo Freites, E. (1973) 'Estatutos de la Guardia Nacional'. *Revista de la Escuela Superior de las Fuerzas Armadas de Cooperación* 2: 463–510.

Aniyar de Castro, L. (2003) *Entre la Dominación y el Miedo. Nueva Criminología y Nueva Política Criminal*. Mérida, Venezuela: Ediciones Nuevo Siglo C.A.

Antillano, A. (2006) 'La Policía en Venezuela: Una Breve Descripción', in S. El Achkar and L.G. Gabaldón (eds) *Reforma Policial: Una Mirada desde Afuera y Desde Adentro*. Caracas: Comisión Nacional para la Reforma Policial: 133–138.

Antillano, A. (2007) 'Características de la policía venezolana', in L.G. Gabaldón and A. Antillano (eds) *La Policía Venezolana: Desarrollo Institucional y Perspectivas de Reforma al Inicio del Tercer Milenio*, Vol. 1. Caracas: Comisión Nacional para la Reforma Policial: 64–158.

Birkbeck, C. (1982) 'La Planificación de la Política Antidelictiva en Venezuela: Balance y Perspectivas', *Revista Cenipec* 7: 67–123.

Birkbeck, C. (1992) 'Crime and Control in Venezuela', in H.-G. Heiland, L.I. Shelley and H. Katoh (eds) *Crime and Control in Comparative Perspectives*. Berlin/New York: Walter de Gruyter.

Birkbeck, C. (2003) 'Venezuela', in *World Factbook of Criminal Justice Systems*. Washington, DC: Bureau of Justice Statistics. Online. Available http://www.ojp.usdoj.gov/bjs/pub/ascii/wfcjsvz.txt (accessed 25 June 2007).

Birkbeck, C. (2007) 'Police Use of Force and Transnational Review Processes: The Venezuelan Police Under the Inter-American System', in A. Goldsmith and J. Sheptycki (eds) *Crafting Global Policing*. Oxford: Hart: 357–388.

Birkbeck, C. and Gabaldón, L.G. (1996) 'Avoiding Complaints: Venezuelan Police Officers' Situational Criteria for the Use of Force Against Citizens', *Policing and Society* 6: 113–129.

Birkbeck, C. and Gabaldón, L.G. (2002) 'Estableciendo la Verdad Sobre el Uso de la Fuerza en la Policía Venezolana', *Nueva Sociedad* 182: 47–58.

Birkbeck, C., Gabaldón, L.G. and Monsalve, Y. (2005) 'Use of Non-Lethal Force in Venezuela', paper presented at Conference on Policing, Dutch Police Academy, April 2005. Online. Available http://www.policeuseofforce.org/Presentations2005/Venezuela.pdf (accessed 25 June 2007).

Borrego, C., Sifontes, M. and Villarroel, A. (2007) 'Marco Jurídico de los Cuerpos Policiales de Venezuela', in L.G. Gabaldón and A. Antillano (eds) *La Policía Venezolana: Desarrollo Institucional y Perspectivas de Reforma al Inicio del Tercer Milenio*, Vol. 1. Caracas: Comisión Nacional para la Reforma Policial.

Bowling, B. (1999) 'The Rise and Fall of New York Murder: Zero Tolerance or Crack's Decline?', *British Journal of Criminology* 39(4): 531–554.

Briceño-León, R., Camardiel, A., Avila, O. and E. De Armas (2003) '¿Tiene la Policía Derecho a Matar a los Delincuentes?', in R. Briceño-León and R. Pérez Perdomo (eds) *Morir en Caracas*, Caracas: Universidad Central de Venezuela: 179–192.

Briceño-León, R., Camardiel, A. and Ávila, O. (2006) 'Attitudes Toward the Right to Kill in Latin American Culture', *Journal of Contemporary Criminal Justice* 22(4): 303–323.

Bureau for International Narcotics and Law Enforcement Affairs (BINLEA) (2007) *International Narcotics Control Strategy Report. Vol. 1. Drug and Chemical Control*. Washington, DC: United Status Department of State, Bureau for International

Narcotics and Law Enforcement Affairs. Online. Available http://www.state.gov/documents/organization/81446.pdf (accessed 4 September 2007).

Carreño, P. (2007) *Venezuela Inmoviliza a Narcotraficantes*. Caracas: Oficina Nacional Antidrogas. Online. Available http://www.ona.gob.ve/Noticias/28082007_1.HTM (accessed 4 September 2007).

Central Intelligence Agency (CIA) (2007) *The World Factbook*. Washington, DC: CIA. Online. Available https://www.cia.gov/library/publications/the-world-factbook/geos/ve.html (accessed 8 June 2007).

Chávez, H. (2007) *Ahora la Batalla es por el Sí. Discurso de Presentación del Proyecto de Reforma Constitucional Ante la Asamblea Nacional*. Caracas: Ministerio del Poder Popular del Despacho de la Presidencia. Online. Available http://www.venezuela.gov.ve/reforma/reforma_constitucional_web.pdf (accessed 3 September 2007).

Coronel, G. (2006) *Corruption, Mismanagement and Abuse of Power in Hugo Chavez's Venezuela*. Washington, DC: Cato Institute, Center for Global Liberty and Prosperity, Development Policy Analysis, No. 2. Online. Available http://www.cato.org/pubs/dpa/dpa2.pdf (accessed 4 September 2007).

Crespo, F. (2006) 'Institutional legitimacy and crime in Venezuela', *Journal of Contemporary Criminal Justice* 22(4): 347–367.

Defensoría del Pueblo (2004) *Informe Anual de la Defensoría del Pueblo. Año 2004*. Caracas: 2004.

Economic Commission for Latin America and the Caribbean (ECLAC) (2007) *Statistical Yearbook for Latin America and the Caribbean, 2006*. Santiago, Chile: ECLAC. Online. Available http://www.eclac.cl/publicaciones/xml/3/28063/LCG-2332B_2.pdf (accessed 8 June 2007).

*El Universal* (3 March 2001) 'Bratton Llega Hoy a Caracas', *El Universal*, Caracas. Online. Available http://buscador.eluniversal.com/2001/03/03/ccs_art_03402BB.shtml (accessed 21 June 2007).

*El Universal* (21 August 2002) 'Alcaldía Mayor Inicia Fase Dos del Plan Bratton en Caracas', *El Universal*, Caracas. Online. Available http://buscador.eluniversal.com/2002/08/21/ccs_art_21460CC.shtml (accessed 21 June 2007).

*El Universal* (16 April 2006) 'Comisión Nacional de Reforma Policial', *El Universal*, Caracas. Online. Available http://buscador.eluniversal.com/2006/04/16/pol_art_16161C.shtml (accessed 22 June 2007).

*El Universal* (26 May 2006) 'Se "Perdieron" Cinco Kilos de Heroína en el CICPC', *El Universal*, Caracas. Online. Available http://buscador.eluniversal.com/2006/05/26/ccs_art_26481C.shtml (accessed 4 September 2007).

*El Universal* (1 February 2007) 'Presidente Chávez Promulgó Ley Habilitante', *El Universal*, Caracas. Online. Available http://buscador.eluniversal.com/2007/02/01/pol_ava_01A830929.shtml (accessed 3 September 2007).

*El Universal* (27 May 2007) 'Plan de Policía Comunitaria', *El Universal*, Caracas. Online. Available http://buscador.eluniversal.com/2007/05/27/pol_apo_plan-de-policia-comu_300962.shtml (accessed 21 June 2007).

Energy Information Administration (EIA) (2007) *Top World Oil Producers, 2006*. Washington, DC: U.S. Department of Energy, Energy Information Administration. Online. Available http://www.eia.doe.gov/emeu/cabs/topworldtables1_2.html (accessed 8 June 2007).

Gabaldón, L.G. (2004) 'Policía y seguridad ciudadana en Venezuela entre 2002 y 2004', *Nueva Sociedad*, 191: 65–77.

Gabaldón, L.G. (2006) 'Derecho penal, criminalidad y castigo en Venezuela', in *Temas de Derecho Penal Económico, Homenaje a Alberto Arteaga Sánchez*, Caracas: Universidad Central de Venezuela: 901–912.

Gabaldón, L.G. and Antillano, A. (eds) (2007) *La Policía Venezolana: Desarrollo Institucional y Perspectivas de Reforma al Inicio del Tercer Milenio, Vols. 1 and 2*. Caracas: Comisión Nacional para la Reforma Policial.

Gabaldón, L.G., Birkbeck, C. and Bettiol, D. (1990) *La Policía en el Vecindario*. Mérida, Venezuela: Gobernación del Estado Mérida/Universidad de Los Andes.

Gabaldón, L.G., Monsalve, Y. and Boada, C. (1996) 'La Policía Judicial en Venezuela: Organización y Desempeño en la Averiguación Penal', in P. Waldmann (ed.) *Justicia en la Calle: Ensayos Sobre la Policía en América Latina*, Medellín: Colombia: Biblioteca Jurídica Diké: 185–213.

Gabaldón, L.G., Benavides, D. and Parra, Y. (2007) 'Victimización delictiva y percepción de la Policía', in L.G. Gabaldón and A. Antillano (eds) *La Policía Venezolana: Desarrollo Institucional y Perspectivas de Reforma al Inicio del Tercer Milenio, Vol. 1*, Caracas: Comisión Nacional para la Reforma Policial: 307–341.

Hernández, T. (1977) *La Ideologización del Delito y de la Pena*. Caracas: Universidad Central de Venezuela.

Human Rights Watch (1997) *Punishment Before Trial: Prison Conditions in Venezuela*. New York: Human Rights Watch.

Instituto Nacional de Estadística (INE) (2006) *Reporte Social. No. 3, Año 2006. Edición Especial 1er Semestre 1998–1er Semestre 2006*. Caracas: INE. Online. Available http://www.ine.gov.ve (accessed 20 August 2007).

Instituto Nacional de Estadística (INE) (2007) *Proyecciones de Población. Población Total por Sexo, 1990–2015 (base Censo, 2001)*. Caracas: INE. Online. Available http://www.ine.gov.ve/poblacion/distribucion.asp (accessed 6 June 2007).

Monsalve, Y. (2006) 'Castigo Policial y Valoración Moral del Infractor', in S. El Achkar and L.G. Gabaldón (eds) *Reforma Policial: Una Mirada desde Afuera y Desde Adentro*. Caracas: Comisión Nacional para la Reforma Policial: 175–180.

Monsalve, Y. (2007) 'Visión de los Policías sobre su Función y Desempeño', in L.G. Gabaldón and A. Antillano (eds) *La Policía Venezolana: Desarrollo Institucional y Perspectivas de Reforma al Inicio del Tercer Milenio, Vol. 1*. Caracas: Ministerio del Interior y Justicia, Comisión Nacional para la Reforma Policial: 267–304.

Morais, M.G. (2006) 'Breves Notas sobre la Seguridad Privada en Venezuela', in S. Achkar and L.G. Gabaldón (eds) *Reforma Policial: Una Mirada desde Afuera y Desde Adentro*. Caracas: Comisión Nacional para la Reforma Policial: 115–120.

O'Donnell, G. (1992) *Delegative Democracy?* Notre Dame, IN: Helen Kellogg Institute for International Studies, Working Paper No. 172. Online. Available http://kellogg.nd.edu/publications/workingpapers/WPS/172.pdf (accessed April 5 2007).

Parra, A.V. (2004) *Extorsión: Vacuna de Vehículos en el Estado Zulia*, paper presented at the annual meeting, Venezuelan Criminology Forum, Mérida, Venezuela, November, 2004.

Programa Venezolano de Educación-Acción de Derechos Humanos (PROVEA) (2003) *Situación de los derechos humanos en Venezuela. Informe Anual. 2002–2003*. Caracas: PROVEA. Online. Available http://www.derechos.org.ve/publicaciones/infanual/2002_03/16seguridaCIUDADANA.pdf (accessed 12 September 2007).

Programa Venezolano de Educación-Acción de Derechos Humanos (PROVEA) (2006) *Situación de los derechos humanos en Venezuela. Informe Anual. 2005–2006*.

Caracas: PROVEA. Online. Available http://www.derechos.org.ve/publicaciones/infanual/2005%5F06/ (accessed 8 June 2007).

Rico, J., Piris, A. and Salas, L. (1991) *Informe sobre la Policía en Venezuela. Para el Ministerio del Interior.* Miami, FL: Florida International University, Center for the Administration of Justice.

Robinson, L. (2003) 'Terror Close to Home'. *U.S. News and World Report*, October 6 2003. Online. Available http://jewishpoliticalchronicle.org/dec03/Terror%20close%20to%20home.pdf (accessed 4 September 2007).

Romero Salazar, A., Salas, J.J., García Pirela, A. and Luna, C. (2001) 'El Miedo a la Violencia y el Guachimanismo: Instrumentalidad vs. Conformidad', *Capítulo Criminológico* 29 (2): 25–51.

Transparency International (2007) *Transparency International Corruption Perceptions Index 2006.* Berlin: Transparency Internacional Secretariat. Online. Available http://www.transparency.org/policy_research/surveys_indices/cpi (accessed 3 September 2007).

Ungar, M. (2003) 'La Policía Venezolana: El Camino Peligroso de la Politización', *Revista Venezolana de Economía y Ciencias Sociales* 9(3): 205–229. Online. Available http://redalyc.uaemex.mx/redalyc/pdf/177/17709310.pdf (accessed 15 June 2007).

United Nations (UN) (1999) *Global Report on Crime and Justice.* New York: Oxford University Press.

Venezuela (1962) *Código de Enjuiciamiento Criminal.* Caracas: *Gaceta Oficial No. 748, Extraordinario, de 3 de Febrero de 1962.*

Venezuela (1998) *Código Orgánico Procesal Penal.* Caracas: *Gaceta Oficial, 23/01/1998, No. 5208, Extraordinario.*

Venezuela (1999) *Constitución de la República Bolivariana de Venezuela.* Caracas: *Gaceta Oficial, 30/12/1999, No. 36.860.*

Venezuela (2001) *Decreto con Fuerza de Ley de Coordinación de Seguridad Ciudadana.* Caracas. Online. Available http://www.mintra.gov.ve/legal/leyesordinarias/leycoordinaciondeseguridadciudadana.html (accessed 22 June 2007).

Webb-Vidal, A. (2006) 'South American Cocaine Trafficking Shifts Operations Towards Venezuela'. *Jane's Intelligence Review* (May): 36–40. Online, Available http://www.derechoshumanos.gov.co/shared/venezueladrugs.pdf (accessed 4 September 2007).

World Bank (2007) *06 World Development Indicators.* Washington: World Bank. Online. Available http://devdata.worldbank.org/wdi2006/contents/Section2.htm (accessed 20 August 2007).

World Institute for Development Economics Research (WIDER) (2007) *World Income Inequality Database.* Helsinki: United Nations University, WIDER. Online. Available http://www.wider.unu.edu/wiid/wiid.htm (accessed 8 June 2007).

# 9 Who polices the police?

## The challenges of accountability in democratic Mexico [1]

*Diane E. Davis*

The challenge of establishing police accountability in new democracies is immense, especially in those countries where democratic transition has come incrementally rather than through an abrupt break with an authoritarian past. When the country also faces major economic challenges ranging from growing income inequality to sustained un- or under-employment and rising informality, increased violence linked to cross-border drug trade, and a history of corruption, human rights abuses, and police impunity, this task is even more daunting. This is nowhere more evident than in Mexico.

The transformation of one-party rule into a more democratic and competitive political system has unfolded slowly over the last two decades, leaving many of the same institutions intact, including key elements of the police, who are slow to shed the long-standing mantle of corruption and human rights. In the same period, Mexico's economy has changed in ways that contribute to income inequality, unemployment, and crime, much of it concentrated in urban areas. The latter problems are fueled not only by social and economic polarization associated with economic liberalization, but also by the concentration of ever more citizens in cities, where low-wage service jobs and informality are increasingly seen as the principal source of employment. As of 2006, 76 percent of Mexicans resided in cities, and 18 percent (nationally) lived below the poverty line—despite the fact that Mexico hosts some of the world's wealthiest entrepreneurs (World Bank 2006). While the decline in percentage of GDP in industrial manufacturing (from 24.8 percent in 1986 to 17.8 percent in 2006) was matched by an increase in services for the same period (from 54.8 percent to 69.4 percent), much of this new service-related employment is in the informal sector, where economic productivity remains low and income is not always sufficient to cover basic needs (World Bank 2006).[2] Smuggling and other forms of illegal trade also are on the rise (Andreas 1998). As a result, many Mexicans face downward pressure on wages and income, more poverty, and greater economic insecurity, leading to an increase in criminality (Davis and Alvarado 1999; Alvarado 2000; ICESI 2005; Pansters and Castillo 2006).

In key cities across the country, the management and regulation of informality and illegality, coupled with rising criminality, have put a strain on policing services (Bailey and Godson 2000; Davis 2007). This is so not just because of the person power needed to monitor the production and consumption of informal goods, but also because the world of informality so easily nestles in a world of illegality where the import and trade of illicit goods like drugs, guns, and other forms of global contraband predominate. For many police, the volumes of money involved in these illegal activities are too tempting to bypass, especially given their chronically low wages, and as a result police themselves often become involved in criminal activities. In response, citizens in Mexico have called on their newly elected officials to establish an effective and accountable police force, capable of guaranteeing public security and the rule of law. They have been joined by several multi-lateral organizations, not just Amnesty International, but also the Lawyers' Commission for Human Rights, and other global advocacy groups. The US Congress has even passed legislation to enable support for the Mexican government to deal with this array of problems, ranging from corruption within the police and military to the global drug trade.

Yet even with an organized citizenry clamoring for change, concerted international pressure, and open recognition on the part of the government that problems of insecurity are among the nation's top priorities, scholars still describe Mexico as a place where "impunity is the rule and legality is the exception" (Pardinas 2003; see also Amnesty International 2002). Remedying this situation has been extraordinarily difficult. Mexican officials have intro-duced reform after reform of police institutions, hierarchies, and practices since the late 1990s, only to see few positive results and a stubborn resilience of police corruption (Davis 2006a; Bailey and Flores-Macías 2007). Why? Part of the answer is that roots of impunity run deep, and given the newness of the democracy, elected officials often lack the institutional and/or political capacity to effectively purge police of their corrupt elements.

The latter problems result partly from the existent structure of policing, which is relatively fragmented and in which control over different police institutions rests in the hands of separate authorities and is spread across divergent levels of government. One observer has gone so far as to suggest that if someone actually "tried to plan a *lack of control* over public security forces, not only in Mexico City but also in a good part of the rest of country, they could not have done it better" (Alcocer 1997: 49). Mexican police fall into two general categories, preventative and judicial police, with the former charged with protection or vigilance duties and answering to elected author-ities, and the latter charged with prosecutorial rights and obligations, making them connected to the judicial branch of government. These two sets of forces co-exist in the same territorial spaces, but with different degrees of authority and influence, a situation which drives conflict and competition for control of the streets even as it inspires inter-organizational tensions within the police leadership.

Complicating matters, both the preventative and judicial police operate at local and federal levels, with the federal police often charged with involvement in local affairs—particularly when it comes to drug operations and other activities that are classified as federal offenses, despite their local operations. This bureaucratic structure of the organizations exacerbates competition and overlap in policing services, limiting the scope for cooperation on issues of police reform and accountability. When democratic elections bring different political parties to power locally and federally, the tension accelerates and cooperation remains more elusive. When in response both local and federal authorities try to create new police organizations to supersede old ones, as occurred under the prior presidential administration of President Vicente Fox with the creation of a new federal security apparatus, the bureaucratic picture becomes even more fragmented (Davis 2006a).

But organizational disarray is not the only problem. Much of the failure to make headway on police accountability has to do with the newly democratic environment and citizen responses. Citizens have become disheartened about the state's capacity to remedy security problems and make police accountable. Many are distrustful of the government and pessimistic about democracy's prospects. As a consequence, citizens readily turn to "private" policing and other alternative means for achieving public security—ranging from the employment of private security services and vigilantism to the criminalization of everyday behavior. Yet when citizens take matters into their own hands, or when the definition of criminal acts becomes so wide-ranging that police have ever greater powers to arrest, public police are further let off the hook in terms of accountability. The global embrace of privatization as an ideology further sustains this tendency to turn to the market rather than the state for solutions. And when privatization occurs in policing services, private police then act without coordination and at the service of their clients, who often seek revenge as much as protection. The rule of law is often the first casualty. This was most clear in a spate of lynchings undertaken by enraged citizens against criminals and the police in Mexico City (*La Jornada*, July 5, 2001; *CNI en Linea*, January 19, 2005).

In a downward spiraling environment of insecurity and disorder, the question of who "polices the police," whether public and/or private, and for what larger social or democratic purpose, becomes a central theoretical and policy question with serious implications for democracy, as well as social and political order. In the absence of effective reform, and with police impunity a persistent concern, oversight and the capacity to discipline or punish egregious police behavior is one of the few means available for insuring a modicum of accountability. Yet, any effective "policing of police," whether undertaken by citizens, the state, or both, entails a commitment to larger principles of rights, accountability, and authority that may not be shared by all constituencies. Confounding matters, the mere act of "policing police" often involves a degree of centralization that, when undertaken by the state, can undermine rather than strengthen democratic principles, although for civil society the dilemma is often the opposite. That is, democratic principles generally support a territorial decentralization of decision-making in civil society that can make it difficult, if not impossible, for citizens to truly police the police in any effective way.

In what follows, I examine the trade-offs between deepening democracy and ensuring police accountability, ascertaining how and why Mexico arrived at this difficult situation, and asking what measures are available today to ensure an accountable policing system that will also maintain democratic principles. The chapter draws its materials and insights from a focus on the Mexico City police who are the largest and most important police force in the country, where impunity is great, and where citizens have been involved in efforts to make police more accountable. I argue that the recent political and economic transformations have reinforced—rather than reversed—past patterns of impunity in such a way as to severely limit the capacities of either formally democratic mechanisms or civil society to ensure police accountability.

## From present to past: the weight of revolutionary history sets the stage

One of the main obstacles to police accountability is the culture of corruption and impunity in Mexico. These problems have deep historical roots, back to the post-revolutionary period and to the trade-offs made between revolutionary leaders and Mexico City police in their efforts to defeat counter-revolutionary forces associated with loyalists to the dictatorship of Porfirio Díaz. In fact, there is some evidence that it was the corruption within the police, as well as between the police and the state set in the immediate post-revolutionary period, that laid the foundation for more endemic corruption in the state apparatus in subsequent years, and not necessarily vice-versa. Although it is difficult to tease out cause and effect in terms of the origins of corruption, the record suggests that connections between a corrupted police force and the Mexican state have existed for decades.

These connections trace to the years following the 1910 Revolution, when many elements in the military sided with the dictatorship and other counter-revolutionaries, thereby forcing the Revolution's main protagonists to seek other "coercive" allies, among them police and armed peasants or workers. Because the future of the new revolutionary state depended upon whichever political faction controlled the means of coercion in the capital city, Mexico City police were key allies for the revolutionary leadership. The country's aspiring leaders depended on local police forces loyal to pro-revolutionary populations who were willing to demonstrate such sympathies by arresting or harassing counter-revolutionaries or others considered politically dangerous by the revolutionary leadership. For this reason, in the immediate revolutionary aftermath the country's new political leaders gave Mexico City police—individually and as an institution—extraordinary leeway to persecute political enemies, in return for protection from prosecution. Over time, these practices of "political policing" helped institutionalize the police's "autonomy" from citizens, and later from the state itself, conditions that made bribery and corruption possible while also limiting efforts to professionalize the police and/or make them accountable.

The institutional roots of these problems originate in the period between 1910–1918, when the military (under Carranza) usurped Mexico City policing functions in order to consolidate the revolutionary leadership's power over citizen militias and local municipalities, who sought to maintain a locally-controlled system of policing (see Davis, in press). They also reflect the slow but steady centralization of Mexico City police, first under the jurisdiction of the city government, and then to the national state and the military, which was followed by a reform to the 1917 Constitution that established separate police functions. Only judicial police had the power to arrest and take suspects to court, while preventative police (i.e. beat cops) kept the peace and prevented crime.

The initial rationale for separating police powers and functions was political: to give President Carranza more control over who could be legally prosecuted, since judicial police—who alone had the right to arrest—answered to a federal ministry under the supervision of the president's office. This meant that lines of accountability were shifted away from the courts to the federal executive, primarily to the president (Picatto 2001). In addition to empowering the police who were most linked to the presidency, and distancing them both from the citizenry and the courts, this 1917 constitutional reform also laid the foundations for greater corruption in the entire system of policing because it pitted judicial and preventative police against each other in the search for rent-seeking, producing competition between them over the capacity to extort citizens.[3]

These changes also reduced citizen confidence in the police, leading to reduced accountability as both citizens and police became ever distant from each other. Once citizens saw that they could not count on the police for protection, either because they were the subject of bribery or because the police were more interested in political policing, they increasingly failed to turn to the police to uphold the rule of law. As citizens became ever more distrustful not only of police, but of most legal institutions, this in turn increased the incentive to all to resolve violations of the law at the "street level" through coercive bribery rather than through juridical procedures guaranteed by the formal system of justice. These informal practices fueled an even more vicious cycle of police corruption–judicial weakness that served to legitimize an alternative or unofficial system of "everyday justice" while also undermining the courts and the rule of law (*Reforma*, January 18, 2003; Picatto 2004) and providing disincentive to struggle for police accountability.

## The military–police nexus and reduced accountability

The military was a key actor in the growing centralization of the police, in no small part because of the strong relationship between the military leadership and the national executive immediately following the Revolution. But the military's role was by no means uncontroversial. After the Mexico City police joined in the campaign to route counter-revolutionaries, the focus of the federal executive and the military soon shifted from policing counter-revolutionaries to policing other revolutionaries and partisan political opponents. Yet as the state's political objectives shifted, so too did the actions of the police. In the long run, this brought conflict and tension within and between the Mexico City police, the military, and the state; and in this environment, mistrust and violence became the *modus operandi* of political rule and the institutions of the police themselves became the battleground for power. Over time these tensions led to reforms in police structures that further reinforced the authoritarian character of the state and reduced police accountability to citizens.

These developments were perhaps clearest during the administration of President Lázaro Cárdenas (1934–1940). Cárdenas came to power faced with several key concerns, not the least of which was unparalleled police corruption. By 1930 corruption had reached such heights that high level police personnel were publicly known—and affirmed in secret police internal reports—to be involved in criminal activities, including one infamous high-profile auto theft gang known as the *Banda de Automobile Gris* that counted on Mexico City's police chief as a principal interlocutor.[4] A second key concern for Cárdenas involved rising police repression against labor and other independent political movements pushing for more democracy. By 1934, the year Cárdenas became president, the instances of armed conflict within and between contending political parties and police were generating considerable public outcry, while also further tarnishing the police's reputation.

In response, President Cárdenas promised to purify the notoriously corrupt police apparatus in the capital city, and to purge elements responsible for labor and peasant repression. Attacking the existent structure of policing, however, required support from political allies both within and outside the military, as well as in civil society. These needs led him to introduce three key reforms.

The first entailed an expansion of the city's police force to include semi-private security forces that had been operating parallel to the preventative police. With a new infusion of non-state security forces in the public police ranks, Cárdenas had a greater chance of limiting the overall relative institutional influence of the highly corrupted officer corps. Just as important, he hoped to offer the city's residents a renovated new police force, many of whose members had a reputation for being responsive to the citizenry. Last, by bringing private police into the city's public policing services as an auxiliary force, he strengthened his own ideological position within the conflictive revolutionary family at large. These new police officers, now called *Policia Auxiliar*, were known to be extremely loyal to Cárdenas and his political ideals, and they were both organized and self-identified as part of his larger working-class movement.

A second major initiative sought the reorganization of police in order to reflect their class, employment, or state-worker status, putting them in sync with all others employed by the state. With this legislation, police were to be treated as just another form of state worker, a shift that in organizational and identity terms would help link police to the citizenry in a way that might also facilitate greater accountability. They also were given the right to strike. However, both of these reforms met serious political limits. For one thing, they gave the newly incorporated rank-and-file police powerful tools to expose the corrupt hiring and firing practices used by the existent cadres of police officials. For another, they created new tensions within the police, especially between the "new" auxiliary and the "old" preventative police, and between some elements of the police and the military.

Faced with opposition, President Cárdenas eventually backed down on plans to extend state worker legislation to the police. To repair the damage inflicted on police–military relations by the state worker debate, Cárdenas introduced a third and final reform of the police: its "militarization." Militarization meant organizationally subordinating the police to the military, and endowing all police with the same juridical status as military personnel (who were neither allowed to strike nor hold superiors accountable for employment decisions). In the short term, these reforms gave Cárdenas considerable leeway to purify and discipline the corrupted police force; but in the long term they limited police accountability to citizens and helped establish conditions in which *greater* corruption and more unconstrained political policing would flower.

## Administrative fragmentation and reduced accountability

There is little doubt that diminished police accountability stemmed from the declining democratic potential of the one-party dominated political system, and not merely from the development of a more militarized police apparatus that remained at the frontline of political policing in subsequent decades. But the increasingly fragmented and overlapping administrative structure of policing, coupled with the increasingly complex network of semi-autonomous police services that offered very little scope for citizens to hold individual police or their leaders to task for abuses, also took their toll.

Part of the fragmentation in policing services also stemmed from the ways the government responded to citizen demands for a less corrupt and repressive police. When citizens protested about abusive police actions, the government could not dismiss old forces in their entirety, primarily because of longstanding complicities between police and the revolutionary state (or different factions of it). Thus the government needed to create new police forces that would co-exist with the old corrupted police (contributing to fragmentation). This often required the establishment of more centralized police "oversight" so as to monitor existent cadres of corrupted police. This task usually fell into the hands of the secret police, who were charged with monitoring and rooting out internal corruption.[5] But the extent of corruption was so great that the secret police themselves usually succumbed to the cycle of impunity and extortion, thereby forcing the government to continually re-organize and restructure them by varying their lines of authority. New secret police forces generally answered directly to the president or military, while other police answered to either the mayor or the military. Fragmentation and overlap in administrative authority also contributed to a confusing array of police services that answered to a variety of local and national agencies.[6] And once fragmentation became vertical—or spread across various agencies and levels of government—as much as horizontal, that is between judicial and preventative police at the city level, it was even more difficult for the state to coordinate police services, as the rank-and-file police answered to their own sub-leadership.

The upshot was that by the 1930s, police services were organized around just about every functional basis *but* territory, and they answered to myriad state agencies and officials, both local and national. This meant that within Mexico City, there was no single police authority to whom local residents could turn to complain about general servicing; nor could they make claims at the level of the neighborhood, because police services were not territorially organized.

Still, the most serious structural obstacles to establishing police accountability to either citizens or the national state rested in the militarization of the police, and the key role that military generals played as police chiefs in the institutional evolution of policing services and as administrative overseers of the police. The 1939 decision by Cárdenas to subordinate Mexico City police to the military meant that, institutionally speaking, by the 1940s the ruling party was bypassed almost altogether as a site for posting complaints about the police. So, too, the Mexico City mayor's office was no longer responsible for disciplining police; and the national government, for its part, was only indirectly responsible, by virtue of its more vertical relationships with the military. The upshot was that with the military responsible for police organization, but formally absent in corporatist bodies and representative political institutions of the PRI, over the 1950s, 1960s, and 1970s there was increasingly less scope for citizen demand-making to either the military or the police with respect to police accountability.

Combined with the fragmentation of policing and the overlaps of local and national coercive apparatuses, these historical legacies set the stage for the repressive political policing and abuses of power that materialized in the 1960s, leading to the 1968 student crisis, in which hundreds of protesting students were shot by special police forces answering to a military leadership that deemed student unrest a threat to national security (Aguayo 1998). The "political policing" of protesting students not only revealed the Mexican state's true authoritarian face, despite the formal absence of military rule; the need to cover up military and state-dictated police abuses in subsequent years further undermined the political system's overall legitimacy. Both fueled the emergence of an active and mobilized civil society in the 1970s and 1980s (Hellman 1978; Zermeño 1978), leading to successful struggles for the democratization of the Mexican political system by the 1990s.

## Democratization: a break with the past or more of the same?

So did the successful democratization of the political system put an end to the problems of police corruption, impunity, violence, and limited accountability? Hardly. By 1994, just around the time Mexico City residents were finally granted rights to democratically elect a mayor, the country found itself awash in robberies, kidnappings, stolen car rings, extortion, and other forms of violent and non-violent crime, including rape and homicide, much of it concentrated in the capital city (Davis and Alvarado 1999). From an average annual rate of 1,700 crimes (per 100,000 inhabitants) in 1993, by 1995 the rate in Mexico City had reached 2,835, with violent crimes growing at a rate of 500 percent from 1990 to 1996 (Zurita and Ramirez 1999: 12–13). Between 1995 and 1998 alone, the overall crime rate in the capital nearly tripled (*Fundación Mexicana Para la Salud* 1997: 16).

Much of the increase in crime was fueled by criminal gangs, who dominated robbery and assault rings as well as in extortion rackets—including kidnapping. Between 1990 and 1996 reported rates of robbery, property damage, fraud, and extortion more than doubled from 1,059.0 to 2,434.3 incidents per 100,000 inhabitants (ibid.: 16). In this same time period, the percentage of robberies involving violence increased from 38.5 percent to 55.5 percent (ibid.: 17). Official statistics show that of the 1.5 million crimes committed yearly in Mexico City in that period, only 7 percent of reported crimes were ever resolved.[7]

Even with crime on the rise, did democratization make it possible to change the institutional context of police authority in ways that allowed greater reciprocity between police and citizens, or even new measures for oversight that would allow citizens or the newly democratic state to "police the police," corrupt as it still was, despite the limited headway being made on crime itself? Unfortunately, progress on this front also was much less than most hoped for, primarily mainly because it was so difficult to change institutions and practices on the ground, given the weight of political history noted above, despite the advent of formal democratization.

First, the police's own proclivities to operate above the law did not disappear just because elections became democratic in the mid- to late-1990s. High levels of police corruption remained, evidenced by a 1997 United States Foreign Military Studies Office study of the city contending that in the Federal District close to "6 of every 10 crimes involve(d) policemen" themselves.[8]

Second, the long durée of institutionalized police corruption in Mexico made citizens understandably distrustful of police motives and legal institutions, giving additional incentive to citizens themselves to resort to time-worn practices of resolving violations of the law at the "street level," through coercive bribery rather than through juridical procedures guaranteed by the formal system of justice (*Reforma*, May 19, 2003; Picatto 2004). Third, democratization of governance turned out to be part of the problem of accelerating violence, security, and declining accountability, not the solution.[9]

Without the longstanding PRI (*Partido Revolucionario Institucional*) at the helm in the capital, and weakened by electoral defeat, neither police nor citizens counted on the same informal practices of patronage and authority that in prior decades gave the state a modicum of oversight, imperfect and partial as it was. Nor did the newly elected government leadership have the institutional capacity to impose authority on a police system that was already so fragmented and out of control. Accordingly, transformations within the state produced by the democratization had the paradoxical effect of reducing rather than enhancing police accountability. How and why this happened is well exemplified by the first major efforts to reform police in Mexico City, during the first phase of democratic transition between 1997 and 2000.

When 1997 elections in Mexico City brought Cuauhtémoc Cárdenas (son of Lázaro Cárdenas, responsible for the militarization of the police in the 1930s) as mayor on the ticket of the PRD (*Partido de la Revolución Democrática*), citizen expectations rose dramatically. Like his father he was committed to democracy and police reform, and one of his first objectives was to establish a capable and trustworthy police force, purged of old and corrupted elements and replaced with those loyal to the PRD rather than the PRI. Unlike his immediate predecessor, Cárdenas insisted that he would not "militarize" the police. However, some of his most loyal political allies remained in the military, owing to his father's legacy, and immediately upon coming to office he appointed a retired military man as the first police chief (López Montiel 2000).

This not only generated considerable public skepticism about his capacity to depart from business as usual, it also showed how hard it was to seek a reform of the police without bringing the military into the picture. Yet given the military's reputation as conservative and coercive, and as stained by its show of force against Zapatista rebels and other dissidents, public outcry pushed Cárdenas to reverse his initial decision. He soon appointed two civilians to head the police and spearhead reform efforts.

With two civilians at the helm, Cárdenas introduced new structures for hiring and formulated alternative mechanisms for much stronger oversight of the police, measures he hoped would help create a more accountable police force. Changes included lie detector tests for new and returning police personnel, forced resignations among the judicial police (those empowered with bringing criminals to court), and a new system of tracking preventative police (i.e. beat cops, or those entrusted with guaranteeing social order) by neighborhood. The reform's ineffectiveness was visible almost immediately, however, owing in no small part to the institutional legacies created by his father's reforms fifty years prior.

First came opposition from leading police officials, one of whom went directly to the press to vigorously defend the "moral quality" of the city's police—despite these officials' simultaneous public acknowledgement of the "occasional" problem of "judicial police . . . linkages with mafia dedicated to the robbery and reselling of automobiles and autoparts" (*La Jornada*, August 25, 1999a). Second, beat cops also protested against the new government's anti-corruption measures by "withdrawing" their services completely. With foot-dragging from both the police leadership and rank-and-file, crime rates immediately went through the roof, a direct product of police inaction—and perhaps even concerted action, seen in the form of blatant involvement of police in criminal acts as a form of retribution. The level of calculated impunity in the first several weeks after the reform was introduced was so extreme that police chief Gertz Manero was compelled publicly to acknowledge that Mexico City's "40,000 member force (wa)s out of control" (Gregory 1999: 4).

This situation of open rebellion was a product not only of the unparalleled power of police and police institutions reinforced over close to half a century, but also from the fact that reform of the police did not touch the heart of the problem: government incapacity to legally indict criminal elements so as to get to the source of violent disorder and criminality. Problems at "upper" ends of the administration of justice system stemmed in part from the fact that most beat cops refused to cooperate with the state in investigating drug and other gang-related crime, in protest at reform-fueled threats to their own livelihood. They also stemmed from fact that Cárdenas' strong-armed efforts to purify the judicial police had alienated key elements in that next stage of the administration of justice, the courts. In short, the fragmentation of the policing and justice system established in earlier historical periods not only remained; after democratization there was even less cooperation between these different groups than before. This problem was acknowledged publicly by the city's police chief, who lamented a lack of institutional or legal "coordination which [could] link [crime] prevention with investigation" or "articulate civil, business, and penal codes" (*La Jornada*, March 9, 1999b).

But a disarticulated and corrupted legal system was only part of the problem. Democratic transition also created a new environment in which political competition among parties vying for electoral success had reached such heights that it was difficult to reach congressional compromise on legislation or policy to enable police or military reform, let alone revamp the entire administration of the justice system. While democratization did give the newly-elected PRD government in Mexico City incentives and a public platform to rein in the police, democratization also meant that political conditions and institutional goals on the national level did not follow suit. During all of Cárdenas' term in office, the PRI still maintained its monopoly on the national executive, and with it a reservoir of institutional capacities that could be used to undermine police reform efforts in the capital. This included a system of PRI-dominated federal police forces—still tied to the national executive—with a history of intervening in Mexico City affairs; a military bureaucracy still answering to the PRI and also increasingly worried about what would be exposed in terms of federal armed forces' complicity and impunity if Mexico City police were purged; and considerable federal (i.e. PRI) control of local finances—in the form of a budgetary veto on Mexico City expenditures.

Also, the Constitution set clear limits on the mayor's capacity to name his own police chief, with any appointee needing to be jointly supported by the president and approved by national congress. In such conditions, it was very difficult for the Mexico City mayor to make much headway on local police reform. In short, the fact that many local police still had strong connections to the PRI reinforced the federal "safety net" that kept the city's mayor from successfully penetrating and purging the ranks of local police, even though in Mexico City he had the PRD-dominated local legislature behind him. And all this meant that despite the changes in political culture and party strengthening in Mexico City, both wrought by democratization, the existent structure of the state (and particularly, the balance of local and national authority guaranteed by the Constitution) did not change that much, nor did the social networks and political relations among police and persons of influence within the party and the state. The persistence of these structures and practices constituted a non-trivial barrier to reform.

But why then did the PRD not successfully compensate for these failures when Andres Manuel López Obrador, also of the PRD, became mayor in 2000 at a time when the PRI was then defeated at the national level? One explanation is that even with the PRI purged from the national executive, yet another political party—the *Partido Acción Nacional* (PAN) had gained control of the presidency, and it too had limited networks of control over either the police or the military. The only institutions it controlled were national agencies answering to the presidency, many of which were also wracked by their own problems of intensifying corruption which had worsened in the years even before the PAN came to power, owing to the acceleration of military involvement in both drugs and policing. Yet national efforts to struggle against corruption and public insecurity entailed a centralization of institutions and efforts close to the president's office, in individuals and agencies whom the new president could trust (Davis 2006a). This may have opened up new possibilities for facilitating top-down efforts to make the police accountable, seen in new federal efforts to "police the police," but such measures did very little to help make the police accountable vis-à-vis the citizenry.

Complicating matters, top-down efforts at police reform emanating from the office of the president alienated Mexico City officials. The PRD had its own networks, orientations, and partisan goals in Mexico City, especially with respect to public insecurity, and its local ties with the citizenry could have facilitated greater accountability among the police. But with competing local and national political constituencies—tied to different political parties emboldened by the competitive democratic environment—competition rather than cooperation prevailed. In the low grade conflict that ensued, with the PAN and the PRD struggling for the hearts and minds of the Mexico City citizenry, both sets of authorities faced limited maneuvering room for enacting serious or substantial police reform.

To be sure, there were some gains, despite this circumscribed space for action. In Mexico City, Mayor López Obrador and his police chief offered the following reforms: 1) renaming old police forces with new citizen friendly titles, such as the *Policía Comunitaria*; 2) appointing new police leadership and recycling corrupt police out of the force, but keeping old organizational structures intact (Sarre 2001); and 3) developing more community-run policing programs built around PRD ideals of citizen participation, but with the aim of bringing citizens into the front line of crime-fighting. The latter reform came closest to establishing greater accountability vis-à-vis citizens. But the larger effects of this change were counter-balanced by the more systemic problems of police corruption, by the fact that most police were still organized at the level of function rather than territory, and by the non-cooperation from federal authorities. In this environment, community policing efforts only dealt with a small number of police, and their main function was public relations.

On the national level, as well, there were some gains in tackling corruption, yet most came in tandem with greater centralization, which fueled further police corruption and violence even as it backtracked on decentralized democratic ideals (Davis 2006a). Centralized efforts to shut corrupted police out of the state and punish them for past abuses drove some high-ranking police and military officials directly into the criminal world (Hernandez and Joiner 2003; *CNI en Linea*, December 12, 2004; *New York Times*, February 7, 2005; *CNI en Linea*, February 14, 2005). And in a vicious cycle, such developments further pushed the federal government to find greater means of hierarchical control to rein in the problem, including the use of highly specialized military personnel—clandestine and not—against the police and other potential suspects (Hernández 2003b: 14). The use of authoritarian-era militarized tactics to get the problem under control served to undermine the democratic franchise and to alienate citizens from the administration (*CNI en Linea*, December 12, 2004). It also led to bureaucratic fragmentation and infighting among the myriad of new and old federal-level agencies being created in such a relatively short amount of time. This did not bode well for efficiency of police reform efforts, as conflict, competition, and ambiguity about which police forces were supposed to be where, doing what, and why has continued to stymie results.

Combined with a centralization of power in the national state that limited the power of local authorities in sub-national jurisdictions like Mexico City, these changes called into question the coherence and efficacy of many governing structures, as well as the longstanding constitutional precedents and the legal code separating these aspects of police power. Additionally, the problems of bureaucratic infighting and incompetence created problems of transparency—not to mention legitimacy and trust—vis-à-vis civil society. In this environment, it was not unreasonable for the average citizen to ask who was answering to whom and with what accountability, especially with state institutional dynamics shifting from administration to administration, from year to year, and from month to month. In sum, the question of who was "policing the police" became more pressing as time went on.

## Privatization of policing and the question of accountability

The limited progress in establishing clear advances on the issue of police accountability, and the attendant failure to reform the corrupted policing system, had its impact on civil society. With years passing and democratic governments failing to make headway on crime because of past legacies, civil society started to take matters into its own hands. In Mexico City, a 2004 demonstration of 200,000 marching in the name of public security, inspired by no particular event so much as the accumulation of robberies, assaults, and kidnappings over the prior half decade, brought attention to the fact that citizens felt betrayed by their government and were clamoring for change. But the fact that citizens used the route of social mobilization rather than the formal political process showed them to be disenfranchised if not cynical about the possibilities of true reform.

In the absence of concrete gains in police reform or rooting out corruption, citizens also developed their own alternative means to deal with police corruption and the lack of police accountability. Their responses ranged from contracting their own private police to vigilantism, which can be seen as a form of informal or substitute policing. Stated differently, citizens and businesses began to absorb the servicing and protection duties that had long been the legitimate charge of "public" police. This was reflected in the unprecedented explosion in private policing in Mexico, starting in the 1990s. The economic liberalization and commercial opening of the country further contributed to the proliferation of private security forces, mainly because it allowed foreign companies to offer security services. Lucrative profits and a relative low investment were some of the benefits of this business. Citizens, for their part, were eager to hire their own police because this seemed to be one of the few ways to establish some accountability.

To coordinate the explosion of private security forces in this period, in 1994 Mexico City's authorities created the *Dirección de Registro de Servicios Privados de Seguridad*—a Private Security Services Registration Department— which in its first year of operation counted a total of 2,122 registered private security firms within the Federal District. Officials subsequently acknowledged that there were a lot more "pirate" companies that failed to register and thus remained beyond government scrutiny; but among those who did register, almost half (1,123) were subsequently closed because of irregularities in their functioning—i.e. no permits for use of firearms, lack of registration of all firm personnel, etc.[10] By 2002, the number of private security firms operating in the capital neared 1,000, and these companies together employed approximately 22,500 private security guards.

Citizens cannot be faulted for turning to the private sector to solve problems that the newly democratic government proved itself incapable of tackling. Yet the decision to bypass public police in favor of one's own private security forces has its darker side, not just for democracy but also for accountability. For one thing, the turn to private policing can inadvertently let corrupted police off the hook, and diminish public demands for oversight. This is so when citizens no longer direct their attention to reforming the public police or by-pass efforts to change them. There is also the question of to whom private police are accountable, and what this means about democracy, equality, and the rule of law more generally? When individuals start bearing arms as a condition of their employment in private security services, and residents or their "employees" start to carry guns for protection from criminals and police alike, violent "resolutions" to questions of public insecurity become the norm, thereby fueling the vicious circle of insecurity. In addition to reduced public police accountability, this also has driven a degree of impunity and abuse of power within the private police. A 2002 survey of national political cultural and citizen practices found that 45 percent of Mexican citizens believed neither citizens nor authorities respected the law (Secretaría de Gobernación 2002: 137). The recourse to lynchings and the emergence of vigilante attitudes among citizens has thus become the logical extension of this mentality.

Protagonists in such events justify their behavior in terms of the total break-down of policing and the rule of law, a claim that is not that far from the truth. Notably, vigilante responses also seem to emerge frequently among low-income communities where accountability is minimal and the police have long abused the citizenry, as well as where the costs of professionalized private policing prices such services beyond their reach. In this sense, when both state and market failures in police servicing leave citizens vulnerable, they have little recourse but to act on their own. Yet, the overall security situation can deteriorate further when communities or "private" police compete with "public" police for a monopoly over the means of violence and the legitimate use of force. In Mexico City, there have been instances of public and private police forces (not to mention communities themselves) engaging in struggle with each other, fueling an environment of fear and insecurity. This dynamic may partly explain why in the last several years, as the number of private police has risen, citizens have started making formal complaints against them as well.

The magnitude of the problem and the volume of complaints still do not match that leveled at the public police, of course. But as a trend it is noteworthy. In 2002, when statistics were first compiled, Mexico City governing officials saw more than a four-fold rise (from 5 to 22) in monthly complaints against private police in a seven-month period. The fact that private police frequently are comprised of ex-military or ex-police may account for some of the "transference" in impunity and frequent human rights abuses to within the ranks of private police.[11] Whatever the source, accounts of private security forces thwarting public police, and vice-versa, are routinely reported by citizens and officials alike.

For many citizens, one seemingly positive sign on the horizon is the rise of new social movements and other non-governmental organizations devoted to questions of public security, as noted above. Many grassroots groups are taking the problems of police corruption and public insecurity to heart, seeking alternative solutions and community practices at the neighborhood level. In this sense, citizens are both building on and reinforcing the democratic practices and advances that resulted from many years of struggle against authoritarianism. Over the last several years, the Mexico City government has supported citizen security meetings at the level of the delegation, with the goal of bringing residents and police together in democratic dialogue about how to best guarantee public security. The results have been limited, however, for obvious reasons. Citizens do not speak frankly about police misconduct in their neighborhood when those very same police are sitting across the table, armed with their badges and note pads (identifying citizens by face, street, etc.). As such, a certain degree of police reform must already been in place before grassroots citizen participation can make a serious difference.

Given the limits to individual and even neighborhood action, among those social organizations making most headway in tackling police corruption are those operating on a city-wide basis, something which guarantees a larger scale and scope for action and organization. Yet this means that smaller, community-based organizations—the bread and butter of much civil society activism and the scale upon which accountability can be greatest—are relatively insignificant in tackling the problem. Instead, the most high-profile organizations that operate on this scale tend to work in collaboration with private sector businesses. In Mexico, one such high profile organization funded by the private sector, called ICESI, has developed a massive public relations campaign about police corruption, and its efforts have included the publication of names of police officials known to be involved in illegal activities.

Organizations like ICESI have considerable clout because of their connections to wealthier elites in society, and a great deal of legitimacy because they are independent from the institutions of government. But such organizations also have a narrowly-defined view of the problems of insecurity, why they occur, how best to solve them, and to whom reformers should be accountable. Indeed, those linked to business chambers of commerce and other private sector organizations often care mainly about problems like crime and police corruption because they create an environment in which economic gains are put in jeopardy, either by creating location disincentives for private investors, or by driving away potential consumers. Within this framing, concerns about justice and human rights are not so central, and the techniques these organizations favor are more consistent with an authoritarian, eliminate-the-problem-no-matter-what-it-takes ethos that includes pushing for harsher legislative penalties against criminals and greater powers of arrest for police. In this environment, police no longer need to be accountable to the poor and would-be criminals, only to the wealthier middle-class organizations that support the hard line approach.

This is not to say that all civil society organizations involved in fighting police corruption have appropriated the businessman's agenda of stopping crime at all costs. There are a number of the civil society organizations in Mexico that take a human rights approach to the problem. But those organizations committed to human rights seem to be declining in number, compared to the more "anti-crime fighting" NGOs and citizen organizations, several of which are now working with police departments in the Mexico City area to up the ante in terms of restrictions of individual liberties. Significantly, most newfound citizen activism for hard-line measures against crime suspects is openly encouraged by the police, who have a vested interest in blaming criminals for the current situation—thereby diverting attention from their own unaccountability and corruption.

As citizen support grows for such hard-line measures, the sky seems to be the limit, as evidenced by recent efforts in Mexico to install the death penalty. In a move that suggests that authoritarian tendencies are alive and well despite the competitive electoral opening, support for this position is now advocated by some members of the PRI (Pardinas 2003), who through their recent victories in the State of Mexico have found themselves competing with PRD loyalists for the hearts and minds of the metropolitan citizenry. Differentiating themselves politically in terms of who is tougher on crime seems to be the latest salvo launched in a tight electoral field in which all parties are desperate to guarantee their political future.

The power to change endemic police corruption and the downward spiraling situation of insecurity in Mexico rests partly in civil society's institutional capacity to transform system police practices and the overall administration of the justice system, and this requires, among other things, legislative and policy actions in which the state and political parties join together to insist on greater police accountability. But again, the paradox of democracy looms large: such goals are difficult to realize in a virulently competitive democratic context when the vying political parties are unwilling to cooperate with each other and in which citizens routinely bypass formal political routes for evoking change. As little progress is being made on effective measures to "police the police," and as citizens and the state disagree over who should manage this process, both public and private police remain relatively unaccountable to just about everyone, except perhaps their direct superiors and in many cases, not even them.

## Signs of hope? Some concluding remarks on new directions in accountability

In light of these developments, it is hard to be optimistic about a way forward toward a stable and accountable system of policing in Mexico, despite the clear democratic gains in recent years. What is clear is given the political and economic history bequeathed by authoritarianism, reformers are in for a rough time. Even so, in the last several months there are signs of hope on the horizon, even in Mexico City, the locale that has suffered so greatly from the long history of police corruption. The current mayoral administration of Marcelo Ebrard has built on prior efforts at police reform, many of them imposed under his watch as police chief during the prior administration, to break the stranglehold of corruption and introduce new means of making police more accountable. He has done so by creating new programs and political alliances that wreak havoc in old hierarchies of power in longstanding police institutions, while also linking previously antagonistic state and civil society actors together in a common project of reducing crime.

Specifically, Mayor Ebrard has empowered a new political authority in Mexico City (called the *Autoridad del Centro Histórico*) charged with problems of policing, crime, downtown renewal, and overall urban quality of life in a highly circumscribed but critical and economically vibrant area of downtown near the historic center of the city. The targeted area, which is home to a burgeoning informal sector and other service activities linked to illegal trade in contraband, guns, drugs, and clandestinely imported manufactured products, is known to be a center for crime and has a long history of police corruption. Yet this area is also the setting for recent real estate efforts to "rescue" downtown and its built environmental heritage so as to increase property values, upgrade the commercial clientele, bring tourist and other affluent populations downtown, and minimize crime by offering new sources of income and employment to local residents.

As such, the *Autoridad del Centro Histórico* has been given the task of managing and coordinating all activities that occur within this circumscribed area, from policing to street cleaning to granting of construction permits to monitoring air quality to regulating transport to accommodating cultural tourism (Ruiz Healy 2007). It supersedes all prior institutional hierarchies and established levels of governance, and does so for an area long overwhelmed by crime and police corruption. For example, the police in this newly targeted area are expected to support all anti-crime policies established by the *Autoridad*, and there is a special police force and command structure for doing so. The same form of regulation and reform in lines of accountability accrues to other public services offered in this area, which in the past were coordinated sectorally and at the level of the city (i.e. the *Distrito Federal*) or possibly even the federal government, but not at this sub-territorial level. Finally, the coordination and regulation of these public activities is undertaken in conjunction with private sector developers and NGO activists who are driving new investment and cultural or social projects in the area.

So far, this experiment has been relatively successful in eliminating old institutional practices in urban public service delivery, and in bettering the conditions of public security in key downtown areas. In the past year, citizens have come back to the historic center to shop, eat, and live in ever greater numbers, and the general sense is that crime in this area has stopped accelerating. But more important, this experiment has offered a new model for enhancing police accountability, both vis-à-vis citizens and authorities, leading to a less corrupt police force and greater confidence in the local police. Some of this comes from the fact that the special police force has oversight of the historic area only, and many of these police personnel are there because they have personal ties to the current mayor. This not only brings them higher salaries and special privileges, which can reduce the temptation to corruption; it also means that they are tied to a political team that wants this experiment to succeed. Some of it owes to the fact that the installation of surveillance cameras to protect tourists has also allowed the *Autoridad* to monitor the police. And some of it also owes to the fact that the new head of the *Autoridad* is a respected scholar and historian with a long resume of accomplishments in the city whose loyalty to the mayor is unquestioned, who has strong personal relations with the private sector, and who has few personal political ambitions herself (*Milenio* 2006). This small team of connected and committed folks have joined together in alliance against behemoths of power in the city that made reform so difficult in the past.

What also is important about this experiment is the ways that the new lines of authority attributed to the *Autoridad* are able to cross-cut old corrupted institutions so as to diminish the individual and institutional influences of the past, as well as the current lines of patronage policies. This is true not just with respect to the police, which are effectively wrenched out of old, still-corrupted structures of policing. It also is true with respect to all other services in the city, and the way decisions are made at a much smaller territorial scale than in the past. For decades, decisions about policing and other downtown services were made at the level of the city (and in the authoritarian period, at the level of the nation), giving life to large "mafias" of service providers and patronage networks of loyalty and employment that made institutional reform difficult to implement because of the numbers and large flows of resources involved. Because these servicing decisions were made at the level of the city in its entirety, moreover, they were not tailored to the problems and concerns of neighborhoods and more localized areas. With such a large scale of decision-making and so many powerful networks and bureaucratic influences involved, accountability was difficult and power was entrenched. This was so not just with respect to police, but also with transport providers and other purveyors of urban services.

In contrast, in this current experiment the much more circumscribed and smaller scale of action allows for greater accountability and more visible impact. Decisions are made for a territorial unit smaller than the city, but larger than the neighborhood, and in such a way as to bypass old patronage power networks (and longstanding political jurisdictions) reinforced through decades of authoritarian rule. In this environment, there is scope for new horizontal connections of reciprocity to grow. In other words, it is not just that the *Autoridad* operates in a "new" political world where policy making does not coincide with established electoral authority (because its new jurisdiction doesn't match any existent politico-territorial unit). To the extent that this authority also has the power to coordinate *among* urban servicing sectors (security, transport, zoning, etc.) for this new jurisdiction, it is further able to break old vertical structures of patronage and decision-making linked to formal politics or bureaucratic authority that kept reform and accountability vis-à-vis citizens at bay.

That these new bonds of reciprocity engage both public and private sector actors—ranging from government officials, local residents, NGOS, private developers, the police, and other culture and service providers—in a common project to transform a key but manageable territorial location in the city, also is important to the success of the experiment. This has meant that old vertical hierarchies of patronage and politics have been further demobilized, at least with respect to decisions about this part of the city; enough that old political ideologies and longstanding political "bedfellows"—like the police and the state—are no longer the most relevant or politically expedient basis for making policy decisions. These new horizontal networks of reciprocity free the *Autoridad* and its partners from falling into the cracks of those old political alliances which limited reform efforts in the past, and allows them to engage in dialogue and reform efforts that best promote their shared objectives of transforming this specific part of the city. In many ways, this is the ultimate accountability—a horizontal set of networks and reciprocities among a wide range of divergent public and private actors who all care deeply about this particular space. Because police are merely one of the "horizontal" actors in this experiment, they are no more significant that others. As a result, they also are less capable of demanding impunity and more capable of acting accountably, even if it is just with respect to the other key actors in their horizontal networks of decision-making.

To be sure, such an experiment has its limits, in terms of the breadth and extent of police accountability as well as how much real or lasting impact any gains in the historic center of the city will have on the problems of police corruption and insecurity in the metropolitan area as a whole. After all, to a certain degree this experiment could be understood as a glorified version of a business-improvement district (BID), a program which has been widely criticized in the US and elsewhere for its protection of the private sector and the social and class exclusivity that often results. Is the *Autoridad* and its horizontal network of partners, including the police, really more accountable to the local residents, or just to its business-investing partners and their urban redevelopment concerns? Moreover, how big an impact can changes from just one small area of the city have on the larger problems of police lack of accountability in the overall system of policing, which remains massive and fragmented? These are difficult questions to answer.

While this program clearly is no magic bullet for change, the symbolic, economic, and political importance of the historic center suggests that any successes in this area may actually have a demonstration effect for the public and for the city as a whole. Even more significantly, because of the history of this area and the important actors and institutions involved, ranging from the police to the private sector, these small-scale changes may produce a ripple effect in those political networks, hierarchies, and jurisdictions that in the past held dominion over the center. Maybe challenging power structures and creating new room for maneuver within these old structures and institutions, while also providing a space for creating new relationships and reciprocities in which police are merely another "interest" group, is enough to lead to the de-legitimization of old corrupt practices and to increased police account-ability. While change in police behavior may not be immediate, it might be slow and steady enough to re-invigorate a sense of hope and optimism about reversing impunity and jumpstarting its eventual demise in a city where such sentiments have been in short supply. Only time will tell. But even a sym-bolic victory is better than a defeat, and any gain is an improvement in a system where conditions have only worsened over time.

## Notes

1  Portions of the research for this paper were supported by grants from the John D. and Catherine T. MacArthur Foundation and the Carnegie Corporation of New York. Address all inquires to: dedavis@mit.edu.
2  In Mexico City alone, estimates suggest that close to 65 percent of the labor force is employed in the informal sector. For more specific figures see Baroni (2007: 8).
3  The legal separation of functions increased incentives for bribery, especially among beat cops (preventative police), as citizens learned that if they were to avoid judicial police and a court date, a small payoff to the beat cop would suffice. These restrictions motivated both sets of police to transcend their legal limits of action, further undermining the rule of law.
4  Crooks like this did not last long in their posts. Most were recycled out of leadership positions; but recycled police chiefs rarely disappeared entirely. Most just found other lucrative positions elsewhere in the administration—either in another police agency, in the military, and/or in other higher levels of the state (a favored posting was in Customs, where rent-seeking potential was great and corruption also flowered). These dynamics help explain the transfer of cultures of corruption from the police to other arms of the state.
5  That is, the secret police (*Policía Secreta*) were initially formed in the 1920s to "police the police." The formation of secret police, and their fragmentation and expansion over time, strengthened the authoritarian ethos within the Mexican state apparatus.
6  In the late 1960s, one newspaper listed upwards of 24 forces operating in the capital city, empowered by local and federal authority, not including private forces or the large subcategory of preventative police (divided by task, like

firefighting, riot, street vending, etc.) See Carlos Ravelo, *Excelsior*, 31 October 1968.
7  Smith, "Mexico City's Battle to Beat Crime," n.p.
8  Turbiville, "US Army on Law Enforcement and the Mexican Armed Forces", c.f. Anozie *et al.* (2004: 2).
9  Some of these problems also stemmed from a call by the city's last PRI-appointed mayor to "militarize" the city's police force, using the army to purge the corps of its most corrupt elements (López Montiel 2000). Such measures created new conflicts within and between police and the military, further fueling an environment of insecurity as these two sets of forces struggled over dominion and singular control of illegal networks that in the past they jointly shared.
10  Data on private police drawn from interviews and documentation provided by the Secretaría de Seguridad Pública in Mexico City during summer 2002.
11  Statistics from the Registration Office suggested that one-third of the personnel (30 percent) in private security forces came from the military and police ranks. In personal interviews with several representatives from private security firms, the numbers were closer to 50 percent. Interview with Adriana Robles Zapata, SOMESCA.

## Bibliography

Aguayo, Sergio. 1998. *1968: Los archivos de violencia*. México, DF: Grijalbo.

Alcocer V., Jose. 1997. "Inseguridad Pública." *Proceso*, September 28: 49–51.

Alvarado, Arturo. 2000. "Seguridad Pública en la Ciudad de México" in Gustavo Garza (ed.), *La Ciudad de México en el fin del segundo milenio*. Mexico, DF: El Colegio de Mexico-Gobierno del Distrito Federal.

Amnesty International. 2002. *Summary of Amnesty International's Concerns on Mexico* (available at http://web.amnesty.org//library/Index/ENGAMR410372002/).

Andreas, Peter. 1998. "The Political Economy of Narco-Corruption in Mexico." *Current History* 97 (April): 160–170.

Anozie, Valentina, Juhie Shinn, Katy Skarlatos, and Julio Urzua. 2004. *Reducing Incentives for Corruption in the Mexico City Police Force*. Monograph. La Follette School of Public Affairs, University of Wisconsin-Madison. International Workshop, *Public Affairs* 869, Spring.

Bailey, John. 2003. *"Introduction: New Security Challenges in the South–North Dialog"* in Working Paper: "Public Security in the Americas: New Challenges in the South–North Dialog" (http://www.georgetown.edu/pdba/Pubsecurity/pubsecurity.html).

Bailey, John and Roy Godson (eds). 2000. *Organized Crime and Democratic Governability: Mexico and the U.S.–Mexican Borderlands*. Pittsburgh: University of Pittsburgh Press.

Bailey, John and Gustavo Flores-Macías. 2007. "Violent Crime and Democracy: Mexico in Comparative Perspective". Paper presented at the Annual Midwest Political Science Association Conference, Chicago, IL, April 12–15.

Baroni, Bruno. 2007. *Spatial Stratification of Street Vendors in Downtown Mexico City*. Thesis, Master of City Planning (MCP), Department of Urban Studies and Planning, Massachusetts Institute of Technology.

Bliss, Katherine E. 2001. *Compromised Positions: Prostitution, Public Health, and Gender Politics in Revolutionary Mexico City*. University Park: The Pennsylvania State University Press.

Bodemaer, Klaus, Sabine Kurtenbach, and Klaus Meschkat. 2001. *Violencia y regulación en América Latina*. Caracas: Asociación Aemana de Investigación sobre América Latina-Adlaf.

*CNI en Linea*. 2005a. "Confirman vinculos de Nahún Acosta con narcotráfico." February 14 (http://www.cni.tv/nacional).

*CNI en Linea*. 2005b. "Indigará PGR detención de agentes de la AFI en Edomex." January 19 (http://www.cni.tv/nacional).

*CNI en Linea*. 2004. "Acto autoritario, destitución de Ebrard: Victor Hugo Cirigo." December 12.

Cross, John. 1998. *Informal Politics: Street Vendors and the State in Mexico City*. Stanford: Stanford University Press.

Davis, Diane E. in press. "Policing and Populism in the Cárdenas and Echeverría Administrations," forthcoming in William Beezley (ed.) *Cárdenas, Echeverría and Revolutionary Populism*. Arizona: University of Arizona Press.

Davis, Diane E. forthcoming. "The Political and Economic Origins of Violence and Insecurity in Contemporary Latin America: Past Trajectories and Future Prospects," forthcoming in Desmond Arias and Daniel Goldstein (eds) *Violent Pluralisms*. Durham, NC: Duke University Press.

Davis, Diane E. 2007. "Insecure and Secure Cities: Towards a Reclassification of World Cities in a Global Era." *Sociologia Urbana e Rurale* 29 (82): 67–82.

Davis, Diane E. 2006a. "Undermining the Rule of Law: Democratization and the Dark Side of Police Reform in Mexico." *Latin American Politics and Society* 48 (1) (Spring): 55–86.

Davis, Diane E. 2006b. "Conflict, Cooperation, and Convergence: Globalization and the Politics of Downtown Development in Mexico City." *Research in Political Sociology* 15: 143–178.

Davis, Diane E. 1999. *Urban Leviathan: Mexico City in the Twentieth Century*. Philadelphia: Temple University Press.

Davis, Diane E. and Arturo Alvarado. 1999. "Descent into Chaos? Liberalization, Public Insecurity, and Deteriorating Rule of Law in Mexico City." *Working Papers in Local Governance and Democracy* 1(99): 95–197.

Fruhling, Hugo and Joseph Tulchin (eds) *Crime and Violence in Latin America: Citizen Security, Democracy and the State*. Washington, DC: Woodrow Wilson Center Press Baltimore: The Johns Hopkins University Press.

*Fundación Mexicana para la Salud*. 1997. *La Violencia en la Ciudad de México: Análisis de la magnitud y su repercusión económica*. Mexico City: *Fundación Mexicana para la Salud*.

Goldstein, Daniel M. 2003. "In Our Own Hands: Lynching, Justice, and the Law in Bolivia." *American Ethnologist* 30 (1): 22–43

González Ruiz, Samuel, Ernesto López Portillo V. and Jose Arturo Yáñez. 1994. *Seguridad pública en México: Problemas, perspectivas, y propuestas*. Mexico, DF: Universidad Nacional Autónoma de México (UNAM).

Gregory, Joseph R. 1999. "Mexico: A Call to Fight Crime." *New York Times*, February 27, p. A4.

Hellman, Judith Adler. 1978. *Mexico in Crisis*. New York: Holmes and Meyer.

Hernández, Vicente 2003a. "Ofrece Macedo de limpiar la PGR en cuatro años." *Milenio*. January 19, p. 12.

Hernández, Vicente 2003b. "El Ejército desmanteló las instalaciones de la FEADS." *Milenio*. January 17, p. 14.

Hernández, Vicente and Alfredo Joyner. 2003. "Limpia a toda la PGR, advierte el procurador." *Milenio*. January 24, p. 14.

Hinton, Mercedes S. 2006. *The State on the Streets: Police and Politics in Argentina and Brazil*. Boulder, CO: Lynn Rienner.

Huggins, Martha K, Mika Haritsos-Fatouros, and Philip Zimbardo. 2002. *Violence Workers: Police Torturers and Murderers Reconstruct Brazilian Atrocities*. Berkeley, CA: University of California Press.

Huggins, Martha. 1998. *Political Policing: The United States and Latin America*. Durham, NC: Duke University Press.

Instituto Ciudadano de Estudios Sobre la Inseguridad (ICESI). 2005. *Tercera Encuesta Nacional sobre Inseguridad 2005 (ENSI-3): Analisis de resultados*. Mexico, DF: ICESI, A.C.

Knight, Alan. 1986. *The Mexican Revolution (Vols I & II)*. Cambridge: Cambridge University Press.

Knight, Alan and Will Pansters (eds). 2005. *Caciquismo in Twentieth-Century Mexico*. London: Institute for the Study of the Americas.

*La Jornada*. 1999a. "Defienden *calidad moral* de jefes policiacos." August 25, p. 64.

*La Jornada*. 1999b. "Aplica la SPP plan de emergencia de control de 37 mil policía." March 9.

*La Jornada*. 2001. "Asaltan judiciales Mexiquenses a dos policias del DF." July 5, p. 38.

Lear, John. 2001. *Workers, Neighbors, and Citizens: The Revolution in Mexico City*. Lincoln and London: University of Nebraska Press.

Leeds, Elizabeth. 1996. "Cocaine and Parallel Polities in the Brazilian Urban Periphery." *Latin American Research Review* 33(3): 47–83.

López Montiel, Gustavo. 2000. "The Military, Political Power, and Police Relations in Mexico City." *Latin American Perspectives* (Special Issue on Violence, Coercion, and Rights in the Americas) 27 (2): 79–94.

López Portillo, Ernesto. 2003. "La policía en Mexico: function política y reforma" in *Crimen Transnacional y Seguridad Pública*. Mexico, DF: Plaza y Janes Editores.

Lupsha, Peter A. 1996. "Transitional Organized Crime versus the Nation-State." *Transnational Organized Crime* 2 (1) (Spring): 21–48.

Meade, Teresa A. 1997. *"Civilizing" Rio: Reform and Resistance in a Brazilian City 1889–1930*. Philadelphia, PA: The Pennsylvania State University Press.

*Milenio*. 5 de Diciembre 2006. Dirigirá Alejandra Moreno la nueva Autoridad del Centro (http://www.milenio.com/index.php/2006/12/05/20784/).

Moser, Caroline O. N. 2004. "Urban Violence and Insecurity: An Introductory Roadmap." *Environment & Urbanization* 16 (2): 3–16.

*New York Times*. 2005. "Mexico Says Drug Cartel Had Spy in President's Office." February 7, p. 3.

Oszlak, Oscar. 1981. "The Historical Formation of the State in Latin America: Some Theoretical and Methodological Guidelines for its Study." *Latin American Research Review* 16(2): 3–32.

Oxhorn, Philip D. and Graciela Ducatenzeiler (eds) 1998. *What Kind of Democracy? What Kind of Market? Latin America in the Age of Neoliberalism*. Philadelphia, PA: The Pennsylvania State University Press.

Pardinas, Juan E. 2003. "Empollando a Díaz Ordaz." *Reforma*, June 8.

Pansters, Wil and Hector Castillo Berthier. 2006. "Insecurity and Violence in Mexico City" in Kees Koonings and Dirk Kruijt (eds.), *Fractured Cities: Social Exclusion, Urban Violence and Contested Spaces in Latin America*, London, Zed Books.

Pereira, Anthony. 2005. *Political (In)justice: Authoritarianism and the Rule of Law in Brazil, Chile, and Argentina*. Pittsburgh. University of Pittsburgh Press.

Picatto, Pablo. 2004. "A Historical Perspective on Crime in Twentieth Century Mexico City." Paper presented at the Janey Conference on *Security and Democracy in the Americas*, New School University, Graduate Faculty, April 2 (text version available at http://repositories.cdlib.org/usmex/prajm/picatto).

Piccato, Pablo. 2001. *City of Suspects: Crime in Mexico City, 1900–1931*. Durham, NC: Duke University Press.

*Reforma*. 2003. "Recetan a policía del DF: Proponen fusionar a preventivas y judiciales para garantiza la prevención e indagación del delito." January 18, p. 14a.

Rotker, Susana (ed.). 2002. *Citizens of Fear: Urban Violence in Latin America*. New Brunswick, NJ: Rutgers University Press.

Ruiz Healy, Eduardo. 2007. "Las noticias de hoy." 24 de enero de 2007 (http://www.radioformula.com.mx/noticias/rf2101.asp?ID=55813).

Sarre, Miguel. 2001. "Seguridad ciudadana y justicia penal frente a la democracia, la división de poderes y el federalismo" in Arturo Alvarado and Sigrid Arzt (eds) *El desafío democrático en Mèxico: Seguridad y estado de derecho*. Mexico, DF: El Colegio de Mèxico.

Secretaria de Gobernación. 2002. "Conociendo a los ciudadanos Mexicanos: Principales resultados de la encuesta nacional sobre cultura política." *Revista Este Pais* 30(2) (August).

Smith, Gerri. 2003. "Mexico City's Battle to Beat Crime." *Business Week Online*, August 20 (available at http://www.businessweek.com/bwdaily/dnflash/aug2003/nf200330820_5793_db017.html).

Smulovitz, Catalina. 2003. "Citizen Insecurity and Fear: Public and Private Responses in Argentina" in Hugo Fruhling and Joseph Tulchin (eds) *Crime and Violence in Latin America: Citizen Security, Democracy and the State*. Washington, DC: Woodrow Wilson Center Press Baltimore: The Johns Hopkins University Press.

Ungar, Mark. 2002. *Elusive Reform: Democracy and the Rule of Law in Latin America*. Boulder, CO: Lynne Rienner Publishers.

Wallace, Claire and Rossalina Latcheva. 2006. "Economic Transformation Outside the Law: Corruption, Trust in Public Institutions and the Informal Economy in Transition Countries of Central and Eastern Europe." *Europe-Asia Studies* 58 (1 January): 81–102.

World Bank. 2006. "Mexico Country Data Profiles." *Mexico Data*. Washington, DC: The World Bank (available at: http://web.worldbank.org/website/external/countries/lacext/mexico/).

Zepeda Lecuona, Guillermo. 2004. *Crimen sin castigo: Procuración de justicia penal y ministerio público en México*. Mexico, DF: Fondo de Cultura Económica.

Zermeño, Sergio. 1978. *México: Una democracia utópica. El movimiento estudiandial de 1968*. México, DF: Siglo XXI.

Zurita, Beatriz and Teresita Ramirez. 1999. *Trends and Empirical Causes of Violent Crime in Mexico*. Washington, DC: The World Bank/Mexican Health Foundation.

# 10 Police and state reform in Brazil

## Bad apple or rotten barrel?

*Mercedes S. Hinton*

## Introduction

Violence is ubiquitous in Brazil. Extermination of street children, police participation in death squads and crime rings, and violent land conflicts are the kinds of law-and-order headlines that reoccur at a disturbing rate. Homicides are the number one cause of death for 15–44-year-olds in Brazil, surpassing killings by disease or accident (UNCHR 2007). For citizens of Brazil, fear of violence is exacerbated by widespread anxiety over predatory police forces and unresponsive governments.

Some of the tensions surrounding crime, policing, and government in Brazil are illustrated by events that took place just prior to the historic elections of October 2002, in which Luiz Inácio da Silva, better known as Lula, was elected president of Brazil. Lula had originally stood at the forefront of the workers' movement that had organised in staunch opposition to the Brazilian military regime of 1964–85 – a regime that had come to power originally to curb labour militancy and stymie threats of communism. The presidential victory by this former left-wing union organiser and his Workers' Party, after three previous failed attempts, was thus widely hailed as the triumph of popular democracy in Brazil. Moreover, President Lula's ascent from humble origins as a shoeshine boy in one of the world's most unequal countries was a veritable rags-to-riches story, giving hope to the poor throughout the country.

In the weeks leading up to Lula's election, however, there were some very dark events unfolding in Rio de Janeiro that received far less international attention. Just a few days before the first round of the elections, Rio drug lords issued an order that the city should close down or face the consequences.

The threat was not taken lightly: the text of the drug lords' communiqué was broadcast by radio and television, published in newspapers and spread by personal messengers. On what became known as 'Black Monday', even the most affluent areas of the city submitted to the will of the drug traffickers. Banks, schools, public transportation, and commerce shut down, and Rio's streets emptied out. Faced with this situation, the governor of Rio was forced to call on the federal government to send in 40,000 army troops to ensure that voters would be safe to go to the polls in the coming elections.

The events of Black Monday immediately raise several troublesome questions. First, why did the population at large heed the orders of the drug lords? To put it simply in Weberian terms, isn't a monopoly over the legitimate use of force the defining characteristic of the state? One must also wonder why, more than 20 years on from the transition from military rule, troops were necessary to preserve basic electoral freedoms in Brazil's second most important city. In a democracy, shouldn't the population be able to look to the police rather than the military for protection on local streets? And if not, what does this tell us about the status of the police as the state's primary legal enforcers? Indeed, as British police specialist Robert Reiner has argued, 'policing is both source and symbol of the quality of a political civilization' (2000: 8). Even though the police role in any democracy is bound to be contentious, the police should provide the quintessential public service – the protection of life and property (Reiss and Bordua 1967). How the police discharge their duties has a profound impact on public trust in the system, the legitimacy and authority of the state and law, and basic democratic freedoms such as freedom of assembly and the right to vote. Thus the events of Black Monday suggest something deeply amiss.

While policing is never without controversy, even in the most homogeneous and politically stable societies, one hallmark of a democracy is that the population is able to look to the police to provide a modicum of assistance and reassurance to the public. One would also expect that they provide some measure of redress by supporting the rest of the criminal justice system through arrests and investigations and that their actions and presence provide a minimum threshold of deterrence to dissuade crime. Instead, we find that Brazil's police are non-universalistic in law enforcement, violent, corrupt, predatory, and often so ineffective that their deterrent capabilities are in doubt.

The first half of this essay will focus on these problems, following a brief discussion of the organisation of policing and general crime context. The second half will seek to identify the main factors that have perpetuated this state of affairs even into President Lula's second administration.

## The organisation of policing

The police in Brazil are convened primarily at the state (provincial) level, where they are overseen, staffed, trained, and paid under the jurisdiction of each of the country's 26 state governors plus the governor of the capital district, Brasília. Within each state there are two separate police forces responsible for day-to-day policing. The uniformed Military Police (PM) is responsible for patrol, emergency response. and arrests of crimes in progress; PM officers number 390, 451 across Brazil. The larger states of São Paulo and Rio have 79,812 and 43,774 PMs respectively (SENASP 2007).[1] The second state police force, the Civil Police (PC), is essentially a plainclothes judicial force that is responsible for investigations and judicial proceedings; nationwide they number 115,960, while São Paulo and Rio's respective PC force strength stands at 32, 623 and 11,230 (SENASP 2007).

Control over the police can be considered to be relatively centralised, even if more decentralised politically than in countries with single national police forces because each state represents a very large geographic area. Eighteen of Brazil's states are each a larger territory than the whole of England and Wales. The state of São Paulo alone has 40 million people and is about 1.6 times geographically larger than England and Wales in square kilometers. And yet São Paulo has two main territorial police forces as compared to the 43 found in England and Wales. If in Britain there are constant and heated debates about whether the police are too centralised to meet local needs, one can imagine the difficulties of police administration, management, and territorial coverage in Brazil simply because of its size, to say nothing of its challenging political and socioeconomic environment.

Of greater local controversy than the fact that the police are managed at the state (provincial) level is the division between patrol and judicial policing. This division of labour between the two police forces is prescribed by the Brazilian constitution and is a matter of long-running debate in Brazil, as it is widely believed that this dual structure perpetuates a host of coordination problems, duplication, and expense.

In addition to the two main state police forces, in some large cities Brazil has small municipal police forces that are under the control of local mayors, but their powers are quite limited. The federal government also has a small FBI-style Federal Police force under its control, and this force is responsible for federal investigations in areas such as terrorism, fiscal crimes, forced labour, electoral or political crimes, and drug trafficking, in addition to border control and passport regulation. It has about 10,000 sworn officers. Drug trafficking is also a major issue and focus of attention for the state police forces, and this overlap in function generates some tensions, not least because federal investigators sometimes uncover state forces' complicity with local traffickers.

## The general crime context

The policing environment in Brazil, as suggested in the introduction, is an extremely challenging one. Brazil is a country of 183.9 million, over 55 per cent of whom live in households that are under the poverty line (IPEA 2005). Crime and violence, particularly on the periphery of major urban centres, are inescapable features of daily life. Analyses based on Ministry of Health data reveal that there were 48,000 homicides in Brazil in 2004. This represents a rate of 27 per 100,000 inhabitants and an increase of 16 per cent from 1994 (OEI 2007: 21).

Given Brazil's large population and extensive rural areas, the national homicide rate belies the levels of crime and violence going on in Brazil's main cities. As shown in Table 10.1, the homicide rate in Brazil's top ten largest cities is far higher than the national rate.

The causes of the spike in violent crime in Brazil that began in the mid-1980s are complex. An important factor is the process of urbanisation in the 1960s and 1970s. During this period, the military regime was engaged in an industrialisation drive that produced Brazil's 'economic miracle'. To provide workers for the country's factories the government encouraged rapid rural migration to the cities, such that Brazil's urban dwellers more than doubled between 1967 and 1985 (Hinton 2006: 95). The majority of these newcomers settled in squatter settlements on the hillsides and peripheries of major cities. These squatter settlements, known as *favelas*, were characterised by crumbling and unstable dwellings, squalid conditions, and few public services. Today about 85 per cent of Brazilians live in urban areas, and an estimated 55 per cent work in the informal sector (IPEA 2007).

With this disorderly and rapid urbanisation came the breakdown of many informal social controls and enormous population pressures on metropolitan public services. When economic slowdown hit with the onslaught of the international debt crisis in the 1980s, Brazil was in the midst of a transition from military rule and was not positioned economically, or politically, to begin to deal with the combustive situation in the *favelas*.

With the rise of the drug cartels in the 1980s in neighbouring Colombia and Peru, Brazil became attractive for the drug trade, as its extensive and porous borders offered numerous opportunities for trans-shipment. Its growing internal market for drugs and the low levels of state presence in the *favelas*, moreover, offered numerous opportunities for bases of local dealing. These events were of course occurring against a backdrop of Brazil's extremely unequal pattern of income and land tenure, the implications of which will be addressed further below.

*Table 10.1* Homicide rates and levels in Brazil's ten largest cities, 2004

| Size rank | City | Number of homicides | Rate per 100,000 inhabitants |
|---|---|---|---|
| 1 | São Paulo | 4,275 | 39.8 |
| 2 | Rio de Janeiro | 3,174 | 52.8 |
| 3 | Salvador | 739 | 28.5 |
| 4 | Belo Horizonte | 1,506 | 64.7 |
| 5 | Fortaleza | 654 | 28.5 |
| 6 | Brasília | 815 | 36.5 |
| 7 | Curitiba | 693 | 40.8 |
| 8 | Recife | 1,352 | 91.8 |
| 9 | Porto Alegre | 566 | 40.3 |
| 10 | Manaus | 410 | 26.2 |
| **Ten-City** | **Average** | **1,418** | **45.0** |

*Source:* Ministry of Health Data (cited in OEI 2007).

Certainly the police are not responsible for the complex social and economic factors that contribute to Brazil's high levels of violent crime. But the police exacerbate already existing levels of insecurity, rather than dampen them as one would expect the police to do in a democracy.

Of course no police force, no matter how well managed or accountable, can prevent all crimes, let alone detect or investigate all crimes that occur. But a democratic police service should be able to lend an important measure of assistance, protection, and psychological reassurance to the public and support to the rest of the judicial system (Hinton 2006). They contribute to crime deterrence and the provision of redress to victims of crime by helping to ensure that perpetrators will receive some form of punishment for wrongdoing. In Brazil, the police are struggling to provide all of these – reassurance, investigative capacity, and deterrence – intensifying the perception and indeed the reality of public insecurity.

## Assistance and reassurance?

In a democracy, the frequent presence of police officers on patrol, coupled with rapid and effective police responses to distress calls, can provide a significant degree of the psychological reassurance to the public that is required to prevent fear of crime. But throughout Brazil, public confidence in the police is undermined by negative interactions with the police and by stark media and NGO depictions of police corruption and violence. Documented abuses range from petty forms of corruption, such as bribery to turn a blind eye to traffic violations, street vending, and informal transport, to direct involvement in serious forms of organised crime relating to prostitution, car theft, drugs, kidnapping, and arms dealing. Extortion of criminals, drug users, prostitutes, and the working poor is rampant, as is police involvement in acts to destabilise political opponents and rivals. While not all individual officers are involved in these activities, these problems have become so pervasive that they undermine public confidence in the police as a whole.

To be sure, tourists and more affluent Brazilians experience a more courteous and less adversarial side to law enforcement. The affluent are also better able to insulate themselves from street crime by means of private security guards for their homes and businesses, gated communities, private transport, bulletproof vehicles, and GPS tracking devices. But whatever limited reassurance and protection the police do provide to the general public is generally not felt in poorer neighbourhoods, as *favelas* do not receive routine policing.

One can picture the Brazilian *favela* as groupings of precarious and claustrophobic shacks within or at the periphery of a city, encroaching on hillsides and forests and areas where land lies fallow. Similar shantytowns are indeed found throughout the developing world. The working poor living in these densely populated areas are effectively squatters on the edge of a city, functioning as a supplement to formal industry and services, as fuel for the informal sector, and as a means of self-help for the rural and urban poor.

Individuals who live in these shantytowns typically do not own their land or property and have little formal access to basic public services. Space pressures and governmental complicity have created a situation in which many *favela* residents pay sizable rents to individuals who have illegally staked a claim to these areas and who exploit the situation by charging user rights. The infrastructure and public services that reach these overpopulated areas are oversubscribed and poorly maintained. Electricity is typically poached, running water is not always available, and basic sanitation is lacking, resulting in open sewers and the burning of garbage.

A lack of routine police presence in *favelas* throughout Brazil has contributed to the spread of criminal gangs in these neighbourhoods and has impeded more systematic service provision. In Rio, the city government estimates that there are some 1.1 million residents (about 20 per cent of the population) living in the city's 750 *favelas* (Prefeitura da Cidade do Rio de Janeiro 2006). And yet the state does not require universal policing coverage of these areas, although the high crime rate in these regions has long been apparent. Instead, the police make what could be termed *periodic incursions* – usually to contain crime that has spilled out to more affluent neighbourhoods. Things have gotten so dangerous that when the police do enter they arrive as an occupying army might. I remember seeing in one *favela* a flag planted at the top of the highest hill by the SWAT team that entered. This was not just any flag but the black flag of Rio SWAT team or (the battalion of special police operations BOPE), which depicts a skull impaled on a sword, backed by two gold pistols.

The Rio state government's 2006 official description of what the symbol represents did little to dispel the ominous visual implications.[2] The police website publicly interprets the symbols in the following way: The 'skull symbolises death'. The sword in the centre of the insignia 'signifies combat weapons; when pointed downwards impaling the skull, it represents war,' while the black colour of the symbol 'represents grief and mourning' and the red colour 'represents combat and war'. Finally, the gold pistols in the centre are 'the logo of the Military Police' (of which the SWAT team is part). Such an insignia is hardly the ideal emblem of civilian, democratic police force, and yet it appears not only on flags raised in 'occupied' *favelas* but also on the doors of the vehicles used by the SWAT team when they enter the *favelas*.

Police 'occupations' have intensified over the years. At least since 2003, the Rio police have been entering *favelas* with military assault vehicles, known colloquially as the *caveirão* – literally, 'the big skull'. These vehicles, which can carry up to twelve heavily armed police officers, resemble a small tank and feature a rotating turret that can turn 360 degrees and firing positions running along the body. Amnesty International, which has issued numerous complaints about the use of these vehicles and their terrorising effect on children, estimates that by 2006 the Rio state government had bought ten *caveirões* at a cost of $62,000 US each and had plans to increase the fleet (Amnesty International 2006b: 1).

With no routine police presence, only temporary militarised police occupations or sweeps, the *favelas* have been prey to control by drug gangs. Residents are all too often caught in the middle of armed battles between rival traffickers or between these gangs and the police forces that enter to fight them, only to leave later. This violence in itself has been a major deterring factor to the systematic provision of municipal public services such as sanitation, lighting, transport, health, and postal services to these communities. Civilian ambulances will not enter most *favelas*, and only the most committed physicians are willing to attend basic medical clinics in these areas. Since politicians, officials, and staff of NGOs dare not enter most *favelas* without obtaining a safe-conduct from a local drug baron, it is obvious who is in control of what, how, and when something is done in these communities.

In this climate of fear and intimidation, freedom of movement is dramatically impeded, as is residents' ability to travel to work and school, let alone to organise and sustain local associations. The negative impact this has on the capacity for political voice within the *favelas* dramatically impedes robust democratic political oversight of local, state, and federal authorities, particularly the brutal and corrupt police officers, who have more direct and immediate capacity for reprisals than do civilian state officials and bureaucrats. In this context, the police are notoriously heavy-handed in their use of force.

Dangerous working conditions for the police, inadequate police numbers, and daily confrontations with a heavily armed criminal element brandishing automatic weapons, grenades, and even rocket launchers and hiding easily in the labyrinthine maze of the *favelas* feed a siegelike police mentality and violence on all sides. Compounding these factors is the belief within many sectors of the PM and public that Brazil's investigative police, prisons, and courts suffer from laxity, corruption, and inefficiency. These factors have spurred the spread and perpetuation of death squads in Brazil, with disgruntled officers banding together to exterminate suspected criminals and derelicts, intimidate witnesses, mete out reprisals for police killings and encroachment on turf, and provide vigilante protection of neighbourhoods and private property.

In recent years, paramilitary organisations known as *milícias*, composed of police and security sector personnel with direct ties to key politicians and businessmen, have begun to arise within the slums to exterminate drug traffickers. This has been a slippery slope, resulting in police and paramilitary takeover of and profit from aspects of the drug trade under the guise of law and order and in widespread human rights abuses. *Milícia* groups have also begun to impose extortionary protection 'taxes' on slum residents in addition to charging illegal user rights for alternate transport and poached electrical connections.

Further enabling the situation are very weak or nonexistent governmental controls on police discharge of weapons, poor police training, and insufficient capacity to investigate suspected police malfeasance. Police lethal force on or off the job is typically justified as self-defence, and a lack of systematic attempts to ascertain the veracity of these claims has led to impunity.[3] Between 1999 and 2004, a total of 9,000 killings were carried out by police in the states of São Paulo and Rio de Janeiro (Amnesty International 2006a: 1).

In 2006, police statistics showed 1,063 police killings in the state of Rio de Janeiro, which the government classified as acts of self-defence (CESEC 2006). To give a sense of the magnitude of this figure, it represents nearly three times the 376 police homicides that took place in the entire United States that same year (FBI 2007), despite Rio state's population of 15 million as compared to the US population of 300 million. Certainly, some of this is a function of the fact that homicides overall in Rio and Brazil are much higher than in the United States, and indeed Brazil's criminal justice system in Brazil is overloaded by the sheer volume of cases.

Nevertheless, if one looks at the ratio of civilians to police officers killed, as expert on police violence Paul Chevigny (1991) has advocated, the police in Rio are making disproportionate use of force. Chevigny argues that when the ratio of civilians to police officers killed exceeds 10: 1, it suggests that deadly force rather than self-defence is being employed (1991: 192). What is notable here is that the Rio PM and PC in 2006 killed more than 37 times the number (29) of police officers who were killed while on duty.

Police violence and death squad activity are not isolated to Rio and São Paulo. In November 2006 a parliamentary commission of inquiry in the Brazilian Congress detailed death squad activity in all nine of Brazil's north-eastern states. The commission of inquiry, which lacks powers of prosecution, found links between state officers, police, business interests, and organised crime in this region (Amnesty International 2006a: 1). Many of the violent conflicts in rural areas are over land rights. Activists seeking to accelerate the pace of land reform frequently come into conflict with wealthy landowners and the local police officers who support them. According to the Pastoral Land Commission of the Catholic Church, between 1985 and 2006 there were 1,464 killings of land activists in a total of 1,104 violent conflicts over land. Only 85 of these cases proceeded to trial, and 94 per cent of the perpetrators enjoyed impunity (CPT 2007: 1).

## Investigations and criminal deterrence

Against the backdrop of the preceding discussion, it is of perhaps little surprise that police involvement in supporting criminal investigations is very problematic. As already mentioned, Brazil's policing is divided between two forces, a judicial police and a uniformed police. Their functions are theoretic-ally complementary: the PM is charged with keeping order and arresting criminals where there is an arrest warrant or where they are caught *in flagrante delicto*, while the plainclothes PC is charged with criminal investigation *post facto*.

In practice, however, the two are bitter rivals, operating under a veil of mutual suspicion and secrecy and sharing information only rarely. Their statistics are separate, as are their training and the police precincts. Police statistics are frequently unreliable, and crime categories are often blurred. Mishandling of investigations and crimes in progress is another factor that has stoked public insecurity.

An outgrowth of low public confidence in the police, non-universal police coverage, and poor performance in investigations is police inability to provide an adequate minimum threshold of criminal deterrence, even as their violent tactics endeavour to compensate. In most societies, informal mechanisms of social control, such as the family, moral values, culture, and religion, are buttressed by formal social controls applied by the criminal justice system through arrests, fines, criminal penalties, and imprisonment, to create an atmosphere of deterrence. The dissuasive effectiveness of formal social controls is very much affected by criminal calculations of the likelihood of apprehension and of the application and severity of criminal penalties (see von Hirsch *et al.* 1999).

While Brazil's police do arm themselves with heavy artillery, engaging in heavy use of lethal and non-lethal force and torture, arguably part of a bid to boost their deterrent role, the police often find themselves outgunned. Drug traffickers are heavily armed with automatic weapons and hand grenades, and the drug barons are known to patrol openly with their weapons in military fatigues in the *favelas*. Pay is so low that there have been numerous police strikes in Brazil, and police officers often have to buy their own bullet-proof vests, have outdated equipment, and are exhausted and demoralised from long shifts, extra working hours, long commutes to work, and difficult working conditions. In cities like Rio and São Paulo, more often than not, police officers moonlight as private security guards, where controls over their activities are even more tenuous because of poor governmental regulation of the private security sector. Many studies done by human rights organisations have shown that while working as private security guards, police often use firearms and lethal force to protect the property, store, home or institution they are guarding, and they face a high risk of being killed or seriously wounded themselves. Indeed, 117 off-duty police officers were killed in 2006 as compared to the 29 killed while on duty (CESEC 2006), suggesting that many were working as private security guards or were engaged in vigilante or other illegal activity.

In a context where there is such a lack of public confidence in the protective capacities of the police, where there is widespread involvement in crime rings, and where the police are all too often overwhelmed and overpowered by levels of crime and violence, it is little wonder that there is scant cooperation with public investigative efforts. Information released by Brazil's National Security Secretariat in March 2007 indicated that there were some half a million outstanding arrest warrants in the country for suspects involved in such crimes as kidnapping, robbery, and murder (Xinhua News Agency 2007).

When suspects are apprehended, the penalties are harsh, at least for small-time criminals, as Brazilian prisons are notoriously violent and severely over-crowded institutions where riots and torture are rampant and where prisoners must often buy their own food. As of June 2007, Brazil's prisons (including those housed in police custody) were at an overcapacity of 132,556 inmates; the overall prison population was 419,551, representing a rate of 224.6 per 100,000 inhabitants (MJ 2007).

The rehabilitative function of prisons, which is questioned even in highly industrialised societies, are virtually nil in Brazil, given the gross overcrowd-ing, disease, and lack of investment. Instead, individuals behind bars are further brutalised in prisons and presented with new opportunities for crim-inal networking. When Thomas Bastoz was minister of justice, he himself referred to Brazil's criminal justice system, particularly its youth detention facilities, as a 'production line for crime' that 'graduates criminals' (*Globo* 2003).

Those who administer Brazilian prisons, moreover, have done little to prevent crime bosses from continuing to orchestrate their criminal enterprises from behind bars, with the assistance of cell phones and prison guard and administration corruption. Prison breaks are also virtually routine. Indeed, things have deteriorated to such a point that in May 2006 Brazil's most economically important state, São Paulo, was paralysed by simultaneous uprisings in 45 prisons: inmates took guards and administrators hostage, destroyed infrastructure, killed guards and criminal rivals, set fire to prem-ises, and in many instances escaped en masse.

The ostensible catalyst of the riots was the leak of the prison administra-tion's 'secret' plans to transfer several hundred members of the criminal gang First Command of the Capital (PCC) to a maximum-security prison in the interior of the state. As if a timed and coordinated uprising across the peniten-tiary system were not shocking enough, these prison rebellions were coordin-ated with a series of lethal drive-by shootings of police officers, bus hijackings, and shootings and bombings of bank branches and police installations.

This wave of attacks and subsequent retaliatory counterattacks by the police paralysed much of São Paulo, Latin America's most economically important city, for over a week, left nearly 200 dead, and caused over $1 billion of damage (LABSCR 2006). The events appeared to have surprised authorities even though there was a precedent: São Paulo had faced coordinated attacks in 29 prisons back in 2001.

## Why so little progress?

The picture of crime and policing in Brazil is thus very dramatic. While high crime levels cannot be blamed on the police, it is clear that police actions are not effectively contributing to a pacification of the population as one would hope. The police often fail to adequately respond and protect, and when they do, they are often brutally repressive and violent, acting with impunity.

Involvement in corruption, crime rings, and death squads further impedes real hopes of democratic policing.

What explains the lack of progress in this arena in the 20 years following the end of military rule? It is not that Brazil has failed to seek police reform over the past two decades. To the contrary, in the aftermath of the dictatorship toward the end of the 1980s, when violent crime began to reach alarming proportions in Rio, São Paulo, and other major cities, a range of initiatives were undertaken at the national and state level. If one was to peruse Brazilian policy statements, governmental programmes, legislation, and the press over the past 15 years, one would perceive a frenzy of governmental activity on police reform, human rights, and crime reduction.

Many First World reformers have suggested that the solution lies in the improvement of police management techniques. William Bratton, for example, has suggested that solutions to Latin America's policing problems 'lie in decentralization and localization of police resources' so as to allow police departments to better 'connect to local communities'. He argues that 'the police methods that worked in New York City can work in Latin America' and advocates that Latin American police departments 'establish management systems that allow top managers to detect corruption and misconduct, allocate resources and drive forward a citywide effort to defeat the criminals' (Bratton and Andrews 2001). Others have suggested that the problem is underfunding or police resistance to reform. For some, such as Rio's governor Sergio Cabral (2007–present), the problem is quite simple: 'We have new instructions for the police, they don't go out there on shooting rampages anymore' (Reuters 2007).

The very extreme nature of the problems described in the preceding sections should in itself give the lie to such facile solutions. Nevertheless, a 'magic wand' approach to reform has proved ever popular. The reform efforts that have been launched nationally and locally have generally aimed at improving police funding, infrastructure, and equipment and have sought to hire more men, fire the bad apples, and simply ban punitive practices without appropriate guarantees of compliance. Other reform efforts have brought in new institutions such as police ombudsmen or parliamentary committees to improve oversight, or have encouraged community councils to improve the relationship between the population and the police.

On the whole, however, reforms have made very little impact, because of three basic interlinked issues. First, the problem has deep historical roots; second, personalistic and partisan patterns of police governance and symbolic initiatives have not succeeded in overturning the traditional police role; and third, deficits in democratic accountability and checks and balances at all levels of the state prevent effective responsiveness to the needs of the majority population and to effective governmental self-policing. Each of these issues is addressed below.

## Historical roots

The adversarial and violent nature of policing in Brazil is a deep-seated issue. Throughout the nation's history, both civilian and military governments have utilised the police as an instrument of social and political repression. Certainly the police in all societies serve a function of social control to varying degrees. But the situation in Latin America is much more extreme owing to the region's deep and persistent social divisions and to its fractured experience of democracy.

In Brazil, the police were initially organised in Rio de Janeiro during the early 1800s, at a time when about half of the Rio population was enslaved. In this context, the police were primarily a means for containing the threat of slave revolts and for preventing and punishing insurrection and escape. But even long after Brazil abolished slavery in 1888 (being the last country in the Americas to do so), in a context of deep inequality, privileged Brazilians faced the problem of how to keep the poor from interrupting their lives, and the police were a useful tool for the purpose (Hinton 2005: 81).

Brazil remains one of the world's most unequal countries. Stark inequities are present not only in income and land ownership but also in gender, racial, and educational realms, as well as between urban and rural dwellers and northern and southern states (Hinton 2006: 159). In 2005, while the top 10 per cent of households controlled 45.3 per cent of the nationwide household per capita income, the bottom 50 per cent accounted for just 14 per cent (IPEA 2005). Patterns of unequal land ownership aggravate these problems. About 45 per cent of all land is owned by 1 per cent of landowners. If one considers that 60 per cent of privately owned Brazilian land lies fallow, the concentration of land in the hands of a few is all the more unjust, aggravating Brazil's widespread problems of homelessness, urban poverty, underemployment, and landlessness (UNCHR 2004: 11–12).

In an age of mass media, the disparities between the First World consumption standards of the Brazilian elite and the majority of the population have become all the more visible to those on the bottom rungs of Brazilian society, generating a number of crime-accelerating pressures. In addition to the problems that Brazil suffers from its own levels of inequality, the country must deal with the related spill-over problems of its unequal Latin American neighbours, a number of whom are plagued by extreme levels of corruption, coca production, drug trafficking, and low-intensity guerrilla conflict and civil war. Brazil shares borders with 11 of South America's 13 countries (Chile and Ecuador are the only non-border countries), a fact worth mentioning given that Latin America is 'unambiguously' the region with the highest levels of income inequality in the world (World Bank 2004: 27). While the extent to which inequality generates crime is difficult to quantify – given that crime responds to a complex mix of economic and social factors that include formal and informal social controls, demographics, urbanisation, and employment – it undoubtedly plays an important role. Perhaps even more significant is the fact that stark levels of inequality generate schizophrenic consumption and economic pressures that have a tendency to skew and corrupt a society's power relations, generating enormous pressures to maintain the status quo against numerical odds.

In their role as hedge between affluent and poor, the police developed an historical trajectory of involvement in the monitoring of political and social threats. For this reason, the police also developed very close ties to the military. To provide an indication, in Rio the police force responsible for day-to-day policing did not have a career police chief until 1983; prior to that year all chief commissioners had come from the military. If one reflects on the fact that Brazil underwent military coups in 1930, 1945, 1954, 1955, and 1964, this becomes less surprising. During the 21 years of the most recent military dictatorship, which lasted until 1985, not only were all legal and political institutions systematically weakened, but the police were formally placed under military control and were trained in a climate where adherence to due process, whether in investigations or arrests, was not expected or demanded (Hinton 2006).

More specifically, the police were trained in the use of torture and illegal surveillance to combat the spread of communism and political dissidence – both real and imagined – at a time when containing the communist threat was paramount for the Brazilian military regime and for the United States. While the middle class bore the brunt of political repression, the regime also closely monitored the *favelas* in key urban centres to ensure that they were kept free of 'communist infiltration' (Ramsdell 1990: 167).

Once military rule ended, control over the police was again shifted to civilian provincial governors. This divestiture, however, did not do much to restore professionalism or public confidence in a force heavily tainted by involvement in death squads, repression of protests and political activity, arbitrary arrests, and abusive treatment of the poor. The aforementioned dramatic escalation in violent crime that occurred following the exit of the military from power would further undermine public trust in the police, as they would be perceived as incapable or unwilling to protect the population. These historical factors bring us to more recent developments.

## Personalistic police governance and symbolic initiatives

The second factor important to understanding the obstacles to democratic policing in contemporary Brazil is that civilian authorities have not yet significantly overturned traditional particularistic and overtly politicised forms of police governance. Admittedly, such a shift is especially arduous in any country with an authoritarian past; consider the challenges that democratic police management poses even in long-established democracies of the First World.

But because of the degree to which policing can be disruptive of political and civil liberties, personal privacy, and physical security because of its coercive potential, it is essential that civilian authorities seek to place the police under effective forms of democratic control and that they take corrective actions when lapses occur. Yet civilian governments in Brazil are far from overturning the traditional police role.

The federal government has not successfully demanded compliance with its laws at the state level, nor has it provided the leadership to appropriately modernise and professionalise the country's police forces though monitoring, regulation, prosecutions, financial carrots and sticks, or direct intervention. A case in point was Brazil's National Program of Human Rights, launched by President Fernando Henrique Cardoso (1995–2002). Launched in May 1996, shortly after Cardoso came to power, it was seen as a landmark plan that was to address many of the international human rights complaints about Brazil. The plan had been drafted by the Ministry of Justice in conjunction with broad consultation with civil society and was an ambitious programme that included more than 200 measures. Yet its impact was stymied by the fact that most of the clauses were recommendations rather than legal requirements. Even in the few cases where they were made law, enforcement of the legislation was left in the hands of provincial governors with little federal oversight, and thus the effect was often negligible.

The 1997 torture code, for example, criminalised the use of torture. More than three years later, however, the UN Special Rapporteur on Torture determined that the law had been 'virtually ignored', noting that no convictions had taken place between 1997 and March 2000 and finding that police use of torture to obtain information, coerce confessions, punish, intimidate, and extort was systemic (UNCHR 2001: 53–55). In a 2006 follow-up investigation of the implementation of the 1997 law, the United Nations found that the government's anti-torture hotline and other programmes still failed to meet the special rapporteur's guidelines for safe reporting and prosecution of cases, such that 'impunity continues to be the norm' (UNCHR 2006: 6). In response, in June 2006 the Brazilian government created the National Committee for the Prevention and Control of Torture within Brazil's Special Human Rights Secretariat to monitor and curb torture throughout the country by means of inspections and audits of detention centres, improved data collection and management, and research on new means to reduce torture. Whether this new institution of oversight will be effective is too soon to tell, but the fact that it took nine years after the law was passed for these basic steps to be taken is telling.

Similarly, the federal government began to make systematic attempts to collect state-level police and crime statistics only in 2003, more than 20 years after the transition from military rule presented the opportunity for doing so. Given the infancy of these attempts, today the government is still a long way from amassing the cornucopia of data that industrialised countries collect, let alone analyse. With such weak collection and analysis of even the most basic forms of crime data, there are few systematic official statistics on arrest rates, percentage of crimes that proceed to court, arrests for misdemeanours, racial and age categorisation, and clear-up rates for police investigations at the local level or nationally.

Centralised data collection, further, is just one of a whole complex of data-related practices that Brazil has yet to develop. Poor training and manipulation contribute to unreliable local recording of statistics, even where these are forwarded to central government authorities. Even police homicide statistics, which in most countries are considered to be the most reliable indicator of violent crime because of the difficulty of hiding bodies, are extremely mismatched with public health data: whereas Ministry of Health data show a total of 48,000 homicides for the year 2004, for example, the National Secretariat of Public Security reports that the police recorded 20,825 homicides nationally (SENASP 2006). Some of this discrepancy is doubtless a function of the fact that three states, Rio de Janeiro, São Paulo, and Rio Grande do Sul, did not forward their homicide statistics to the federal government in 2004 or 2005. A particularly egregious inaccuracy is the federal government's claim that the police in Rio killed no civilians in 2004 or 2005, when separate statistics published by the state of Rio indicate that 983 and 1,098 were killed in these years respectively (SENASP 2006; CESEC 2006). The same federal government report indicates that another six states claimed zero such deaths for 2005 while 13 others failed altogether to send their police lethal force statistics.

The broad patterns of symbolic action plans, campaigns, and legislation and very selective and politically convenient application and enforcement of the laws has continued since the first National Plan of Human Rights was launched in 1996. Its successor plans, the National Public Security Plan (June 2000, 124 proposals) and the National Program of Human Rights II (May 2002, 518 recommendations), contained several hundred recommendations between them, most of which followed similar patterns to the 1996 plan. President Lula's most recent action plan, the National Program of Public Security and Citizenship (PRONASCI), was launched in October 2007 and contains 94 proposals. The plan pledges about $3.3 billion to target the root causes of violence and at-risk youth in the 11 most violent Brazilian metropolitan areas. It foresees a host of measures ranging from psychological support for at-risk youth to urban renewal, construction of schools and prisons, and police scholarships and salary increases. Whether and how the numerous innovative approaches will be implemented will need to be assessed in future.

For now, police governance remains ad hoc and consists primarily in the appointment of a police chief by local state governors. Appointments are made for partisan and personalistic reasons and rarely are based on professional benchmarks. Those in positions of authority are seldom held responsible for the actions of their subordinates. A government minister, undersecretary, or police chief may be fired or tender a resignation in the face of a major police, crime, or corruption scandal with significant media import, but these officials are unlikely to be held criminally or financially liable and are often able to move on to a new office after a short period of time has elapsed.

A case in point has been the investigation and trial of the notorious October 1992 massacre at Carandiru Prison in São Paulo, where 7,000 inmates were crowded into a facility designed for half that number. When a rebellion broke out in one section of the prison on the eve of municipal elections, riot police were sent in. The repression that unfolded was so savage that it resulted in the death of 111 prisoners (with no police losses) and an equal number wounded in the space of half an hour.[4] The next morning, the governor of the state attempted to minimise what had take place, declaring police action to have been 'appropriate' (Carvalho and Gomes 1992). Official news bulletins conveniently spoke only of the death of eight prisoners until the municipal elections were nearly concluded, to mitigate the potential damage for candidates who were the governor's allies. Later, when the gravity of the situation emerged, the police command was replaced.

The attempt to criminally prosecute São Paulo metropolitan police commander Coronel Ubiratan Guimarães (who had been in charge of one of São Paulo's most repressive police squads during the dictatorship), who ran the operation, floundered for nine years in the face of lack of political support and intimidation of prosecutors. The trial was further delayed because Guimarães was subsequently elected to the São Paulo state legislature, which conferred on him parliamentary immunity from criminal prosecution. After he lost his bid for re-election, he was tried and sentenced in 2001 to 632 years in prison. He was immediately released from prison, however, pending appeal. Five years later, in 2006, the São Paulo Supreme Court annulled his conviction, finding that he had acted in accordance with his official duties. No other police officer or overseeing civilian authority has been brought to trial for the Carandiru massacre; overcrowding remained severe at the prison until it closed ten years after the massacre, in September 2002.

Criticism from international human rights groups over such protracted cases such as these prompted the federal government to pass a law in November 2004 by presidential decree allowing cases involving grave human rights violations to be transferred from state courts to federal jurisdiction. Thus far, however, no cases have been thus federalised.

In the absence of effective federal oversight and activism, compliance with federal legislation related to policing that does get passed is patchy, and management of the police remains very politicised. In Rio de Janeiro, for example, during 18 months between 2003 and 2004 the police were under the direct control of of Anthony Garotinho, himself the previous governor, who had been named state public security secretary by his wife, Governor Rosinha. This husband-and-wife control of public security in Rio followed a long period of politicised management of the police, during which each new elected governor would come in and completely undo the policies of his predecessor (Hinton 2005). While the husband-and-wife team initiated a period of greater stability in personnel, it was hardly to progressive effect, at least as concerns policing and human rights.

Indeed, in the last year of Governor Rosinha's administration 29 people were indiscriminately killed in one night of March 2005 by a death squad in the Baixada Fluminense, an impoverished neighbourhood within the greater Rio metropolitan area; authorities admitted that this murderous spree had probably been carried out by elements within the police.[5] More recently, Alvaro Lins, who was chief of the Civil Police during much of Governor Rosinha's tenure and her husband's preceding governorship, was placed under federal investigation for overseeing a crime ring centred on illegal slot machines. After Lins was elected to the state legislature in 2006, however, he secured parliamentary immunity from prosecution.

The politicised and personalistic forms of control that prevail perpetuate susceptibility to bribery and political favours on matters ranging from cover-up of both petty and serious crimes to active efforts to destabilise political opponents. Low police salaries are a factor that facilitates this kind of political manipulation. At least for certain sectors, low salaries can be seen to serve a perversely useful purpose, given that they ensure that the police remain malleable to political favours and open to bribery by the elite.

In such a context it is perhaps of little surprise that the police constantly face allegations of political destabilisation. Accusations abound that elements within the police intentionally stage criminal acts or fail to investigate them properly, turn a blind eye to certain crimes with political import, or deliberately apply excessive force in certain situations to tarnish political images. A case in point are the São Paulo prison riots of May 2006, mentioned earlier. At the time President Lula was running for re-election against Geraldo Alckmin, who had resigned the governorship of São Paulo State to seek the presidency. In the wake of the riots and co-ordinated criminal attacks throughout São Paulo, Lula's opponents alleged that Lula's party had deliberately used its contacts in the criminal underworld to create the chaotic situation so as to tarnish the record of the governor (who was responsible for oversight of the state's police and penitentiary system) and destabilise his presidential bid. Whether this is true is difficult to ascertain, but similar dramatic crime episodes have surfaced along with allegations of deliberate plots around the time of nearly every major political contest in Brazil. Black Monday, discussed at the beginning of this chapter, is another such case, as it occurred shortly before the October 2002 elections and effectively derailed the gubernatorial bid of the governor in charge of Rio at the time, Benedita da Silva, who was an ally of Lula and member of his party.

## Political game

While one could blame rogue or mercenary elements within the police for illegal, violent, and negligent acts, it is important to highlight more systemic issues. Indeed, if one were examining any state bureaucracy from top to bottom, it is difficult to imagine a situation of probity at the lowest rungs of the bureaucracy if the same were not true at the highest levels. This brings us to the third main factor involved in the failure of most police reform efforts to date in Brazil: *all* levels of the Brazilian state, not just the police, operate in a climate of deficient checks and balances and pervasive corruption.

For example, before the end of his first term in office, President Cardoso, who was anxious to secure passage of a constitutional amendment that would allow his re-election, was implicated in a vote-buying scandal. Five congressional deputies admitted to having sold their vote of support for several hundred thousand dollars, and Cardoso's minister of communications and close friend was implicated in the bribery in May 1997. Support for a full congressional inquiry was later blocked. Later, during Cardoso's second term (1999–2002), a web of fraud and influence-peddling schemes implicated the president's former chief of staff and ultimately brought down three senators and a senior judge in spin-off cases.

I have written elsewhere that Brazil is characterised by a political game, or enduring ethos permeating national life, marked by tolerance for corruption, low levels of public accountability, and intense, destructive, and protracted political contests (Hinton 2006). These factors produce particularistic, venal, or elite-interest capture of public policy, such that the government fails to respond appropriately to the needs of the majority population.

Brazil's judicial system is deeply affected by the political game and is prone to corruption, nepotism, extensive backlog, long delays, and exclusionary access. While a nation's judicial system should provide the average citizen with a means of holding the government accountable for its actions, 'in a society like Brazil's in which there is so much inequality, the poorest, excluded people do not have enough information [regarding] how to claim their rights through the judicial system' (UNCHR 2005: 8) – to say nothing of time, resources, or skills. And while organised civil society has endeavoured to advocate on behalf of the poor, these organisations do not possess the numbers, unity, or resources to compensate for the many shortcomings of the state.

Unequal power relations are reproduced throughout the system, and, as has already been suggested, the system is prone to impunity for the crimes of the powerful, whether they involve fraud, money laundering, corruption, organised crime, or even murder. Corruption at Brazil's highest levels has hardly dissipated, despite the election of a working-class president who promised to break with traditional patterns of politics. In 2004, the Lula administration became embroiled in an ever-widening corruption scandal involving illegal party financing schemes, money laundering, kickbacks, vote buying, a political assassination, and other abuses. A congressional panel of inquiry that published its findings in August 2006 found that 72 legislators were involved in bribe taking and a complex fraud ring dubbed Operation Bloodsucker, leading the panel to recommend expulsion of more than one-tenth of the Congress.

Two weeks before voters went to the first-round polls in September 2006 to decide on whether to give President Lula a second term, a new scandal erupted, forcing the replacement of Lula's campaign manager after two

Workers' Party operatives (one of them a former police officer) were arrested with nearly $800,000 of cash on them. This cash was allegedly to be paid to the holders of a dossier meant to incriminate an ally of Lula's opponent.

Initially, Lula argued that he had been betrayed by his aides, but he went on to say, 'I don't admit that I chose my associates badly. There are many people who realise after one year of marriage that their wife was not the ideal woman . . . that is part of life' (quoted in Dias Leite 2006). Later, he claimed that the corruption of which his administration was accused was no different from what politicians in Brazil had traditionally done and that 'the same elite that has dominated [Brazil] for 500 years' engineered the scandal to prevent him from working to help the poor (quoted in Rother 2006). Despite the scandals, Lula won a thunderous victory and with it a second term.

## Conclusion

More than two decades since Brazil's transition from military rule, even with the hope for change brought in by Lula's ascent to the presidency in October 2002, we see a frightening and intensifying continuity in the state's inability to guarantee necessary levels of physical security and human rights to the population, without which democracy is hollow. In November 2007, the United Nations Human Rights Council again issued scathing criticism of Brazil, declaring that 'the people of Brazil did not struggle valiantly against 20 years of dictatorship . . . only in order to make Brazil free for police officers to kill with impunity in the name of security.' In fact, the number of the 'disappeared' during the years of democracy has already dwarfed the number of political disappearances during the military dictatorship: in contrast to the 136 disappeared nationally during the 21 years of the dictatorship, the police recorded 10,464 disappearances due to crime and destruction of bodies in the state of Rio alone in the 14 years between 1993 and 2007 (Rocha *et al.* 2007). Yet this has not generated the same level of national scandal.

Brazil is now the tenth economy of the world (World Bank 2007) and has made impressive gains in many other aspects of public administration and economic life. The country has established an enviable system of electronic voting, even as the United States struggles to modernise its system of balloting. Brazil also benefits from impressive hydroelectric infrastructure, an impressive aerospace industry that competes with Canada's, tremendous natural resources, and First World technologies in bio-fuels. While the United States is only now scrambling to make use of bio-fuels, Brazil had already developed sugar cane-based ethanol for airoplanes and cars in the 1970s and is the world's leader in its production.

Nevertheless, Brazil's achievements involve First World enclaves premised upon a highly exclusionary system buttressed by repressive policing. While there have been a number of individually positive police reform efforts, the lack of coordination or efforts to guarantee and monitor the implementation of progressive legislation has made for extremely patchy and ad hoc reform efforts. There have been few real efforts to depoliticise the management of the police to create a universalistic public service orientation. And indeed, the frightened population is all too often supportive of violent police operations and extra-legal forms of 'justice'. International reformers who seek to apply pressure or contribute to change all too often fail to make a realistic assessment of the overall political and social context, focusing instead solely on the police.

In the context of few systematic attempts to deal with inequality, social exclusion, or massive political corruption at all levels of the state, it is unrealistic to expect that the police could become a vanguard of democratic values and probity. If elected officials routinely get away with stealing millions, what is to deter a police officer earning a pittance from supplementing his income through any means available? The tone has long been set by Brazil's political leadership.

At his January 2007 inauguration following his re-election, President Lula declared that the 'barbarity in Rio de Janeiro cannot be treated like common crime. It is terrorism and must be dealt with by the strong hand of the Brazilian state'. While Lula appears interested in applying the firm hand of the Brazilian state only to those outside his inner circle, he is certainly not the only high official to benefit from the Brazilian political game. Former president Fernando Collor de Mello (1990–1992), for example, was impeached for corruption in 1992. The judgment was hailed as a turning point for Brazil. But while Collor's impeachment banned him from running for political office for eight years, he was acquitted of criminal charges; no prison time was served and no funds were returned. In 2007 he managed to re-emerge on the political scene by winning a Senate seat. Upon accession to office, he declared that his impeachment had been an attack 'without proof' and that the 1992 move to oust him was 'a great farce' (quoted in Sequera 2007).

In view of the situation described in this chapter, one begins to wonder whether Brazil's corruption allegations, investigations, human rights scandals, action plans, resignations, and purges are simply a revolving door. One hopes not.

## Notes

1   Figures on police strength in the text are from 2003, the latest available from the federal government.
2   See http://www.policiamilitar.rj.gov.br/bope/.
3   As police killings are placed in the category of 'records of resistance' or 'resistance followed by death', moreover, they often are not incorporated into recorded homicide levels, which thus significantly under-represent the picture of violent crime.
4   It later emerged that 80 per cent of those killed in the prison during the massacre had not yet even been convicted of their crimes; they had been in preventive imprisonment pending trial (Global Justice 2001).
5   One entry-level police officer, out of the ten military police officers and one former police officer who were originally arrested for the crime, was subsequently convicted in August 2006.

# References

Amnesty International. 2005. *Brazil: Briefing on Brazil's Second Periodic Report on the Implementation of the International Covenant on Civil and Political Rights.* London: Amnesty International.

——. 2006a. *Amnesty International Report 2006: Brazil*, London: Amnesty International.

——. 2006b. *Brazil: 'We have come to take your souls' – The Caveirão and Policing in Rio de Janeiro.* London: Amnesty International.

Bratton, William, and William Andrews. 2001. 'Driving Out the Crime Wave: The Police Methods That Worked in New York City Can Work in Latin America.' *Time,* July 23.

Carvalho, Joaquim de, and Marcos Emílio Gomes. 1992. 'Cadavares sob a urna.' *Veja,* October 14.

Centro de Estudos de Segurança e Cidadania (CESEC). 2006. *Registros de ocorrência da Polícia Civil, dados mensais divulgados pelo ISP entre 2000–2006.* Rio de Janeiro: CESEC, available at http://www.ucamcesec.com.br/.

Chevigny, Paul G. 1991. 'Police Deadly Force as Social Control: Jamaica, Brazil, and Argentina.' In *Vigilantism and the State in Modern Latin America: Essays on Extralegal Violence*, ed. M. K. Huggins. New York: Praeger.

Comissão Pastoral da Terra, Secretaria Nacional (CPT). 2007. 'Dados da CPT revelam que impunidade mantém violência no campo.' Press release, Assessoria de Comunicação, April 13.

Dias Leite, Pedro. 2006. 'Lula culpa Berzoini por usar "bando de aloprados".' *Folha de São Paulo,* September 26.

U.S. Federal Bureau of Investigation (FBI). 2007. 'Expanded Homicide Data Table 13: Justifiable Homicide by Law Enforcement, U.S. Department of Justice: By Weapon, Law Enforcement 2002–2006.' In *Crime in the United States 2006*, available at http://www.fbi.gov/.

Global Justice. 2001. *Massacre at Carandiru Prison: A Report from the Commission to Observe the Carandiru Trials.* Rio: Global Justice.

*Globo.* 2003. 'Thomas Bastos: Cria cadastro único para correntista.' April 24, available at http://www.globo.com.

Hinton, Mercedes S. 2005. 'A Distant Reality: Democratic Policing in Argentina and Brazil.' *Criminal Justice* 5, no. 1: 75–100.

——. 2006. *The State on the Streets: Police and Politics in Argentina and Brazil.* Boulder, CO: Lynne Rienner Publishers.

Instituto de Pesquisa Econômica Aplicada (IPEA). 2005. 'Pobreza – número de pessoas em domicilios pobres.' In *IPEAdata: Indicadores sociais*, available at http://www.ipeadata.gov.br.

——. 2007. *PNAD 2006: Primeiras análises.* Brasilia: IPEA.

Latin American Brazil and Southern Cone Report (LABSCR). 2006. 'Lack of Political Will Links Violence to Corruption in Brazil.' August.

Ministério da Justiça (MJ). 2007. 'População Carcerária, Junio 2007.' Brasilia: Sistema Integrado de Informações Penitenciárias (InfoPen), available at http://www.mj.gov.br/depen/default.htm.

Organização dos Estados Ibero-Americanos para a Educação, a Ciência e a Cultura (OEI). 2007. 'Mapa da violência dos municípios brasileiros.' Brasilia: OEI.

Prefeitura da Cidade do Rio de Janeiro. 2006. 'Favelas Cariocas: Comparação das areas ocupadas, 1999/2004.' *Rio Estudos N. 233*. Rio de Janeiro: Instituto Periera Passos.

Ramsdell, L. 1990. 'National Housing Policy and the *Favela* in Brazil.' In *The Political Economy of Brazil: Public Policies of an Era in Transition*, eds L. S. Graham and R. H. Wilson, 164–85. Austin: University of Texas Press.

Reiner, R. 2000. *The Politics of the Police*. Oxford: Oxford University Press.

Reiss, A. J., and A. J. Bordua. 1967. 'Environment and Organization: A Perspective on the Police.' In *The Police: Six Sociological Essays*. New York: John Wiley and Sons.

Reuters. 2007. 'Rio Governor Says Legalise Drugs to Fight Crime.' March 2.

Rocha, Carla, Amora Dimmi, Fabio Vasconcellos, and Ramalho Sérgio. 2007. 'Tortura: Uma prática que não acabou.' *O Globo*, August 20.

Rother, Larry. 2006. 'As Brazil Prepares to Vote, Scandal's Taint Seems to Fade.' *New York Times*, September 25.

Secretaria Nacional de Segurança Pública (SENASP). 2006. *Perfil das vítimas e agressores das ocorrências registradas pelas Polícias Civis (janeiro de 2004 a dezembro de 2005)*. Brasilia: SENASP.

——. 2007. *Relatório descritivo (perfil das organizações de segurança pública*. Brasilia: SENASP.

Sequera, Vivian. 2002. 'Collor Returns to Brazilian Senate.' *Associated Press Newswires*, March 15.

United Nations Commission on Human Rights (UNCHR). 2001. *Civil and Political Rights, Including the Questions of Torture and Detention: Report of the Special Rapporteur Nigel Rodley's Visit to Brazil*. Geneva: UN Commission on Human Rights, Economic and Social Council.

——. 2004. *Report of the Special Rapporteur on Adequate Housing as a Component of the Right to an Adequate Standard of Living, Miloon Kothari: Mission to Brazil*. Geneva: UN Commission on Human Rights, Economic and Social Council.

——. 2005. *Report of the Special Rapporteur on the Independence of Judges and Lawyers, Mr. Leandro Despouy: Mission to Brazil*. Geneva: UN Commission on Human Rights, Economic and Social Council.

——. 2006. *Follow-up to the Recommendations Made by the Special Rapporteur in the Report of His Visit to Brazil in August and September 2000*. Geneva: UN Commission on Human Rights, Economic and Social Council.

——. 2007. Press statement from Professor Philip Alston, Special Rapporteur of the United Nations Human Rights Council on Extrajudicial, Summary or Arbitrary Executions.

Von Hirsch, Andrew, Anthony E. Bottoms, Elizabeth Burney, and P.-O. Wikström. 1999. *Criminal Deterrence and Sentence Severity: An Analysis of Recent Research*. Oxford: Hart.

World Bank. 2004. 'Different Lives: Inequality in Latin America.' In *Inequality in Latin America and the Caribbean: Breaking with History?* Washington, DC: World Bank.

——. 2007. World Development Indicators Database. Washington, DC: World Bank. Available at http://www.worldbank.org/.

Xinhua News Agency. 2007. 'Half a Million Criminal Suspects at Large in Brazil: Study.' March 27.

# Part IV

# Africa

# 11 Policing in Kenya

## A selective service[1]

*Alice Hills*

In 2003, 40 years after independence from Britain, the Kenya Police announced an ambitious plan to transform itself from an incompetent, corrupt and often brutal force into a professional and democratic service that responds to 'the needs and expectations of its customers' (Kenya Police Service 2003: 15). Recognising the central role played by public police in democratic criminal justice systems, the police aimed to ensure their own accountability by introducing measures such as transparent management systems and an independent oversight body capable of monitoring performance and investigating misconduct.

No one doubted that reform was needed. Kenya is one of Africa's more politically stable countries, but the previous 20 years had seen its police system deteriorate to the point where the government could no longer guarantee security. Multi-party democracy was restored in 1992 amidst violent protests and international pressure, but little changed in policing, and ten years later President Kibaki's National Rainbow Coalition (NARC) was able to win a landslide electoral victory on the basis of a pledge to deal with the country's corruption, crime and poverty. However, none of these contingencies changed the essential nature of policing in Kenya, and the police remain subject to 'low morale, lack of professionalism, inadequate resources, political interference and endemic corruption' (Kenya Police Service 2003: 8).

This chapter argues that the situation the police find themselves in is typical of the problems confronting public police in developing democracies (especially those with Anglophone legacies). Additionally, Kenya is representative in that it is under pressure from donors to tackle corruption, crime and terrorists, all of which impact on policing; the USA, EU and UK repeatedly warn that aid will be cut if corruption is not tackled.

Although no one single factor can explain policing standards in such societies, let alone the extent of corruption, the critical one affecting policing, in Kenya as elsewhere, is the role played by the political elites to whom the police are effectively answerable. Not only are the police vulnerable to intimidation and interference by politicians and rich businessmen, but also the constitution legitimises presidential (i.e. political) control over police operations and personnel. Little has changed since 1969 when Potholm noted that Africa's police are 'consistently involved in the output side of the political process', and by their action and inaction enforce decisions taken by political elites (Potholm 1969: 142, 157). For good or bad, policing standards in Kenya reflect those of society more broadly.

## Context of policing

Like most former British colonies in Africa, the Republic of Kenya, East Africa's regional finance and trade hub, inherited – and quickly rejected – a Westminster-style system of security governance. A year after independence, the Kenyatta government used constitutional amendments to remove police autonomy and consolidate power into the hands of the president. Since then, Kenya's history has been one of autocratic, or one-party or (since the elections of 1992) multi-party rule against a backdrop of violence, corruption, and incompetent policing (Kenya Police Service 2003: 1–5; CHRI 2006: 3–8).

Kenya is a mix of contradictory tendencies. It is a vibrant if inconsistent democracy that legally guarantees many human rights, but such laws are selectively enforced. It is a republic consisting of executive, legislative, and judicial branches of government, which are effectively accountable to a president who is elected by popular vote and serves a five-year term as the chief of state and head of government. However, 'while diverse political points of view are increasingly tolerated, the nation's fragile institutions are continually undermined by a closed system of patronage and graft. The government has established numerous commissions to investigate major cases of corruption . . . but no one has been held accountable' (Human Rights Watch 2002). Additionally, Kenya is one of the most unequal countries in Africa in terms of national income distribution. The per capita income is approximately $360 a year, and approximately half of Kenya's 35 million population live below the poverty line, many of them in slums that are amongst the biggest in Africa (Earthtrends 2003; USAID 2006). For example, in 2001 there were approximately 700,000 people living in the 1.5 square miles of Kibera, a slum four miles from the centre of Nairobi (BBC 2001). Declining economic performance, combined with rapid population growth, ensures continuing poverty and unemployment, and high prices for everyday goods such as cooking oil.

As a result of such trends, Kenya is marked by two factors: corruption and presidential influence. Both affect policing and can be considered as environmental.

Corruption is embedded in both state and society. Further, it is insidious, for unlike corruption elsewhere in the region, Kenyan corruption is driven by a combination of fiction and tolerance of the third rate, rather than by natural resources as is common elsewhere. As the *Economist* has noted, the notorious Goldenberg scandal, which cost Kenya perhaps $1 billion in the 1990s, involved the illegal export of fictitious gold and diamonds, not real ones' (*Economist* 28 January 2006). But above all, the *Economist* continued, 'shoddiness is the key' because trade in 'third-rate goods allows large margins on corrupt deals'. At the level of the state this manifests itself as ministers and civil servants either paying over the odds for imaginary or inferior goods, or fleecing businesses. It means that police stations and transport routes receive state cash, but are not upgraded; stations are squalid and it costs more to ship a tonne of grain from Mombassa to the Ugandan capital Kampala than from Chicago to Mombassa.

Ironically, Kibaki won the presidency as a result of widespread disgust with the policing tolerated by his predecessor, Daniel arap Moi, who regarded the police as a tool for suppressing political opponents (Adar and Munyae 2001). By 2001 it was clear that traditional policing methods had failed to curb crime, and the police were openly criticised for complicity with criminals and extra-judicial killings. Amnesty International, for example, estimated that 'scores of people' were killed during 2000 by extrajudicial executions or the indiscriminate use of force (Amnesty International 2001a; 2001b). According to figures from Nairobi's city mortuary (which examined all gun-shot victims from the surrounding towns), 232 people were shot dead by police in 2001, compared to 23 killed by criminals (BBC 2002). Retribution may have played a part in this; figures are not available but officers no doubt died as a result of the increased availability of small arms. Nevertheless, there was little debate about the probable reasons. According to an internal police report, it was the result of poor management, corruption, indiscipline and a disregard for rules (Human Rights Watch 2001).

Kibaki's government quickly developed a number of strategies and programmes for police reform, and in 2003 a police task force was established. Donor support increased and anti-corruption campaigns were initiated. Yet nothing really changed, and by 2004, donor countries and agencies openly expressed their concern about the government's failure to address high-level corruption and take legal action against Moi. Indeed, Kibaki and his closest associates were by then widely seen as corrupt as Moi – which was unsurprising given that the same class of politicians, civil servants and businessmen dominated the governments of both men (Brown 2004). Kibaki responded by appointing a team led by John Githongo (who had previously headed the local office of Transparency International) to investigate high-level graft, but it was not long before politicians and their cronies again began looting public funds. Githongo resigned as permanent secretary for ethics in February 2005, fleeing to the UK when Kibaki failed to defend him against the ministers who warned him (Githongo) to back off. This prompted the United States and Germany to cut their aid budgets to Kenya. Githongo later produced a report accusing a number of cabinet ministers of corruption worth tens of millions of pounds, but no senior politicians were charged. Several years on, and many scandals later, Kenya is 'a quagmire of social, political, and economic turmoil' (CHRI 2006: 8).

The second environmental factor affecting policing results from the influence exerted on the institution, its senior officers, and its operations by the president. Regardless of the police's theoretical priorities, everything depends on the president's personality and political calculations because the Kenyan system is one of presidential control. Constitutionally, Kenya's police answer to the president, whose intent is channelled through his commissioner. Article 108(1) of the Kenyan constitution gives the president absolute power to appoint and dismiss commissioners, who are his conduit to the institution. Not only does Kenyan law provide no criteria for presidents to follow, but also parliament has no legal role (consultative or otherwise) in a commissioner's appointment or removal. Additionally, the constitution allocates presidents unlimited authority to control police operations. Unsurprisingly, internal and external accountability mechanisms are weak, laws are restrictive, and there is a strong culture of secrecy within the police.

## Models of policing

Environmental factors are key to understanding developments, but Kenya's style of public policing is further shaped by three main trends. Today's police are partly the result of the way in which successive governments adapted Kenya's colonial legacy to independent statehood, partly by their need to be seen to confront some forms of crime on some occasions, and partly by their need to make tactical concessions to influential international actors. In other words, Kenya's police model is the result of a series of adaptations to political contingencies, some of which are little more than tactical concessions in the face of unavoidable pressures. This pattern is traceable throughout the history of Kenya's police.

When Kenya gained independence in 1963, the organisational, operational and legislative norms and practices of the new police were those imported by the UK and adapted to the circumstances of an East African colony over the course of 70 years. In other words, the new state inherited a relatively mature, coherent and resilient policing model.

As far as London was concerned, imperial policing was a matter of control and regulation, and Kenya's model of policing was accordingly based on the organisational and operational practices associated with the export version of the Royal Irish Constabulary (Anderson and Killingray 1991; Anderson and Killingray 1992; Clayton and Killingray 1989; Deflem 1994). Acting in this light, the Imperial British East African Company (which administered British East Africa) recruited the first police in 1887 to provide security for company stores in Mombassa, though it was not until 1906 that a Police Ordnance legally constituted the first Kenya Police. It was this force that became the Kenya Police Force when the British East African Protectorate became a colony in 1920. By the early years of the twentieth century, the police protected Europeans and their property, patrolled urban areas, detected property crimes, enforced labour laws, and executed death sentences. Meanwhile, the criminal law they enforced was imported from British India. It was originally intended that this should conform to British codes, but preference was soon given to Indian law which (being codified) was thought to offer a more effective means of controlling Africans.

As this suggests, policing was characteristically paramilitary (though there were concerns about police performance as early as 1909, when it was noted that the military element had been promoted at the expense of police training). It was also comparatively well organised. The police had expanded their facilities and manpower during the interwar years as crime became increasingly organised, and this trend gained momentum in the late 1940s. For example, a mounted branch was created for patrol and pursuit work, an emergency company was established to handle strikes in cities such as Mombassa (1947) and Nairobi (1949), and most of the activities of the old Tribal Police forces were taken over by the regular police. By 1949 some 5,000 constables were African.

This model of policing proved resilient, as its response to the Mau Mau movement of the 1950s showed. Mau Mau gangs used terrorism, murder and arson in their campaign to overthrow British rule, and one of their tactics was to withhold from the police information on crimes involving Africans. The state of emergency declared in October 1952 placed the police at the heart of the government's response, and conventional policing was of necessity sacrificed as the police worked more closely with the army and its intelligence officers. A Special Effort Force was established, and Special Branch was expanded, as was the number of ordinary police; by 1954, there were approximately 14,000 policemen for a population of about 5,000,000. The Mau Mau was eradicated in 1957, but Kenya experienced considerable disorder in the early 1960s. At that point Africanisation was increased, and the tribal composition of the police adjusted to take account of Kenya's ethnic composition.

Independent Kenya thus inherited a model of policing capable of dealing with insurgency, disorder, unemployment, economic stagnation, and ethnic disturbances. Conventional police duties continued in the aftermath of independence, but in Kenya, as in most newly independent countries, Westminster models of policing were rapidly adapted to suit the personal requirements of the new rulers. And a primary requirement of the Kenyatta regime was that the police should fulfil a political intelligence role, thereby increasing its ability to control political opponents. More generally, the conventional capacity of the police to detect or prevent ordinary crime declined as experienced expatriate officers retired or were dismissed.

As a result of such trends, Kenya's current model of policing shares most of the characteristics of police systems elsewhere in Africa. It is in many respects a relatively mature and bureaucratic system, but it is also politicised, unaccountable, under-resourced, ineffective, incompetent, corrupt and often brutal. Partly because of this it is resilient, for such a model has always suited Kenya's political and security elite whereas an effective or accountable police would not be in their interests. Resilience is further reinforced by the general utility the police offer to politicians who must deal with political opponents, and by the functional continuities underpinning coercive institutions.

The Kenyan model's maturity and adaptability are evident from the legislation governing the police. The continuities are strong; the police are governed by the Police Act of 1961, and by Police Regulations (first published in 1961), which are clarified by Standing Orders (originally drafted in 1962) that regulate routine operational and administrative procedures, and are issued by the commissioner. Now, as then, the police maintain order, regulate certain activities, and represent the regime. At the same time contemporary requirements are accommodated. The Police Act may define police functions as the maintenance of law and order, and the preservation of the police, but this is balanced by the promotion of 'community policing', and by instructions insisting that officers called upon to answer complaints made against them 'will adopt a quiet and courteous manner' (*Police Act* 1988: Chapter 2, section 12).

Institutionally, the police adhere to the hierarchical model common to police in formerly Anglophone countries. The constitution provides that the police commissioner is appointed by and under the command of the president, and that he retains overall control of the police. The commissioner is assisted by a secretariat that is situated centrally at headquarters, as is Special Branch, the Criminal Investigation Department, transport, signals and the quartermaster. The country is divided into eight policing provinces, and a railways and harbours police. Each province is subdivided into divisions, which are controlled by a divisional commander who is answerable to the province's senior officer. A chief inspector or inspector heads most stations, while police posts are the responsibility of a sergeant or corporal. There are no plans to civilianise the rank structure's 14 levels.

The police also conform to the predominant model of policing in that they contribute to Kenya's main civilian intelligence organisation, the National Security Intelligence Service (NSIS). NSIS was developed from Kenya's Special Branch (security intelligence service) in the aftermath of the 1998 bombing of the US embassy in order to monitor potential subversives, and is trained in urban counter-insurgency and counter-terrorism strategy by US Federal Bureau of Investigation (FBI) agents. An NSIS graduate training programme was introduced in 2003.

## Police–military relations

One further aspect of Kenya's police model that deserves note is the police's relationship with the Kenyan military (that is, the army). The relationship between the two is difficult to assess accurately, but, broadly speaking, it is typical of the region in that it is uneasy.

The two forces share similar approaches to functional issues such as recruitment, with both recruiting from a small number of ethnic groups. During the colonial period recruitment to both was politically designed in that certain ethnic groups were thought to be more martial or reliable. Today's imperatives may be different, but both forces remain as ethnically imbalanced as a result of historical socioeconomic distributions of opportunities and governmental recruitment strategies as they were in the 1970s (Enloe 1976: 25–38). Indeed, it is arguable that ethnic origin in the upper ranks at least is more important now than it was 10 years ago, for the current political system is ethnicised, and political rivalries and promotions are often drawn along ethnic and regional lines. For instance, Kibaki's closest advisers – his 'Mount Kenya mafia' – are, like him, Kikuyu; at 21 per cent, Kikuyu are the country's largest ethnic grouping (the next largest are the Luhya at 14 per cent). On the other hand, Kenya has more than 40 ethnic groups, and no one group dominates; coalitions and alliances are essential. Further, although the police recruit from a small number of ethnic groups, issues of ethnic identity rarely arise in current analyses of police reform; Amnesty International may argue that certain groups are singled out for brutal treatment, but the Commonwealth Human Rights Initiative (CHRI) rarely discuss such issues.

But ethnic preference is probably as far as commonality between the police and the military extends, for in Kenya as elsewhere the status of the military is higher than that of the police. This is partly the result of the military's greater budget and resources (the military are relatively small and well-trained) and partly the result of the police's operational record. Accurate crime statistics are not available, but most commentators believe there has been a marked increase in violent crime such as armed robbery in recent years, and a corresponding decrease in public confidence in the police, who are seen as ineffective.[2] The reasons for the increase are debatable. Most commentators agree that societal and institutional weaknesses are influential, but disagree about the impact of urbanisation, structural adjustment and Moi's legacy. In a survey of crime in Nairobi in 2002, the UN suggested that crime had increased because 'the social control that operates through formal institutions (police, justice, family, schools etc.) and informal institutions (civil society organisations, solidarity networks etc.) is broken or weakened' (UNDP/UN-Habitat 2002: 2). Their Kenyan respondents, meanwhile, blamed unemployment and poverty for forcing people into crime in order to 'survive' (UNDP/UN-Habitat 2002: 31). In rural areas, access to small arms may explain the increased incidence of stock theft.

In such circumstances the military are seen to provide more effective and robust forms of control. For example, in November 2006 it took hundreds of riot police five days to stop widespread rioting between rival gangs in Mathare (a slum in the north-east of Nairobi), prompting the Kenya National Commission on Human Rights (KNCHR) to petition Kibaki to invoke the Armed Forces Act so that the military could be mobilised. Its commissioner in charge of complaints and redress, Fatuma Ibrahim, argued that the Army should replace the police in crime prone areas because

> The President having been sworn into office to protect the constitution of this country must as soon as possible reassure the public on their security.

> Kenyans are dying because of the inaction or inability of the security apparatus which, despite the huge tax allocation, appear negligent and incapable of containing insecurity.
>
> (*Kenya Times* 2006a)

As Ibrahim's words suggest, the relationship between the two forces is often tense, especially when, as in Kibaki's early days, the police investigate senior military officers. Thus many people saw the police's investigation of officers in 2003 as part of the government's purge of senior officials and civil servants inherited from Moi's regime; that is, as politically motivated (BBC 2003). The officers were alleged to have allocated Land Rovers to the banned Mungiki sect, which had campaigned against the NARC during 2002's general election.

Tensions are accentuated by African police's paramilitary characteristics and by its militaries traditionally fulfilling an internal security role. The British conception of colonial policing always implied that policing would gradually shift away from a paramilitary force designed for territorial control to a police designed for civil duties, but in Kenya this was always tempered by the insecurity generated by the Mau Mau, the secessionist Shifta movement in North Eastern, Eastern and North Coast provinces in 1963–69, large-scale stock theft and localised banditry and smuggling, and (as in December 2006) fighting along Kenya's porous 1,500 kilometre border with Somalia. When, for instance, attempts to disarm cattle rustlers in western districts failed in early 2006, the police were required to work with the military and its police in a massive disarmament operation.

In such cases the police's 5,000-strong paramilitary internal security force, the General Service Unit (GSU), is used. Originally formed in 1948, the semi-autonomous mobile GSU (which is notorious for extrajudicial killings and torture) handles violent crime, outbreaks of communal violence, demonstrations, and, since 2003, some counterterrorism functions. Some GSU officers were co-opted into general duties as part of Kibaki's reform measures of 2005, but Kenya's police, like all public police, still needs a rapid response capacity. This is particularly so in the north. Consequently, responding to banditry and 'terrorist' attacks in northern border regions usually involves the military and paramilitaries, leaving the police to deal with enforcement tasks such as money laundering, corruption investigations, smuggling and the movement of illicit drugs.

The 40,000-strong police appear to accept their secondary role. Witness the failure of most senior police officers to build personal or political power bases comparable to those of the military. Unable or unwilling to operate as independent political actors, they are, in Kenya as elsewhere, typically adjuncts to groups that control resources more directly. In Kenya, however, the situation is particularly complex and interesting because the current police commissioner is a career army officer.

Kibaki's administration came to power in 2001 on a platform to fight crime and improve standards of living. The extent to which Kibaki is genuinely concerned by Kenya's crime rates is debatable; clamping down on ordinary crime offered him an opportunity to crush troublemakers, but his own aloofness and tolerance of corruption is notorious. Whatever the reason, there was a complete overhaul of the police's senior ranks in March 2004, and Brig Hussein Ali was appointed commissioner in April 2004. At the same time an unknown number of officers were arrested and prosecuted for human rights abuses, while police salaries were increased by 115 percent in order to reduce incentives for corruption.

In retrospect, it was probably the political implications of crime and his lack of faith in the police leadership, rather than political machinations or the threat of disorder, that prompted Kibaki to replace his civilian commissioner, Edwin Nyaseda, with Ali. The official line was that the change was aimed at injecting new blood into the police, and addressing rising crime. And it was a popular move, given Kenyans' concerns over the ineffectiveness of their police in the face of murder, manslaughter, rape, armed robbery, carjacking, drug trafficking, and corruption, and the proliferation of illegal small arms. Indeed, in April 2005, an MP said it was as if the country was at war, insisting that the police should therefore be allowed to shoot-to-kill criminals (*East African Standard* 2005). Ali's appointment was widely welcomed on the basis that he would introduce the discipline and professionalism that the police lacked.

Another factor influencing Kibaki may have been President Museveni's successful appointment to the Uganda Police of a former commander of Ugandan forces in Congo. In 2001 Maj Gen Edward Katumba Wamala became the 16th inspector general (IG) in the 15,000-strong 99-year old Uganda Police as the direct result of a commission of inquiry that found the police to be ineffective, under-funded, under-staffed and corrupt. In the event, Katumba (who wore a senior police officer's uniform while IG, and whose deputy was a career police officer) reduced drunkenness and corruption during his four-year tenure, and was replaced by another military man, Brig Kale Kayihura. Kayihura's appointment had not been expected, so it was widely assumed that Katumba had displeased Museveni in some way, or that Kayihura's appointment was connected to the potentially explosive 2006 general election, or was an attempt to intimidate the police. One politician was reported as saying that Museveni had never 'been bedfellows with the police . . . The only way for him to keep them in check is [therefore] to appoint his person to oversee them' (*Sunday Monitor* 2005). The police were, he thought, likely to resist Kayihura. Kibaki's calculations were probably different. Certainly his situation and personality are different to Museveni's. But the key point is that Kibaki, like Museveni, was able to impose an army officer.

The implications of Ali's appointment for police–military relations are as yet uncertain. Ali's own record is mixed. Certain types of crime have fallen, but he has not gained public – or police – confidence. The unresolved killings of government opponents during 2005's referendum campaign,[3] and a series of scandals involving a corrupt recruitment campaign and various suspicious arrests soon led to calls for his resignation or dismissal. Further, he, like his predecessors, accepts the limits of his legal and operational authority. Although public policing is a primarily urban phenomenon, he tolerates swathes of Nairobi operating outside the state. Like his peers, he seemingly accepts the state's minimal role in areas such as Kibera:

> it provides no water, no schools, no sanitation, no roads, no hospitals. Security comes from vigilante groups – who, for a price, will track down thieves and debtors. Usually, the Nairobi police are too scared to come here. But if they do, they're just looking for bribes.
>
> (BBC 2002)

Like his Ugandan colleagues, Ali conscientiously attempts to fulfil the remit given to him. Like them he has sought to improve or 'professionalise' policing standards, though he has avoided overtly intimidating or identifying with the police. He evidently retains his military standards and, no doubt, aspirations, but the Kenyan police institution remains less militarised than many. Ali's appointment is unlikely to affect the existing balance between police and military, or, indeed, the police and criminal-justice system's place within the security sector more generally.

## Democratic-style policing

Unlike many governments in developing countries, the NARC government publicly acknowledges that policing is only one aspect of the administration of justice. The Governance, Justice, Law and Order Sector (GJLOS) reforms introduced in November 2003 are evidence of their preferred cross-sectoral, multi-agency approach. In reality, however, this simply means that policing must be placed in the broader context of a flawed criminal-justice sector.

As with its police, the structure and norms of Kenya's criminal-justice system are typical of those in Anglophone Africa's politically stable democracies. The system is institutionally and procedurally standard in that the police must – in theory – co-operate with the courts, prisons and probation department, all of which are overseen by the Ministry of Home Affairs. The sector's staff are civil servants, though the pay, conditions and allowances of the police, prisons services and National Youth Service differ from those received by other workers in the public sector. Their salaries do too. In 2003, the then head of the Kenya Anti-Corruption Commission (KACC) was reported as receiving the equivalent of US$32,000 a month, i.e. 500 times what a constable earned (*East African* 2003).

Kenya's criminal-justice system is also typical in that its working practices and standards fall far short of what donors regard as appropriate. Just as extortion, intimidation, forced confessions, and extra-judicial killings by police are common so too are corruption, incompetence, inefficiency, and executive interference in court cases. Kenya's prisons and penal policy are relatively humane in comparison with those in, say, Nigeria or Zimbabwe – rehabilitation is theoretically incorporated into policy – but chronic over-crowding, understaffing and casual brutality exacerbate the usual problems of grossly inadequate health, nutrition and sanitation provision. More than 50,000 prisoners are held in 92 prisons, the capacity of which is 19,000:

> despite some reforms, prison conditions remained harsh . . . Understaffed and poorly trained prison wardens used excessive force to control inmates. People die in custody, allegedly as a result of ill treatment. Forty-five inmates reportedly died in suspicious circumstances in Meru prison during the first nine months of 2004, with 14 deaths recorded in September alone.
>
> (Amnesty International 2005)

As this suggests, the local challenges to achieving democratic-style policing are significant. In particular, it is the lack of accountability that allows prison and police officers to act with impunity. Indeed, much of the criticism the Kenyan criminal-justice system attracts amongst donors and NGOs such as CHRI and the Kenya Human Rights Commission (KHRC) focuses on the police's lack of accountability to elected and/or accountable civilian groups or organisations. Many police officers of all ranks acknowledge the accuracy of NGO criticism, and recognise the need for reform, but corrupt, brutal or incompetent police are rarely called to account for their actions. Hence CHRI's assessments that 'Police criminality and misconduct are based in impunity. The police are charged with protecting the public . . . however rife criminality within police ranks reflects a belief that police illegality will go unchecked. The state is either complicit in or acquiescing to police criminality' (CHRI 2006: 25).

The local obstacles confronting reformers are major regardless of the government's stated commitment to institutional and functional change. The relative importance of individual variables naturally varies according to standpoint. On the one hand it is arguable that this situation reflects Kenya's inequality, poverty, general insecurity, and violence; corrupt and polarised societies tend to have corrupt and brutal police, and policing will not change until societal attitudes change. Also, resources and economic constraints as such are rarely the cause. CHRI, meanwhile, offers a variant understanding by blaming the current situation on the police's 'colonial birth'. According to their assessment, the police's historical and cultural legacy ensures that 'illegitimate political interference is embedded in its culture' (CHRI 2006: 27). This is implausible, not least because it absolves successive governments of all responsibility for decision-making since independence. Alternatively, it may be argued that police behaviour must first change. But whatever the most plausible explanation (or sequencing) most commentators agree that genuine reform requires political will on the part of the government concerned. This is missing. Despite Kibaki's electoral victory of 2002, there is little evidence to suggest that he and his government wish to promote democratic forms of accountability. The two key challenges confronting reformers are thus political leadership and endemic corruption at the highest levels.

Attempting to distinguish between the two is unprofitable, as Kibaki's own position makes clear. First of all, the Kenyan system of presidential control means that political interference is to some extent legitimate, as well as entrenched in law and habit, so it is misleading to categorise it (CHRI 2006) as legally illegitimate *per se*.

Second, although Kibaki has initiated reforms and appointed inquiries into corruption, he operates within a system that instrumentalises, rather than criminalises, corruption (Chabal and Daloz 1999; contrast Bayart *et al.* 1999). Further, Kibaki is deeply involved in scandals such as the Anglo Leasing affair whereby millions of dollars of government money was (according to John Githongo (CHRI 2006)) paid to businessmen close to the ruling elite, who then re-directed some of it back to the government for political campaigning. The networks underpinning such activities were evident in the Goldenberg scandal of 2005–6. Those implicated in the export of non-existent gold and diamonds included a former head of Special Branch, several of Moi's children and one of his aides, a prominent businessman, and a former vice-president and minister, George Saitoti, who resigned after the commission of inquiry appointed by the government presented its report to Kibaki (*Africa Research Bulletin* 2006: 16546).

## External influences

From a Kenyan perspective, the most serious security threats confronting policing are internal, rather than regional or international. Policing is accordingly affected and constrained primarily by national issues, actors, responses, resources and scandals. Regional factors occasionally play a secondary role, but their impact is usually local, as when the GSU are called on to act against cattle rustling and cross-border incursions on Kenya's borders with Ethiopia, Somalia and Tanzania that could affect Kenya's territorial integrity. International issues and actors affect policing superficially and temporarily.

Recent developments in Kenya support the thesis that the threat perceptions prompting specific policing-related responses are location specific, rather than a reflection of global trends as such. This applies to every level of policing. For example, in theory the appointment and policies of Ali should have been influenced by global concerns such as international terrorism. Not only did al-Qaeda sponsor attacks on the US embassy in Nairobi in 1998, but also four years later an Israeli-owned hotel was bombed in Mombassa, and an attempt made to bring down an Israeli charter plane. Kenya is, moreover, viewed by the Bush administration as a weak link in the so-called war on terror because of its proximity to Somalia, which Washington regards as a sanctuary for al-Qaeda. America's envoys repeatedly offer 'any and all assistance Kenya needs' in the 'fight against terrorism', yet in reality Kenya's security assessments are dominated by state and sub-state concerns such as the flow of illegal small arms, the presence of foreign refugees, stock theft, armed robbery and tribalism (Krause and Otenyo 2005; Rosenau 2005; US Embassy 2005).

In practice, ethnic tension is a particularly significant source of internal unrest (especially in productive areas), and is a major factor underpinning risk assessments and policing styles. Ali and internal security minister John Michuki may have criminalised 2006's Nairobi riots, and dismissed claims that they were tribally inspired (*Kenya Times* 2006b), but Kibaki repeatedly warns politicians not to incite hatred. Ethnic tension is manipulated for political purposes, and neither Kibaki nor Ali will have forgotten that political motives probably lay behind inter-ethnic clashes in the Rift Valley in early 1998. The violence, which displaced some 300,000 people, was probably instigated by the Moi government, for it appeared to be directed against the Kikuyu, many of whom had voted for the opposition (i.e. Kibaki, a Kikuyu) in December 1997's general elections.

This is rational, for Kibaki cannot afford the police to be overwhelmed by such disturbances, which exacerbate Kenya's high rates of robbery, rape and murder. Hence his lack of confidence in the police hierarchy, and his appointment of Ali. The seriousness of the threat is evident from Ali's own record. His period of office began well but he failed to reduce crime significantly, and in April 2005 the chairman of the Parliamentary Committee on Security sought an adjournment motion on the basis that the country was under siege from thugs (adjournment motions are reserved for matters of grave national importance) (*East African Standard* 2005). That Ali's own credibility came under threat in the aftermath of multiple cases of police brutality during political rallies in late 2005 reinforced the domestic focus of Kenyan security assessments.

Political squabbles reinforce this trend. Take the release in 2005 of old Etonian Tom Cholmondeley after he confessed to killing a game warden. This reignited hostilities between Ali and the Director of Public Prosecutions originally caused by the police's incompetent handling of a series of high profile cases, one of which involved the seizure of a tonne of cocaine destined for Europe. On that occasion, the police turned down an offer of international help in investigating the seizure by the United Nations Office on Drugs, Crime and Money Laundering (UNODC). Kenyan policing's domestic focus should, however, be seen in context – it is the norm in the UK and USA, as well as Africa. African officers attending Interpol conferences may talk about globalisation's challenges, but the politicians who fund policing are more concerned with stock theft, banditry and illegal migrants.

There is little evidence that the police look beyond Kenya's borders. Kenya is a member of the East Africa Police Chief's Co-operation Organisation (EAPCCO) and the East African Community (EAC), both of which are relatively active participants in regional developments, but the obstacles to effective regional policing are many, as is evident from the profitability of cigarette smuggling. For example, an 'Eastern Africa Anti Illicit Trade' workshop, organised by British American Tobacco (BAT) in Uganda in November 2005, was attended by delegates from Kenya, Uganda, Rwanda and the Democratic Republic of Congo (DRC), all of whom emphasised the need for regional co-operation (*Daily Monitor* 2005). As the then minister of finance noted, illicit cross-border trade between Kenya and Uganda represented a major security threat, ranking third after corruption and crime. However, he also argued that 'most officials' collude with illicit traders, thus acknowledging that the police response is negligent (*Monitor* 2005). But the police have few incentives to do otherwise because Kenya has little reason to prevent the trade. Smuggled Kenyan cigarettes may represent 20 per cent of the cigarette market in Uganda, but it is Uganda that loses Shs2 billion a year as a result of the difference in tax regimes, not Kenya. Kenya's compliance with international schemes and agreements designed to reduce corruption is (like that of its EAPCCO neighbours) accordingly marginal (Goredema and Botha 2004: 5–7).

In practice, the interface between the national and the international is minimal and limited to the transfer of jargon and training, as can be seen from the following three examples.

First, the police have adopted the language of international policing. Thus 2003's *Strategic Vision* states that 'The Police Service will endeavour to endear itself to its stakeholders by being fair, honest, loyal, humane and accountable' (Kenya Police 2003: 15). Similarly, the NGO Saferworld runs small but established community policing training programmes, launched by Kibaki in 2005 (Saferworld 2008).

Second, the impact of Kenya's former colonial masters' liberal norms is, despite their best efforts, limited. Hence in 2004, the then UK high commissioner Sir Edward Clay went so far as to accuse Kibaki's government of 'vomiting on the shoes' of donors. Two years later Kim Howells, the UK's foreign minister whose portfolio includes counter-terrorism and narcotics, said during an official visit to Nairobi that 'people can be bought, right from the person who works at the docks in Mombassa up to the government . . . You can buy off politicians, you can buy off policemen' (BBC 2006b; *Guardian* 2006a). Howells described Kenya as a major transit point for cocaine and heroine, but said that the government was not serious about tackling the problem. He noted that although Kenyan police destroyed more than a tonne of cocaine early in 2006, 'tonnes' of drugs moved through the country, and senior officials were implicated: 'They [the government] talk the talk but when it comes to action it's very disappointing. There is clearly complicity at very high levels.'

Similar considerations apply to the third example, which concerns the limited impact of the Bush administration's war on terror. Kenya may have direct experience of al-Qaeda-related terrorism, but Kibaki and Ali have more immediate priorities. By early 2006, for example, it had become increasingly difficult for Kibaki to distance himself from scandals such as the Anglo Leasing affair, let alone from the political intrigue surrounding the deportation of the two Armenian brothers rumoured to have organised raids by police commando units against opposition media offices (BBC 2006a). Ministers claimed that the operations were carried out on security grounds. However, questions arose once it became clear that not only were the brothers protected by powerful government figures (i.e. Kibaki), but also no one had told Ali of the operation.

The government's response to pressure for more effective counter-terrorism follows a fixed pattern: senior politicians and officers accommodate the demands which suit them, and adapt, subvert or obstruct those which they cannot ignore. Similarly, international pressure for functional reform or more effective policing inevitably founders on the police's low morale, bad conditions, and lack of training and resources; in 2005, many of the counter-terrorism unit's officers were 'due for retirement', and the unit's 'strategic plan' consisted of a ' "wish list" of equipment' (Rosenau 2005: 7). The government accepts this situation because it finds effective policing a threat; effective policing is tolerated only when it can be used politically. Hence Kenya's security service (NSIS) is operationally more impressive than the police mainly because its principal purpose is to act on behalf of the president against his potential opponents.

## Reform's place on the agenda

No one factor explains why police reform rose up the national agenda in the late 1990s and early 2000s, but it did so only when it became symbolic of the need for broader political reform, which the then government was pressured into accommodating. Two additional factors are noteworthy. First, agitation for reform became politically important only when it occurred in Nairobi and urban centres such as Mombassa. Second, there was no consensus on what reform involved. To some (such as Kenya's embryonic human rights community) it referred to the introduction of standards and processes based on liberal ideas of human rights and accountability, but to others (including Kibaki) it meant the introduction of new blood and policing capable of dealing with violent crime.

Calls for reform arose from political developments in the mid 1990s. Kenya's first multi-party elections since 1961 had been held in 1992, when Moi's Kenyan African National Union (KANU) won amidst scenes of police violence and intimidation. Moi made some presidential concessions in the mid decade, as in 1996 when a Standing Committee on Human Rights was established, but Kenya's political system remained that of a one-party state reliant on police complicity and violence. Despite this, domestic pressure for constitutional reform grew, with co-ordinated national strikes and regular demonstrations. KANU won the 1997 elections but was unable to crush calls for constitutional review. A number of (minimalist) recommendations were published in the ensuing three years, which resulted in the establishment of a Constitution of Kenya Review Commission (CKRC), which published its findings in October 2002. It recommended that the role played by police corruption and brutality in societal insecurity should be acknowledged, and that police independence should be constitutionally established.

Two months later, Kibaki led the NARC to electoral success on a programme that included police reform as a means to improve living standards. In other words, the main prompt for placing police reform on the national agenda was politicians' recognition of the potential political consequences of rising crime. However, the reverse also holds true: police reform slides down the agenda when politicians lose interest. Thus Kibaki's government quickly developed an ambitious range of strategies and policies for reforming the police, including a task force, an increase in police salaries, and the introduction of community policing. Yet nothing fundamental changed.

Public policing in Kenya, as elsewhere in Africa, is an urban phenomenon, as is politically significant disorder, so calls for reform in both senses of the word become politically meaningful only when discontent with the police takes the form of urban-based protests and strikes. And there is scope for this because more than a third of Kenya's population – and probably a higher percentage of its police – live in urban areas, with the greatest concentration in Nairobi (or 'Nairobbery,' as it is popularly known), which is plagued by burglary, armed robbery, and vehicle hijackings. At best Kenya's police-to-citizen ratio is approximately 1: 811, rather than the internationally recommended 1: 450. These variables explain why police reform slipped down the agenda after 2003.

Nairobi's politicians and police have more pressing priorities than introducing programmes for democratic policing. In the autumn of 2006, for example, members of the Mungiki sect and the so-called Taliban were at the centre of slum clashes in Nairobi that led to some 40 people being hacked or beaten to death by gangs or mobs (BBC 2006c). In November 2006, ethnic tensions in Nairobi's Mathare Valley slums resulted in eight deaths, the heavy deployment of the GSU and the regular police, and the flight of thousands of people. Local newspapers reported that Kibaki was not in control, having 'taken a lax attitude' and left the matter to his internal security minister Michuki and to Ali, who were squabbling and would not work together (*Nation* 2006).

Reform's low priority is evident from a statement by Nairobi Provincial Commissioner, James Waweru, who attributed the insecurity to hawkers in the central business district and the re-emergence of outlawed gangs in Nairobi's 'informal settlements'. He condemned government officers for colluding with or protecting offenders, but, more significantly, Waweru told police commanders that the proliferation of illegal small arms and gangs were the main causes of violent crime, and called on them to eliminate outlawed sects (*Kenya Times* 2006a).

Outside urban areas, the most prevalent form of serious crime is stock theft and banditry, often linked to ethnic feuds or land disputes. This has left much of the North-Eastern Province and parts of the Coast and Eastern Provinces ungovernable. Calls for democratic reform have little resonance in such an environment.

## Reform processes underway

Despite this situation, some reforms are underway. In 2003, the police published an ambitious four-year plan for transforming itself into a modern, efficient and effective institution, working through partnerships and responsive to the needs and expectations of the public (Kenya Police Service 2003; Kagari 2003). The plan advocated individual and institutional accountability, which was to be achieved through the establishment of performance standards, transparent performance management systems, a police service commission, and an independent oversight body capable of monitoring performance, investigating misconduct and taking action.

Quite why police leaders chose to initiate such a programme is difficult to tell, but the answer matters because it is indicative of the nature of the reforms currently in progress. Many of the most senior and junior ranks were reported as having accepted the need for change on the basis that the police's politicisation, corruption and culture of impunity had alienated the population, and thereby undermined its position in Kenya's rainbow democracy. Yet it is difficult to believe that engagement in democratic institutional reform was fully accepted by either the institution or its members. The police had little to gain from the plans, which would shift policing's focus from regime support to providing a service to all Kenyans for which they would be institutionally and individually accountable to external assessors. At best the plan's emphasis on modernisation and professionalism (both of which are contested notions) could mean an increase in human and material resources – the plan prioritised modernising the force as a major strategy for bringing about reform.

The plan's acceptance by some (perhaps many) senior officers was no doubt sincere, but it is probable that the more influential will have seen it as a tactical concession in the face of unavoidable political pressure, for the plan was driven by the political calculations of Kibaki's NARC government which, as this chapter has shown, soon reverted back to more traditional political concerns. Further, police reform, which played a central role in Kibaki's comprehensive reform programme of November 2003, was usually seen into its broader context. In one sense this was admirable, for policing cannot be treated in isolation, and the cross-sectoral and multi-stakeholder programme focused on reforming the police as one (albeit critical) aspect of the governance, justice, law and order sector (GJLOS) as a whole. However, it also enabled the police to obscure their response, intentionally or unintentionally, especially once Kibaki's own interest in reform evaporated, crime rates failed to improve, and the ideal of working with communities to provide a safe and peaceful environment in major urban areas seemed increasingly fanciful.

In principle, Kenya's numerous NGOs are well-placed to influence this situation. Some (e.g. the KHRC) played a major role in the taskforce set up by the NARC government in 2003, but many more promote police account-ability or work on police related issues such as medico-legal support (CHRI 2006: 56–57). They act as witnesses and advocates and mobilise public opin-ion. Their commitment facilitated some of the government's early achieve-ment, such as 2003's series of workshops, constitutional review processes and the National Constitutional Conference (NCC), which was designed to ensure the legal and institutional environment necessary for reform. It was NCC delegates who agreed that an independent and transparent Kenya Police *Service* should be established (*Daily Nation on the Web* 2006). But they did not identify specific actions for ensuring transparency or accountability. More importantly, they failed to evaluate the police's capacity for change, or to identify leaders and supporters capable of driving change (*Daily Nation* 2004). On balance, civil society's political influence is negligible, and many NGOs are subject to systematic police harassment; their meetings are dis-rupted, their representatives arrested and their offices broken into.

In fact the record is uneven. A number of procedural and functional reforms have been initiated, ranging from the introduction of a clear chain of command that gives the commissioner a genuine role and a substantial increase in police salaries to the introduction of community policing strat-egies. In April 2005, for example, the government launched the National Comprehensive Community-Policing Programme, which promotes increased collaboration between the police and citizens in the pursuit of a safer society; every police division must adopt a community-oriented approach within its area of jurisdiction. But such initiatives have been offset by the political distractions and crime rates referred to earlier, by the absence of police in rural areas, and by vigilantism in urban areas where the state does not operate. Also, ambiguity in concepts such as community policing mean that in prac-tice reforms reinforce Kenya's undemocratic and oppressive structures (Ruteere and Pommerolle 2003). A few officers have been dismissed, or arrested and charged for misusing their power, but this is offset by deep-seated trends.

Like most African police, the Kenya Police remains a secretive institution which offers little information about itself (though at the time of writing in April 2007 its Internet website was accessible more frequently than most). Management procedures are at best opaque, and training sessions on human rights are little more than a public relations exercise. Modernisation has yet to take place, with training courses and all forms of equipment in short supply – primarily because billions of shillings allocated for procurement have been misappropriated. Public confidence in the institution is low.

## Prospects for reform

The prospects for fundamental reform are limited. As the East African Community Customs Union noted in June 2006, the challenges to policing in Kenya (as in neighbouring Uganda and Tanzania, and, indeed, Africa more generally) include brutality, corruption, politicisation, militarisation, inadequate training and resources, partial recruitment processes, poor working conditions and the failure of reform in the criminal justice sector more broadly (Kiguta 2006).

Far from becoming a responsive and professional service capable of facilitating social, economic and political development, the police head Transparency International's national bribery league (Transparency International Kenya 2007; Kenya Police Service 2003: 6). Not only do officers ask for bribes on Fridays, which are their 'pay days', but also many of TI's Nairobi respondents attribute one in three crimes to them. Many officers acknowledge the need for reform while doing their best in difficult circumstances, but arbitrary arrests and intimidation are amongst the policing techniques commonly used (*Standard* 2006a). The incidence of violent crime remains high.

The environmental, managerial and cultural problems of Kenya's police are as challenging in 2007 as they were in 2003. The reasons for this are debatable. Most explanations focus on the police as an institution. This is understandable, given the notorious difficulty of changing their institutional culture and individual attitudes while mitigating public mistrust. Nevertheless, it is probable that the primary reason for the lack of reform arises from the fact that the police are part of a political system and society that is, for a variety of reasons, corrupt. Whether the police are a primary cause, or merely an expression, prompt or facilitator of corruption and its associated insecurity is debatable, as is the sequencing required to address it, but two things are clear: first, a police's standards, values and behaviour reflect those of its political masters and host society, and second, police reform cannot take place in a societal or political vacuum. In other words, police reform is only one aspect of the institutional and societal problems confronting Kenya.

The government acknowledges the significance of the problem. Not only is it under pressure to stamp out corruption and nepotism, but also its 2006 *Economic Recovery and Wealth Creation Strategy* prioritises improving policing and security as a means to ensure economic growth. Indeed, in October 2006 Ali cited joblessness and poverty as the main obstacles in the fight against insecurity: 'What you see in the society is as a result of joblessness and poverty, but we are trying to deal with it' (*Standard* 2006b). Genuine reform projects have been initiated too. Police salaries – and numbers – have doubled, more vehicles have been allocated, and community police have been introduced as a means to improve police–public relations (*East African Standard* 2006b). However, Ali's own priority was always that of crime control, rather than anti-corruption measures or accountability campaigns; he illustrated his understanding by reference to skirmishes in Kuresoi, illegal hawkers in Nairobi, and cattle rustling in Marsabit. As far as Ali was concerned, 'we are on top of things'.

Such measures go some way towards giving ordinary Kenyans the crime control they want, but they cannot be categorised as reform in the sense promoted by donors. Further, they cannot overcome the two linked factors that obstruct fundamental reform: corruption and the lack of political reform.

Of the two, corruption is the most fundamental because it undermines any attempts at reform and intensifies the impact of other obstacles. Thus corruption is not only part of the crime problem, but also is part of the usual solution to crime; little will change while Kenyans pay bribes in order to buy security or go about their daily business. More importantly, corruption means that 'ordinary' Kenyans are probably incapable of realistically managing the country's lavishly rewarded and deeply distrusted politicians. It also means that politicians have no incentive to reform the system they profit from. All politicians received big salary increases in December 2006, with Kibaki awarding himself a 186 per cent increase. This brought his basic salary to £14,600 a month (*Standard* 2006c; *Guardian* 2006b).

The prospects for police reform would improve if the direction and administration of the police were uncoupled from the political process. But this is unlikely to happen when the President's Office controls police funding and administration, and uses public funds in ways that are opaque and unaccountable. Further, Kibaki's response to political pressure from his opponents was by late 2006 increasingly intolerant, with all that this implies for accountable styles of policing. The prospects for political reform look increasingly unlikely under Kibaki.

And it is unlikely that the situation will change with his departure. For his successor will inherit chronic corruption, decaying infrastructure, a sluggish agriculture-based economy, high poverty rates, ethnic tensions between coastal Muslims and other Kenyans, tribal issues and potential terrorism, all of which are exacerbated by HIV/AIDS (*Africa Confidential* 2006). Further, reform is expensive. The 52 billion shillings required to roll out 2003's *Strategic Plan* represented a significant proportion of the government's projected revenue at a time when public funding initiatives for free primary education, a new healthcare strategic plan and infrastructure development also demanded attention.

On the other hand, the institutional politics associated with political change offers opportunities to introduce reform. The potentially catalytic role played by intrigue cannot be discounted either, as in late 2006, when the police's institutional unity was threatened by the plots surrounding an elite police unit linked to a raid on Standard Group offices implicated in corruption scandals (*East Africa Standard* 2006a).

To conclude. Policing standards in developing democracies such as Kenya rarely conform to liberal ideals. Reform programmes can result in projects addressing specific resource and training inadequacies, but these are usually superficial and short-term in nature. There are two main reasons for this.

First, police standards reflect the social and political order sustaining them. Second, there can be no genuine reform without political reform, yet most reform projects require that the police should be made accountable to civilian authorities while ignoring the reality that police are already accountable to political elites. For such reasons, the prospects for genuine lasting reform are questionable.

## Notes

1  The Kenya Police motto is 'Service to all'.
2  According to statistics released in July 2007, 4,410 cases of crime were recorded in June, a fall of 12 per cent from April–May. In contrast, murders increased by 24 to 146 (*East African Standard* 2007). The actual figures may be higher, for police do not report crime they themselves are involved in, while public apathy ensures that many crimes are never reported.
3  Nine died at rallies organised by groups opposing the introduction of a new constitution designed to reinforce presidential powers. Voting in November's referendum was seen as a measure of confidence in Kibaki's leadership, so the proposal's resounding rejection was regarded as a protest vote ahead of 2007's general elections.

## References

All websites were accessed in April 2007.

Adar, K. and Munyae, I. (2001) 'Human Rights Abuse in Kenya under Daniel Arap Moi, 1978–2001', *African Studies Quarterly* 5 (1): 1. <http://web.africa.ufl.edu/asq/v5/v5i1a1.htm>

*Africa Confidential* (2006) 'The anti-corruption collapse', 20 October. <www.africa-confidential.com>

*Africa Research Bulletin*: National Security (2006), 1–28 February.

Amnesty International (2001a) *Amnesty International Annual Report 2001*. <http://web.amnesty.org/web/ar2001.nsf/webafrcountries/KENYA?OpenDocument>

Amnesty International (2001b) *Kenya: Ending the Cycle of Impunity*, London: AI.

Amnesty International (2005) *AI Report 2005: Kenya*. <http://web.amnesty.org/report2005/ken-summary-eng>

Anderson, D. and Killingray, D. (1991) eds., *Policing the Empire: Government, Authority and Control, 1830–1940*, Manchester: Manchester University Press.

Anderson, D. and Killingray, D. (1992) eds., *Policing and Decolonisation: Politics, Nationalism and the Police, 1917–1965*, Manchester: Manchester University Press.

Bayart, J.-F., Ellis, S. and Hibou, B. (1999) *The Criminalization of the State in Africa*, Oxford: James Currey.

BBC (2001) 'Kenya's slum war', 7 December. <http://news.bbc.co.uk/2/hi/africa/1697809.stm>

—— (2002) 'Police are Kenya's top killers', 14 January. <http://news.bbc.co.uk/1/hi/world/africa/1759421.stm>

—— (2003) 'Kenya police probes army', 31 January. <http://news.bbc.co.uk/1/hi/world/africa/2714371.stm>

—— (2006a) 'Kenya inquiry on airport security', 13 June. <http://news.bbc.co.uk/1/hi/world/africa/5074276.stm>

—— (2006b, 10 November) 'Kenya corruption "threatening UK" ', <http://news.-bbc.co.uk/1/hi/uk_politics/6135244.stm>

—— (2006c) 'Effort to halt Kenyan slum battle'. 9 November <http://news.-bbc.co.uk/1/hi/world/africa/6132776.stm>

Brown, S. (2004) 'Theorising Kenya's Protracted Transition to Democracy', *Journal of Contemporary African Studies* 22, 3: 325–342.

Chabal, P. and Daloz, J.-P. (1999) *Africa Works: Disorder as Political Instrument*, Oxford: James Currey.

Clayton, A. and Killingray, D. (1989) *Khaki and Blue: Military and Police in British Colonial Africa*, Athens, OH: Ohio University Center for International Studies.

Commonwealth Human Rights Initiative and Kenya Human Rights Commission, (CHRI) (2006) *The Police, The People, The Politics: Police Accountability in Kenya*.

*Daily Monitor*, Kampala (2005) 'Kayihura vows to fight illicit trade', 30 November. <http://www.monitor.co.ug/business/bus11302.php

*Daily Nation*, Nairobi (2004) 'It's time for radical police reforms', 4 February. <http://www.nationaudio.com/News/DailyNation/04022004/Comment/Comment040220044.html>

*Daily Nation on the Web* (2006) 16 November. <http://www.nationaudio.com/News/DailyNation/04022004/Comment/Comment04022>

Deflem, M. (1994) 'Law Enforcement in British Colonial Africa: A Comparative Analysis of Imperial Policing in Nyasaland, the Gold Coast, and Kenya.' *Police Studies* 17(1): 45–68.

Earthtrends (2003) 'Economic Indicators: Kenya'. <earthtrends.wri.org/pdf_library/country_profiles/eco_cou_404.pdf>

*East African*, Nairobi (2003), 'Kenya's Filthy Rich Civil Servants', 3 November.

*East African Standard*, Nairobi (2005) 'Crime by the numbers', 10 April. <http://allafrica.com/stories/200504110177.html>

—— (2006a) 'Kenya: Internal Wars Threaten Police Force Unity', 16 October. <http://allafrica.com/stories/200610160458.html>

—— (2006b) 'Kenya: New Tactics Needed in Anti-Crime War', 29 October. <http://allafrica.com/stories/200610300238.html>

—— (2007) 'Kenya: Crime Goes Down As Cases of Murder Rise', 3 July. <http://allafrica.com/stories/200707021714.html>

*Economist* (2006) 'Caught in the act', 28 January.

Enloe, C. (1976) 'Ethnicity and Militarization: Factors Shaping the Roles of Police in Third World Nations', *Studies in Comparative International Development*, 11: 25–38.

Goredema, C. and Botha, A. (2004) 'African Commitments to Combating Crime and Terrorism: A review of eight NEPAD countries', AHSI Paper 3, July.

*Guardian* (2006a) 'Our man in Africa: lovely country, it's just a pity you're corrupt from head to toe', November 11. <http://www.guardian.co.uk/kenya/story/0,,1945416,00.html>

—— (2006b) 'Kenya's costly politics and Kabila's challenge in the DRC', Letter from Edward Clay, 12 December.

Human Rights Watch (2001), *World Report 2001: Kenya*. <http://www.hrw.org/wr2k1/africa/kenya.html>

Human Rights Watch (2002) *Kenya's Unfinished Democracy: A Human Rights Agenda For The New Government*. <http://hrw.org/doc/?t=africa_pub&c=kenya>

Kagari, M., CHRI (2003) 'The Kenya Police Service Strategic Plan 2003–2007: A Commentary'. <http://www.humanrightsinitiative.org/programs/aj/police/ea/

articles/-strategic_plan_analysis.pdf>

Kenya Police Service (2003) *Strategic Plan 2003–2007*. Draft 2. <http://www.humanrightsinitiative.org/programs/aj/police/ea/articles/draft_strategic_plan_2003-07.pdf>

*Kenya Times* (2006a) 'Anti-Ali plot?', 9 November. <http://www.timesnews.co.ke/09nov06/nwsstory/topstry.html>

——— (2006b) 'Kibaki tough stand', 11 November. <http://www.timesnews.co.ke/11nov06/nwsstory/topstry.html>

Kiguta, P. (2006) 12 June. http://64.233.161.104/search?q=cache:mHpXwf5WcLYJ:www.commonwealthp...watch.org/public_eye.htm+policing+in+kenya&hl=en&gl=uk&ct=clnk&cd=4

Krause, V. and Otenyo, E. (2005) 'Terrorism and the Kenyan Public', *Studies in Conflict and Terrorism* 28: 99–112.

*Monitor*, Kampala (2005) 'Kenya, Uganda Lose $140m in illicit trade', 9 May. <http://allafrica.com/stories/printable/200505050183.html>

*Nation*, Nairobi (2006) 'Kenya: Kibaki Meets Police Chief Over Slum Crisis' 10 November. <http://allafrica.com/stories/200611100032.html>

*Police Act* 1988 (Kenya) Chapter 2, section 12. Quoted in CHRI Initiative eMagazine (2006) *Commonwealth Police Watch* 'About a Police Force'. <http://www.commonwealthpolicewatch.org/abt_police_force.htm>

Potholm, C. (1969) 'The Multiple Roles of the Police as Seen in the African Context', *Journal of Developing Areas* 3: 139–58.

Rosenau, W. (2005) 'Al Qaida Recruitment Trends in Kenya and Tanzania,' *Studies in Conflict and Terrorism* 28: 1–10.

Ruteere, M. and Pommerolle, M.-E. (2003) 'Democratizing Security or Decentralizing Repression? The ambiguities of community policing in Kenya', *African Affairs* 102: 587–604.

Saferworld (2008) 'Implementing community-based policing in Kenya'. London: Saferworld. <http://www.saferworld.org.uk/publications.php/306/implementing_community_based_policing_in_kenya>

*Standard* (2006a) 'Kenya Police unit tops list of human rights abusers', 18 September. <http://www.eastandard.net/hm_news/news.php?articleid=1143958374>

*Standard* (2006b) 'Poverty fuelling crime, says police chief', 26 October. <http://www.eastandard.net/hm_news/news.php?articleid=1143960127>

*Standard* (2006c) 'MPs sign off more cash for "big men" ', 8 December 2006. <http://www.eastandard.net/archives/cl/hm_news/news.php?articleid=1143962211&date=8/12/2006>

*Sunday Monitor* (2005) 'Is Museveni deliberately militarising the police?', 1 December. <http://www.monitor.co.ug/sunday/insights/ins11272.php>

Transparency International Kenya (2007) 'FAQs', point 13, 5 January. <http://www.tikenya.org/faqs.asp>

UNDP/UN-Habitat (2002) *Crime in Nairobi: Results of a Citywide Victim Survey*. Nairobi.

USAID (2006) *Budget*. <http://www.usaid.gov/policy/budget/cbj2006/afr/ke.html>

US Embassy (2005) 'U.S. Independence Day Remarks', 4 July. <http://usembassy.state.gov/nairobi/wwwhjuly405.html>

# 12 The building of the new South African Police Service

## The dynamics of police reform in a changing (and violent) country

*Antony Altbeker*

## Introduction

Policing in South Africa is something of a national obsession largely because crime is one of the country's most pressing policy problems. This fixation may or may not be healthy or appropriate because, as students of the subject will know, the extent to which policing impacts on crime levels is by no means well-established. This is certainly true of the developed world where scholarly debate about the role of the police in preventing crime has produced many a peer-reviewed article, but in the developing world, matters are, if anything, worse. In developing countries, after all, crime problems are often far worse than in the developed world, and police services are frequently staffed by poorly trained personnel, usually lack basic resources and infrastructure, and suffer from severe deficits in both discipline and professional integrity.[1] That being so, the link between policing and crime levels in the developing world should be even less clear.

Nevertheless, for better or worse, South Africa's crime problems are generally understood by much of the public to be a marker, almost a gauge, of the extent to which policing has failed. For this reason, police reform (sometimes called 'transformation', a word that in South Africa also carries with it the implication of changing the demographic make-up of the Service) has been high on the policy agenda ever since the inauguration of democracy in 1994. Indeed, within months of the new, democratically-elected government's coming to power, a Green Paper – in effect, a draft policy document, released for public comment before a final policy paper is developed – was produced by the Ministry for Safety and Security (Ministry for Safety and Security, 1994).

To say the least, this document set out an ambitious agenda for change. It argued that policing in South Africa was, and always has been, characterised by a lack of social and political legitimacy because of the role the police had played in implementing and enforcing the hated policies of apartheid, and trying to put down the popular resistance to that system of government during the 1970s and 1980s. The effect of the latter was worsened by the fact that it relied on the use of draconian security legislation as well as illegal tactics of torture and assassination. This lack of legitimacy, so it was argued in the Green Paper, meant that the principle challenge for policing in a democratic society was the building of the organisation's popular legitimacy. This, in turn, required a number of changes to policy and practice, as well as to the shape of the organisation and the demographic profile of those who staffed it. In addition, much more rigorous and vigorous oversight of policing was required, necessitating the creation of a range of state institutions to fill this function. Finally, and in some ways most fundamentally, it argued that policing had to develop new methodologies based on a philosophy of community policing and crime prevention, counter-posing these to the law-enforcement models that had driven police thinking about their work for generations.

On a less abstract plane, the Green Paper also argued that the fragmentation of policing that the new South Africa inherited, a result of the artificial and illegitimate division of the country into the Republic of South Africa and 10 ethnically-defined 'independent' Bantustans, had to be brought to an end. Following the provisions agreed during constitutional negotiations that led to democracy, policing was to be centrally-controlled by national government, with only nominal powers to direct and oversee policing delegated to the nine newly-created provincial governments.

That the first democratic government should feel that the Police Service in South Africa was in need of fundamental reform is hardly surprising, of course, given the role historically played by the police, and the security forces more generally. Before reviewing the politics and practicalities of police transformation, then, it is crucial that policing in South Africa be located in its social, political and historical context.

## A (brief) history of policing in South Africa

As in any society, the role of the police under apartheid was shaped in large measure by the character of the state of which it was part. In South Africa, a country whose boundaries were defined by its colonial masters and whose state from earliest colonial times was dedicated to maintaining a deeply iniquitous system of national oppression and economic exploitation, coercion was central to the practice of government. Inevitably, policing was implicated in this after 1912, when the national police force was first established. This act was itself a function of the creation of what was then called the Union of South Africa and which brought together what had been, until then, four separate states, two of which were colonies of Britain and two of which had been independent 'Boer' republics.

Although the Union was granted the power to make its own laws and run its own affairs, South Africa was still a colony of the British Empire, a status it would retain until the early 1960s when it became a Republic. Like all colonies, the logic and content of government's programmes were driven by the interests of the ruling minority, and, in the case of South Africa, with its abundant mineral resources and rapidly developing agricultural sector, that meant that the social structure was built essentially around the need to ensure that labour was cheap and docile. In addition, beginning in 1913 with the passage of the Land Act, parts of the country were set aside for the indigenous population, and a system of pass laws was introduced which made it illegal for African people to live in 'white' areas if they were not employed there. Eventually, some 13 per cent of the country's land mass was set aside for Africans although they made up 80 per cent of the population. The remainder was reserved for the white minority, with the implication that black people living in those areas could never become full citizens in the areas in which they lived. In the process, whole communities were forcibly relocated to these areas and those who offended against the pass laws were arrested, tried and imprisoned. Inevitably, all of this meant that policing played an irreducible role in shaping the nature of South African society.

The erection of this racialised and racist social formation accelerated sharply in 1948 when the National Party came to power with its stated policy of implementing *apartheid*. This, too, had consequences for the manner in which policing was conceived by the state and, indeed, the way police officers conceived themselves.

### Policing and resistance to apartheid

If policing was crucial to the erection of the structure South African society and its state, it was also central to the defensive reaction of that state to the resistance mounted by the dispossessed and disenfranchised majority.

For the first half of the twentieth century, this resistance was largely – but not exclusively – peaceful in character. It did, nevertheless, occasionally result in violent responses from the state. Thus, in Galeshewe, a black township outside Kimberley, in 1952, 13 people were killed by police officers at a demonstration during the Defiance Campaign. By far the most famous example of deadly police action, however, occurred in March 1960 in Sharpeville, a ghetto near Johannesburg, when police opened fire on a crowd symbolically burning their pass-books as an act of defiance of apartheid laws. Sixty-nine people were killed, many shot in the back, and the massacre precipitated a decision by the African National Congress (ANC) – the principal voice of the dispossessed majority – to commit itself to an armed struggle after nearly 50 years of more-or-less fruitless peaceful protest. Six months later, the first bombs in a campaign of 'armed propaganda' exploded, and the ANC, along with other liberation organisations, was formally banned.

Although armed struggle was one of the principal strategies of resistance, police harassment using increasingly severe security legislation meant that the ANC was never able to mount a military insurrection that posed a serious military threat to the apartheid government. Starting in June 1976, however, when protests by school children in Soweto against the imposition of Afrikaans as the language of tuition prompted a deadly response by the security forces, popular revolt bubbled through many of South Africa's black urban townships. This led to daily confrontations between security forces and demonstrators who were generally unarmed, but amongst whom were often some individuals who would throw stones or petrol bombs. The rising incidence of these confrontations led to the imposition, from 1983 onwards, of a series of States of Emergency which sharpened police powers of detention: upwards of 80,000 people were detained without trial for periods ranging from weeks to years. It would almost be no exaggeration to say that, throughout this period, the only axis of police–community relations for the majority African community was across the barrel of police weapons. In 1985 alone, official police figures put the number of African adults killed at over 500, while a further 187 children died; in addition, 2,300 people were wounded by police actions (Brogden and Shearing, 1993: 18).

By the late 1980s, apartheid, and the resistance it generated, had become too costly for the South African government, which began tentatively to explore the possibilities of a negotiated settlement. The led to the unbanning of liberation movements, the release of political prisoners (most famously, Nelson Mandela in February 1990), and the commencement of a process of negotiation which led to constitutional change and democratic elections in April 1994.

The four years during which the new constitution was negotiated were marked neither by reduced violence nor increasing levels of public confidence in the police. Indeed, these years were probably the most violent in the country's history, with what was blithely labelled by government 'black-on-black' violence reaching appalling levels in some parts of the country. At the very best, South African policing proved incapable of preventing these clashes, and a great deal of evidence now exists that some police officers actively stoked these conflicts acting alone in accordance with official policy (TRC, 1998: 211), by arming the more conservative forces aligned with the Inkatha Freedom Party (ibid.: 339) and engaging in anonymous acts of terror including facilitating terror attacks on commuter trains in which scores of people died (ibid.: 581).

Given the history of police–community relations, then, it is unsurprising that one of the central tasks the newly-elected government set itself for the transformation of policing in South Africa, was to create a basis on which the police could build public legitimacy and credibility. This was seen as a precondition for effective policing and resulted in a number of processes. Among the most important of these processes were the work of the Truth and Reconciliation Commission (TRC) and the associated processes of rooting out the worst offenders from the ranks of the police. The other critical elements – to be dealt with in subsequent sections – were the restructuring of policing and the adoption of community policing as a guiding philosophy for the organisation.

## Policing, police legitimacy and the TRC

One of the key agreements reached during constitutional negotiations in the early 1990s related to the twin questions of the continuity of employment in the public service of those who had served under apartheid (which a 'sunset provision' in the constitution guaranteed for a minimum of five years) and the stipulation that those who had committed 'gross violations of human rights' would be entitled to amnesty for their acts, but only if they came forward and disclosed fully the circumstances of the crime. In effect, in order to increase the willingness to contemplate democracy among previously-privileged groups (and reduce the risk of rebellion by the old elite), existing civil servants were guaranteed their jobs. In addition, in order to foster reconciliation, those who had committed 'gross violations of human rights' were also offered amnesty from prosecution in return for the truth. Hence some have argued that the 'dominant logic' of the model of transitional justice in South Africa emphasised truth and reconciliation over justice and accountability (Rauch and van der Spuy, 2006: 42).

Institutionally, the power to grant amnesty was conferred on the TRC. However, despite the pleas of the newly appointed National Commissioner of the Police Service, George Fivaz, only a few police officers applied for amnesty, doing so very late in the process and only after the successful prosecution of a former policeman, Eugene de Kock, for scores of crimes including murders, assault, theft and fraud. In all, only about 300 of the 7,000 amnesty applications that the TRC received came from police officers, with about 70 per cent of these being granted.

The small number of amnesty applications was a function of the fact that the TRC's terms of reference meant that they could offer amnesty only for 'gross violations of human rights'. This meant that only the most egregious incidents would qualify, while the day-to-day human rights violations inherent in policing apartheid would not be considered. More to the point, though, the act in question also had to be illegal at the time it was committed for the 'perpetrator' to be at risk of prosecution. Because most forms of police action, no matter how unpleasant or unjust, were not illegal at the time, they were not brought to the TRC. Indeed, at least by the permissive standards of the criminal and security legislation of the day, the vast majority of even the deaths caused by the police were not unlawful. The result was that amnesty applications related, in the main, to police-initiated executions, as well as the death or torture of detainees and prisoners. The many thousands of deaths caused by police shootings, to say nothing of the detentions and the routine humiliations attendant on enforcing apartheid's laws, were not criminal acts and did not qualify as 'gross violations of human rights'. For the most part, then, even those who had killed protestors while defending apartheid had no reason to apply for amnesty.

It is arguable, therefore, that the TRC and the amnesty process played little role in changing policing in South Africa. While there is some merit in this claim – and the TRC's final recommendations on the reform of policing are, in fact, relatively weak and uninspired – it is important not to conflate the impact of the TRC on policing with the degree to which police officers embraced the amnesty-for-honesty deal that was offered. This is because the

TRC's most profound impact – on society in general, as well as on the police itself – was felt through the very public process in which some victims of gross violations of human rights testified to their experiences. These were broadcast live and were also packaged for a weekly half-hour long television programme. The effect on the national psyche, as well as on the psyche of the police, of hundreds of people testifying about the brutality of apartheid and its enforcement cannot be quantified. Nevertheless, it must have played an important role in preparing the ground for subsequent efforts to reform policing. After the TRC, it was simply impossible for anyone – including the most insistent of police officers and their apologists – to profess a belief that all was well with policing. It meant also that when the new cadre of police managers spoke about policing under apartheid, they had little choice but to condemn its excesses and to present themselves as advocates of radical change. Indeed, the catch-phrase of the newly appointed National Commissioner – a white career police officer who had in his day almost joined the dreaded Security Branch, the most explicitly political of the police force's divisions – was the importance of policing's making 'a clean break from the past'.

If the TRC did not lead to the rooting out of all those who had committed egregious violations of human rights, the changing atmosphere in the police – the result in part of the TRC and, in larger measure, of the attitude and approach of new police leadership – did, in fact, lead to large numbers of police officers leaving the organisation. This was actively encouraged by government which offered generous 'voluntary severance packages' to long-serving officers in the hope that those whose politics and attitudes were most offensive to the new values would choose early retirement. The result was that large numbers of police officers left the force, with employee numbers falling from about 145,000 in 1994 to under 119,000 in 2000.[2] That those departing were predominately middle-ranking white officers is demonstrated by the fact that in 1995, the ratio of white middle-ranking officers to black was almost 8:1, but, as early as 1999, this had shrunk to less than 2.5:1, even as the overall number of officers in the police declined (Rauch and van der Spuy, 2006: 29).

It seems conclusive, then, that despite the very limited number of prosecutions of apartheid's police officers for crimes committed in those years, the limited impact of formal TRC processes, and the decision to avoid the lastration of officials who had served apartheid, only a few years after the death of apartheid, the racial composition of senior ranks of the Police Service had changed beyond recognition. This is a result of two inter-related factors: the increasing discomfort of old order, principally white, police officers with the new Police Service, and the aggressive programme of affirmative action, dubbed in South Africa, 'transformation'.

## Police restructuring and transformation

The transition from apartheid had enormous implications for policing. By far the most important of these was that the kind of policing used to defend an unjust social structure which generates high levels of political conflict and widespread disorder was hopelessly ill-suited to the challenges of policing a democracy, albeit one with high levels of crime. This is a subject to which we will return below. On the other hand, however, there were a variety of 'purely' organisational issues which also demanded the attention of policy-makers and senior police management. The two most important of these were the restructuring of the police organisation and the need to ensure that the new Police Service would be representative of the demographic make-up of South Africa.

## Restructuring

One of the most highly contested issues during constitutional negotiations in the early 1990s was the extent to which state power and authority would vest in the central government or at lower levels of government. Throughout the negotiations, the ANC regarded those who advocated a relatively high level of devolution and decentralisation as attempting, consciously or unconsciously, to limit the ability of the soon-to-be elected government of South Africa to effect change. Largely for this reason, the constitution eventually agreed upon placed a preponderance of state power in the hands of a central, national government, with much weaker authority granted to nine provincial governments and the hundreds of municipalities. This was true of the distribution of powers across all government functions, but, in the case of policing, the justification for the decision to centralise authority rested on other considerations as well. One of the most important of these was the desire to prevent a fragmented Police Service being dragged into any political conflict that might erupt after the transition.

The concern about the potential for decentralised, autonomous police agencies to be dragged into any potential conflict was not unreasonable in the context of a fraught transition to democracy. This was, after all, a time of immense uncertainty and insecurity, as well as of violence. Indeed, in an act of terrifying brinkmanship, one of the most significant political forces in the country – the Inkatha Freedom Party – threatened to boycott the 1994 elections and contest their outcome, violently if necessary, if it felt its authority in the Bantustan of KwaZulu was threatened. In the circumstances, it was hardly surprising that constitutional negotiators would fear the consequences of a local or provincial government dominated by factions such as these having a Police Service at their disposal. This would have increased the potential lethality of any violence that might occur and, as important, may have made more bold and aggressive those with a desire to carve out independent fiefdoms in which they might rule. Unsurprisingly, it was felt that a central government ought to control those functions of government the devolution of which could increase the risk of violence.[3]

These pragmatic considerations about whether it was responsible to allow the fragmentation of coercive authority in a fragile transition were, at the same time, reinforced by an unarticulated sense that the imperatives of nation building after centuries of divide-and-rule required the building of truly national institutions. To my knowledge, this argument was never made explicitly, but it is intuitively plausible that much of the political energy associated with the desire to forge a single national Police Service (as well as other national institutions) had as much to do with the emotional energy attached to the qualifiers 'single' and 'national' as it had to do with any genuine concern about the potential for a political break-away.

In practice, the decision to forge a single national Police Service, however, meant that much of the time, energy and resources of both the political and operational leaderships of the Police Service was consumed by the practical questions that would have to be addressed in the building of such an institution – questions of organisational structure, of rank titles and of the design of uniforms, of pay scales and career paths (see Eloff, 2006). These were hard questions to answer, but, however loudly they were trumpeted as signs of reform and progress, the implementation of these developments on their own could never be made to resonate either with rank-and-file police officers or, indeed, with members of the public; it made the reform of policing seem at once bureaucratic and superficial.

### Transformation

In addition to the commitment to a single national Police Service answering to the central government, a second organising principle for institutional change in the Police Service was the need to ensure that its membership, and especially its leadership, would become more representative of the population as a whole. In effect, the objective was to ensure that police management, historically virtually the preserve of white, male police officers, would become increasingly black. As already described, one mechanism for achieving this was the offering of generous severance packages to officers who would choose to leave the organisation before reaching their retirement age. Another was – and remains – an aggressive programme of affirmative action.

The argument for changing the demographic make-up of the Police Service has always been about two inter-related issues: the impact of the Service's demographic representivity on its public legitimacy, and the rights of its employees, black and white.

In relation to the role of transformation in increasing public legitimacy, the argument has always been that a Police Service associated with the upholding of apartheid which also remained dominated by white officers, would forever lack credibility in black communities. In addition, for various reasons ranging from the prosaic (e.g. the inability of most white South Africans to speak any of the African languages) to the more subtle (e.g. the more limited ability of white police officers to develop a 'street sense' about social dynamics in black areas), the ability of the Service to police effectively also required changes in the profile of its officers. One difficulty with this argument that has never been resolved satisfactorily, however, is that for historical reasons, white police officers have attracted the lion's share of both training and managerial experience in the organisation, leading to some concerns that the transformation of the Service would inevitably lead to some degree of reduced operational performance. Indeed, for some sectors of public opinion, the rise in violent crime after 1994 is the direct result of decreased police effectiveness, a process sometimes ascribed to the implementation of affirmative action.

The issue of the rights of employees of the Police Service has also affected the debate about, and implementation of, affirmative action. Much of this debate has been instigated by white police officers and their unions, which have mounted a number of law suits, some of which have been successful, against the process. While this might have been the more dominant strand of the debate in recent years, in the mid-1990s a commission of enquiry appointed by the Minister for Safety and Security found that promotion policies in the police had historically been grossly discriminatory. For many years, for instance, it had been official police policy that white police officers could never be under the command of black officers. In addition, the manner in which examinations were structured and interpreted, and the way in which promotions boards deliberated, had systematically denied black officers equal rights to promotions. Inevitably, these kinds of practices had created a range of problems in the organisation. Inevitably, also, redressing these created a degree of resentment on the part of white police officers, whose career prospects worsened as those of black officers improved. Finally, it also created a degree of organisational instability as middle- and senior-ranking white officers left and new appointments were made.

## A new philosophy of policing

If the TRC had been the principal vehicle for exploring and addressing police abuses, and the restructuring and transformation of the Service were intended to create an organisation better suited to the needs of the new South Africa, the third and most ambitious leg of police reform has been the attempt to develop and operationalise a new approach to policing. Drawing on a range of ideas from the international literature on 'community policing', 'problem-oriented policing' and 'crime prevention', a domestic version of community policing was premised on the idea that the approach to policing which had governed the Service under apartheid, with its emphasis on law enforcement, as well as the social and political distance between the police and the policed, was ill-suited to South Africa's needs.

Perhaps the most obvious reason why community policing was seen as the most suitable model for the Police Service was the complete absence of community trust for, and support of, the police in most communities in South Africa. For this reason, in addition to the elements of community policing models adopted elsewhere – such as stepped-up foot and vehicle patrol work, and partnerships with organised civil society – the local model of community policing was built around the statutorily-mandated establishment of Community Police Forums (CPFs) at every police station. In terms of the relevant laws, these structures were to represent the community in order to ensure that its needs and priorities were taken on board in the development of station-level strategic and operational planning. In addition, CPFs were granted certain limited powers of oversight over the police, and also became a vehicle through which complaints about service delivery and performance could be channelled.

The oversight role of CPFs, it should be noted, was necessitated in part by the decision to establish a single national Police Service, a decision which had the inevitable consequence of denying a role to local communities in the oversight of policing through locally-elected politicians. By its nature, a national Police Service is a large – indeed, in South Africa, an enormous – organisation of (at the time of writing) over 160,000 people operating in wildly diverse social conditions and servicing very different communities. With no institutional channel through which local communities could be consulted on their needs, it is hard to see how such an organisation of this kind could possibly tailor its activities to local circumstances. In this regard, however, the balance of authority between a local CPF, on the one hand, and a police station's managers in Pretoria, on the other, has, in the past few years, shifted decisively in the favour of officials in police headquarters. As a result, there is now a widespread conviction that CPFs have proved to be deficient as a structure for consultation and oversight. Indeed, even the ruling party, the ANC, in a policy paper circulated before its most recent congress, suggested that 'only a handful [of CPFs] are truly functional and, in the main, those are structures that were established and work in the more affluent areas of the country'. The paper goes on to argue that the whole business of CPFs had been a 'blunder' from the start, blaming the fact that it had been the police, rather than the communities themselves or their elected representatives, who had be responsible for their establishment. This had resulted in the compromising of CPFs' ability to fulfil their oversight functions (ANC, 2007).

This assessment of CPFs is only partially accurate, however (Altbeker, 2007b). Perhaps more important than the locus of responsibility for the establishment of CPFs in explaining subsequent disillusionment with these institutions, has been the gap between the promise of community policing and the reality that the experience of policing in post-apartheid South Africa has been affected by the persistence and growth of violent crime. This has both affected public confidence in the police (and, by extension, in community policing), as well as having led to repeated efforts to reconfigure both the police organisation and the manner in which it approaches its appointed tasks.

## Crime and policing in post-apartheid South Africa

If the distance between the police and the communities they served was the principal reason for the adoption of community policing as the organisation's guiding philosophy, a second reason was that it was believed that this would be the most effective way of addressing the increasingly serious crime problems confronting the country. Whatever the relationship between policing in general and crime levels, and however well or poorly community policing has been implemented in South Africa, one thing is certain: if crime levels are any gauge of the question, police reform in South Africa has not met public expectations or demands. Consider, for instance, a list of the 10 countries with the highest mortality rates from violent crime as estimated by the World Health Organisation (WHO) (see Table 12.1).[4]

As this list demonstrates, levels of lethal violence in South Africa are very high by international standards, putting the country, by these measures, in the same league as the failed and war-ravaged states of Sierra Leone, Angola, Somalia and Liberia, the narco-state of Columbia, as well as Russia and some of the more troubled states in Latin America. Even within this group, in 2002, lethal criminal violence was estimated to be over 30 per cent more common in South Africa than it was in Somalia, Russia and Liberia.

These sorts of figures are the reason why crime and policing command so much attention in policy debates about the priorities and performance of government and, most especially, the police in South Africa. It is not, after all, as if the country is under-policed. Indeed, at around 300 police officers per 100,000 people, South Africa sits somewhere in the middle of world police-per-capita rankings, while, at 3 per cent of GDP, the country spends about twice the international norm on criminal justice (Altbeker, 2005b: 17). Given this, and given the enormous energies devoted to changing the Police Service, the fact that the country is also one of the most violent countries in the world, one that compares on this score with some failed states, might be interpreted to mean that policing and police reform have failed.

This interpretation may be unfair, however, and for two reasons. The first is that it is far from obvious that the best use a policy-maker or analyst can make of the murder rate is to use it to assess the quality of policing. Levels of violence, after all, are a function of a vast range of factors such as the age

*Table 12.1* Mortality rates from violence in 2002, selected countries

| | |
|---|---|
| Colombia | 72.4 |
| Sierra Leone | 50.3 |
| South Africa | 43.2 |
| Angola | 39.6 |
| El Salvador | 38.4 |
| Guatemala | 37.1 |
| Venezuela | 35.2 |
| Somalia | 33.1 |
| Russia | 32.9 |
| Liberia | 32.8 |

*Source:* WHO (2004: 120–125)

structure of the population, the level of poverty and inequality, the extent of social exclusion, as well as softer 'cultural' factors such as the manner in which men express or fail to express physical aggression, amongst many, many others. Thus, it is grossly unfair to assess the impact of police reform on the basis of the absolute level of lethal violence.

In this respect, it is worth noting that South Africa's demographic, social and economic profile are characterised by the kind of patterns that are widely believed to cause crime, especially violent crime. The country is, for instance, extremely young, with more than half the population aged 24 or younger and a third being younger than 14 (The Presidency, 2006: 39). Unemployment levels are very high, ranging between 25 per cent (on a strict definition of unemployment) and 40 per cent (using a wider definition), as is the level of poverty, with 43 per cent of the population living on less than R3,000 (about $420) a year (The Presidency, 2007: 23). In addition, despite some improvements in recent years and extensive redistribution through progressive taxation and government programmes, income distribution in South Africa is extremely unequal. Indeed, income inequality is regarded as among the most extreme in the world. Even at less abstract levels than these, social patterns are criminogenic: South Africa has one of the highest rates of alcohol consumption per drinker in the world and consumption patterns, which include 'bingeing', make this phenomenon even more conducive to crime. Given all of this, given the history of violence and the easy access to firearms, the impact of the police on violent criminality is never likely to be more than marginal.

The second reason for using South Africa's high levels of lethal violence to assess the impact of policing and police reform is that, over the past decade, per capita murder rates in South Africa have fallen by almost 40 per cent. Having peaked at over 67 per 100,000 in the mid-1990s, they had fallen to about 40 per 100,000 in 2006 and 2007. This is obviously far higher than international norms, but it does represent improvements in levels of safety.

In contrast to the declining murder rate, however, another significant trend in post-apartheid criminality has been the rapid rise in robbery. This is a crime which is under-reported (and even under-recorded) in every jurisdiction (Alavazzi del Frate and Van Kesteren, 2004), and so there have been some rather half-hearted attempts to argue that the rise in robbery is merely a statistical illusion, the result of increased reporting rates attendant on the improved accessibility and legitimacy of the police for most South Africans. Increased reporting (Leggett, 2002), however, is almost certainly not the reason why the robbery rate, as reflected in police statistics, rose by over 60 per cent between 1994 and 2004 (from 302 per 100,000 to 503 per 100,000) before dropping by 16 per cent over two years. There are a number of reasons why this seems likely, the most important being the fact that a national victimisation survey in 2003 found that only 29 per cent of robbery victims had reported the matter to the police, down from the 41 per cent recorded five years earlier (Burton *et al.*, 2004: 107). Another is what appears to have happened in the case of rape, a crime that is also notoriously under-reported and under-recorded. Police statistics suggest that this crime has hovered between 110 and 120 per 100,00 since 1994, a stability that is hard to reconcile with the idea that increased police legitimacy was increasing reporting rates.[5]

If continuously-increasing reporting rates do not explain the rise in robbery, and if, therefore, the increase reflected in police figures reflects an underlying reality, that would go a long way to explaining the fraught politics of crime (and policing) in post-apartheid South Africa. This is especially so because the increase in robbery has been accompanied by a dramatic shift in the spatial patterns of victimisation as it has moved into the middle-class suburbs of the cities. Because the middle classes in South Africa remain predominantly white, the shift is not just spatial in character, but is also a change in the race and class profile of the victims of predatory crime. Given that one of the consequences of apartheid was the erection of a security bubble around white South Africans, the explosion of robbery after 1994, and its dramatic shift into the suburbs, has meant that for many in the middle classes, crime and, by extension, law enforcement, have become litmus tests of the capacity and legitimacy of democracy itself. This is reflected also in two other trends: the rising use of private security services to provide static and mobile patrols as well as armed response services in the suburbs, as well as the apparent rise in incidents of vigilantism. It has been argued that while the

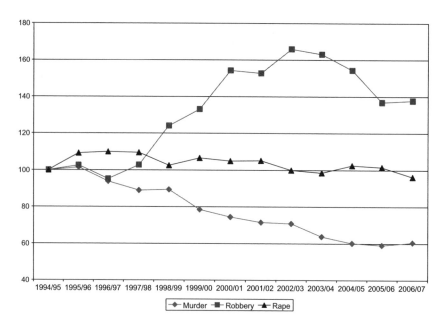

*Figure 12.1* Trends in post-apartheid crime per capita (1994 = 100).

*Source:* SAPS Annual Reports, various years

latter trend has usually been ascribed to a lack of faith in the criminal justice system, it has also been driven by the widening of class differences in previously disadvantaged communities. This has led those whose incomes have risen to use vigilantism as a means to distinguish and protect themselves from those who have been left behind by development programmes (Jensen, 2007).

This may or may not be entirely fair, but government's response to the crime wave has not always helped raise confidence. In the first few years after 1994, public statements about crime from government tended to acknowledge the scale of the problem and would often be accompanied by the assurance that efforts and resources were being deployed to address the causes of crime (which were understood to be the appalling material conditions in which far too many people lived their lives) and into the reform of the police. In the late 1990s, however, a Cabinet reshuffle and the appointment of a new National Commissioner of the police, saw a change in government rhetoric. The signature tune of the new minister, Steve Tshwete, was that the police would 'treat criminals as a bull dog treats a bone'. At the same time, the new Commissioner, Jackie Selebi, put in place a police strategy – dubbed Operation Crackdown – that emphasised quasi-military style operations in urban areas. These would see literally hundreds of police officers being deployed for cordon-and-search operations in which whole city blocks might be closed down and every person and residence in the area would be searched. This was a far cry from the philosophy of community policing to which the Service still professed its adherence. Despite this divergence, however, public support for these measures was high. Nor was this support confined to areas in which the police refrained from these kinds of operations: in one survey in a high-crime ghetto outside of Cape Town, 80 per cent of respondents said they would happily submit to monthly searches of their homes if it would reduce crime (Steinberg, 2004).

Unfortunately, there is little evidence that these operations, which are expensive and which drain human resources out of other areas, achieve anything apart from a brief suppression of criminality, with crime levels returning to previous levels shortly after. Indeed, if the trendlines of murder and robbery offer only ambiguous evidence (at best) of the success of community policing, the same is true in relation to Operation Crackdown-style activities. These operations, which were a staple of policing under apartheid, had never fallen out of the Service's repertoire, but they were significantly stepped up after 2000. That they do not appear to have dealt with the problem of violent crime is evident, however, in that fact that the decline in murder began well before 2000 and the rise in robbery persisted after it.

## Police reform and the investigation of crime

If there are real doubts about whether post-apartheid police reform has helped to prevent crime, the extent to which it has affected the ability of the police to investigate crime successfully is just as uncertain. Organisationally, the transformation of policing has been, if anything, more difficult and traumatic in the Detective Service than in any other division of the institution, with two distinct waves of structural reform, together with a plethora of changes to the law, affecting the confidence of the Detective Service and the morale of its members.

The first and most jolting of the structural changes made to the Detective Service was initiated in 1996 and consisted in the amalgamation of the command of the uniformed branch of the police and the detectives based at police stations under the authority of the local Station Commissioner. This move was justified on the basis that the previous arrangement, which saw detectives at a police station answering to their own commanders at higher levels of the Police Service rather than to the commander of the station itself, left the Station Commissioner with too little authority over a crucial police function. Besides, if he was supposed to be accountable to the CPF, but had no authority over 'his' detectives, the oversight function of CPFs would be greatly compromised. In addition, it was felt that the absence of a unified command implied a lack of coordination between 'proactive' (or uniformed) and 'reactive' (or investigative) policing.

While there is much merit in these arguments, my own research with detectives suggest that these structural changes were deeply traumatic. They were perceived as an assault on the professional independence and status of detectives. In addition, because of the historical animosity between uniformed and investigative branches of the Service, the changes were also often accompanied by Station Commissioners (who were almost invariably from the uniformed branch) choosing to reallocate resources to the uniformed members and away from the detectives (Altbeker, 1998). One result of this has been that the Detective Service, once regarded as an elite within the police, has struggled to attract and retain members.

The second major wave of restructuring within the Detective Service commenced in 2002 and was aimed at rationalising the number of specialised units within it. What distinguished these units from the bulk of detectives who were and are deployed at police stations is that their mandates directed their attention at specific kinds of crime, and their geographical jurisdictions extended beyond the boundaries of any individual police station. Thus the Family, Child and Sexual Violence Units were tasked with investigating serious crimes committed against women and children, the South African Narcotics Bureau investigated drug offences, the Murder and Robbery Units investigated cases deemed to require specialised attention either because of their seriousness or because of the complexity of the matter. In addition to these units, there were literally scores of other units, each investigating a sub-set of criminality.

The restructuring of these units was justified on the basis that 'all crime is local', and that it would make more sense to capacitate local police stations to investigate these matters, and, in the process, to strengthen them, rather than to denude the stations of these skills. In addition, the specialised units, because they seemed to operate in an oversight shadow, had a reputation for abuse: the Murder and Robbery Units were alleged to use torture as a matter of investigative routine, while the activities of the Narcotics Branch were thought to have been deeply compromised by corruption. Under those circumstances, breaking up the units created the potential for casting some sunlight into the shadows.

Once again, however, members of the Detective Service, including some of its most senior officers, have reported that these changes have been dislocating and have undermined efficiency and effectiveness. In my own experience, for instance, former members of the Narcotics Branch who were relocated to police stations, now routinely refuse to investigate drug crimes on the somewhat petulant basis that the organisation obviously deems them to be ineffective in this task or it would not have closed down the units in which they were doing it.

It is very hard to measure what the impact of these changes has been since the Police Service does not release statistics on conviction rates, and those statistics it does release about the extent to which cases go to court are not particularly satisfactory measures of the quality of cases. There is, however, evidence that since the mid-1990s, a larger and larger number of cases have entered the court rolls, suggesting, perhaps, that effectiveness has risen. There is also evidence that between 1994 and 2005, the number of convicted prisoners in South Africa's prisons increased at about 5 per cent per year. Because the growth in prisoner accommodation was much less modest, this had the effect of increasing levels of overcrowding from less than 20 per cent of capacity in 1996 to nearly 70 per cent in 2005.

Whatever the impact of the rise in prisoner numbers on overcrowding, it also suggests increased effectiveness on the part of the criminal justice system. More recently, however, the mass commutation of sentences that was instituted in mid-2005 in order to reduce overcrowding in prisons, and which reduced the number of convicts from 134,000 to nearly 110,000 virtually overnight, has not been followed by continued growth in prisoner numbers. This suggests that the number of convicted prisoners entering South Africa's prisons has fallen, and poses real questions about the effectiveness of South Africa's detectives.

Trends in the number of cases going to court and in the population of convicted prisoners is not an ideal measure of the quality and productivity of a Police Service's detectives, of course. For one thing, many arrests are made by uniformed members in the course of their patrol work, so some proportion of the rise or fall in cases and in the number of convicted prisoners may reflect changes in the quality of proactive work. Another factor is that the number and quality of prosecutors and the availability of sufficient court hours also affects the number of successful prosecutions every year. Nevertheless, the apparent collapse in the number of convicted prisoners entering prison is a great concern in a country with very high levels of violent crime.

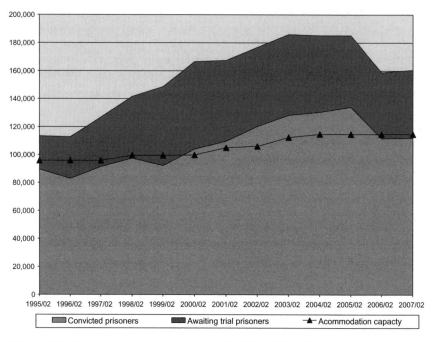

*Figure 12.2*  The prisoner population in South Africa (Feb. 1995 to Feb. 2007).

## Conclusion: explaining the disappointments of police reform

There is little doubt that public perception about policing and police reform in South Africa, while not uniformly negative, does reflect a degree of disappointment in the apparent inability of the Police Service directly to prevent crime or, by arresting a sufficiently large number of offenders, to create sufficient deterrence. These disappointments, it must immediately be added, may do a disservice to the police since the degree to which policing can roll back a crime wave of the nature and size of post-apartheid South Africa's, remains an open question. Nevertheless, given the reputation for ruthless effectiveness that the police under apartheid had, there are many people – in government as well as out – who regard the failure of the police to control crime as both unexpected and disappointing. And, the fact is that police themselves have often struggled to explain this apparent contradiction.

But perhaps the challenge of explaining the gap between the effectiveness of the police in combating resistance to apartheid and combating ordinary criminality is not, after all, entirely insurmountable given the profound differences in the nature of the two problems.

There are any number of differences between the 'revolutionary activity' – as the apartheid police dubbed it – and 'ordinary' criminality, but, from a policing point of view, perhaps the most striking is the degree of organisational structure and coherence that the two kinds of challenge reflect. Although it was never centrally-planned and directed, in the nature of things, popular resistance to apartheid was led by activists and organisations. However careful the individuals might have been to avoid becoming targets of police activity, people playing these kinds of roles would inevitably have some kind of public profile, whether at a national level or just in a local community. This meant that policing could always be directed at identifiable targets. Add to that the permissive legal environment – especially under the States of Emergency, when due process considerations were repudiated – and the policing of this threat becomes reasonably straightforward, at least in comparison to the policing of the unstructured threat posed by swarms of thousands of unconnected criminals.

Law enforcement, which might be characterised as the act of directing the coercive might of the state at those who violate the law, is much easier when those who violate the law must, in the process of doing so, also make themselves known. A structured, organised political threat, in other words, is much easier to police than is an unstructured, unorganised crime wave. The latter challenge is objectively more difficult. And this leads to a second problem: a police organisation which has devoted decades to combating one kind of threat may not be particularly adept at finding the strategies and tactics that are appropriate to new ones. This is partly an issue of the lack of appropriate skills, of course, but it is also a function of the way in which organisations cultivate their leaders: tightly organised hierarchical organisations, like a highly-militarised police force, seldom produce leaders who are innovators. It may be, therefore, that the leadership which the Police Service inherited after apartheid was poorly equipped to deal with the challenges of the new order. In addition, it may be that the Police Service was always bound to struggle with the crime problems of the new South Africa, and that only time, combined with appropriate organisational incentives, will allow more appropriately skilled officers to rise to the top.

## Notes

1   One example will serve to demonstrate this point. At the time of writing (November 2007), the National Director of Public Prosecutions, the country's top prosecutor, is serving a suspension. Although government insists that this is because of a breakdown in relations between him and the minister to whom he answers, it is widely believed that the real reason for his suspension is that he had approved a request for an arrest warrant for the National Commissioner of the Police Service – the country's top cop – who is rumoured to have close links to organised crime (Wines, 2007).
2   Personnel numbers include both police officers and civilians employed in the SAPS. The figures for 1994 are 'soft' because some of the police agencies amalgamated into the SAPS in 1994 (about which I will have more to say below) had relatively large numbers of 'ghost employees' on their books.
3   Running somewhat against the trend of centralising authority over the police has been the establishment of a number of municipal police services. These

institutions, despite having legal authority for 'crime prevention', are almost exclusively devoted to traffic policing. Despite this limited *de facto* mandate, there is a strong view in the highest ranks of the SA Police Service and the ANC that these should now be incorporated into the national Police Service (ANC, 2007).

4   In the WHO's estimates, deaths from violence, the data for which are reflected in this table, are a sub-category of all deaths from injuries but are distinguished from deaths as a result of self-inflicted injuries and those that arise from acts of war. Precisely how, in war-torn countries, one distinguishes between deaths from war and deaths from non-war violence is a question best directed at the authors of the WHO's reports. The figures supplied by the WHO are an outcome of work done estimating the causes of death by disease – infectious and non-infectious – as well as from non-natural causes. In all counties, these figures are estimates based on the best available data. Naturally, the better the national data, the better the WHO estimates. For details on this, see the Explanatory Notes to the statistical annex of WHO (2004: 93–111).

5   It may be pedantic to note that, since South African law defines rape in a way that makes it impossible to define attacks on men and boys as rape, it may be more accurate to report that rape hovered between 220 and 240 attacks per 100,000 women and girls.

## References

African National Congress (ANC) (2007) 'Peace and Stability' in *Commission Reports and Draft Resolutions for the ANC Policy Conference 2007* (ANC: Johannesburg) available at http://www.anc.org.za/show.php?doc=ancdocs/policy/2007/conference/commission.pdf (last accessed 8 Nov 2007).

Altbeker, A. (1998) 'Solving Crime: The state of the SAPS Detective Service' *ISS Monograph 31* (Institute for Security Studies: Pretoria) available at http://www.iss.co.za/
index.php?link_id=3&slink_id=502&link_type=12&slink_type=12&tmpl_id=3.

Altbeker, A. (2005a) *The Dirty Work of Democracy: A year on the streets with the SAPS* (Jonathan Ball: Johannesburg).

Altbeker, A. (2005b) 'Paying for Crime: South Africa's expenditure on criminal justice' *Occasional Paper 115* (Institute for Security Studies: Pretoria).

Altbeker, A. (2007a) *A Country at War with Itself: South Africa's crisis of crime* (Jonathan Ball: Johannesburg).

Altbeker, A. (2007b) 'Community police forums' in O. Edigheji (ed.) *Rethinking South Africa's Development Path: Reflections on the ANC's Policy Conference Discussion Documents* (Centre for Policy Studies: Johannesburg).

Alvazzi del Frate, A. and Van Kesteren, J. (2004) 'The ICVS in the Developing World', *International Journal of Comparative Criminology* 2(1).

Brogden, M. and Shearing, C. (1993) *Policing for a New South Africa* (Routledge: London and New York).

Burton, P., du Plessis, A., Leggett, T., Louw, A., Mistry D. and Van Vuuren, H. (2004) *National Victims of Crime Survey: South Africa 2003* (Institute for Security Studies: Pretoria).

Eloff, L. (2006) 'Transformation of the South African Police Service (SAPS): An insider's view' in Rauch and van der Spuy (op. cit.).

Jensen, S. (2007) 'Through the lens of crime: Land claims and contestations of citizenship on the frontier of the South African state' in L. Buur, S. Jensen and F. Stepputat (eds) *The Security–Development Nexus: Expressions of sovereignty and securitisation in Southern Africa* (HSRC Press: Pretoria).

Leggett, T. (2002) 'Improved crime reporting: Is South Africa's crime wave a statistical illusion?', *SA Crime Quarterly*, No. 1 (Institute for Security Studies: Pretoria).

Ministry for Safety and Security (1994) *Green Paper on Safety and Security: Change* (Ministry for Safety and Security: Pretoria).

Rauch, J. and van der Spuy (2006) *Police Reform in Post-Conflict Africa: A review* (Idasa: Pretoria).

South African Police Service (SAPS) (various) *Annual Report of the South African Police Service* (SAPS: Pretoria) available at www.saps.gov.za.

Steinberg, J. (2004) 'Holding ground means losing ground when it comes to policing' in *Business Day* 23/08/2004 available at http://www.businessday.co.za/Articles/TarkArticle.aspx?ID=1170611.

The Presidency (2006) *A Nation in the Making: A discussion document on macro-social trends in South Africa* (The Presidency: Pretoria).

The Presidency (2007) *Development Indicators: Mid-term review* (The Presidency: Pretoria).

Truth and Reconciliation Commission (TRC) (1998) *Final Report of the Truth and Reconciliation Commission* (TRC: Pretoria).

Wines, M. (2007) 'Party power struggle enthrals South Africa', *New York Times 12/10/2007* available at http://www.nytimes.com/2007/10/12/world/africa/12safrica.html.

World Health Organization (WHO) (2004) *World Health Report 2004: Changing History* (WHO: Geneva).

# 13 Policing Nigeria

## Challenges and reforms

*Kemi Asiwaju and Otwin Marenin*

## Introduction

The Nigeria Police Force (NPF) is the only full service conventional police force in this most populous African country. The NPF is responsible for enforcing laws and maintaining order; investigating, solving and prosecuting crimes and threats to public security; providing protection services for the political leadership; enforcing traffic regulations and road safety; preparing police contingents for international service; and collecting and analyzing intelligence related to crime and national security threats—all this while also being responsive and accountable to the political leadership in power and the independent Police Service Commission for its conduct. Clearly these are large organizational and operational challenges in a country of about 140 million people which is sparsely and unevenly policed, a ratio of about 1 to 446 in 2005 (NPF, 2006: 3).

Nigeria's history since independence in 1960 has been a turbulent one, with existing police forces continually caught in political cross-fires and conflicting social demands. Political instability has been the norm—cycles of military and civilian regimes, coups and countercoups (some quite violent), a series of new constitutions, an increase in the structural components of the federal system inherited by the British colonizers from three regions to now 36 states (in response to group demands for a share of control over the state, the main employer and the distributor of oil wealth to the states by a complicated formula), and an attempted secession and civil war (Biafra) which threatened the very existence and identity of the country.

Despite, or because of, being the seventh largest producer of oil in the world, the Nigerian people live with growing economic inequalities among the ostentatiously rich and the vast numbers of poor who barely survive in the rural areas by subsistence farming and in the sprawling slums which surround the major cities by menial labor and semi-legal activities. The average per capita GDP is about US$675, yet "about 52 percent of the population lives on less than 1 dollar a day" (WorldBank, 2007). Economic development has been stymied as much of the oil wealth has been squandered or stolen by civilian and military regimes. In consequence, Nigeria has gained an international reputation as being one of the most corrupted countries in the world today.

Relations between the state and civic society have been contentious. The Nigerian state and its rulers are seen by much of the public and interest groups as self-serving, prebendal, and unwilling to address the corruption, misconduct and malfeasance of military and civilian members of the ruling regime (Joseph, 1987). The police suffer from their association with the state, but also add to the malign image of the state by their own actions.

Nigeria is an artificial country, divided ethnically among three majority groups (Hausa/Fulani, Yoruba, Igbo) and about 250 so-called 'minorities' (some quite large). Public perceptions of and judgments about politics, economics, social relations, or the distribution of government services and benefits (e.g., admission to higher education, jobs in government, or access to government contracts) are always filtered through the lens of group identifications, most of these ethnic identities but also including regional (especially North–South; in the North further divided into the Far North and the Middle Belt, and in the South into East, Midwest and West), states in the federal system, and communal affiliations and loyalties. Nigerians can always tell you, when asked, where politicians, economic elites or military leaders come from and it is commonly assumed that identification with Nigeria, and citizenship, is weak and less salient than sub-national identities; that who decision-makers are will have a profound impact on how they see and treat other Nigerians.

Political instability, and the failure by government to provide even basic services, build and maintain the needed infrastructures, promote economic growth, and distribute the oil wealth equitably has contributed to a rise in criminal violence and identity based group conflicts. Group violence has been endemic, with the Biafran war which led to the death of about 2 million people during the fighting between the secessionists and the central government forces and by starvation, the most prominent example. Large-scale riots erupt routinely in various parts of the country, which often include attacks on the police and lead to injuries and deaths when the NPF attempts to control and stop civil disturbances. Many riots arise from sectional conflicts of long standing: between Christians and Muslims over real and imagined slights, between soldiers and communities (in situations when a soldier has been injured or killed in some personal confrontation and his fellow soldiers descend en masse on the offending location and run rampant), among students and the police, among villagers fighting over land ownership (Tamuno, 1991) and during election campaigns. Most recently, the country has seen sustained campaigns of violence by insurgent groups against foreign oil companies (and criminal gangs using the instability as cover for extortion and murder) leading to police and military deployment to protect oil company personnel and property in the Niger Delta region. This set of conflicts stems mainly from the massive environmental degradation created by foreign oil companies' policies and the lack of resources flowing back from central and state governments to the area which produces most of Nigeria's wealth (*The New York Times*, April 21, 2007, A1ff).

Though riots are normally discussed in the Nigerian press and among scholarly observers as reflecting specific underlying identities, Paden (2005: 4) argues that it "makes no sense to debate whether such events are political, religious, or socioeconomic in nature. The answer is all of the above." Social identities in Nigeria are more flexible and overlapping than believed in public stereotypes and described by pundits. In Nigeria there have always been political alliances and personal relations and marriages which cross ethnic, religious and regional lines.

The police are enmeshed in these complex societal contexts from which they cannot detach themselves. They have been used routinely by political factions seeking victory in electoral contests before and after independence; they were willing, and sometimes, reluctant accomplices in silencing critics of political regimes; they became tightly enmeshed in the cycles of military coups and civilian regimes which have characterized Nigeria's post independence history; and they are now faced, in addition to group violence, with an exploding violent crime problem and informal vigilante efforts by communities and interests groups (e.g., merchants, market women or community leaders) to provide security, a task that the NPF does not seem to be able to accomplish.

The public image of the NPF is dismal. Few people in Nigeria have a high opinion of the NPF as a whole or of individual officers. In Nigeria, everyone—commentators, academics, reformers, politicians, traditional rulers, economic elites, and the public at large—has an opinion on the NPF and voices it. The media, which is pretty free from government control, reports voluminously on the police, and is not intimidated, despite periods, especially under the military, when severe constraints were imposed on media outlets and individual reporters.

Complaints about the police are widely circulated in traditional media outlets and, now, on the internet.[1] The public litany of what is wrong with the NPF, is lengthy, and centers on corruption, abuse of powers, lack of discipline and integrity, the seeming inability or unwillingness to control crime, and lack of commitment to service. The public generally tries to avoid contact with the police believing that little good will come of it (e.g., Africa Leadership Forum, 1994; Ajomo and Okagbue, 1991; Alemika, 1997, 2005; Alemika and Chukwuma, 2000; Alemika *et al.*, 2006; CLEEN and NHRC, 1999; CLEEN, 2006; Human Rights Watch, 2005; Igbinovia, 1980; Lawyers' Committee for Human Rights, 1992; Muhammad, 1972; Odekunle, 1979; Olurode, 1991; Osoba, 1994; Yakubu, 2000).

What explains this negative perception of the NPF? Can the NPF shed its reputation as a tool of local and national political regimes and become a democratically controlled and accountable police force? While one could point to a range of factors such as deficiencies in police culture, recruitment, training, and leadership and to overwhelmed police capacity, the lack of substantive progress is more deep rooted. We argue that the police, in facing the challenges posed by their societal environments and their own history, are constrained by three basic factors: their colonial origins and past policies which continue to shape the culture and practices of the NPF; the consistent interference in their work by military and political leaders and civic society; and the sheer difficulties of administering a large organization in the absence of much needed resources.

The police are a colonial creation and, despite it being nearly 50 years since Nigeria gained independence on October 1, 1960, and despite numerous crises, reform efforts, minor changes in their legal powers and roles, and occasional progressive leaders, the NPF still struggles with an image derived from its colonial origins as a repressive, brutal, semi-military, politically controlled force which served the interests of the colonial British administration and, after independence, the new political elites.

Closely related to the colonial origin and past practices of the police in Nigeria is the highly hierarchical structure of the Force. This structure encourages seniority and rank over performance, competence and merit. This culture has prevented younger and junior ranking officers from developing fresh ideas that could facilitate innovative reform initiatives in the NPF. Most of the time, the senior officers cynically tell the bright junior officers to 'wait for their turn' in order to implement their bright ideas.

Second, the NPF has been hampered by the consistent interference in their work by the state and political leadership and by civic society groups and members which have never desired a NPF which acts impartially, abides by the rule of law, treats all people it encounters and deals with equitably and fairly, and has the resources to effectively control crime and disorder. The NPF has been surrounded by a societal and political culture which sees control of the state, and the police, as a means to private and group enrichment. In encounters with police, people will routinely appeal to shared identities to mitigate problems. The police, in turn, reflect in their occupational culture, institutional arrangements, and operational practices values and norms which are strongly entrenched within their society and which have consistently complicated and distorted their goals and work.

One persistent influence is the military which often conducts domestic security operations for personal or organizational reasons when a crisis or perceived need arises, without including the police. Such incursions by the military into the domestic security sphere severely compromise the authority and ability of the NPF to do its work, with little the police can do about being turned into hapless bystanders.

Third, managing a large organization with few resources while also lacking essential information about the most basic deployment and performance measures, has been a difficult task which has overwhelmed administrative capacity and ambitions. Implementing needed reforms has been stymied by the inability to control and change work behavior throughout all rank levels, especially street behavior which is encountered by the public.

## Origins and historical developments

Nigeria did not exist as one country until 1914, when the British colonial power consolidated the northern and southern sections of Nigeria into one unified administrative and political whole. The British imposed their own political and policing structures on existing security systems, but in different ways.

### The colonial period

In the northern areas above the Niger and Benue rivers, under a system of indirect rule devised by British administrators, local rulers, whose authority rested on political and religious status, were allowed to maintain existing institutions and practices, as long as these did not conflict with minimal standards of justice and good conscience as defined by the British. Effective administrative systems for tax collection, the organization of large scale slave-based agricultural production, and the enforcement of the rulers' decrees and Islamic law and norms had evolved and become institutionalized in complex status and authority hierarchies centered on the rulers' court (Smith, 1960). Under the imprimatur of British tolerance, existing 'police' were converted into Native Authority (the then name for local government districts) police working at the behest and under the control of traditional rulers and village elders.

In other areas, depending on the level of institutionalization of government, police were attached to local political structures (as Native Authority forces, mostly in the western region of the south). In 'stateless' societies and village communities typical of the South-Eastern region of Nigeria, artificial authority structures—warrant chiefs—were appointed to act as representatives of the colonial power and were given some policing and order maintenance and law enforcement authority.

The first colonial police force was the Hausa Police[2] established in 1861 in the commercial center, Lagos, to protect the property and the lives of merchants and colonial administrators against local protests and crime. Other, essentially private, police forces were created to protect trading routes and depots which had developed in the interior, missionaries attempting to convert local people to their form of Christianity, and adventurers seeking to unveil the mysteries of the 'dark continent'. As the colonial administrative system matured, police under the control of local District Officers were used to extend the reach of the colonial power through pacification campaigns, when local communities protested against British encroachment, the enforcement of tax collection, and the promotion of moral and physical hygiene appropriate to more 'civilized' British standards (Ahire, 1991; Alemika, 1993; Marenin, 1985; Rotimi, 2001; Tamuno, 1970; Tamuno *et al.*, 1993).

*The pre-independence period*

The run-up to independence during the 1950s engendered mass protests by local people, agitations by the educated elites demanding the return of sovereign power to themselves and their followers, and much social turbulence and conflict as the British moved towards establishing a Westminster model of government prior to independence. The intensity of party competition and thuggery which accompanied much campaigning can be judged from the list of 'Eight Don'ts' issued by the Inspector General of the NPF, Louis Edet, during the 1964 electoral campaigns, which included these admonitions:

> don't set fire to the motor vehicle of your political opponents; don't overindulge yourself in alcohol . . . or Indian hemp for the purposes of whipping up 'Dutch courage' to tackle your thuggery duties efficiently; [and] don't arm yourself with broken bottles, matchets, sticks and so on when accompanying your political leaders.[3]
>
> (cited in Diamond, 1988: 209, 338; also see Okoigun, 2000)

The image of the police and relations with civic society continued to be shaped by their political subservience to political masters, now central and local elites instead of colonial administrators.

*Post colonial developments*

The police were one of the last vestiges of colonial rule to be indigenized. Many British remained in high-level positions within the force and the first Nigerian Inspector General of the NPF, Louis Edet, was not appointed until 1964. Efforts by the central government, first under civilian and later military rule to consolidate political control, and control over the police, led to the establishment of the 'Gobir' Commission (Nigeria, 1967) which recommended that the Native Authority Police forces be abolished and those qualified by minimal levels of education, literacy and propriety be absorbed into the NPF. This was accomplished during 1969/1971, leaving the NPF as the only legitimate and legal police force in the country.

## Institutional arrangements and powers of the NPF

Since that time, the NPF has experienced a steady growth leading, with a sudden spurt, to its current strength of about 370,000 members following a recruitment drive ordered by President Obasanjo in 2000 (Alemika and Agugua, 2001: 34). There had been a hiring freeze during the previous five years, leaving the personnel strength of the NPF severely depleted. Under both civilian and military rule and within the basic norms of different constitutions, the police are governed by the Police Law written by the British in 1943. The NPF has retained the organizational structures, ranks and entry levels inherited from the British. A variety of external, differently-named police commissions were charged by successive civilian and military regimes with establishing basic regulations on recruitment, training, discipline, accountability and salaries.

Nigeria is a federal system. The NPF is administered from the center, under the leadership of the Inspector General appointed by the president or ruling military council, yet significant operational control remains at the level of states and is heavily influenced by state governors. Formally, Section 6 of the 1943 Police Act provides that the Force shall be under the command of the Inspector General, and that contingents of the Force stationed in a state shall be subject to the authority of the Inspector General but also be under the operational command of the police commissioner of that state. The issue of overlapping authority and operational command of the police in a federal system has been of long standing (Ohonbamu, 1972), and centers on how to resolve the potential conflict between the center (the NPF and the President) and the states (whose governors are elected and may belong to a different party than the ruling party at the center) over who has the authority to command the local police and tell them what to do, such as what party will get permission for an assembly during election campaigns or which public figure will be investigated for corruption. The balance of political control between the center and the states is negotiated and negotiable, with control of the police a major object of desire. In a political process which is seen as a zero-sum game, the police have remained a powerful resource, tool and protector of particularistic interests, at the expense of service to civic society as whole. Success in politics matters greatly. Winners gain everything and the losers are out, in exile or in prison. Control of the police helps ensure that you end up on the winning side, and that the police will not be used against you once, as they always arise, accusations of abuse and corruption are leveled against those in power.

At various times during military periods, other police forces which are directly responsible for state security have been established, and abandoned. As some states in northern Nigeria adopted *sharia* law in the 1990s, 'morality' police to enforce Islamic norms of public behavior by men and women were created, but these have no legal standing under the hegemonic centralized legal and control system. Nonetheless, conflicts over jurisdiction do occur and have to be dealt with by the NPF, the central government and state governors.

### Current structure and powers of the Nigeria Police Force

The Nigeria Police Force is charged with various police duties and extra police functions. Section 4 of the Police Act highlights the (conventional) functions of the Nigeria Police Force: prevention and detection of crime; apprehension of offenders; preservation of law and order; protection of life and property; enforcement of all laws and regulations with which they are charged; and such military duties within or without Nigeria as may be required of them. They are also responsible for marine and joint border patrol and liaison with the Independent National Electoral commission sections.

In order to discharge their numerous functions, the police in Nigeria are accorded wide powers. These include the usual powers of arrest, crime prevention and investigation, but also the authority to conduct prosecutions; to serve summons; to release on bail persons arrested without warrant and to grant bail to suspects pending investigation or arraignment in court; to regulate processions and assemblies; as well as other administrative and regulatory functions, such as issuing international driving permits or registering firearms.

The NPF, in 2005, had an establishment of 417,608 and actual strength of 309,049 personnel across its 22 ranks, the main shortfall being at the corporal and constable ranks (NPF, 2006: 4). Personnel are deployed across the 36 states of the Federal Republic, the Federal Capital Territory (Abuja), and Railroad, Airport and PAP (Ports Authority Police) contingents. The Force HQ is located in Abuja. State commands are headed by a commissioner. States are grouped, for administrative purposes, into 12 zones; additionally, deployment is divided into 123 area commands, 1,202 divisions, 1,03 police stations, and 2,797 Police Posts (NPF, 2006: 36–37). Its budget for 2005 was 84.4 billion Naira—about 670 million US dollars (NPF, 2006: 26).

Functionally, the NPF is organized into six Departments: General Administration (A), Operation (B), Logistics and Supply (C), Criminal Investigations (D), Training (E), and Planning and Policy (F). (For further details see the NPF website at www.nigeriapolice.org.)

The crime control workload in 2005 was 180,295 reported offenses: 71,796 against persons, 95,736 against property (armed robbery is included under property crimes), 9,691 against lawful authority (e.g., breach of peace, bribery and corruption, gambling, counterfeiting), and 3,072 against local acts (e.g., firearms, traffic, liquor or narcotics offences). Offenses against persons included 2,074 classified as murder, a decrease of 476 from 2004. Arrests totaled 215,882 persons, of which 156,059 were prosecuted and 45,636 were convicted in 2005 (NPF, 2006: 191).

These are remarkably small (and one suspects basically inaccurate)[4] reported crime numbers for a country of about 140 million people; indeed Nigeria's 2005 recorded homicide rate per 100,000 inhabitants (1.6), by police statistics make the country safer than Canada (2.05) (see Table 1.4 in the Introduction to this volume). The numbers attest that members of the public, even when victimized, are reluctant to report crimes to the police. They are afraid that they will be accused of having committed the reported crime, that they will be asked for a bribe, and they believe that not much will happen to solve the crime in any case. The arrest and conviction figures leave little doubt that the NPF is not efficient and effective in crime control.

Officially, the comparative crime rate for Nigeria is low and rising slowly, but most people will tell you that certain kinds of personal and property crime (e.g., armed robbery, organized theft) are on a fast and steady rise. The most fear-creating crime for the middle/upper class is carjacking, a common form of armed robbery, along major roads between and within cities; as well as police roadblocks where, according to public beliefs, people who refuse to pay the bribe are routinely killed by the police (even though there are few hard data or accurate accounts of such killings).

The NPF Annual Report (2006) blames failures in crime control on resource constraints, lack of equipment and inadequate salaries. The report adds that "the dynamics of pluralistic nationalities and technological advancements pose serious challenges to policing," specifically, that "traditional courses with near obsolete syllabuses need an urgent review in line with the realities of modern policing," that "there is need for adequate logistical and infrastructural equipment of the Force in line with the Police of civilized countries of the world," and "since the best of equipment and gadgets cannot operate themselves, the welfare of the Police should be revisited in terms of provision of decent barracks accommodation, comfortable remuneration, constant kitting and provision of welfare schemes to enhance the future of the personnel" (p. 236). Nonetheless, the report concludes, somewhat weakly, "it is not unsafe to conclude that apart from professional lapses and incapacitations, Police has always achieved remarkable results" (NPF, 2006: 21).

President Obasanjo directed the Minister of Police Affairs in January 2006 to establish a Presidential Committee on Police Reforms (the Madami Commission) to examine how the NPF could be reformed (*Police News*, 2006, 1, 4: 24). The committee was to review the organization, administration, operations, recruitment, training, remuneration, and control of the NPF and suggest ways to improve police efficiency and service delivery, enhance public confidence, reduce corruption, raise police morale and assess the potential for community policing.

The Committee reported its findings and recommendations in early 2007. These included an increase in police resources; appropriate printing and distribution of vital books and working manuals to all commands and training institutions; a new, flatter rank structure and improvement in conditions of service (pay, housing, office space, equipment) by means of internal reforms and greater financial support from the legislature and the creation of a privately supported Police Trust Fund. Indeed the police had long complained of having to buy their own uniform and private phones and phone cards in order to communicate. But the Committee refused to address the long-standing issue whether control of the police should be shared between the central governments and the states (Agbaegbu, 2007: 26). The central government is clearly unwilling to give up control of the police.

### Oversight of the Nigeria Police Force

The third schedule of the 1999 Constitution created two organs for the governance of the NPF: the Police Council and the Police Service Commission.

## The Nigeria Police Council

The Police Council is the central policy and supervisory unit for the NPF, and consists of the President as Chairman, the Governors of the States, the Chair of the Police Service Commission, and the Inspector General of Police. The remit of the Police Council covers all aspects of the organization and administration of the NPF (except matters relating to the use and operational control of the Force or the appointment, disciplinary control and dismissal of members of the force); the general supervision of the Nigeria Police Force; and advice to the President on the appointment of the Inspector General of Police.

## The Police Service Commission

The Police Service Commission was inaugurated on November 28, 2001 as an external institutional mechanism for holding the NPF leadership accountable to both members of the public and its own personnel (Police Service Commission, 2006). Prior to its establishment, citizens who were aggrieved by an act of police misconduct and had neither money nor time to engage the judicial process were left with no other alternative than to go back to the police (Chukwuma, 2001). This approach was found wanting because of widespread citizens' dissatisfaction with the internal disciplinary procedures of the police force and departments (Police Service Commission, 2006; Chukwuma, 1994) and the decrepit workings of Nigerian courts. The degree of dissatisfaction with internal disciplinary procedures extends to rank-and-file personnel who question the fairness of the internal processes through which they are sanctioned, demoted or dismissed from service (Police Service Commission, 2006). Without an independent body to lodge complaints, there was little recourse for police officers who felt that they were unjustly disciplined.

The membership of the Police Service Commission includes the Chair and eight other members representing the judiciary, retired police officers, women's interest groups, media, non governmental human rights organizations and the organized private sector. All the members of the Commission are appointed by the President, who has to ensure that membership reflects the 'federal character' of Nigeria, and must be confirmed by the Senate. There is security of tenure for members who can only be removed for good cause, for financial and criminal malfeasance, incapacitation, or serious misconduct in relation to duties.

The Commission has the responsibility of appointing and promoting all officials of the NPF (other than the Inspector General of Police); dismissing and exercising disciplinary control over the same persons; formulating policies and guidelines for the appointment, promotion, discipline and dismissal of officers of the NPF; formulating and implementing policies aimed at efficiency and discipline within the NPF; "performing such other functions as, in the opinion of the Commission, are required to ensure optimal efficiency in the NPF; and carrying out such other functions as the President may, from time to time, direct." In short, the formal powers of the Commission are substantial and if effectively exercised could significantly improve police accountability in Nigeria. In a conversation by one of the authors with members of the Commission (Abuja, January 2007), when asked whether and how many of the functions assigned to the Commission were being implemented, members of the Commission agreed that, being new, much work still had to be organized and accomplished.

The Police Service Commission in Nigeria has been involved in activities since its inception to ensure that these contribute to the police reform process in the country. In 2003, the Commission in collaboration with international organizations and local civil society groups, such as the Centre for Law Enforcement Education (now CLEEN Foundation, a leading and well-respected human rights and police reform NGO), developed guidelines for monitors sent by the Commission to the different States and the Federal Capital Territory to observe the activities of the police deployed for electoral duty. The guidelines were disseminated through the Police Area Commands/ State Commands structure. A checklist was also developed and reproduced for the electoral monitors to take into the field and use during the monitoring exercise. The report of the exercise was printed in National Newspapers and it was also produced in book form to ensure that members of the public have access to it (Police Service Commission, 2006).

Yet the run-up to and conduct of the state and federal elections (in April 2007), which resulted in an overwhelming victory by the ruling party, were beset by extensive violence, corruption, intimidation of voters, ballot stuffing and outright fraud (charges well documented by local and international observers), allegations which question the accuracy and legitimacy of the conduct and outcomes of the elections, undermine the public's trust that small steps toward democracy can be achieved within the current political climate, raise fears that the military will step in (again), but also placed the NPF in a tight and delicate situation. No matter what they did or did not do, they are being criticized by one side or the other, and their credibility is undermined.

### Legislative oversight

In a presidentialist system such as Nigeria's, where power is tilted towards the executive, legislative oversight tends to concentrate on revisions to the legal framework governing the police. An interagency committee was set up by the House Committee on Police Affairs in November 2004 to review the 1943 Police Act. Inputs into the proposed bill were made by stakeholders across the country through an extensive consultative process. The new Police Bill was submitted to the House Committee and has gone through its second reading. A new policing philosophy based on democratic principles—efficiency and effectiveness; political accountability; and protection of human rights and fundamental freedoms—is being introduced with the Bill. The specific objectives are to establish a Police Service that is seen as a friend rather than an enemy of the people; that embodies in its operations the values of fairness, justice and equity; makes the police responsive to the citizens and the needs of the community; respects the dignity of citizens; and efficiently and effectively prevents crimes without unduly threatening the values of liberty and privacy. The details of the final legislation are not yet available (as of May 2008).

## Reforms and implementation strategies

There have been numerous attempts to reform the NPF. These have been encouraged and implemented both by the government and non-governmental organizations that are involved in the justice sector from both the supply (police) and the demand (civic society) side of justice sector reform. The most salient attempted reforms have been these.

### *The community policing strategy*

In 2004, the NPF adopted community policing as its dominant strategy and ideology, a position urged by international donors and civic society groups.

The CLEEN Foundation (Alemika and Chukwuma, 2000), based on extensive research, had recommended the creation of periodic police–community interactions. To convert rhetoric into practice, the CLEEN Foundation helped the NPF establish Community Policing Partnership Forums in 14 local governments spread across the six geopolitical zones in the country. As a result of the challenges and the lessons learnt from the initial phase of the community policing project, model community policing partnership fora were implemented in two local government areas of Lagos State. The idea was to provide routinized opportunities for interactions between the police and the community to ensure that issues that could lead to breakdown of law and order, and possibly violence, be identified and resolved at an early stage. Yet, so far, apart from the pilot projects, no fora for direct community interaction with the police as modeled by CLEEN have been created elsewhere.

A second reform program, funded through the foreign aid office of the British government (DFID), sent a project team of seven senior Nigerian police to the UK to undertake an intensive study of how community policing was conducted there. The team produced a Project Plan on the content and implementation steps of a community policing model suited for Nigeria. The model stressed these key principles: "active partnership between the police and community," providing high quality service as the main role and goal of the police, the development of "appropriate skills, attitudes and behaviours of police personnel" to achieve high quality service, a proactive problem solving approach to work, and police–community consultation on policing priorities (British Council, 2007: 1).

Operationally, reforms have focused on changing the existing occupational culture, through seeding prepared community policing developers (CPDs) as trained trainers into local contingents and through reforms of the method-ologies of teaching and the content of curricula, supported by improvements in the data collecting, processing and analytical capacities of the force at all levels. The Community Police reforms being started by the British Council rightly focus on police culture as the crucial element in sustainable reforms, an indirect indication that the people in charge of the program are fully aware that the current police culture is not conducive to either community service or the adoption of democratic policing values. They describe the current culture as reinforced by "military conditioning, hierarchical rigidity, lack of empowerment and 'siege syndrome' defensiveness," leading to an absence of meaningful communication from the bottom up and top down "management by intimidation" NPF (British Council, 2007: 3, 6).

By the beginning of 2007, about 1,000 CPDs had been trained and deployed; over 600 officers had attended short courses on human rights, vigilante support (see below) and community safety; about 400 area and divisional commanders had participated in management and leadership development seminars; and about 40,000 police had attended one day sensi-tization workshops (British Council, 2007: 5). The numbers of officers par-ticipating given in the NPF Annual Report for 2005 (NPF, 2006: 184) are slightly lower. Surveys conducted by CPDs in consultation with a research forum, as well as face-to-face meetings with members of the public, have established a baseline of public opinion. In the original meetings with public groups, the police were most frequently described as "brutal, corrupt and ineffective," yet the project leaders also think that "the very fact of having their opinions honestly sought has started the process of repairing negative perceptions" (British Council, 2007: 5).

Preliminary evaluations of progress so far point to the beginnings of change in the thinking and operations of the police who have been through the training and experience of community policing: latent abilities and potential have been liberated and begun to empower lower-level rank officers, reform the organizational culture, reduce corruption and abuses of power, and enhance respect and support from the community (British Council, 2007: 10–11). A survey in a pilot project in Enugu State found a decrease in the fear of crime, a "lowering in the citizens' personal experience of police corrup-tion," an increase in police visibility on patrol, and improvements in police performance (NPF, 2006: 185) which seems to be associated with community policing efforts.

Similar steps towards greater transparency were registered in 2006 during the Police Station Visitors' Week 2006 carried out by the Altus Global Alliance through its member organizations all over the world; 163 visitors including school children visited 34 stations in five states in Nigeria. They assessed the conditions of police stations, the fundamental connecting link between the police and the public. Overall assessments of Nigerian stations visited ranged from 34/100 (totally inadequate) to 74/100 (more than adequate), with an average score of 50/100 (inadequate). The lowest score was 'inadequate' for equal treatment and 'adequate' for community orientation (Altus, 2006: 18). Good practices noted by the visitors included community Policing Forums run at some stations, human rights desks located in stations, and suggestion and complaints boxes available to the public (pp.18–20). Though one can question the precision and validity of the evaluations, or how much the police were prepared for visits (since these had to be approved from HQ), and how formalized receptions of visitor teams were (pictures included in the report depict organized meetings), nonetheless the evaluations done by members of the public are useful and valuable to the police and to reformers. In the end, the judges of the quality of policing are members of the public, and untrained though they are, they can use their common sense to observe what is going on. The permission given to conduct visits does indicate some movement toward transparency for the NPF.

Despite the enthusiasm with which domestic reformers and international assistance programs have greeted community policing programs, some observers (e.g., Brogden and Nijhar, 2005) have expressed serious reservations as to whether a complicated policing model such as community policing, which expands the roles and domain of police work into new tasks and previous private spheres of life, can or even should be implemented in conditions of insecurity, less than democratic governance, constrained legal system and strained police–community relations typical of developing or transitional countries. A much simpler, local needs-based model (Horn, 2004) might be more appropriate as the starting point for reform. Yet in all reforms, especially if the starting point is extremely low, one can find initial signs of improvement in whatever elements of police work and management are measured. The question remains whether reforms can be sustained once pilot projects, with the attention and resources and publicity they receive, are completed—whether new practices and attitudes can be routinized, can become part of the normal work habits of the police. The evidence on that is less clear.

### *Mainstreaming gender in the Nigeria Police Force*

Gender mainstreaming is a strategy that has been accepted globally for promoting gender equality as central to all activities—policy development, research, advocacy/dialogue, legislation, resource allocation and planning, implementation and monitoring of programs and projects.

A study carried out by the CLEEN Foundation (Alemika and Agugua, 2001) found that police officers are aware of discrimination in the Nigeria Police Force and that women are grossly under-represented in the police. In 1993, 4,578 out of 137,734 personnel were women (3.37 percent) who worked mostly in rank-and-file, at inspector and lower ranks (4,053); the highest ranked female police officers then were two Assistant IGS (Alemika and Agugua, 2001: 34–35). By 2005, the numbers and ratios had improved somewhat. Of the 309,049 actual strength in 2005 (NPF Annual Report, 2006: 4) about 50,000 are women. (The NPF 2006 Annual Report does not give the number of female officers; the 50,000 number was mentioned a number of times in talks with the NPF leadership, Abuja, January 2007.) If correct, the percentage of women in the force has grown to 16 percent, largely as result of the recruitment drive initiated by the Obasanjo regime in 2000. Civil society has also pressed for increased gender representation in the NPF.

Increasing gender representation in the NPF has been urged by civic society groups and the police leadership. In 2005/2006 CLEEN worked in collaboration with the Police Service Commission and the Open Society Justice Initiative (OSJI) to develop equitable human resource guidelines. The Commission advocated the "enlistment of more women into the Nigeria Police Force by ensuring that a minimum of 10 percent of the police workforce is comprised of women." IG Ehindero, in 2005, directed that in all "appointments and postings, there must be at least 20 percent women representation. This is just a minimum requirement" (Agbaegbu, 2007: 27; Police Service Commission, 2006: 33).

A major reason, however, for the continuing lack of female officers are the current Police Regulations in force. Though there are no significant distinctions in recruitment criteria, the only roles female police can be assigned to are "duties which are concerned with women and children" (e.g., investigations of sexual offenses against women and children, attendance while women are interviewed by male police officers, school crossing duties or the searching and escorting of women prisoners), and women may be permitted, in "order to relieve male officers from duties," to assume clerical, telephone and officer orderly duties (Section 121, 122, cited in Alemika and Agugua, 2001: 41). Other differences compared to male officers are that women officers need permission to marry, they are discharged for becoming pregnant, are not eligible for employment if they are married, and do not have the right to bear arms on duty. Alemika and Agugua (2001: 73–75) suggest that discrimination against women in the NPF reflects larger patterns and norms in Nigerian society—entrenched patriarchy, sexism, stereotyping of gender roles— and will not be expunged easily. They suggest changes in the Police Regulations which currently limit the work and promotion opportunities of women in the force, positive recruitment actions to increase gender numbers, and changes in academy curricula and police facilities to accommodate women officers.

The legislature reviewing the existing police law will examine the roles of female officers in the NPF and will seek to remove discriminatory sections related to gender. As well, a continued strong commitment by civic society groups will be needed to sustain whatever changes in law and regulations will be adopted.

# Continuing challenges

## *Personnel issues*

Recruitment into the NPF is bifurcated. There are minimum height requirements for men and women (1.68/1.63 meters). Candidates for direct entry or
promotion from within the force to the officer corps (ASP and higher) must
be physically, medically and mentally fit, be of good character and possess a
Bachelor's Degree from a recognized university or other institution of higher
learning in "any discipline that is relevant to police duties" (NPF, 2006: 173).
Entry at the rank-and-file level (constable) requires the same physical and
mental fitness traits but only a formal secondary education.

The stress on formal diplomas and certificates, accurately called the
'diploma disease', as minimal requirements for entry into government service
bedevils every recruitment effort, and prevents individuals, no matter
how suited they could be for police work (and that is not tested) from even
applying to the NPF since they lack the required formal qualifications and
certificates. Formal schooling is class based and reinforces class distinctions
and a sense of entitlement and superiority, sentiments which then are
reflected within the organization of the NPF. Police officers also complain
that promotions are not based on merit but on social connections and
patronage.

## *Training*

Recruitment and training are centrally controlled, and deployment to states is
done on the basis of needs without regard for individual identities. There exist
no studies on the content and impacts of training, but is seems that training
of lower ranks focuses on physical drills and basic skills, with little follow-up
through on-the-job training or specialized workshops. The introduction
of Community Policing, though, has led to more emphasis on re-training and
changes in content.

Training for managers seems to be more knowledge based, and some
higher level officers will be offered the opportunity to attend command col-
leges in other countries.

## *Deployment*

The police in their routine work tend to protect the powerful. Most patrol
officers are deployed to protect the persons and property of the well-off (who
also use their own resources to buy private protection or fortify their homes),
while the poor are left to fend for themselves by creating and supporting their
own informal control mechanisms (Alemika and Chukwuma, 2004). It is
almost a tradition that once a citizen becomes a public figure, her/his first
official correspondence on assuming duty is to write to the Inspector General

of Police to ask for an orderly and policemen to guard her/his house. To most political figures the police are a status symbol, yet the welfare of the police is deplorable and such demands, which are typically agreed to, detract from the effective utilization of police for their real jobs.

In addition, police are assigned to work that has no real connection to their formal functions. It is not uncommon to see the wives of police officials being escorted by police officers as they go shopping and to see the police carry the loads to the car. There may be a security justification for this practice (and that says something about the fear of crime which now hovers over the social landscape), but the impact on public perceptions and the officers themselves is that they are treated like servants by the higher-ups. One can argue that there is little organizational identity shared between rank-and-file and officers, which creates problems for supervision, internal accountability, commitment to police work and performance.

The diversion of police resources to serve the powerful and well-off is massive, though hard to document. A report by the British Council (2007: 6) found a "lack of meaningful performance indicators in the police organization." In effect, police managers are flying blind; planning and policy development have little empirical basis; and evaluation of how well officers or the organization perform is impossible in any systematic way. When one adds the informal corrupt activities by the police to deal with their under-resourced status, low salaries and living standards, and poor training, one could argue that very little of what would be considered conventional police work actually gets done.

### Corruption

The real extent of corruption and abuse of force in the NPF, as in any other police force, is unknown. Most Nigerians and outside observers believe that corruption is extensive, from top to bottom in the NPF, as it is thought to be in all sectors of Nigerian society. Corruption across ranks differs only in opportunities and scale.

At the street level, a tactic of long standing that has probably contributed more to the image of the NPF as a corrupt force, are roadblocks which can be found along all major highways connecting cities and within cities, and are rightly seen by the public and the media as 'tax collection' enterprises which serve no other purposes. Most susceptible to the demands by the NPF for bribes (currently the 20 Naira note, leading to the nickname for police as '20 Naira men') are people who make a living driving the road (taxis, trucks, buses) and cannot earn the small incomes they do unless they can travel freely. They are stuck. One can always tell when there is a problem collecting the 'tax' as passengers are unloading their luggage and standing around while the police check, slowly, all belongings and the vehicle particulars. The police have time on their side but passengers and drivers do not. The problem is pervasive. Two recent surveys conducted in 2005 in 18 states found that

"54% and 50% (respectively) of all Nigerians had been asked to pay N20 'dash' in the previous 6 months" (British Council, 2007: 8). Sixty-five percent of respondents in another survey stated that they had been solicited by the police for a bribe (Alemika, *et al.*, 2006: 21), a substantial percentage of which must have occurred at roadblocks.

The police are quite resourceful in finding a violation which will require a fine, to be paid on the spot to the police. In the 1980s, every car was required to carry a fire extinguisher, which was not a normal item in most cars, but gave the police a pretext for a fine. A recent issue of the *Police News* (2006, 1, 4: 46), includes the question "what particulars [documents] need to be presented if asked at a roadblock." The answer lists the necessary documents and adds that "you are not required to carry vehicle purchase documents, or proof of ownership." Clearly, the police have been asking for those. A later answer suggests that "if you are eventually made to part with a bribe, note the time, location, any other information you can safely memorize and file a complaint with the local head of the NPF." The phrase "safely memorize" means don't ask the police at the roadblock for their names or other identifying information and get yourself in even more trouble. The NPF leadership knows what is normal police behavior at roadblocks. IG Ehindero, shortly after taking office in 2006, noted that "of course you know what they do at those checkpoints; we are more than ever prepared to bring sanity to that sector of this country" (cited in Onyeozili, 2005: 43); he ordered that all road blocks be removed, unless there was a real security reason for establishing one on a temporary basis, such as a report of a fleeing bank robber, and that officers caught setting up a roadblock would be arrested and dismissed. But it remains to be seen how successfully that order will be implemented.

Another common abuse and public irritant is detention at police stations. The current regulations state that 'bail is free' (and signs stating so are posted in the stations), but asking for bail requires a 'fee'. Not being let go, or not being able to pay to get the free bail, means staying in filthy police cells, a fate which hits the poor the hardest.

Mobile police officers, who are frequently deployed to deal with disorder, riots and personnel shortfalls may, unless supported by the area commands to which they are ordered for work, in IG Ehindero's words "be exposed to the temptations of poverty" and "in order to survive indulge in all forms of corrupt practices" (*Police News*, 2006, 1, 4: 3). Being armed and feared, members of this elite force can easily succumb to their temptations. Their behaviour, in many cases, has cast doubt on "matters relating to honesty, effectiveness and reliability. This is supported by the abundant evidence of their involvement in criminal activities as reflected in the spate of extra judicial killings, armed robberies and like offenses that are traceable to them" (*Police News*, 2006, 1, 4: 19; these are remarks made by the Deputy IG in charge of the Mobile Force).

At the top, as the dismissal of IG Tafa Balogun in 2006 indicates, corruption is lucrative and largely undetected or seriously sanctioned. Tafa Balogun was removed from office, tried and sentenced for diverting police funds into accounts in Nigeria, Switzerland, and London, of which about 1.9 billion Naira (about 24 million US dollars) were recovered, and for receiving payoffs from politicians and criminal gangs "to alter justice in favor of the highest bidder" (Onyeozili, 2005: 42–43). In a surprising twist, his successor, IG Sunday Ehindero, who was generally considered an honest cop, was accused of stealing money from the police budget, an allegation he denies. It is not yet clear exactly how and why these allegations came to light right after his replacement by the new IG.

The perception by the public and observers that impunity for misconduct is the norm, is supported by data on disciplinary actions taken during 2005, at a time when the force numbered about 300,000 personnel and corruption was endemic. A total of 1,116 officers in all ranks were disciplined, 721 by dismissal and 309 by compulsory retirement. The rest were reprimanded in various forms, but none were turned over for any kind of criminal prosecution (Police Service Commission, 2006: 29).

In sum, the managers of the NPF, as much as is the public, the media and reform NGOs, are well aware of the corrupt practices of their officers but seem to be unable to do much about it except exhort their troops not to give in to temptations. Nor is corruption a one-way street. Bribes are offered to the police by the public, almost routinely. One of the strategies IG Ehindero endorsed is that the public should not arrive at roadblocks with a 20 Naira note already in hand, ready to pay the 'tax'. Make the police ask for it (Talk, Abuja, January 2007).

### Rules on deadly force

The most significant power of the police is their authority to use force, including the legal right to kill. The Police Regulations allow the use of deadly force in cases of self-defense or in defense of the lives of others, but also to disperse rioters or prevent them from committing a serious offense against life or property, to stop a person in lawful custody from escaping, and to prevent, if other means fail, a person to be arrested from taking flight but only "if the accused may be punished with death or imprisonment of 7 (seven) years or more" (*Police News*, 2006, 1, 4: 46). In the words of the United Nations Special Rappoteur on extrajudicial, summary and arbitrary executions, "these rules practically provide the police carte blanche to shoot and kill at will" (in CLEEN, 2006: 157). CLEEN (2006: 160) cites an interview given by a representative of the Legal Defense and Assistance Project (a human rights NGO) to a local newspaper which stated that the NGO recorded 997 extrajudicial killings in 2003 and 2,987 cases in 2004.[5] Official disaggregated statistics on deadly force, or lesser levels of force, and systematic investigation of the circumstances in which it is employed do not exist, however. But one can assume, with some confidence, that the use of force is extensive, discretionary and largely unrestrained by norms of professional ethics or sanctioned by code of conduct violations. Indeed, since forensic, investigative and interrogation skills are minimal, the police depend heavily on extracting confessions, often by torture and abuse.

## Police community relations and vigilantes

Relations between the police and civic society have been antagonistic. The public believes that the police are abusive, brutal, corrupt, lazy and unskilled, while the police think that civic society has little faith and trust in them and gives them little support. One consequence of distrust in and dislike of the NPF has been the emergence of 'vigilante' groups in all parts of the country. A CLEEN (Alemika and Chukwuma, 2004) survey found that 49 percent of respondents had such a group in their locality.

A later survey in January 2007 by the British Council (2007) in six states found response rates ranging from 38 percent in Kano to 82 percent in Benue that vigilante groups existed in the respondents' neighborhoods. The average participation by residents in vigilante activities in the six states was 4 percent ("are you or anyone in your family or household a member of a vigilante group") ranging from 1 percent to 14 percent across the six states. In rural areas, residents tended to band together to form vigilante groups. In urban areas, especially in the South, residents paid voluntary fees to support vigilantes. In no area covered by the surveys did vigilantes extort money from fellow residents. The most common activities engaged in by vigilantes were group night patrol, market security, arrest of armed robbers and of cheats (and the frequent administration of physical punishment to offenders on the spot), and dispute settlement. The types of tasks performed varies by location. Satisfaction with the work of vigilantes was quite high (in the 70 percent–80 percent satisfied range) and much higher than for the NPF, the main reasons being that residents could contact a vigilante group quite easily and quickly and perceived them to be less corrupt and closer to the people than the NPF. Nonetheless, respondents preferred to report crimes to the police because the police have the legal power to deal with crime and criminals. Police and vigilantes do work together (e.g., joint patrols, handing over of criminals to the police) in some locations but not others, based on local histories, personalities and perceived power differences among the police, vigilantes and residents.

Self-help groups, and vigilantes, have a long history in Nigeria and are based on traditional forms of social control. In rural areas, which have always been under-policed, villagers have relied on elders and informal means to deal with crime and violations of norms. Even if the police came, it would take them a long time. In urban areas, and Nigeria has some of the highest rates of urbanization and the most concentrated and dismal slums among Third World countries, government services (water, electricity, garbage removal, security) have been minimal. As settlers moved into the fringes of core cities they had to depend on themselves and developed self-help organizations, generally along ethnic lines, to provide even minimal levels of security and survival (e.g., Baker, P., 1975; Ebbe, 1989).

Most vigilantes are legitimate descendants of self-help activities which fill in for the absence of the state (Baker, B., 2007). Their positive image noted in the surveys cited attests to that, as does the recognition by the NPF and international advisors, that community policing reforms have to work with informal control mechanisms if they are to succeed. The British Council funded reformers concluded that "vigilantes everywhere are regarded as highly effective local organizations delivering a needed service locally," that "much can be learned by the police as to local service delivery from the vigilant phenomena," (e.g., accessibility, non-corruption, closeness to the public) and that "the vigilantes are too wide-spread and important a phenomena in the lives of a majority of people in Nigeria to be disregarded in the design of any new security or local government level programmes" (del Buono and Davis, personal communication, March 2007).

Although vigilantes have a basically positive image in Nigeria, they do represent a human rights challenge given that lynch mobs are known to chase, beat or kill suspected thieves and small-scale criminals. Some organized vigilante groups (such as the Bakassa Boys in Eastern Nigeria), initially created by civic groups for protection or ethnic exclusion, moreover, have turned into criminal gangs living by extortion and violence, a pattern found in other countries as well. Until the state's inability (or unwillingness) to provide adequate policing coverage is addressed, vigilantism is likely to continue, thus further challenging the rule of law.

## Concluding comments

Efforts to reform the police, to face up to challenges, to set in motion processes which over time can lead to genuine reforms continue sporadically. The rhetoric is there. Writings by past high-level police officials (e.g., Atta, 1997; Inyang, 1989; Jemibewon, 2002; Musa 1998; Olewe and Anga, 1994; Oseni, 1993) are replete with the correct aspirational rhetoric, critiques of the current goals, practices and cultures of the force, and exhortations to do better. IG Ehindero, when appointed in 2006, was well aware of the "image crisis of the Force" (Agbaegbu, 2007; Ehindero, 2006b; Ehindero and Alemika, 2005). He proposed a new motto for the NPS, "To Serve and Protect with Integrity," and adopted a ten-point program of action stressing effectiveness, zero tolerance for corruption, better welfare for rank-and-file, and commitment to service and police–public partnerships (NPF, 2005; NPF, 2006: 19–20). Program flyers were widely distributed to the media and are posted prominently in local police stations.

Nigeria has an active civic society—human rights NGO, occupational interest groups, public media—which demands and supports police reforms and has been the driver of many reform initiatives. As well, many international private and public organizations have invested heavily in promoting police reform and enhancing effectiveness in Nigeria.

The real challenge is whether such rhetoric and support and public demands, given the political and policing contexts in which they occur, can be implemented on a sustained basis. Comparative examples are not kind to that notion. Reform of policing is a notoriously difficult process which cannot be achieved in isolation from other changes in societal contexts (Bruce and Neild, 2005; Cawthra and Luckham, 2003; Hills, 2000; Hinton, 2006; Marenin, 1985). The police cannot reform themselves and even small reforms which can be made will only be sustained when supporting societal contexts come into being.

It will be difficult to overcome three basic obstacles: the lack of institutional and operational autonomy of the police, their entrenched public image, and the occupational culture which now pervades the Force. The NPF is beset by consistent and persistent interference in their work by political and societal demands. One indicator is the appointment of the IG, which is the prerogative of the president. The last two IGs have been appointed as 'Acting IGs', clearly a way to check them out before making that decision permanent. Every change in central government leads to a change in the IG as the new president seeks an IG he finds attuned to his visions. The new IG, then, to make a mark will implement his own ideas and priorities (and discard many of the reform efforts of predecessors). There is little continuity in the policies promoted by the leadership. Change is not sustained but set on a different track. Until that pattern changes, the NPF will remain a political organization rather than a professional force concentrating on providing equal and equitable security services, even when leaders within the NPF want to be professional.

The public image of the NPF cannot be changed quickly, no matter what supporters, donors or the NPF wants. Every reform can at best produce small fluctuations in the public's perceptions and judgments of the NPF. Reforms run out of steam quickly if improvements are seen as minor and disappointing. Reforms work when committed reformers see success and continue their efforts without disillusionment. International reformers tend to have short time-spans, resources may not be renewed, and they will go back home. The main hope for sustainability are civic society groups. So far they have remained realistic in their hopes but also optimistic about their ability to promote change.

Finally, and this is the most difficult obstacle for reform, the culture of the NPF will have to undergo fundamental transformation, as will the basic policies on opportunities for meaningful careers by all within the Force. The conditions of that job have to be attractive for those who take it up; and once in the job, the legitimate and legal conceptions of what doing the job entails and how it should be done have to be consistently taught, reinforced and rewarded by managerial practices. For example, corruption will not disappear because the rhetoric says so. Only when impunity for corruption and abuse of powers declines will abuses and corruption decline. Fighting impunity is a policy which police administrators, political leaders, external accountability organizations and civic society must practice, not just state as a goal. The same argument applies to all other reforms. They have to be managed into existence and sustained by reiterative administrative efforts.

Given the difficulty of surmounting these obstacles, it is our view that both Nigeria and the NPF have a long road toward democratic reform ahead of them.

## Notes

1   For a non systematic sample of public opinion, but also some fascinating stories, see the postings to www.nairaland.com/nigeriaextn/ on the topic of "The Nigeria Police Force: How do you view them?"

2   The British, as they did in other colonies, encouraged differential recruitment into the police and military, seeking to staff these forces from the 'martial races,' those suited for discipline, coercion, warfare and obedience. The Hausa police was staffed by police from the North to serve in the South, because they were seen as more controllable than the local Yoruba people and to ensure that police would serve outside their home area. This practice of posting away from home was continued by the Nigerian government to ensure more detachment from local demands but also led to the inability of the NPF to interact with locals for the practical reasons that the police could not speak the local language or know local customs. The ethnic composition of the NPF, though, is unknown at this time since the NPF does not publish those statistics.

3   Fears about the conduct of elections and their likelihood to lead to violence seem not to have changed much. The Prologue to the published proceedings of a Workshop on Public Order (which seems to have been written by an NPF official) states that "political disorders centre around the practice of politics in Nigeria which borders on unbridled lust for power that are exhibited during political meetings, assemblies, rallies, campaigns and processions that turns such events to threats to public peace while the electoral disorders involve the nightmarish wanton manipulation of the electoral process to ensure victory at all costs through legitimate and illegitimate means" (Ehindero, 2006b: 9).

4   As is true for most developing countries, the accuracy of reported official crime and arrest figures is doubtful. In Nigeria, annual police reports which contain these statistics are published irregularly. Officially reported crime data fluctuate wildly from year to year, an indication that it is the level of reporting and the quality of analysis of the data that varies rather than the underlying realities of criminal behavior (Marenin, 1997; Marenin and Reisig, 1995). Much of the knowledge of crime is not derived from systematic studies but is based on anecdotal and widely believed evidence. As with most countries, hidden illegal acts (e.g., corruption or fraud) are hard to measure and not discoverable by common proxy methods such as victimization surveys.

5   It is not clear why the numbers would fluctuate this widely over a one year period, nor are "extrajudicial" killings defined precisely. There are clear cases where the police killed people in their custody, but the number also seems to include any person killed by the police, regardless of circumstance. Annual reports by international NGOs, such as Amnesty International or Human Rights Watch, do not give numbers for police killings for Nigeria and merely note that there are 'many' and 'a large number.'

# References

Agbaegbu, Tobs (2007), "The Most Trying Times of Ehindero," *Newswatch*, January, 16–27.

Africa Leadership Forum, Farm House Dialogue 30 (1994), *Police and Society*, Ota, Ogun State Nigeria: Obasanjo Farms Limited. Edited by Dr. 'Tunji Dare.

Ahire, Philip Terdoo (1991), *Imperial Policing: The Emergence and Role of the Police in Colonial Nigeria, 1860–1960*, Buckingham: Open University Press.

Ajomo, M. Ayo and Isabelle E. Okagbue (1991), *Human Rights and the Administration of Justice in Nigeria*, Lagos: Nigerian Institute of Advanced Legal Studies.

Alemika, Etannibi E.O. (1993), "Colonialism, State and Policing in Nigeria," *Crime, Law and Social Change*, 20, 187–219.

—— (1997), "Police, Policing and Crime Control in Nigeria", *Nigeria Journal of Policy and Strategy*, 12, 1 & 2, 71–98.

—— (2005), "Overview of Patterns of Human Rights Violations by Law Enforcement Agencies in Nigeria," in S.G. Ehindero and E.E.O. Alemika, eds. (2005), *Human Rights and Law Enforcement in Nigeria*, Abuja: Nigeria Police Force, pp. 1–18.

Alemika, Etannibi E.O. and Austin O. Agugua (2001), *Gender Relations and Discrimination in Nigeria Police Force*, Lagos: Centre for Law Enforcement Education (CLEEN).

Alemika, Etannibi E.O. and Innocent C. Chukwuma (2000), *Police-Community Violence in Nigeria*, Lagos: Centre for Law Enforcement Education (CLEEN) and Abuja: National Human Rights Commission, at www.cleen.org.

—— (2004), *The Poor and Informal Policing in Nigeria. A Report on the People's Perceptions and Priorities on Safety, Security and Informal Policing in A2J Focal States in Nigeria*, Lagos: CLEEN.

Alemika, Etannibi, Emmanuel U. Igbo and Chinyere P. Nnorom (2006), *Criminal Victimization, Safety and Policing in Nigeria: 2005*, Lagos: CLEEN Foundation.

Altus Global Alliance (2006), "Police Station Visitors' Week. 29 October to 4 November 2006. Report of Results from Africa," at www.altus.org. (Altus is an alliance of six think tanks/research institutions security and policing in Chile, Brazil, Nigeria, India, Russia and the USA.)

Atta, Aliyu Ibrahim (1997), *Service at Kam Selem House. My Years as Inspector-General of Police*, Lagos: Blowsome Ventures Limited.

Baker, Bruce (2007), *Multi-Choice Policing in Africa*, Uppsala: Nordic Africa Institute.

Baker, Pauline (1975), *Urbanization and Political Change: The Politics of Lagos, 1917–1967*, Berkeley: University of California Press.

British Council (2007), "Security, Justice and Growth Programme. Nigeria: Background Note on Work on Security and Conflict" (draft report written by Vince del Buono and Blair Davis).

Brogden, Mike and Preeti Nijhar (2005), *Community Policing. National and International Models and Approaches*, Cullompton: Willan Publishing.

Bruce, David and Rachel Neild (2005), *The Police We Want: A Handbook for Oversight of Police in South Africa*, Johannesburg: The Centre for the Study of Violence and Reconciliation.

del Buono, Vince and Blair Davis (March 2007), personal communication.

Cawthra, Gavin and Robin Luckham, eds. (2003), *Governing Insecurity. Democratic Control of Military and Security Establishments in Transitional Democracies*, London: Zed Books.

Centre for Law Enforcement Education (CLEEN) and National Human Rights Commission (NHRC) (1999), *Policing a Democracy. A Survey Report on the Role and Functions of the Nigeria Police Force in a Post Military Era*, Lagos and Abuja: CLEEN and NHRC.

Centre for Law Enforcement Education (CLEEN) Foundation (2006), *Opportunity for Justice. A Report on the Justice Olasumbo Goodluck Judicial Commission of Inquiry on the Apo Six Killings by the Police in Abuja*, Lagos: CLEEN.

Chukwuma, I. (1994), *Above the Law: a Report on Torture and Extra Judicial Killings by the Police in Nigeria*, Lagos: Civil Liberties Organisation.

—— (2001), "Guarding the Guardian in Nigeria," *Law Enforcement Review*, June 2001.

Diamond, Larry (1988), *Class, Ethnicity and Democracy in Nigeria. The Failure of the First Republic*, Syracuse, NY: Syracuse University Press.

Ebbe, Obi (1989), "Crime and Delinquency in Metropolitan Lagos: A Study of the 'Crime and Delinquency Area' Theory," *Social Forces*, 67, 751–765.

Ehindero, Sunday Gabriel (2006a), "My Dilemma: Interview with Sunday Ehindero, Inspector General of Police," *Newswatch*, January, 18–25.

Ehindero, Sunday Gabriel, ed. (2006b), *The Nigeria Police and the Public Order Act*, Abuja: Nigeria Police Force; compiled by Femi L. O. Ololeye.

Ehindero, S.G. and E.E.O. Alemika, eds. (2005), *Human Rights and Law Enforcement in Nigeria*, Abuja: Nigeria Police Force.

Hills, Alice (2000), *Policing Africa: Internal Security and the Limits of Liberalization*, Boulder, CO: Lynne Rienner.

Hinton, Mercedes (2006), *The State in the Streets: Police and Politics in Argentina and Brazil*, Boulder, CO: Lynne Rienner.

Horn, Adrian (2004), "Background Paper: Sierra Leone, Commonwealth Community Safety and Security Project," paper presented at Workshop on "Implementing Community Based Policing in Transitional Societies," organized by the International Peace Academy and Saferworld, New York, 22 March 2004.

Human Rights Watch (HRW) (2005), "Nigeria," available at www.hrw.org/english/docs/2005/01/13/nigeri9883.htm (section in the annual report HRW for 2005).

Igbninovia, Patrick E. (1980), "The Police in Trouble: Administrative and Organizational Problems in the Nigeria Police Force," *Indian Journal of Public Administration*, 28, 2, 334–372.

Inyang, Etim O. (1989), "The Nigeria Police Force: Peace-keeping," in Tekena N. Tamuno and J.A. Atanda, eds., *Nigeria Since Independence. The First 25 Years. Volume IV: Government and Public Policy*, Ibadan: Heinemann Educational Books (Nigeria), pp. 65–83. (Etim O. Inyang was the Inspector General of the Nigeria Police Force from Jan. 1984 to Oct. 1986).

Jemibewon, D.M. (2002), *The Nigeria Police in Transition*, Ibadan: Spectrum Books.

Joseph, Richard (1987), *Democracy and Prebendal Politics in Nigeria: The Rise and Fall of the Second Republic*, Cambridge: Cambridge University Press.

Lawyers' Committee for Human Rights (1992), *The Nigeria Police Force: A Culture of Impunity*, New York: Lawyers Committee for Human Rights.

Marenin, Otwin (1985), "Policing Nigeria: Control and Autonomy in the Exercise of Coercion," *African Studies Review*, 28, 1, 73–93.

—— (1987), "The 'Anini Saga': Armed Robbery and the Reproduction of Ideology in Nigeria," *Journal of Modern African Studies*, 25, 2, 259–81.

—— (1997), "Victimization Surveys and the Accuracy and Reliability of Official

Crime Data in Developing Countries," *Journal of Criminal Justice*, 25, 6, 463–475.

Marenin, Otwin and Michael Reisig (1995), "A General Theory of Crime and Patterns of Crime in Nigeria: An Exploration of Methodological Assumptions," *Journal of Criminal Justice*, 23, 6, 501–518.

Muhammad, Alhaji Muazu (1972), "Magisterial Impressions of the Police," in T.O. Elias, ed., *The Nigerian Magistrate and the Offender*, Benin City: Ethiope Publishing Corporation, pp. 74–80.

Musa, Mallam Abubakar Bala, ed. (1998), *For a Better Police Force: Selected Speeches of Retired Inspector General of Police, Alhaji Aliyu Atta cfr, NPM, mni*, Lagos: Neptune Communications Worldwide.

Nigeria, Federal Republic of (1967), *Working Party on Nigeria Police, Local Government and Native Authority Police and Prisons (Gobir Commission): Report*, Lagos: Federal Ministry of Information.

Nigeria Police Force (NPF) (2005), *10-Point Programme for Action. Date of Commencement: 18th January, 2005*, Abuja: Nigeria Police Force.

Nigeria Police Force (NPF) (2006), *2005 Annual Report of the Nigeria Police Force*, Lagos: "F" Department, Nigeria Police Force.

Odekunle, Femi (1979), "The Nigeria Police Force: An Assessment of Functional Performance," *International Journal of the Sociology of Law*, 7, 1, 61–83.

Ohonbamu, O. (1972), "The Dilemma of Police Organization under a Federal System: The Nigerian Example," *Nigerian Law Journal*, 6, 73–87.

Okoigun, R.O (2000), *The Role of the Nigeria Police in Elections*, Lagos: CSS Press.

Olewe, Bernard N. and Jatau Salame Anga, Commissioner of Police (1994), *Command Administration: The Police Perspective*, Enugu: New Generation Books.

Olurode, 'Lai (1991), *The Law and Order Question in Nigeria*, Lagos: Nigerian Law Publications.

Onyeozili, Emmanuel C. (2005), "Obstacles to Effective Policing in Nigeria," *African Journal of Criminology and Justice Studies*, 1, 1, 32–54.

Oseni, Kayode (1993), *Inside Out. (The Circumstance of the Nigeria Police Force)*, Lagos: Raose Nig.

Osoba, S. (1994), "Relevance of Logistics in the Enforcement of Law and Order" paper presented at the joint workshop of the National Orientation Agency and the Nigeria Police Force at the Police Staff College Jos, November 20–December 1.

Oyakhilome, F.E. (1972), "Police Impressions of the Magistrate," in T.O. Elias, ed., *The Nigerian Magistrate and the Offender*, Benin City: Ethiope Publishing Corporation, pp. 81–91.

Paden, John (2005), *Muslim Civic Cultures and Conflict Resolution: The Challenge of Democratic Federalism in Nigeria*, Washington, D.C.: Brookings Institution Press.

*Police News* (2006), 1, 4; special issue on "A New Dawn for the Nigeria Police."

Police Service Commission (2004), *Police and Policing in Nigeria: Final Report on the Conduct of the Police in the 2003 Elections*, Abuja: Police Service Commission.

—— (2006), *2005 Annual Report*, Abuja: Police Service Commission.

Rotimi, Kemi (2001), *The Police in a Federal State: The Nigerian Experience*, Ibadan: College Press Limited.

Smith, M.G. (1960), *Government in Zazzau, 1800–1950*, London: Oxford University Press.

Tamuno, Tekena (1970), *The Police in Modern Nigeria, 1861–1965: Origins, Development and Role*, Ibadan: Ibadan University Press.

—— (1991), *Peace and Violence in Nigeria*, Ibadan: The Panel on Nigeria Since Independence History Project, Ibadan: University of Ibadan Secretariat.

Tamuno, Tekena, Ibrahim L. Bashir, Etannibi E.O. Alemika and Abdulrahman O. Akano, eds. (1993), *Policing Nigeria: Past, Present and Future*, Lagos: Malthouse Press (Produced by the Panel of Policing Nigeria Project for the Nigeria Police Force).

World Bank (2007), "Nigeria. Country Brief," at http://web.worldbank.org/website/external/countries/africaext/nigeriaextn.

Yakubu, J.A. (2000), "Some Problems Associated With Law Enforcement in Nigeria," in J.A. Yakubu, ed. *Administration of Justice in Nigeria*, Lagos Malthouse Press, pp. 36–45.

# Index

eBooks – at www.eBookstore.tandf.co.uk

# A library at your fingertips!

eBooks are electronic versions of printed books. You can store them on your PC/laptop or browse them online.

They have advantages for anyone needing rapid access to a wide variety of published, copyright information.

eBooks can help your research by enabling you to bookmark chapters, annotate text and use instant searches to find specific words or phrases. Several eBook files would fit on even a small laptop or PDA.

**NEW:** Save money by eSubscribing: cheap, online access to any eBook for as long as you need it.

## Annual subscription packages

We now offer special low-cost bulk subscriptions to packages of eBooks in certain subject areas. These are available to libraries or to individuals.

For more information please contact webmaster.ebooks@tandf.co.uk

We're continually developing the eBook concept, so keep up to date by visiting the website.

# www.eBookstore.tandf.co.uk